MEDIEVAL LATIN PALAEOGRAPHY

A BIBLIOGRAPHICAL INTRODUCTION

TORONTO MEDIEVAL BIBLIOGRAPHIES 8

General Editor: John Leyerle

Published in Association with
the Centre for Medieval Studies, University of Toronto

LEONARD E. BOYLE OP

Medieval Latin Palaeography

A BIBLIOGRAPHICAL INTRODUCTION

UNIVERSITY OF TORONTO PRESS
Toronto   Buffalo   London

© University of Toronto Press 1984
Toronto   Buffalo   London
Printed in Canada

ISBN 0-8020-5612-1 (cloth)
ISBN 0-8020-6558-9 (paper)

Canadian Cataloguing in Publication Data

Boyle, Leonard E., 1923-
  Medieval Latin palaeography

  (Toronto medieval bibliographies ; 8)
  "Published in association with the Centre for
  Medieval Studies, University of Toronto."
  Includes indexes.
  ISBN 0-8020-5612-1 (bound); 0-8020-6558-9 (pbk)

  1. Paleography, Latin — Bibliography.
  2. Manuscripts, Latin (Medieval and modern) —
  Bibliography.   3. Transmission of texts —
  Bibliography.   I. University of Toronto.   Centre
  for Medieval Studies.   II. Title.   III. Series.

  Z106.B69 1984   016.471'7   C84-099547-4

Editor's Preface

The study of the Middle Ages has been developed chiefly within university departments such as English or History. This pattern is increasingly being supplemented by an interdisciplinary approach in which the plan of work is shaped to fit the subject studied. The difference of approach is between Chaucer the English poet and Chaucer the civil servant of London attached to the court of Richard II, a man interested in the Ptolemaic universe and widely read in Latin, French, and Italian. Interdisciplinary programs tend to lead readers into areas relatively unfamiliar to them where critical bibliographies prepared with careful selectivity by an expert are essential. The Centre for Medieval Studies at the University of Toronto takes such an interdisciplinary approach to the Middle Ages, and the need for selective bibliographies has become apparent in our work. The Centre has undertaken to meet this need by sponsoring the Toronto Medieval Bibliographies.

In his valuable guide, *Serial Bibliographies for Medieval Studies,** Richard H. Rouse describes 283 bibliographies; the number is surprisingly large and indicates the considerable effort now being made to provide inclusive lists of items relevant to medieval studies. The total amount in print is already vast; for one unfamiliar with a subject, significant work is difficult to locate and the problem grows worse with each year's output. The reader may well say, like the throng in *Piers Plowman* seeking the way to *Treuthe,* 'This were a wikked way but who-so hadde a gyde' (B.vi.I). The Toronto Medieval Bibliographies are meant to be such guides; each title is prepared by an expert and gives directions to important work in the subject.

---

* Publications of the Center for Medieval and Renaissance Studies 3, University of California, Los Angeles (Berkeley and Los Angeles 1969)

Each volume gives a list of works selected with three specific aims. One is to aid students who are relatively new to the area of study, for example Medieval Celtic Literature. Another is to guide more advanced readers in a subject where they have had little formal training, for example Medieval Rhetoric or Latin Palaeography; and the third is to assist new libraries in forming a basic collection in the subject presented. Individual compilers are given scope to organize a presentation that they judge will best suit their subject and also to make brief critical comments as they think fit. Clarity and usefulness of a volume are preferred over any demand for exact uniformity from one volume to another.

Toronto, September 1984

JL

Contents

Abbreviations

Author's Preface

Palaeography means 'old writing,' and so far as we know is a coinage of the Benedictine Bernard de Montfaucon in his *Palaeographia Graeca sive De ortu et progressu litterarum Graecarum* of 1708.

To engage properly in the discipline as we know it today, it is not sufficient to be able to read 'old writing' or simply to analyze it as a handwriting expert does. Writing is a medium of communication, no matter where one finds it: in a lavish codex, a crumpled roll, a scrap of paper, a scribble on a wall, a jagged inscription, the base of an old chalice or drinking cup, the rim of a coin. To understand any given sample as the medium of communication it is, one has to see it in all its circumstances: how it is couched, what the material is to which it is entrusted, where it originated, when it made its first appearance, who its practitioners are, what exactly it communicates, why it is there at all.

The present bibliography attempts to cover all of these, although not under those heads or in that order. Its aim is to present students with as wide a survey as possible of all the aspects they must consider, and of all the tools they should employ, in order to evaluate the communication in the book, document, or inscription from the Middle Ages on which they may be working.

For all seven sections of this bibliography, which roughly embrace the seven classical 'circumstances' of antiquity and the Middle Ages noted above, the term *setting* has been chosen as one elastic enough to represent the variety of angles from which one may view a piece of written communication from the Middle Ages.

To begin with, in approaching a specimen of 'old writing' from those ages the student has to be aware first of all that there is a great amount of scholarship on writing, both medieval and in general, and that there are relevant bibliographies, periodicals, manuals, collections of facsimiles, and historical accounts of the discipline of palaeography and its masters, which he or she cannot afford to ignore. This is the burden of the first section, 'Scholarly Setting.'

Writing, the object of so much scholarly endeavour over the past three centuries since the appearance of Mabillon's *De re diplomatica* in 1681, did not, of course, and does not, take place in a vacuum, nor may it be considered in a vacuum. It is a reflection of various cultures and propensities of various times, and it provides a window on the mentality, preoccupations, and tastes of the people who were responsible for it in its variegated forms. The second and the longest section therefore concerns itself with the 'Cultural Setting' of writing from the earliest times of Latin writing and its vernacular derivatives to the Renaissance and a little beyond. It includes as well some pages on Greek, Hebrew, and other non-Latin alphabets and scripts, since writing in the Middle Ages was a heritage not an invention. But, naturally, the emphasis is medieval, and the section surveys at some length the Latin writing of the Middle Ages as it reflects in turn Roman culture, monastic culture, scholastico-mercantile culture, and humanist culture (a division that is somewhat artificial but has its uses).

Today we would hardly be in a position to benefit from the literary, documentary, and other products in writing of this procession of cultures had not these been passed on to or preserved for us through various institutions such as archives, treasuries, libraries, and collections of the Middle Ages and Renaissance, and their post-medieval and modern successors. An account of the principal guides to and of the general literature on these deposits, whether modern or medieval, is therefore essayed in the third section, 'Institutional Setting.'

These survivals are not disembodied. They have, as the heading of the fourth section indicates, a 'Physical Setting,' a description that has been chosen to avoid the limitations of the much-heralded term *codicology*, since, to put it simply, a *codex* is not the only physical form in which medieval writing survives. In general the section deals with the 'supports' of writing: the material on which it has been transmitted, the medium (ink, etc.) of transmission, the make-up and binding, and the role of all these in cataloguing, dating, and localizing specimens of writing for the general benefit of scholarship and for a better understanding of the culture of the period.

All would be reasonably plain sailing for the reader or student today were these survivals from the Middle Ages or any other period in copperplate or fully written out as these words here are. But they are not. They are often so transmitted that they present barriers to an immediate or full communication. Hence the subject of the fifth section is the 'Human Setting' of writing and the problems of the very human fashion in which

the communication has been wrapped, including decoration, the techniques
and conceits of scribes, and, needless to say, the shorthand they almost
invariably practised.

Scripts, however, and their practitioners, characteristics, and surrounds,
are not there simply to be objects of study or admiration. They are there to
communicate — and on occasion to highlight — some message or other;
and what they have to communicate — the text — is what counts. In fact,
the reason primarily why scripts engage the attention of most scholars and
students is because they are vehicles of some text or other, whether literary
or documentary. All else — the abbreviations, the spacing, the embellishments — is by the way. Hence the section 'Textual Setting,' where works
on the thorny problems of recovering, evaluating, editing, and publishing
texts are listed at considerable length, and the whole process of 'transmission' that gives us these texts is treated on a fairly wide scale.

Finally, in order to make writing from the middle and other ages communicate to the full in all these cultural, institutional, physical, human,
textual, and scholarly settings, one has to have a raft of aids to research at
one's elbow, from books on the Latin and vernacular languages to those on
topography, liturgy, chronology, theology, and the like, the more useful of
which are listed under the final (and the most contrived) heading, 'Research
Setting.'

This last section of all includes an elementary bibliography of diplomatics and kindred disciplines which in one way or another have writing as
their object of study. Writing as it is found in non-literary sources such as
charters, seals, coins, or administrative records is, of course, as much part of
the discipline of 'old writing' as the scripts known as 'bookhands,' and
indeed is accepted as such throughout this volume. But inasmuch as the
disciplines of diplomatics, epigraphy, and sigillography, for example, are
concerned with an historical evaluation of what the writing proper to each
has to say, they will often be of great help to the palaeographer when one
has to turn, as one must, from literary to non-literary scripts and specimens.

In view of the fact that the art of studying 'old writing' has its beginnings precisely within the bounds of diplomatics in Jean Mabillon's *De re
diplomatica,* it is odd to have to note that documentary or diplomatic
writing itself, not to speak of other non-literary scripts, is all too often
ignored by 'bookhand' palaeography. To redress the balance somewhat, I
have not confined this bibliography to medieval bookhands but rather have
included as many collections of facsimiles as I could manage of documentary
writing of any and every kind.

To some it may seem indeed that, on the whole, facsimiles in general are
too much with the present bibliography. I make no apologies. For unless

students are given as many opportunities as possible of becoming as familiar with the word in manuscript in all its manifestations as they are with the printed word, all the bibliographies and learned articles in the world will be of little use, if not a waste of time. In this year, the three-hundredth anniversary of the publication of *De re diplomatica*, the cradle of palaeography, I cannot but make my own some pointed words of Mabillon: 'Rectius docent specimina quam verba.'

Procedures (and Prejudices)

1. As may be evident from the reference above to Mabillon's tercentenary, this bibliography was completed in 1981. That it is only now appearing some three years later is largely due to a reluctance on my part to allow it to go to press. When I had finished it in 1981, I (and others) found it wanting in many respects and even more inaccurate and incomplete than it is at present. On returning to it in earnest some six months ago, I decided that it would be better to secure what I had listed up to 1981 than to attempt to bring the bibliography up to the moment. Many important books or articles have appeared in the interval, a few of which I have managed to squeeze in (sometimes resorting to double entries) without unduly disturbing the order established in 1981. But as a whole the bibliography does not go beyond 1981.

2. I am not a professional bibliographer, nor have I aimed at anything approaching completeness. The present bibliography is a working bibliography for beginners, and little else. It is not meant for scholars or librarians but for students who, if provided with an author's name and the main title of his or her book, may without any undue stress look it up in the card catalogue of a library. In the entries in the bibliography I have noted only essential cross-references, but I have tried in the index to list each author or subject or manuscript as fully as possible. Likewise, in the entries I have provided initials only before or after the family names of authors, but in the index I have given the full first (sometimes second) name of each author, where ascertainable.

3. As noted above, this bibliography is meant for beginners; it is not at all directed to scholars (most of whom in any case will already know it all and much more). And it is designed to give beginners as wide a view as possible of the background one has to have in order to do justice to any piece of old writing. In other words, what I have attempted to present

here is what I may term an 'integral palaeography,' at the centre of
which is a text which one must make to communicate as completely as
possible. Not every palaeographer will share this view. But I write not as
a codicologist, an art historian, a librarian, a researcher, a cataloguer, or
a textual critic, but as a teacher of palaeography whose primary purpose
over the past twenty-three years of teaching in Toronto has been to
ensure first and foremost that his students were enabled confidently to
engage themselves in original research in literary and documentary
material from the Middle Ages, and chiefly in that period from which
there is the greatest survival of all of literary and documentary material
in manuscript – the period, that is, between A.D. 1150 and 1450. Texts
from that period in all their variety were my chief preoccupation, followed inevitably by the often insidious array of abbreviations that im-
pede understanding. For only when one is in complete command of the
text may one turn with full profit to the techniques of, for example,
codicology or art history that can bring the surrounds of the text to life.
For this reason everything in this bibliography is viewed in terms of text
and textual communication. Hence the scripts that convey the text and
are its medium of communication form the core of the work, and codicology, art history, and other disciplines or techniques do not stand on
their own but in an ancillary position (although, of course, as disciplines
or techniques they may be studied individually – and with much profit –
in their own right).

All this single-mindedness may be a cause of concern to some. It has
been suggested to me, for example, that the segment on art history is,
to say the least, perfunctory. Perhaps it is. But this is not a bibliography
of illumination or decoration. It is a bibliography of palaeography; and
I have therefore done no more than indicate some of the works of art
history which a student who has to work on a text in a codex or other
form of manuscript may find useful when faced with the problem of
dating, localizing, or in general describing the codex or document in
question. And if ornamentation and painting are tucked away (1821-68)
under the 'Human Setting' of writing, where, of all things, they rub
shoulders with abbreviations, this is simply because they, like the scribes,
the hands, the abbreviations, belong to the human setting of a text. Like
all of these they are products of a mind, in this case of a mind moved by
the message or solemnity of a text to decorate or illustrate it. No matter
how impressive, they do not exist on their own. They spring from a
text and, at least where painting is concerned, are only intelligible for
what exactly they convey in the light of the text that spurred the artist.

Others have expressed surprise, on the other hand, that so much space is devoted to the transmission, not to speak of the editing, of texts. Subjects such as these, I have been given to understand, belong to philology or a seminar in textual criticism. Again, I can only repeat what I stated above. I do not subscribe to a 'piecemeal' palaeography — one that is content to concentrate on, for example, forms of writing or codicology or art forms or cataloguing or localization, yet ignore or play down the fact that the basic function of palaeography is to address a text as it is transmitted in writing, and to compel it to communicate, as it was meant to do. And since textual transmission is central to the understanding of any given text in any given codex or document, then to pass it over, and with it the principles and the pitfalls of editing, is as destructive of an integral palaeography as is a marked concentration on codicology or art forms to the utter neglect of the text that the codex houses and that the art forms embellish.

4. Since, quite unexpectedly, I am about to leave Toronto and the teaching of palaeography for good, I have had to curtail the finishing touches to the bibliography. Likewise, this part of the preface has been pulled together in some haste and none too coherently. That the volume is to appear at all is due to the kindness and support of many friends, notably Barbara Broden, Anna Burko, Heather Phillips, David Townsend, Annette Vatter, and the Curator of the Bergendal Collection, Joseph Pope, in Toronto; Mary and Richard Rouse in Los Angeles. Originally I had thought to dedicate the work to my own three teachers of palaeography at Oxford, D. A. Callus, R.W. Hunt, and N. R. Ker, all of whom unfortunately are no longer with us; but since my own days of teaching palaeography are now over, I think it only fair to dedicate the volume, imperfect though it is, to the five hundred and five former students who patiently bore with the annual course in integral palaeography at Toronto over the years 1961-1984.

Toronto, 16 April 1984

LEB

MEDIEVAL LATIN PALAEOGRAPHY

A BIBLIOGRAPHICAL INTRODUCTION

Scholarly Setting

While there is no claim here to be complete, it is hoped that this first section covers all the main general works on Latin palaeography. The longest stretch, **160-415**, is that which attempts to list most of the general series of facsimiles. In the case of each facsimile, the aim is to note the present location, length, date, and predominant script of the codex in question, and whether the facsimile is complete (CF) or partial (PF).

BIBLIOGRAPHIES

1
Bayerische Staatsbibliothek, Munich. *Katalog der Handbibliothek der Handschriftenabteilung.* 8 vols. (Wiesbaden 1981-3)
The first two volumes (1981) carry a photographic reproduction of the card catalogue of the MS reference room at the Bayerische Staatsbibliothek, area by area, e.g. Allgemeine Lexika; Buchwesen; Handschriftenkataloge; Schriftgeschichte; Paläographie; Buchmalerei; Handschriftenfaksimiles. The remaining six volumes (Alphabetischer und Schlagwortkatalog, 1982-1983) proceed alphabetically: authors, places, subjects, titles. In effect, all areas of medieval studies are covered.

2
Bischoff, B. 'Paläographie' in *Dahlmann-Waitz, Quellenkunde der deutschen Geschichte: Bibliographie der Quellen und der Literatur zur deutschen Geschichte,* 10th ed., ed. H. Heimpel and H. Geuss; vol. I: *Abschnitt 1 bis 38* (Stuttgart 1969) sec. 14 (no pagination)
A good bibliographical survey.

3

Bonacini, C. *Bibliografia delle arte scrittorie e della calligrafia* (Florence 1953)

Very weak on palaeography. Useful for the works of masters and teachers of calligraphy in the 16th and later centuries.

4

Braswell, L.N. *Western Manuscripts from Classical Antiquity to the Renaissance: A Handbook* (New York 1981)

An annotated bibliography of, in effect, medieval studies in general. Shows marked interest in vernacular literatures. Otherwise covers much the same ground as the present bibliography, though from a different angle. Not always reliable.

5

Brown, T.J. 'Palaeography' in *New Cambridge Bibliography of English Literature* (Cambridge 1974) I, cols. 209-20.

6

Fischer, I. *Die Handbibliothek in Handschriftenlesesälen: Überlegungen zu ihrer Entstehung, Aufgabe, und Benutzung. Mit einem Modellvorschlag für die systematische Aufstellung.* Arbeiten aus dem Bibliothekar-Lehrinstitut des Landes Nordrhein-Westfalen 44 (Cologne 1974)

A concise, well-organized list of books on and aids to MS studies with which a MS reading-room (or indeed a palaeography seminar-room) ideally should be furnished. Less congested than, although obviously not as complete as, 1.

7

Mateu Ibars, J. and M.D. Mateu Ibars. *Bibliografía paleográfica* (Barcelona 1974). 18 pls., mostly of MSS

An interesting introduction on palaeography in general and on Spanish palaeography, pp. v-xx. Especially valuable for catalogues of libraries, medieval and modern, in a variety of countries, and for Spanish bibliography. Nearly 1000 pages in length, it is a mine of information.

8

Nélis, H. *L'Ecriture et les scribes* (Brussels 1918)

Lists writings on palaeography up to 1914. Still useful.

9

Omont, H. *Listes des recueils de fac-similés et des reproductions de manuscrits conservés à la Bibliothèque nationale,* ed. P. Lauer. 3rd ed. (Paris 1935).

10
Sattler, P. and G. von Selle. *Bibliographie zur Geschichte der Schrift bis in das Jahr 1930* (Linz 1935).
11
University of London Library: The Palaeography Collection. 2 vols. (Boston 1968)
An author catalogue, followed by a subject index.
12
Zotter, H. *Bibliographie faksimilierter Handschriften* (Graz 1976)
A listing by library (Aachen – Zürich) of 637 MSS (Latin, Greek, etc.) which have been published in complete (CF) or partial (PF) facsimile. There are lacunae: see E. Irblich in *CM* 2 (1976) 123-4.

PERIODICALS

13
Anglo-Saxon England (Cambridge 1972-)
This annual volume assigns Section 5 of its yearly surveys of bibliography to 'Palaeography, Diplomatic and Illumination.' Cited as *ASE*.
14
L'Année philologique (Paris 1928-)
A magnificent annotated bibliography which annually combs more than 700 periodicals, journals, and collections for anything to do with Greek and Latin studies in any age or discipline, and devotes Section III of each volume to 'Histoire des textes: A. Paléographie; Histoire de l'écriture et des manuscrits. B. Papyrologie. C. Critique des textes.' From time to time other sections should be consulted. In 1977 a serial numeration was introduced.
15
Bibliothèque de l'Ecole des chartes (Paris 1839-)
The oldest journal of its kind. Especially valuable for periodical articles on palaeography and diplomatics, notices of theses defended at the Ecole, and news of additions to MSS collections in the Bibliothèque nationale, Paris. Cited as *BEC*.
16
Bulletin de l'Institut de recherche et d'histoire des textes (Paris 1952-69)

Cited as *BIRHT*. Now replaced by *Revue d'histoire des textes* (Paris 1971-), cited as *RHT*.
17
Bullettino dell' 'Archivio paleografico italiano ' 1st ser., 6 vols. (Rome 1908-19); new ser., 5 vols. (Rome 1955-58/9); 3rd ser., 3 vols. (Rome 1962-4)
Cited as *BAPI*. Now, apparently, replaced by *Scrittura e civiltà* **27**.
18
Cahiers de civilisation médiévale Xe-XIIe siècles (Poitiers 1958-)
The annual bibliographical supplement, with a combined index of authors, places, and subjects, usually carries entries (within the above time limits) on, e.g., 'codicologie,' 'écriture,' 'manuscrits,' 'paléographie'; unlike *Scriptorium* **26**, it does not provide an index of MSS by library.
19
Codices manuscripti: Zeitschrift für Handschriftenkunde (Vienna 1975-)
Provides general coverage, with annual reviews of work on palaeography and codicology in Austria. Cited as *CM*.
20
International Medieval Bibliography (Leeds 1967-)
Produces two volumes a year, each of which has a section (very thin) on 'Palaeography and Diplomatics' and, in the general index, a list of MSS cited in the bibliography.
21
Manuscripta (St. Louis, Mo. 1957-)
Largely concerned with MSS of the BAV, and with the deposit of microfilms of MSS from the BAV in the Pius XII Memorial Library at St. Louis.
22
Medioevo latino: Bollettino bibliografico della cultura europea dal secolo VI al XIII. Appendice bibliografico a *Studi medievali* (Spoleto 1980-)
This new annual bibliography from the Centro italiano di studi sull'alto medioevo at Spoleto, has a section on 'Storia del testo e filologia' with information on, e.g., sale catalogues of MSS, exhibitions of MSS, medieval and modern library catalogues, codicology, transmission of texts, computers, and textual criticism. There is a useful index of all MSS noted in the bibliography. The first volume (Appendice bibliografico a *Studi medievali* XX, 1979) covers 1978 (and on occasion some years prior to that); the second (Appendice bibliografico a *Studi medievali* XXI, 1980, published in 1981) covers 1979, and so on.

23

Quaerendo (Amsterdam 1971-)

A quarterly journal devoted mainly to MSS and printed books from the
Low Countries.

24

Revue d'histoire ecclésiastique (Louvain 1900-)

Three times each year carries a comprehensive (but not annotated) bibliography of books and articles related to church history which has sections on palaeography, codicology, etc., as follows: 'I. Sciences auxiliaires: 2. Bibliographies' and, since vol. 74 (1979), '2A. Inventaires et catalogues.
3. Paléographie; Chronologie; Diplomatique. II. Sources et critique des sources: 1. Sources monumentales. 2. Sources d'archives et Critique diplomatique. 3. Sources littéraires.' And see also under III ('Histoire des sciences et des lettres'). 3.E: 'Archives et bibliothèques. Histoire du livre.' In general, harder to use than *L'Année* **14**. Cited as *RHE*.

25

Ricerche medievali (Pavia 1966-)

An occasional journal devoted to palaeography and diplomatics, chiefly with respect to North Italy. Cited as *RM*.

26

Scriptorium (Antwerp – Brussels 1946/7-68; Ghent 1969-)

An international semi-annual review of MS studies with, since volume 13 (1959), annotated bibliographies in each issue and, annually, an extensive index which includes a list, library by library, of all MSS cited in the periodical itself and in its 'Bulletin codicologique.' From vol. 30 (1976) there are book reviews distinct from the 'Bulletin codicologique.'

27

Scrittura e civiltà (Turin 1977-)

The emphasis is on handwriting as a cultural phenomenon. To some extent succeeds *BAPI* **17**, at least with respect to 'historical palaeography.' Cited as *SC*.

MISCELLANIES

28
[Albareda, A.] *Collectanea Vaticana in honorem Anselmi M. Card. Albareda.* 2 vols. Studi e testi 219-20 (Vatican City 1962).

29
[————] *Didascaliae: Studies in Honor of Anselm M. Albareda, Prefect of the Vatican Library,* ed. S. Prete (New York 1961).

30
Battelli, G. *Scritti scelti: Codici – Documenti – Archivi* (Rome 1975) Collected articles, 1935-73.

31
[————] *Palaeographica diplomatica et archivistica: Studi in onore di Giulio Battelli.* 2 vols. Storia e letteratura. Raccolta di studi e testi 139 (Rome 1979).

32
Bischoff, B. *Mittelalterliche Studien: Ausgewählte Aufsätze zur Schriftkunde und Literaturgeschichte.* 3 vols. (Stuttgart 1966-81) Collected articles, 1928-81.

33
[————] *Festschrift Bernhard Bischoff zu seinem 65. Geburtstag,* ed. J. Autenrieth and F. Brunhölzl (Stuttgart 1971).

34
Bühler, C. *Early Books and Manuscripts: Forty Years of Research* (New York 1973) Collected articles.

35
[Cencetti, G.] *Miscellanea in memoria di Giorgio Cencetti* [ed. A. Pratesi] (Turin 1973).

36
[Chatelain, E.] *Mélanges offerts à E. Chatelain par ses élèves et ses amis* (Paris 1910).

37
[Degering, H.] *Mittelalterliche Handschriften: Paläographische, kunsthistorische, literarische, und bibliotheksgeschichtliche Untersuchungen. Festgabe zum 60. Geburtstag von Hermann Degering,* ed. A. Bömer and J. Kirchner (Leipzig 1926, repr. Hildesheim – New York 1973). 17 pls.

38

Delisle, L. *Mélanges de paléographie et de bibliographie* (Paris 1880)
A set of seven facsimiles illustrating this volume appeared separately as
Mélanges...: Atlas (1880).

39

[De Marinis, T.] *Studi di bibliografia e storia in onore di Tammaro de
Marinis.* 4 vols. (Vatican City 1964); numerous pls. and figs.

40

[Duft, J.] *Florilegium Sangallense: Festschrift für Johannes Duft zum 65.
Geburtstag,* ed. O.P. Clavadetscher et al. (St. Gall–Sigmaringen 1980)
St. Gall is the focus of the contributions.

41

[Ehrle, F.] *Miscellanea Francesco Ehrle: Scritti di storia e paleografia ... in
occasione dell'ottantesimo natalizio dell'e.mo Cardinale Francesco Ehrle.*
6 vols. Studi e testi 37-42 (Rome 1924)
See especially vol. IV, *Paleografia e diplomatica.*

42

Encyclopédie de la Pléiade, XI: *L'Histoire et ses méthodes,* ed. C. Samaran
(Paris 1961)
This brilliant volume of 1770 pages has long and considered chapters on
epigraphy (L. Robert), papyrology (A. Bataille **1511**), diplomatics (G.
Tessier **2174**), and on Greek (A. Dain **115**), Roman (J. Mallon **541**), and
medieval (C. Perrat **128**) palaeography.

43

[Fairbank, A.] *Calligraphy and Palaeography: Essays presented to Alfred
Fairbank on his 70th Birthday,* ed. A.S. Osley (London 1965).

44

[Federici, V.] *Scritti di paleografia e diplomatica in onore di Vincenzo
Federici* (Florence 1944).

45

[Hunt, R.W.] *Medieval Learning and Literature: Essays presented to
Richard William Hunt,* ed. J.J.G. Alexander and M.T. Gibson (Oxford
1976). 28 pls.

46

[Ker, N.R.] *Medieval Scribes, Manuscripts, and Libraries: Essays presented
to N.R. Ker,* ed. M.B. Parkes and A.G. Watson (London 1978). 83 pls.

47

Lehmann, P. *Erforschung des Mittelalters: Ausgewählte Abhandlungen und*

Aufsätze. 5 vols. (Leipzig 1941, Stuttgart 1959-62)
Collected articles, 1910-62.
48
[Lieftinck, G.I.] *Essays presented to* ... see **51-4** below.
49
Lindsay, W.M., ed. *Palaeographia Latina* (Oxford 1922-9, repr. 1974)
An occasional periodical, only six issues of which were published.
50
LITTERAE TEXTUALES
A series on MSS and their texts, ed. J.P. Gumbert, M.J.M. De Haan,
and, since 1976, A. Gruys (Amsterdam 1972-6, Leiden 1976-), with
contributions, some original, some revised, by various authors:
  51
  [1] *Varia codicologica: Essays presented to G.I. Lieftinck/1*
  (Amsterdam 1972).
  52
  [2] *Texts & Manuscripts: Essays presented to G.I. Lieftinck/2* (1972).
  53
  [3] *Neerlandica manuscripta: Essays presented to G.I. Lieftinck/3*
  (1976).
  54
  [4] *Miniatures, Scripts, Collections: Essays presented to G.I.*
  Lieftinck/4 (1976).
  55
  [5] *Codicologica 1: Théories et principes* (Leiden 1976).
  56
  [6] *Codicologica 2: Eléments pour une codicologie comparée* (1978).
  57
  [7] *Codicologica 3: Essais typologiques* (1980).
  58
  [8] *Codicologica 4: Essais méthodologiques* (1978).
  59
  [9] *Codicologica 5: Les Matériaux du livre manuscrit* (1980).
60
Lowe, E.A. *Palaeographical Papers 1907-1965,* ed. L. Bieler. 2 vols.
(Oxford 1972). 150 pls.
61
[————] *Studia in honorem E.A. Lowe,* ed. S.H. Thomson (Boulder,

Colorado 1962) [= *Medievalia et humanistica* 14]:
62
Masai, F. *Miscellanea codicologica F. Masai dicata MCMLXXIX,* ed. P.
Cockshaw, M.-C. Garand, and P. Jodogne. 2 vols. with continuous pagina-
tion. Les Publications de Scriptorium 8 (Ghent 1979). 78 pls.
63
[Mercati, G.] *Miscellanea Giovanni Mercati.* 6 vols. Studi e testi 121-6
(Vatican City 1946)
See especially vol. VI, *Paleografia, bibliografia, varia.*
64
[————] *Studi e ricerche nella biblioteca e negli archivi vaticani in
memoria del cardinale Giovanni Mercati (1866-1957),* ed. L. Donati
(Florence 1959).
65
Morison, S. *Selected Essays on the History of Letter-Forms in Manuscript
and Print,* ed. D. McKitterick. 2 vols. (Cambridge 1981). 126 pls., mostly
of MSS and inscriptions A.D. 200-1500.
66
La Paléographie hébraïque médiévale. Colloques internationaux du Centre
de la recherche scientifique 547 (Paris 1974). 136 pls.
A wide-ranging volume, with some contributions relative to Latin
palaeography.
66a
*Paläographie 1981: Colloquium des Comité international de paléographie,
München 15.-18. September 1981,* ed. G. Silagi (Munich 1982). 38 pls.
67
[Rand, E.K.] *Classical and Mediaeval Studies in Honor of Edward
Kennard Rand,* ed. L.W. Jones (New York 1938).
68
Schiaparelli, L. *Note paleografiche (1910-1932),* ed. G. Cencetti (Turin
1969).
69
[Tisserant, E.] *Mélanges Eugène Tisserant.* 7 vols. Studi e testi 231-7
(Vatican City 1964)
See especially vols. V, *Archives Vaticanes: Histoire ecclésiastique,* and VI,
Bibliothèque Vaticane.
70
Traube, L. *Vorlesungen und Abhandlungen,* ed. F. Boll. 3 vols. (Munich

1909-20)
Collected papers; see especially vol. I, *Zur Paläographie und Handschriften-kunde,* ed. P. Lehmann.

HISTORY OF SCHOLARSHIP

71-4 are in chronological order.

71

Van Papenbroeck, Daniel. 'Propylaeum antiquarium circa veri ac falsi discrimen in vetustis membranis,' *Acta sanctorum, Aprilis* II (Antwerp 1675) pp. I-LII. 6 pls. of samples of writing, etc.
Among other things argues that the handwriting should be examined carefully before an ancient document is accepted as genuine. He was taken up by Mabillon **72.**

72

Mabillon, Jean. *De re diplomatica libri sex in quibus quidquid ad veterum instrumentorum antiquitatem, materiam, scripturam et stilum; quidquid ad sigilla, monogrammata, subscriptiones ac notas chronologicas; quidquid inde ad antiquariam, historicam, forensemque disciplinam pertinet, explicatur et illustratur,...* (Paris 1681, 2nd ed. 1709) with 50 pls., and *Supplementum* (1704) with 8 pls.; repr. with notes and an appendix on the life and works of Mabillon by J. Adimarus (Giovanni Altomare), 2 vols. (Naples 1789)
Although the Jesuit Van Papenbroeck (1628-1714) and the Benedictine Mabillon (1632-1717) were directly concerned with the evaluation of documents (diplomatics), between them they laid the foundations of the study of handwriting as such (to which the name *palaeography* was first assigned by B. de Montfaucon **476** in 1708). Mabillon, who broadly divided scripts in general into 'scriptura forensis seu diplomatica,' 'scriptura litteratoria, quae hominibus litteratis convenit,' and 'scriptura usualis, quae non ita elaborata est atque illa, quae in mss. codicibus reperiri solet' (prologue to Bk. V, p. 343 in Paris 1681 ed.; I, 359 in Naples ed.), was chiefly concerned with pre-Carolingian scripts, which he categorized as 'antiqua romana,' '(antiqua) gothica,' 'langobardica,' '(anglo-)saxonica,' and 'franco-gallica (merovingica).' These and other scripts are discussed briefly in Bk. I, ch. XI (Paris ed. pp. 45-53; Naples ed. I, 46-55); facsimiles,

splendidly engraved by Pierre Giffart (1638-1723), occupy much of Bk. V.
Some examples of 'scriptura litteratoria' are from MSS then at the abbey
of Corbie, where Mabillon lived 1658-63. See also **80, 88, 91-2, 94**.

73

Maffei, Scipione. *Istoria diplomatica che serve d'introduzione all'arte
critica in tal materia* (Padua 1727). 4 pls.
Advocates a study of all types of writing, not just that in charters and
literary productions. Attacks Mabillon **72** for, among other things, his
'national' or geographical categories of scripts, and stresses rather the
continuity of writing. For him it is sufficient to divide scripts simply into
majuscule, minuscule, and cursive. See also **80, 88**.

74

[Tassin, René Prosper, and Charles François Toustain] *Nouveau traité de
diplomatique où l'on examine les fondements de cet art.... Par deux
religieux Bénédictins de la Congrégation de Saint-Maur.* 6 vols. (Paris
1750-65). 100 pls.
In effect a reply to Maffei **73**, defending Mabillon **72**. The chapters on
palaeography are chiefly the work of Toustain (ob. 1754), an amateur
botanist who was much under the influence of botanical writings of Carl
von Linné (Linnaeus). He argues for the classification of writing by species,
'Les marbres et les bronzes d'une part, les manuscrits de l'autre, enfin les
actes et les diplômes....' The *Nouveau traité* was very influential in its day
and, through De Wailly **134**, up to the beginning of the present century.

75

Bischoff, B. 'Deutsches Schrifttum zur lateinischen Paläographie und
Handschriftenforschung, 1945-1952,' *Scriptorium* 7 (1953) 298-318.

76

———. 'Paläographie der abendländischen Buchschriften vom V. bis zum
XII. Jahrhundert' in *Relazioni del X Congresso internazionale di scienze
storiche.* 6 vols. (Florence 1955), vol. I: *Metodologia – Problemi generali –
Scienze ausiliarie della storia* pp. 385-406.

77

Bonelli, G. 'Ludwig Traube e gli studi paleografici,' *SM* [1st ser.] 4
(1912-13) 1-64.

78

Brown, T.J. 'Latin Palaeography since Traube,' *Transactions of the
Cambridge Bibliographical Society* 3 (1959-63) 361-81; repr. with additional notes in **55**, 58-74.

79

————. 'E.A. Lowe and *Codices Latini antiquiores,' SC* 1 (1977) 177-97
See also **89-90** for the American palaeographer and pupil of Traube, E.A.
Lowe (1879-1969).

80

Casamassima E. 'Per una storia delle dottrine paleografiche dall'Umanesimo a Jean Mabillon, I,' *SM* 3rd ser. 5 (1964) 525-78
To be taken with **88**. The promised continuation has not yet appeared.

81

Cencetti, G. 'Vecchi e nuovi orientamenti nello studio della paleografia,'
La bibliofilia 50 (1948) 4-23
Mainly with respect to Mallon **535-7, 581** and Marichal **543**.

82

Colker, M.L. 'Some Recent Works for Palaeographers,' *Medievalia et
humanistica* new ser. 8 (1977) 235-42
Critical comments on, e.g., *Manuscrits datés* **(314-30)** for France, Belgium,
Austria.

83

Costamagna, G. 'Paleografia e scienza,' *Rassegna degli Archivi di Stato* 28
(1968) 293-315; repr. in his *Studi di paleografia e di diplomatica* (Rome
1972) 175-98
Sees palaeography in relation to writing-as-communication, and rejects the
'historical' and 'global' approach of Cencetti **(81, 152-3)** and others.

84

Delaissé, L.M.J. 'Le Premier Colloque international de paléographie,'
Scriptorium 9 (1955) 290-93
On this colloquium of 1953 (see **1701**).

85

Fiero, G.K. 'L.M.J. Delaissé, 1914-1972: An Appreciation,' *Quaerendo*
9 (1979) 69-78.

86

Garand, M.-C. and F. Gasparri, 'Compte rendu des travaux du deuxième
colloque international de paléographie (Paris, 25-27 mai 1966),' *BIRHT*
14 (1966) 109-41.

87

Garand, M.-C. 'Le Catalogue des manuscrits datés en écriture latine,' *CM*
1 (1975) 97-103
See **313-40**.

88

Gasparri, F. 'Remarques sur la terminologie paléographique,' *BIRHT* 13 (1964-5) 111-14.

89

John, J.J. 'E.A. Lowe and *Codices Latini antiquiores*,' American Council of Learned Societies *Newsletter* 20/5 (1969) 1-17.

90

————. 'A Palaeographer among Benedictines: A Tribute to E.A. Lowe,' *American Benedictine Review* 21 (1970) 139-47.

91

Knowles, D. *Great Historical Enterprises* (London, Edinburgh, etc. 1963) On the Bollandists, the Maurists, the Monumenta Germaniae historica, and the Rolls Series.

92

————. 'Jean Mabillon' in D. Knowles, *The Historian and Character and Other Essays* (Cambridge 1963) 213-39.

93

Langeli, A.B. 'Ancora su paleografia e storia della scrittura: A proposito di un Convegno Perugino,' *SC* 2 (1978) 275-94
See **106.**

94

Leclercq, H. *Mabillon.* 2 vols. (Paris 1953, 1957)
The most complete study of Mabillon.

95

Lieftinck, G.I. *Paleografie en handschriftenkunde* (Amsterdam 1963)
His inaugural lecture at Leiden, on how palaeography, once considered 'ancilla philologiae,' has become an autonomous science, and how it has moved recently towards codicology of the medieval book.

96

Lublinskaya [Ljublinskaja], A. 'Les Travaux des savants soviétiques en paléographie latine (1960-1966),' *Scriptorium* 21 (1967) 100-03.

97

Lüfling, H. 'Neuere Literatur zur Schriftgeschichte des späten Mittelalters und der Renaissance,' *Gutenberg Jahrbuch* 48 (1973) 15-36.

98

Marichal, R. *'Codices Latini antiquiores,'* *Scriptorium* 18 (1964) 226-36
A sensitive review of the volumes to date of E.A. Lowe's collection, **251-61.**

99
Masai, F. 'Paléographie et codicologie,' *Scriptorium* 4 (1950) 279-93
On the writings of Battelli **148**, Marichal **544**, and Dain **2004** in particular.
100
————. 'La Paléographie gréco-latine, ses tâches, ses méthodes,'
Scriptorium 10 (1956) 281-302; repr. in **55**, 34-53, with postscript by
A. Derolez, pp. 53-7.
101
Momigliano, A. 'Mabillon's Italian Disciples' in his *Terzo contributo alla
storia degli studi classici e del mondo antico*. 2 vols. Storia e letteratura
108-9 (Rome 1966) I, 135-52.
102
Natale, A.R. *Ludwig Traube e la nuova metodologia paleografica* (Milan
1957).
103
Pasquali, G. 'La paleografia come scienza dello spirito,' *Nuova antologia*
66 (1931) 342-54; repr. in his *Pagine stravaganti di un filologo* (Lanciano
1933) 181-205.
104
Petrucci, A. 'Funzione della scrittura e terminologia paleografica' in **31**,
I, 3-30.
105
Post, G. 'A General Report: Suggestions for Future Studies in Late Medieval and Renaissance Latin Paleography' in *Relazioni* (see **76**) I, 407-22.
106
Pratesi, A. 'Paleografia in crisi?' *SC* 3 (1979) 329-37
Should palaeography give way to a 'sociology of writing' as some claim?
A reply to Langeli **93**.
107
————. 'Giorgio Cencetti dieci anni dopo: Tentativo di un bilancio,'
SC 4 (1980) 5-17
Sober thoughts on the achievements and non-achievements of this
influential palaeographer (ob. 1970).
108
Samaran, C. 'Le Comité international de paléographie: Réalisations et
projets' in *Une longue vie d'érudit: Recueil d'études de Charles Samaran*.
2 vols. (Geneva 1978) II, 767-86
A reprint of an article of 1962 in the *Journal des Savants*.

109
Spunar, P. 'Définition de la paléographie,' *Scriptorium* 12 (1958) 108-10
Considers particularly its relation to codicology.
110
————. 'Die lateinische Paläographie in der Sowjetunion,' *Mitteilungen des Instituts für Österreichische Geschichtsforschung* 76 (1968) 189-94
From the pioneer days of Dobiaš-Roždestvenskaja (see **896**) in the 1920s to Ljublinskaja **(96, 156)**, Kiseleva **(1100)**, and Romanova **(1190)**.
111
Timpanaro, S. 'Angelo Mai,' *Atene e Roma* new ser. 1 (1956) 3-34
Discusses the renowned philologist and palaeographer (1782-1854) and his work on palimpsests. Lists discoveries of palimpsests prior to Mai.
112
Tjäder, J.-O. 'Latin Palaeography, 1975-77,' *Eranos: Acta philologica Suecana* 75 (1977) 131-61; 'Latin Palaeography, 1977-1979,' *ibid.* 78 (1980) 65-97
Detailed and critical bibliographical surveys in English, often with lengthy and highly original asides, in continuation of earlier periodic surveys in Swedish, in *Eranos* 59 (1961)—73 (1975), of selected contemporary writings on palaeography.
113
Traube, L. 'Geschichte der Paläographie' in **70**, I, 1-80.

SURVEYS

114
Bischoff, B. 'Paläographie: Mit besonderer Berücksichtigung des deutschen Kulturgebietes' in *Deutsche Philologie im Aufriss,* ed. W. Stammler, vol. I, 2nd ed. (Berlin—Bielefeld—Munich 1957) cols. 379-452, 10 pls.; also printed separately, with its own columnation (1-74) ibid. 1957, and, with additional matter, 1970.
The author's recent *Paläographie* **159** is explicitly an expansion in manual form of this survey.
115
Dain, A. 'Introduction à la paléographie' and 'Paléographie grecque' in **42**, 528-31 and 532-52.

116

Delitsch, H. *Geschichte der abendländischen Schreibschriftformen* (Leipzig 1928). 104 pls.

117

Fichtenau, H. 'Paläographie' in *Enzyklopädie der geisteswissenschaftlichen Arbeitsmethoden* (Munich — Vienna 1976) 125-50.

118

Galbraith, V.H. 'Handwriting' in *Medieval England*, ed. A.L. Poole. 2 vols. 2nd ed. (Oxford 1958) II, 541-58. 11 pls.

119

Hunt, R.W. 'Latin Palaeography' in *Chambers's Encyclopaedia*, new rev. ed. (Oxford — London etc. 1967) 379-83. 5 pls., 7 figs.

120

John, J.J. 'Latin Paleography' in *Medieval Studies: An Introduction*, ed. J.M. Powell (Syracuse, N.Y. 1976) 1-68. 19 figs. with transcriptions.

121

Leclercq, H. 'Manuscrits' in *Dictionnaire d'archéologie chrétienne et de liturgie* X.2 (Paris 1932) cols. 1603-1714

Contains (cols. 1704-14) a useful 'lexicon' of Latin palaeographical terms. To be taken with his article 'Paléographie,' *ibid.* XIII.1 (1937) cols. 610-736 — a formidable and not well-known contribution.

122

Lehmann, P. 'Lateinische Paläographie bis zum Siege der karolingischen Minuskel' in *Einleitung in die Altertumswissenschaft*, ed. A. Gercke and E. Norden, vol. I, 3rd ed. (Leipzig 1927) ch. 10, pp. 38-68.

123

Lowe, E.A. *Handwriting: Our Medieval Legacy* (Rome 1969)

Reprinted, with additional notes by T.J. Brown and transcriptions of 22 plates by W.B. Ross, Jr., from an article in *The Legacy of the Middle Ages*, ed. C.G. Crump and E.F. Jacob (Oxford 1926) 197-226 with 16 plates.

124

Marichal, R. 'L'Ecriture latine et la civilisation occidentale du Ier au XVIe siècle' in **456**, 199-247.

125

———. 'Paleography, Latin' in *New Catholic Encyclopedia* (New York 1967) X, 879-85.

126

Morison, S. 'Notes on the Development of Latin Script from Early to

Modern Times' in **65**, I, 222-94
An essay of 1949, revised partly to 1962.
127
Natale, A.R. 'Il codice e la scrittura: Avviamento allo studio della paleografia latina' in *Introduzione alla filologia classica,* ed. E. Bignone (Milan 1951) 263-341. 31 pls.
128
Perrat, C. 'Paléographie médiévale' in **42**, 585-615.
129
Pratesi, A. *Elementa artis palaeographicae* (Vatican City 1981)
Discusses aspects of writing up to ca. A.D. 800. No plates.
130
Sabatini, F. 'Dalla "scripta latina rustica" alle "scriptae" romanze,' *SM* 3rd ser. 9/1 (1968) 320-58
On the transition from written Latin to the writing down of vernacular speech.
131
Schiaparelli, L. 'Paleografia' in *Enciclopedia italiana.* 2nd ed. (Rome 1949) XXVI, 39-47. 9 pls., 16 figs.
132
Ullman, B.L. *Ancient Writing and its Influence.* 2nd ed. (New York 1969)
A reprint, with introduction and additional bibliography by T.J. Brown, of this influential and very readable book of 1932 by Ullman (1882-1965). Includes 16 plates. Now reissued as Medieval Academy Reprints for Teaching 10 (Toronto 1980).
133
Urry, W.G. 'Paleography' in *Encyclopedia Britannica,* 15th ed. *Macropedia* XIII (1974) 911-14.

MANUALS

Entries in this section are in chronological order.

134
De Wailly, N. *Eléments de paléographie pour servir à l'étude des documents inédits sur l'histoire de France.* 2 vols. (Paris 1838). 17 pls.
A reworking of the Maurist *Traité de diplomatique* **74** which dominated the

teaching of palaeography until ca. 1900. In five parts, the third of which
treats of 'paléographie proprement dite.'

135

Wattenbach, W. *Anleitung zur lateinischen Palaeographie.* 4th ed. (Leipzig
1886, repr. Graz 1958)
First published in 1866, it was the first serious rival of De Wailly. The part
on the evolution of the alphabet and on abbreviations (pp. 43-106) is
hand-written. See also **587**.

136

Reusens, E. *Eléments de paléographie* (Louvain 1899, repr. Brussels 1963).
60 pls. with transcriptions.

137

Paoli, C. *Programma scolastica di paleografia latina e di diplomatica,* I:
Paleografia latina, 3rd ed. (Florence 1901); II, *Materie scrittorie e librarie*
3rd ed. (1913)
One of the formative influences on palaeographical studies in Italy. There
is a well-known German version of I: *Lateinische Paläographie,* ed. K.
Lohmeyer (Innsbruck 1902).

138

Prou, M. *Manuel de paléographie latine et française du VIe au XVIIe siècle*
(Paris 1889). 23 pls.
The standard edition of this influential manual is the 4th (1924), published
as *Manuel de paléographie latine et française,* with an album of 24 plates
and transcriptions. The edition was done with the collaboration of A. de
Boüard, and is in effect an entirely new work. See also **440**.

139

Thompson, E.M. *An Introduction to Greek and Latin Palaeography*
(Oxford 1912, repr. New York 1975)
For long a standard work, but now out-dated in most respects. Includes
250 facsimiles, with transcriptions. Not to be confused with his *Handbook
of Greek and Latin Palaeography,* 3rd ed. (London 1906, repr. Chicago
1966), which is a reprint of an entry in the *Encyclopaedia Britannica,* 9th
ed. (1885).

140

García Villada, Z. *Paleografía española, precedida de una introducción
sobre la paleografía latina* (Madrid 1923, repr. 1974) with album of 67
pls. (116 samples without transcriptions).

141

Bretholz, B. *Lateinische Paläographie*. 3rd ed. (Leipzig 1926)
Has no facsimiles.

142

Millares Carlo, A. *Tratado de paleografía española: Ensayo de una historia de la escritura en España desde el siglo VIII al XVII*. 2nd ed. (Madrid 1932) with album of 131 pls. with transcriptions.

143

Federici, V. *Paleografia latina, dalle origini fino al secolo XVIII*, ed. S. Mottironi. 2nd ed. (Rome 1935)
The class-notes of a famous diplomatist.

144

Modica, M. *Paleografia latina* (Palermo 1941)
Listed regularly in bibliographies. Without much value.

145

Floriano Cumbreño, A.C. *Curso general de paleografía y diplomatica españolas*. 2 vols. (Oviedo 1946)
Vol. I includes 18 plates of literary texts; II is an album of 39 plates of diplomatic documents with transcriptions.

146

Bonenfant, P. *Syllabus du cours de paléographie du moyen âge* (Liège 1947)
Influential.

147

Foerster, H. *Abriss der lateinischen Paläographie*. 2nd ed. (Stuttgart 1963). 24 pls. (39 samples) with transcriptions.

148

Battelli, G. *Lezioni di paleografia*. 3rd ed. (Vatican City 1949, repr. 1978) A clearly-arranged manual, with many figures, but lacking a companion set of facsimiles. Notable for its insistence on *ductus* and for valuable pages on musical palaeography.

149

Semkowicz, W. *Paleografia lacińska* (Cracow 1951)
Has useful pages (442-79) on Latin and Polish abbreviations.

150

Novak, V. *Latinska paleografija* (Belgrade 1952).

151

Denholm-Young, N. *Handwriting in England and Wales* (Cardiff 1954)

In effect a general manual. Includes 31 plates, with transcription of six.
152
Cencetti, G. *Lineamenti di storia della scrittura latina* (Bologna 1954-6)
Though in typescript, and rather congested, one of the most discursive and
detailed of manuals, with a fine section (pp. 353-475) on abbreviations.
No facsimiles. Summarized handily in **153**.
153
————. *Compendio di paleografia latina per le scuole universitarie e
archivistiche* (Naples 1965)
Now reprinted in the series Guide allo studio della civiltà romana, X, 3:
Paleografia latina, Guide 1 (Rome 1978), with new plates (24) and a
bibliographical supplement (pp. 170-92) from 1962 by P. Supino Martini.
154
Strubbe, E. *Grondbegrippen van de Paleografie der Middeleeuwen.* 2 vols.
3rd ed. (Ghent 1961)
One volume presents the text; the other, 27 facsimiles with transcriptions.
155
Hector, L.C. *The Handwriting of English Documents.* 2nd ed. (London
1966)
A wise introduction to palaeography in a diplomatic setting, with 32
plates and transcriptions, covering ca. A.D. 700-1836.
156
Ljublinskaja, A.D. *Latinskaja paleografija* (Moscow 1969). 40 pls., mostly
from Leningrad MSS.
157
Mazzoleni, J. *Paleografia e diplomatica e scienze ausiliarie* (Naples 1970)
A replacement for a slender volume of the same title (1955), covering palaeography (pp. 1-205); diplomatics, especially Angevin (209-355); various
contributions on auxiliary sciences (359-453). Includes 53 plates (many
derivative), with transcriptions of plates 24-45 (14th-16th centuries).
158
Stiennon, J. with G. Hasenohr. *Paléographie du moyen âge* (Paris 1973)
Very thoughtful. Provides 51 plates with transcriptions and a fine appendix
of medieval texts relative to writing. See the extensive review, with notes
on Arabic numerals, by M.-Th. d'Alverny, 'Un nouveau manuel de
paléographie médiévale,' *Le Moyen Age* 81 (1975) 507-14.
159
Bischoff, B. *Paläographie des römischen Altertums und des abendländischen*

Mittelalters. Grundlagen der Germanistik [ed. H. Moser and H. Steinecke] 24 (Berlin 1979)
Although without plates, a most complete and systematic manual. See the critical review by J.O. Tjäder in *Eranos* 78 (1980) 72-5.

FACSIMILES

Series

160
ARCHIVIO PALEOGRAFICO ITALIANO, ed. E. Monaci, L. Schiaparelli, et al. (Rome 1882-)
15 volumes to date, issued irregularly in fascicules, from the Istituto di paleografia dell'Università di Roma. A magnificent if unruly series which illustrates the full scope of Latin palaeography – inscriptions, documents, codices – although diplomatic samples predominate in what has been published to date:
  161
  I. [Miscellaneo] (Rome 1882-97, repr. Turin 1963-4)
  100 plates in nine fascicules, mainly of charters from A.D. 500-1400. Description and transcriptions in *BAPI* 1st ser. 1 (1908) 5-75 [pls. 1-42]; 2 (1910) 149-226 [43-100].
  162
  II. [Monumenti paleografici di Roma–1] (Rome 1884-1907, repr. Turin 1965)
  100 plates, mainly of charters, but with selections from papal registers and codices written at Rome, A.D. 951-1500.
  163
  III. [Miscellaneo] (Rome 1892-1910, repr. Turin 1968-9)
  100 plates of charters, letters, some codices, from all over Italy, ca. A.D. 700-1594.
  164
  IV. [Miniature] (Rome 1908, repr. Turin 1969)
  38 plates from three codices: the bible of Charles the Bald (A.D. 842-69), the Vallicelliana codex of the Acts of the Apostles (9th century), an Ottobonian Evangelarium (11th-12th century).

165

V. [Iscrizioni] (Rome 1904-67, repr. Turin 1970)
59 plates of inscriptions, graffiti, Pompeii electoral posters, funerary epitaphs, etc., from ca. A.D. 50-1263.

166

VI. [Monumenti paleografici di Roma – 2] (Rome 1906-24, repr. Turin 1972)
100 plates of local charters, papal letters, statutes of comuni such as Tivoli, Senate mandates, Farfa registers, etc., from ca. A.D. 800-1513.

167

VII. [Miscellaneo] (Rome 1906-29, repr. Turin 1975-6)
109 plates, mainly of Ravenna charters of the 8th-13th centuries, but with some diplomata, royal letters, and a cartulary of bishops of Trent (pls. 98-109), for the period A.D. 500-1500.

168

VIII. *Frammenti diversi – Centri scrittorii* (Rome 1908 [pls. 1-17] and 1975 [18-37])
37 plates of classical authors, bibles, homiliaries, collectaria, missals, breviaries, etc., from the 9th-15th centuries.

169

IX. *Diplomi dei Re d'Italia* (Rome 1910-28, repr. Turin 1975)
122 plates of royal diplomata of the 9th and 10th centuries. Transcriptions in *BAPI* 1st ser. 3 (1910) 9-56 [pls. 1-12]; 4 (1911) 57-101 [13-25]; 5 (1913) 103-55 [26-39]; 6 (1919) 157-99 [40-52].

170

X. *Documenti per la storia letteraria italiana* (Rome 1913, repr. Turin 1971 [pls. 1-10]; Rome 1972 [11-31])
31 plates, 1-10 of which run from A.D. 960-1219 (including the famous *Placiti* of Capua, March 960); 11-31 cover various MSS of Dante's *Divine Comedy*.

171

XI. *Documenti di diplomatica comunale italiana* (Rome 1938, repr. Turin 1971 [pls. 1-10]; Turin 1970 [11-20])
20 plates, 1-10 of which illustrate processes, treaties, etc. of the Roman Senate in the 13th century; 11-20 deal with activities of various communes, A.D. 1157-1408.

172

XII. *Documenti del notariato italiano* (Rome 1942, repr. Turin 1969

[pls. 1-15]; Rome 1953, repr. Turin 1970 [16-34]; Rome 1965 [35-46], 1976 [47-67], and 1978 [68-81])
To date 81 plates illustrating notarial practice in Pisa, Bologna, Genoa, Rome, etc., from the 8th-13th centuries. Transcriptions in *BAPI* 1st ser. 7 (1943) 1-39 [pls. 1-15]; 3rd ser. 1 (1962) 135-68 [16-34].

173

XIII. *Documenti di diplomatica vescovile* (Rome 1950, repr. Turin 1967 [pls. 1-16]; Rome 1963 [17-32] and 1979 [33-51])
The plates thus far published cover privileges and letters of various bishops in Italy, A.D. 971-1298, e.g. 'Diplomata episcoporum bononiensium.'

174

XIV. *Diplomata regum Siciliae de gente Normannorum* (Rome 1954-)
39 plates to date from A.D. 1131-1210, with transcriptions in *BAPI* new ser. 1 (1955) 141-86 [pls. 1-39].

175

XV. *Diplomata principum Beneventi, Capuae, et Salerni de gente Langobardorum* (Rome 1956, repr. Turin 1969 [pls. 1-15]; Rome 1961, repr. Turin 1969 [16-27]; Turin 1969 [28-41])
The 41 plates run from A.D. 886-1060 (Salerno, Benevento). Transcriptions in *BAPI* new ser. 4-5 (1958-9) 117-27 [pls. 1-15]; 3rd ser. 2-3 (1963-4) 167-79 [16-27].

176

ARMARIUM CODICUM INSIGNIUM (Turnhout 1980-):

177

[1] *Les Scolies ariennes du Parisinus latinus 8907: Un échantillonnage d'écritures latines du Ve siècle,* ed. R. Gryson and L. Gilissen (1980)
Paris, BN, MS. lat. 8907: text in early Uncial, surrounded in two sections by marginal notes in Later Roman or Common cursive, in which four hands have been discerned by macrophotography (cf. **1657-8**), one being of the early 5th century and contemporary with the Uncial text, the other three from about the middle of the century. Facsimile of the *scholia* pages (some 55).

178

CHARTAE LATINAE ANTIQUIORES, ed. A. Bruckner and R. Marichal (Olten–Lausanne 1954-67, Zürich 1975-)
This series (ChLA) aims to publish in facsimile, transcribe diplomatically, and annotate every surviving non-literary Latin text whether on papyrus or

parchment up to A.D. 800. It complements E.A. Lowe's *Codices Latini antiquiores*, **251-63**. For vols. I-IV introductions and commentary are in English. From V onwards they are in the native language of the editor or commentator:

179
I. *Switzerland: Basle – St. Gall* (1954)
Plates 1-108 (Bruckner).

180
II. *Switzerland: St. Gall – Zurich* (1956)
Plates 109-78 (Bruckner). Has a valuable introduction on 'The diplomatic of early Alemannian charters.'

181
III. [Great Britain] *British Museum London* (1963)
Plates 179-223 (Bruckner, Marichal, J.-O. Tjäder).

182
IV. *Great Britain (without British Museum London)* (1967)
Plates 224-75 (Bruckner, Marichal). Includes good critical notes in introduction on the diplomatic of early Anglo-Saxon charters.

183
V. *The United States of America I* (1975)
Plates 276-308. Largely concerned with Michigan (Ann Arbor) papyri. Introduction and commentaries (now in French) by Marichal.

184
VI. *The United States of America II* (1975)
Plates 309-21 (Marichal): the Dura papyri at Yale University.

185
VII. *The United States of America III* (1975)
Plates 322-54 (Marichal): Dura papyri at Yale.

186
VIII. *The United States of America IV* (1976)
Plates 355-6 (Marichal): Dura papyri at Yale: Rolls of Cohort XX of Palmyra.

187
IX. *The United States of America V* (1977)
Plates 357-406: remainder (nos. 357-95), with index (pp. 82-100), of the Yale Dura papyri (Marichal); other papyri at Yale, New York (Pierpont Morgan Library), and Princeton, N.J. (Marichal, Tjäder). Provides a detailed discussion of palaeography and diplomatics in section 6 of

the introduction, pp. [15]-[19].

188

X. *Germany I: Berlin DDR* (1979)
Plates 407-64 (Marichal).

189

XI. *Germany II: Berlin (West), Bundesrepublik Deutschland und Deutsche Demokratische Republik* (1979)
Plates 465-517 (Marichal), covering West Berlin – Cologne (Köln).

190

XII. *Germany III: Bundesrepublik Deutschland und Deutsche Demokratische Republik* (1978)
Plates 518-48 (Bruckner, Marichal), covering Leipzig – Säckingen.

191

XIII. *France I,* ed. H. Atsma and J. Vezin (1981)
Plates 549-71: charters from the Archives nationales, Paris, from A.D. 584-629 to 690-91. A concordance is provided to previous publication of these charters, e.g. to Lauer and Samaran (see **913**).

192

CODICES E VATICANIS SELECTI PHOTOTYPICE (QUAM SIMILLIME) EXPRESSI...: SERIES MAIOR (Rome 1889-1931, Vatican City 1932- , unless otherwise specified)
In general only Latin texts are noted here, and, where possible, by short title:

193

I. *Fragmenta et picturae Vergiliana codicis Vaticani Latini 3225* (Rome 1899, 2nd ed. 1930; 3rd ed. Vatican City 1945)
The 'Codex Vaticanus,' carrying 50 miniatures. Rustic Capital, 4th or 5th century. 76 folios. CF. For another CF see **213**.

194

II. *Picturae, ornamenta, complura scripturae specimina codicis Vaticani 3867, qui Codex Vergilii Romanus audit, phototypice expressa* (1902)
The 'Codex Romanus.' Rustic Capital, mid-5th century. 309 folios. PF. 33 plates. See also **562**.

195

III. *Le miniature del pontificale Ottoboniano* (1903)
Vatican City, BAV, MS. Ottobonianum lat. 501. Italy, late 15th century. 208 folios. PF. 15 plates, showing 24 miniatures.

196

VI. *L'originale del Canzoniere di Francesco Petrarca, codice Vaticano latino 3195, riprodotto in fototipia* (Milan 1905)
Written A.D. 1366-8 (at Venice?), partly by Petrarch, partly by the scribe John. 72 folios. CF.

197

VII. *M. Cornelii Frontonis aliorumque reliquiae quae codice Vaticano 5750 rescripto continentur* (Milan 1906)
Palimpsest. Uncial, 5th century, and Rustic capital, beginning of the 6th century. 143 folios. CF.

198

XII. *Monumenti Vaticani di paleografia musicale latina,* ed. H.M. Bannister (Leipzig 1913). 132 pls.

199

XIV. *Codex Vergilianus qui Palatinus appellatur,* ed. R. Sabbadini (Paris 1929)
The 'Codex Palatinus.' Vatican City, BAV, MS. Pal. lat. 1631. Rustic Capital, 4th century. 256 folios. CF.

200

XV. *Codicis Vergiliani qui Augusteus appellatur reliquiae,* ed. R. Sabbadini (Turin 1926)
The 'Codex Augusteus.' Vatican City, BAV, MS. Vat. lat. 3256 (8 folios in all). Square Capital, 4th century. CF.

201

XVI. *Regestum D.ni Innocentii tertii PP. super negotio Romani Imperii,* ed. W.M. Peitz (1927)
Archivio Segreto Vaticano, Reg. Vat. 6. Curial Gothic, early 13th century (1199-1209). 44 folios. CF.

202

XVIII. *Terentius: Codex Vaticanus Latinus 3868 picturis insignis,* ed. G. Jachmann (Leipzig 1929)
Caroline, written by the monk Hrodegarius at Corvey, before A.D. 850. 92 folios. CF.

203

XXI. *Dantis Alagherii Monarchiae liber et Epistolae, ex codice Vaticano Palatino Latino 1729,* ed. F.R. Schneider (1930)
Italian Gothic, 14th century. 64 folios. PF (fols. 31-64).

204

XXII. *Il Convivio di Dante Aligherii, riprodotto ... dal codice Barberiniano latino 4086,* ed. F. Schneider (1932)
PF (fols. 7-49).

205

XXIII. *M. Tulli Ciceronis De re publica libri: E codice rescripto Vaticano Latino 5757, phototypice expressi. Prolegomena De fatis bibliothecae monasterii S. Columbani Bobiensis et de codice ipso Vat. Lat. 5757.*
2 vols. (1934)
The celebrated palimpsest. Uncial of the 4th century A.D. under Uncial Augustine, *Enarrationes in psalmos,* of the 7th century. Palimpsested and rewritten at Bobbio. 151 folios. CF. The volume of Prolegomena is by G. Mercati from notes put together by F. Ehrle; it has one plate. See also **255, 795.**

206

XXIV. *La Cronaca figurata di Giovanni Villani: Ricerche sulla miniatura fiorentina del Trecento,* by L. Magnani (1936)
Vatican City, BAV, MS. Chigi L. VIII. 296. Gothic. A copy of the *Cronaca* of Villani (1280?-1348), written and illustrated at Florence in the second half of the 14th century. 332 folios. PF. 49 plates, 98 illustrations.

207

XXVI. *Il Codice Vaticano lat. 3196 autografo del Petrarca,* ed. M. Porena (1941)
Various sonnets, ballads, and canzoni, with annotations (mostly in Latin), all in the hand of Petrarch ca. 1348-68. 20 folios. CF.

208

XXVII. *I due primi registri di prestito della Biblioteca Apostolica Vaticana,* ed. M. Bertola (1942)
Vatican City, BAV, MSS. Vat. lat. 3964, 3966. The first register of borrowers (kept by Bartolomeo Platina) runs from A.D. 1475-87, the second (by Romolo Mammacini) from 1486-1547. Paper in each case: 44 and 128 pages. CF.

209

XXXI. *Kaiser Friedrich II, De arte venandi cum avibus,* ed. C.A. Willemsen. 2 vols. (Graz 1969)
Vatican City, BAV, MS. Pal. lat. 1071. Gothic. South Italy, A.D. 1250-1300. 111 folios. CF. Also found in the series Codices selecti: see **275.**

210

XXXV. *Exultet-Rolle: Vollständige Faksimile-Ausgabe in Original-grösse des Codex Vaticanus latinus 9820 der Biblioteca Apostolica Vaticana,* ed. H. Douteil and F. Vongrey. 2 vols. (Graz 1974, 1975) Beneventan. Written by the priest John for the Benedictine nuns of St. Peter's, Benevento, A.D. 981-7. 20 membranes (a roll measuring 708 x 27 cm.). CF. Also found in the series Codices selecti: see **294**.

211

XXXVII. *Il codice Chigiano L. V. 176: Autografo di Giovanni Boccaccio,* ed. D. de Robertis (Florence 1975) Parchment, ca. A.D. 1363-6. Boccaccio's *Dante e Petrarca* in his small ('littera sottile') Italian Gothic hand. 81 folios. CF (fols. 1r-79r).

212

XXXVIII. *Sacramentarium Gelasianum e codice Vaticano Reginensi Latino 316,* ed. L.M. Tocci and B. Neunheuser (Vatican City 1975) Uncial (Corbie?), a little before A.D. 750. 245 folios. CF.

213

XL. *Vergilius Vaticanus: Vollständige farbige Faksimile-Ausgabe im Originalformat von Codex Vaticanus Lat. 3225,* ed. D. Wright. 2 vols. (Graz 1980) Rustic capital. Italy, 4th-5th century. 76 folios, with 50 miniatures. CF. Also found in the series Codices selecti: see **304**. See also **193**.

214

CODICES E VATICANIS SELECTI PHOTOTYPICE (QUAM SIMILLIME) EXPRESSI ...: SERIES MINOR (Rome 1910-31, Vatican City 1932-) Latin volumes only:

215

II. *Pagine scelte di due codici appartenuti alla badia di S. Maria di Coupar-Angus in Scozia,* ed. H.M. Bannister (Rome 1910) Vatican City, BAV, MSS. Pal. lat. 65 (glossed psalter, 12th century, in an imitative Hiberno-Insular hand; 201 folios), Reg. lat. 694 (Bede, etc., in early Gothic ca. A.D. 1200; 118 folios). 5 plates (4 from Pal. lat. 65).

216

IV. *Biblia pauperum: Riproduzione del codice Palatino latino 143,* ed. L. Donati and L.M. Tocci (Vatican City 1978) CF (99 plates) of a composite codex of the 15th century, only one part of which is manuscript: the third item of four, a genealogical tree of

Christ, with commentary, in German, on 12 folios. The other items,
including an illustrated *Biblia pauperum,* are xylographic productions.

217

CODICES EX ECCLESIASTICIS ITALIAE BYBLIOTHECIS DELECTI PHOTO-
TYPICE EXPRESSI (Rome 1913-31, Vatican City 1932-):

218

I. *Il codice Vercellese con omelie e poesie in lingua anglosassone,*
ed. M. Foerster (1913)
Vercelli, Biblioteca capitolare, MS. 117. Anglo-Insular minuscule.
England, late 10th century. 136 folios. CF. For another facsimile edition
see **754.**

219

II. *Il codice CCCCXC della Biblioteca capitolare di Lucca: Ottantatre
pagine per servire a studi paleografici,* ed. L. Schiaparelli. 2 vols. (1924)
Various scripts, probably written at Lucca. 355 folios. PF. 83 plates.
For content see **820.**

220

III. *Monumenti paleografici Veronesi,* ed. E. Carusi and W.M. Lindsay,
I: *Semionciale di Ursicino (sec. VI e VII)* (1928)
Verona, Biblioteca capitolare, MSS. XXXVII, XXXVIII, etc. Semi-uncial,
6th-7th century. 23 plates. See also **224.**

221

IV. *Le miniature dell'Evangeliario di Padova dell'anno 1170,* ed. B.
Katterbach (1931)
Padua, Tesoro della Cattedrale, MS. s.n. Written and illustrated at Padua
in 1170 by the cleric Isidore. 85 folios. PF. 23 plates.

222

V. *Le miniature dell'Epistolario di Padova dell'anno 1259,* ed. B.
Katterbach (1932)
Padua, Tesoro della Cattedrale, MS. s.n. Italian Gothic. Written and illuminated at Padua in 1259 by the archpriest Johannes Galbanus. 104
folios. PF. 51 plates.

223

VI. *Le miniature del Sacramentario d'Ivrea e di altri codici Warmondi-
ani,* ed. L. Magnani (1934)
Ivrea, Biblioteca capitolare, MS. 86 (Sacramentary). Caroline, before
A.D. 1002. 222 folios. PF. 50 plates.

224
VII. *Monumenti paleografici Veronesi,* ed. E. Carusi and W.M. Lindsay, II: *Vari tipi di scrittura tra Ursicino e Pacifico (sec. VII-IX)* (1934)
23 plates of scripts of the 7th-9th centuries, with transcriptions. See also **220, 1036.**

225
IX. Giovanni Dondi dall'Orologio, *Tractatus Astrarii,* ed. A. Barzon, E. Morpurgo, A. Petrucci, G. Francescato (1960)
Padua, Biblioteca capitolare, MS. D. 39. Gothic. Written at Padua (?), A.D. 1350-1400. 34 folios. CF. 66 plates.

226
CODICES GRAECI ET LATINI PHOTOGRAPHICE DEPICTI, ed. W.N. DuRieu, S. de Vries, and, from vol. XX, G.I. Lieftinck (Leiden 1897-)
Latin MSS only:

227
II. *Augustinus, Beda, Horatius, Ovidius, Servius, alii: Codex Bernensis 363,* ed. H. Hagen (1897)
Bern, Stadt- und Universitätsbibliothek, MS. 363 (olim Bongarsianus). Hiberno-Insular, mid-9th century. 197 folios. CF.

228
V. *Plautus: Codex Heidelbergensis 1613 Palatinus C.,* ed. K. Zange-meister (1900)
Heidelberg, Universitätsbibliothek, MS. lat. 1613. Caroline, 10th-11th century. 238 folios. CF.

229
VII.1. *Tacitus: Codex Laurentianus Mediceus 68 I,* ed. E. Rostagno (1902)
Florence, Biblioteca Medicea-Laurenziana, MS. Plut. LXVIII, 1. Caroline (Tours). France (?), mid-9th century. 138 folios (incomplete). CF.

230
VII.2. *Tacitus Laurentianus Mediceus 68 II,* ed. E. Rostagno (1902)
Florence, Biblioteca Medicea-Laurenziana, MS. Plut. LXVIII, 2, fols. 1-103. Beneventan. Monte Cassino, mid-11th century. Total codex, 191 folios (Tacitus and Apuleius). Here CF of Tacitus.

231
VIII. *Terentius: Codex Ambrosianus H. 75 inf. phototypice editus....*

Accedunt 91 imagines ex aliis Terenti codicibus et libris impressis nunc primum collectae et editae, ed. E. Bethe (1903)
Milan, Biblioteca Ambrosiana, MS. H 75 inf. Caroline. France (?), Speyer (?), beginning of the 10th century. 120 folios. CF.
232

XI. *Livius: Codex Vindobonensis Lat. 15,* ed. C. Wessely (1907)
Vienna, ONB, MS. lat. 15 (olim 626). Uncial, 6th century. 193 folios (*Ab urbe condita* Bks. 41-5). CF.
233

XII. *Lucretius: Codex Vossianus oblongus,* ed. E. Chatelain (1908)
Leiden, BRU, MS. Voss. lat. F. 30. Caroline. France, or possibly Germany, 9th century. 192 folios. CF.
234

XIII. *Isidori Etymologiae: Codex Toletanus (nunc Matritensis),* ed. R. Beer (1909)
Madrid, BN, MS. Tolet. 15. 8. Visigothic, 8th century. 163 folios. CF.
235

XIV. *Tibulli Carmina, Sapphus Epistula Ovidiana: Codex Guelferbytanus 82. 6 Aug.,* ed. F. Leo (1910)
Wolfenbüttel, Herzog August Bibliothek, MS. Aug. 2° 82. 6. Semi-Beneventan. Written by Gioviano Pontano, 15th century. Parchment. 42 folios. CF. See also **247**.
236

XVI. *Propertius: Codex Guelferbytanus Gudianus 224, olim Neapolitanus,* ed. T. Birt (1911)
Wolfenbüttel, Herzog August Bibliothek, MS. Gud. 224. Caroline. France (?), 12th century. 71 folios. CF.
237

XVII. *Cicero: De natura deorum, De divinatione, De legibus. Codex Heinsianus (Leidensis 118),* ed. O. Plasberg (1912)
Leiden, BRU, MS. B.P.L. 118. Beneventan. Monte Cassino, A.D. 1058-1087. 102 folios. CF.
238

XVIII. *Lucretius: Codex Vossianus quadratus,* ed. E. Chatelain (1913)
Leiden, BRU, MS. Voss. lat. Q. 94. Caroline. France (?), 9th century. 69 folios. CF.
239

XIX. *Cicero: Operum philosophicorum. Codex Leidensis Vossianus Lat.*

fol. 84, ed. O. Plasberg (1915)

Leiden, BRU, MS. Voss. lat. F. 84. Caroline. France, 10th century. 124 folios. CF.

240

XX. *Tacitus: Annales (XI-XVI) et Historiae. Codex Leidensis bibliothecae publicae Latinus 16B (Codex Agricolae)*, ed. C.W. Mendell and E. Hulshoff Pol (1966)

Leiden, BRU, MS. B.P.L. 16B. Personal hand (see **333**). Italy (Ferrara?) ca. A.D. 1476. Parchment. 192 folios. CF. See also **247**.

241

XXI. *Catullus: Carmina. Codex Oxoniensis Bibliothecae Bodleianae Canonicianus Class. Lat. 30*, ed. R.A.B. Mynors (1966)

Gothic. Italy (?), before A.D. 1375. Parchment. 38 folios. CF.

242

XXII. *Corpus agrimensorum Romanorum: Codex Arcerianus A der Herzog-August-Bibliothek zu Wolfenbüttel (Cod. Guelf. 36. 23.A)*, ed. H. Butzmann (1970)

Wolfenbüttel, Herzog August Bibliothek, MS. Aug.2° 36. 23. Uncial. N. Italy (?), 5th-6th century. 156 folios (remains of two MSS). CF of part one.

243

CODICES GRAECI ET LATINI PHOTOGRAPHICE DEPICTI, ed. S. de Vries, SUPPLEMENTUM (Leiden 1902-):

244

I. *Hieronymi Chronicorum codicis Floriacensis fragmenta Leidensia, Parisina, Vaticana*, ed. L. Traube (1902)

Leiden, BRU, MS. Voss. lat. Q.110 (6 fols.); Paris, BN, MS. lat. 6400B (14 fols.); Vatican City, BAV, MS. Reg. lat. 1709 (2 fols.). Uncial. Italy (?), 5th century. 22 folios. CF.

245

II. *Miniatures du Psautier de S. Louis*, ed. H. Omont (1902)

Leiden, BRU, MS. B.P.L. 76A. Caroline, end of the 12th century. 185 folios. PF. 25 plates.

246

III. *Der illustrierte lateinische Aesop in der Handschrift des Ademar: Codex Vossianus lat. oct. 15, fol. 195-205*, ed. G. Thiele (1905)

Leiden, BRU, MS. Voss. lat. O.15. Caroline. Written at St. Martial of Limoges in A.D. 1023-5 (see **333**) by Adémar of Chabannes (988-

1034). 212 folios. PF (fols. 195-205). 22 plates.
247
IV. *Taciti Dialogus de oratoribus et Germania, Suetonii De viris illustri-*
bus fragmentum. Codex Leidensis Perizonianus, ed. G. Wissowa (1907)
Leiden, BRU, MS. Periz. Q. 21. Written at Naples in A.D. 1460 by
Gioviano Pontano, in an artificial hand (see **333**). 59 folios. CF. See
also **235**.
248
V. *Alpertus Mettensis: De diversitate temporum – De Theodorico I.*
episcopo Mettensi. Codex Hannoveranus 712A, ed. C. Pijnacker Hordijk
(1908)
Hannover, Landesbibliothek, MS. 712ª. Caroline, after A.D. 1050.
6 folios. CF.
249
VIII. *Miniaturen der lateinischen Galenos-Handschrift der Königl.*
Öffentl. Bibliothek in Dresden Db 92-93, ed. E.C. van Leersum and
W. Martin (1910)
Dresden, Sächsische Landesbibliothek, MS. Db 92-3. Humanist.
Belgium (?), second half of the 15th century. Parchment. 617 folios.
PF. 18 plates and 105 illustrations.
250
IX. *Die Konstanz-Weingartener Propheten-Fragmente,* ed. P. Lehmann
(1912)
Almost CF of fragments of 46 folios from an Uncial codex of the
5th century written in Italy, which belonged to Reichenau from, prob-
ably, the mid-9th century and then passed to Constance Cathedral
where, in the 15th century, it was broken up and used in binding
various MSS, many of which were acquired by Weingarten Abbey in
1630 and are now in libraries at Darmstadt, Donaueschingen, Fulda,
St. Paul in Carinthia, and Stuttgart. See CLA X, pp. [4] and [46].
251
CODICES LATINI ANTIQUIORES: A PALAEOGRAPHICAL GUIDE TO LATIN
MANUSCRIPTS PRIOR TO THE NINTH CENTURY, ed. E.A. Lowe. 12 vols.
(Oxford 1934-72)
This celebrated set of facsimiles (usually abbreviated as CLA) presents at
least one sample in facsimile from every known codex or fragment written
in a literary (or 'library') script from the earliest period of Latin handwrit-
ing to ca. A.D. 800. Each codex is described as fully as possible, with a

minute attention to hands, abbreviations, and peculiarities. Each entry has its own extensive bibliography. Most volumes carry substantial introductions, often with accounts of various writing-centres, lists of dated or datable codices in the given volume, and various palaeographical observations. On occasion some plates illustrate the introductions. See also **89, 90, 98**.

252

I. *The Vatican City* (1934). Plates 1-117.

253

II. *Great Britain and Ireland* (1935, 2nd ed. 1972). Plates 118-277
In the introduction pp. xv-xx carry a survey of Insular palaeography, with 4 plates of three MSS exhibiting Insular and Uncial scripts. At p. 46 of the 1972 edition there is a note of changes in location of MSS since the first edition, and a list of additional items described in other volumes of the CLA.

254

III. *Italy Ancona – Novara* (1938). Plates 278-406.

255

IV. *Italy Perugia – Verona* (1947). Plates 407-516
The introduction has a list of MSS carrying 'corrections' or annotations which specify a location, a list of dated MSS of Italian Uncial, and pages (xx-xxvii) on Bobbio, its scriptorium and palimpsests (see also **205**). At pp. xii-xiv there is an important set of 'assumptions' which Lowe relied upon 'in reaching conclusions as regards the date or origin of manuscripts.'

256

V. *France Paris* (1950). Plates 517-703.

257

VI. *France Abbeville – Valenciennes* (1953). Plates 704-841
In the introduction, which carries 4 plates of four MSS, there are revisions of some dates given in vols. I-V (p. x), a note on the meaning in the volume of 'Caroline minuscule' (p. xii), and an extensive survey (pp. xiii-xxx) of French scriptoria, with lists of surviving MSS (including those carrying 'Nuns' minuscule': see also **259, 910**).

258

VII. *Switzerland* (1956). Plates 842-1023
Pp. ix-x of the introduction discuss briefly Alemannic and Rhaetian scripts and centres, with a list of nine surviving MSS from Ireland at St. Gall.

259

VIII. *Germany Altenburg – Leipzig* (1959). Plates 1024-1229
Includes a list of dated and placed MSS from Germany in the introduction (pp. viii-ix), and additions to the list of MSS of Nuns' minuscule (see **257**).

260

IX. *Germany Maria-Laach – Würzburg* (1959). Plates 1230-1442
Pp. viii-xi provide a survey of German centres (particularly Bavaria).

261

X. *Austria, Belgium, Czechoslovakia, Denmark, Egypt, and Holland* (1963). Plates 1443-1588
Pp. viii-xviii discuss the relationship of the schools of Salzburg and St. Amand, with a list of MSS and (pp. xiv-xv) 2 plates of eight MSS.

262

XI. *Hungary, Luxembourg, Poland, Russia, Spain, Sweden, The United States, and Yugoslavia* (1966). Plates 1589-1670
Pp. viii-ix give a list of MSS of Spanish origin.

263

[XII] *Supplement* (1971). Plates 1589-1811
Covers various libraries: Aachen – Zürich (pls. 1589-1778), Ann Arbor – Weimar (1779-1811). Pp. vii-ix carry a note (with 8 plates of 15 MSS and 2 inscriptions) of 19 MSS (16 Uncial, 3 Semi-uncial) of the 'African School' (texts of Cyprian, Augustine, etc.). In addition to the customary bibliographical notes to the plates (pp. 68-71), there is a 'Selected supplementary bibliography for C.L.A., I-XI' at pp. 43-67, while pp. 73-84 carry an Index of Authors (for I-XI and Supplement), a list of MSS by library (Aachen – Zürich) in all 12 volumes, and a brief Index of Provenances. There is no list of MSS by origin, nor is there an index of scripts.

264

CODICES LITURGICI E VATICANIS PRAESERTIM DELECTI PHOTOTYPICE EXPRESSI (Augsburg 1929-):

265

I. *Missale Gothicum: Das gallikanische Sakramentar (Cod. Vatican. Regin. lat. 317) des VII.-VIII. Jahrhunderts*, ed. C. Mohlberg. 2 vols. (1929)
Vatican City, BAV, MS. Reg. lat. 317. Uncial. Written, probably, for the church of Autun (see CLA I.106). 264 folios (with some 413 decorated initials). CF.

266
II. *Das Professbuch der Abtei St. Gallen,* ed. P.M. Krieg (1931)
St. Gall, Stiftsarchiv, cod. Class. I. Cist. C. 3. B. 56. Professions from
A.D. 720-59 (Abbot Othmar) to the 10th century. Various hands from
ca. 800. 12 folios. CF.

267
CODICES SELECTI PHOTOTYPICE IMPRESSI, ed. F. Sauer (from vol. 3)
and J. Stummvoll (Graz 1960-)
Generally only Latin volumes are noted here, and, where possible, in a
short-title form. Each text is accompanied by a commentary, sometimes
in a separate volume. For the sake of brevity, all commentators, etc. are
treated as editors:

268
I. *Sacramentarium Leonianum,* ed. F. Sauer (1960)
Verona, Biblioteca capitolare, MS. LXXXV (olim 80). Uncial. Possibly
as early as mid-6th century A.D. (Verona?). 139 folios. CF.

269
III. *Codex epistolaris Carolinus,* ed. F. Unterkircher (1962)
Vienna, ONB, MS. lat. 449. 99 letters of popes Gregory III—Hadrian I
(A.D. 731-95) to Charles Martel, Pepin, and Charlemagne. Caroline.
Cologne (?), second half of the 9th century. 98 folios. CF.

270
VI. *Tacuinum sanitatis in medicina,* ed. F. Unterkircher, H. Saxer, and
C.H. Talbot. 2 vols. (1965, 1967)
Vienna, ONB, MS. Series nova 2644. Gothic, N. Italy (Verona?), end
of the 14th century. 111 folios, illuminated. CF.

271
X. *Millstätter Genesis und Physiologus Handschrift,* ed. A. Kracher.
2 vols. (1967)
Klagenfurt, Landesarchiv für Kärnten, Sammelhs. 6/19. In Middle-
High German. The earliest example of a richly illustrated codex in
German. Gothic. Carinthia (?), A.D. 1180-1200. 167 folios. CF.

272
XIII. *Krumauer Bilderkodex,* ed. G. Schmidt and F. Unterkircher.
2 vols. (1967)
Vienna, ONB, MS. lat. 370. *Biblia pauperum* and legends. Gothic.
For the Franciscans of Krumau (Bohemia), ca. A.D. 1358. 172 folios,
illuminated. CF.

273

XIV. *Gebetbuch Karls des Kühnen vel potius Stundenbuch der Maria von Burgund*, ed. F. Unterkircher and A. de Schreyver. 2 vols. (1969) Vienna, ONB, MS. lat. 1857. Written at Ghent, A.D. 1475-7, by David Aubert, with miniatures by Nicolaus Spierinc (?) and Liévin van Lathem (see the study of the illuminations by de Schreyver). 186 folios. CF.

274

XV. *Das Wiener Fragment der Lorscher Annalen: Christus und die Samariterin. Katechese des Niceta von Remesiana*, ed. F. Unterkircher (1967) Vienna, ONB, MS. lat. 515. Caroline. Reichenau, 10th century. 8 folios. CF.

275

XVI. *De arte venandi cum avibus* ... see **209**.

276

XVII. *Comes Romanus Wirziburgensis*, ed. H. Thurn (1968) Würzburg, Universitätsbibliothek, MS. M. p. th. f. 62. Copy of a Roman lectionary ('Comes Romanus') of ca. A.D. 645, of which it is the earliest witness. Anglo-Insular minuscule. Rome or England, mid-8th century. 16 folios. CF.

277

XX. *Alkuin-Briefe und andere Traktate*, ed. F. Unterkircher (1969) Vienna, ONB, MS. lat. 795. Has a famous set of runes. Caroline. Salzburg, A.D. 799, for or by Archbishop Arn, Alcuin's pupil. 205 folios. CF. See also CLA X.1490.

278

XXI. *Antiphonar von St. Peter*, ed. F. Unterkircher and O. Demus. 2 vols. (1969, 1974) Vienna, ONB, MS. Series nova 2700. Late Caroline. Salzburg, ca. A.D. 1160. 423 folios, illuminated. CF.

279

XXII. *Francesco Tranchedino: Diplomatische Geheimschriften*, ed. W. Höflechner (1970) Vienna, ONB, MS. lat. 2398. A collection of the cryptographic signs used by the Sforza dukes of Milan for their diplomatic correspondence in the second half of the 15th century, compiled by Tranchedino (ob. ca. 1496) at Milan. 169 folios. CF.

280

XXIV. *Sancti Bonifatii Epistolae,* ed. F. Unterkircher (1971)
Vienna, ONB, MS. lat. 751, fols. 1-77. Contains 35 letters of Boniface
and 12 to him. Late Caroline. Mainz (?), mid-12th century. CF (fols.
1-77).

281

XXV. *Karolingisches Sakramentar Fragment,* ed. F. Unterkircher (1971)
Vienna, ONB, MS. lat. 958. Caroline. N. France, second half of the 9th
century. 8 folios, illuminated. CF.

282

XXVII. *Medicina antiqua: Libri quattuor medicinae,* ed. C.H. Talbot
and F. Unterkircher. 2 vols. (1972)
Vienna, ONB, MS. lat. 93. Gothic. Sicily, first half of the 13th century.
161 folios, illuminated. CF.

283

XXVIII. *Sakramentar von Metz Fragment,* ed. F. Mütherich (1972)
Paris, BN, MS. lat. 1141. Caroline. Written and illuminated for (probably) Charles the Bald ca. A.D. 870. 10 folios. CF.

284

XXX. *Otfrid von Weissenburg, Evangelienharmonie,* ed. H. Butzmann
(1972)
Vienna, ONB, MS. lat. 2687. Caroline. Written at Wissembourg, A.D.
863-71, by Otfrid, a pupil of Hrabanus Maurus, with Otfrid's own
marginal annotations. 194 folios, 4 picture pages. CF.

285

XXXI. *Reichenauer Evangelistar,* ed. P. Bloch. 2 vols. (1972)
Berlin, Staatsbibliothek der Stiftung Preussischer Kulturbesitz, Kupfer-
stichkabinett, MS. 78 A 2. Caroline. Written and illuminated at
Reichenau, second half of the 11th century. 91 folios. CF.

286

XXXII. *Speculum humanae salvationis,* ed. W. Neumüller. 2 vols.
(1972)
'Codex Cremifanensis': Kremsmünster, Stiftsbibliothek, MS. 243.
Gothic. Raum Bodensee (?), Weissenau (?), first half of the 14th
century. 62 folios, illustrated. CF.

287

XXXIII. *Hrabanus Maurus, Liber de laudibus sanctae crucis,* ed. K.
Holter. 2 vols. (1972)

Vienna, ONB, MS. lat. 652. Caroline. Mainz or Fulda, after A.D. 847.
50 folios, illustrated. CF.
288

XXXVII. *Le Psautier de Saint Louis,* ed. M. Thomas (1970)
Paris, BN, MS. lat. 10525. Gothic. Paris, A.D. 1253-70. A facsimile
edition in colour of all full-page miniatures (78) and of pages with
initial letters. A volume of commentary is promised. 260 folios. PF.
184 plates.
289

XXXIX. *Das ältere Gebetbuch Kaiser Maximilians I,* ed. W. Hilger (1973)
Vienna, ONB, MS. lat. 1907. Bastarda. Written and illuminated shortly
after A.D. 1486, probably at Bruges. 91 folios. CF.
290

XL. *Bible moralisée,* ed. R. Haussherr. 2 vols. (1973)
Vienna, ONB, MS. lat. 2554. Gothic. Possibly Paris, ca. A.D 1220-30.
131 folios, all illuminated. CF.
291

XLI. *Wiener 'Hispana'-Handschrift,* ed. O. Mazal (1974)
Vienna, ONB, MS. lat. 411. A copy of the collection of ecclesiastical
canons known as 'Hispana.' Early Caroline, 'written presumably in
East France near the Rhineland' (CLA X.1477). 315 folios. CF.
292

XLII. *Sammelhandschrift Diez B Sant. 66: Grammatici Latini et
Catalogus librorum,* ed. B. Bischoff (1973)
Berlin, Staatsbibliothek der Stiftung Preussischer Kulturbesitz, MS.
Diez B. 66. Caroline, shortly after A.D. 796, possibly from the court of
Charlemagne at Aachen. The list of books there may be that of the
palace library. 182 folios. CF. See **917.**
293

XLV. *Codex Millenarius,* ed. W. Neumüller and K. Holter (1974)
Kremsmünster, Stiftsbibliothek, MS. Cim. 1, fols. 17-348 ('Codex
Millenarius Maior'). Four Gospels. Caroline. Written and illustrated at
Mondsee or Kremsmünster ca. A.D. 800. CF.
294

XLVII. *Exultet-Rolle...* see **210.**
295

XLVIII. *Trierer Apokalypse,* ed. R. Laufner and P.K. Klein. 2 vols.
(1975)

Trier, Stadtbibliothek, MS. 31. Caroline. Tours, ca. A.D. 800. 74 folios, all illustrated. CF.
296
XLIX. *Drogo-Sakramentar,* ed. W. Koehler and F. Mütherich. 2 vols. (1974)
Paris, BN, MS. lat. 9428. Caroline. Metz, A.D. 845-55, for Drogo, bishop of Metz. 130 folios, illustrated. CF.
297
L. *Mosaner Psalter-Fragment,* ed. H. Swarzenski. 2 vols. (1974)
Berlin, Staatsbibliothek der Stiftung Preussischer Kulturbesitz, Kupfer-stichkabinett, MS. 78 A 6. Late Caroline. Maas (Meuse) area, A.D. 1160-70. 10 folios, 29 miniatures. CF.
298
LI. *Das Verbrüderungsbuch von St. Peter in Salzburg,* ed. K. Forstner (1974)
Salzburg, Stiftsbibliothek St. Peter, MS. A. 1 (olim a.XI.13), fols. 1r-20r. Caroline. St. Peter's, Salzburg; begun ca. A.D. 784, continued to mid-13th century. CF. 80 plates.
299
LVI. *Vergilius Augusteus: Vollständige Faksimile-Ausgabe im Original-Format. Codex Vaticanus latinus 3256 der Biblioteca Apostolica Vaticana und Codex latinus fol. 416 der Staatsbibliothek Preussischer Kulturbesitz,* ed. C. Nordenfalk (1976)
An edition, with commentary, of seven folios — four in Vatican Library, three in Berlin — that survive of a famous codex in 'Square' capital, dating, according to Nordenfalk, from the time of Pope Damasus (A.D. 366-84) or, according to Petrucci **558**, from between 495 and 530. CF.
300
LX. *Die Goldene Bulle: König Wenzels Handschrift,* ed. A. Wolf. 2 vols. (Graz 1977)
Vienna, ONB, MS. lat. 338. Gothic. Done for Wenceslaus of Bohemia (German emperor, 1378-1419), ca. A.D. 1400. 80 folios, 50 miniatures. CF.
301
LXIII. *Werdener Psalter: Aus dem Besitz der Staatsbibliothek Preussi-scher Kulturbesitz,* ed. H. Knaus. 2 vols. (1979)
Berlin, Staatsbibliothek der Stiftung Preussischer Kulturbesitz, MS. theol. lat. fol. 358. Caroline. Werden, ca. A.D. 1039. 118 folios, 6 full-

page miniatures, 190 gold or silver initials. CF.

302

LXIV. *Reiner Musterbuch*, ed. F. Unterkircher. 2 vols. (1979)
Vienna, ONB, MS. lat. 507. Gothic. Model book from the monastery
of Rein (Reun, Steiermark), first half of the 13th century. 13 folios.
CF.

303

LXIX. *Der Goldene Psalter: 'Dagulf Psalter,'* ed. K. Holter (1980)
Vienna, ONB, MS. lat. 1861. Written at the order of Charlemagne, probably in the palace school, as a present for Pope Hadrian (ob. 795). The
main scribe is Dagulf. 'A milestone in the history of Caroline minuscule'
(CLA VIII.1504), with five ornamental pages on purple and the whole
text written in gold letters. The ivory tablets which originally belonged
to the codex are now in the Louvre, Paris. 161 folios. CF.

304

LXXI. *Vergilius Vaticanus*... see **213**.

305

HENRY BRADSHAW SOCIETY (London 1890-)
Facsimile volumes only:

306

4, 10. *The Antiphonary of Bangor*, ed. F.E. Warren. 2 vols. (1893, 1895)
Milan, Biblioteca Ambrosiana, MS. C 5 inf. Hiberno-Insular minuscule.
Written at Bangor, Co. Down, A.D. 680-91. Later in the library at
Bobbio. 36 folios. CF. 71 plates, with transcriptions. See also CLA III.
311.

307

21. *Facsimiles of Horae de Beata Maria Virgine from English MSS of the
Eleventh Century*, ed. E.S. Dewick (1902)
28 plates, with transcriptions, from London, BL, MSS. Royal 2 B V
(Winchester, mid-11th century) and Cotton Tiberius A. III (Canterbury,
mid-11th century). Anglo-Caroline script.

308

31-2. *The Stowe Missal*, ed. G. Warner. 2 vols. (1906, 1915)
Dublin, Royal Irish Academy, MS. 1238, fols. 12-67. The oldest known
missal of the early Irish church. Possibly connected with Tallaght, Co.
Dublin. Hiberno-Insular majuscule, ca. A.D. 792 (thus CLA II.268).
Total MS is 67 folios. CF (of missal). 112 plates (including 9 of metal
cover), with transcriptions.

309

36. *Facsimiles of the Creeds from Early Manuscripts,* ed. A.R. Burn (1909), with palaeographical notes by L. Traube
24 plates with transcriptions.

310

47-8. *The Psalter and Martyrology of Ricemarch,* ed. H.J. Lawlor. 2 vols. (1914)
Dublin, Trinity College, MS. 50 (= A. 4. 20). Written in Wales, probably at Llanbadarn Fawr in Cardiganshire in or about 1079 for Ricemarch (Rhygyfarch), one of the four sons of Sulien, bishop of St. David's (ob. 1091), by the scribe Ithael in 'calligraphic Welsh minuscule' (with large illuminated letters by John, Ricemarch's brother). 159 folios. PF. 78 plates. See also **692**.

311

53, 58, 61. *The Bobbio Missal,* ed. E.A. Lowe. 3 vols. (1917-24) with notes by A. Wilmart and H.A. Wilson
Paris, BN, MS. lat. 13246 (with other items). The total MS was written in the 8th century in mixed Uncial and minuscule, probably in South-East France. The lower script of the palimpsested section (fols. 296-300) is small Semi-uncial of the 5th century, probably written in Italy. 300 folios. CF. Full transcription. See also CLA V.654.

312

55. *The Calendar of St. Willibrord,* ed. H.A. Wilson (1918)
Paris, BN, MS. lat. 10837, fols. 34v-40r. Anglo-Insular majuscule. Written before A.D. 728, probably at Echternach in Luxembourg. CF (fols. 34v-40r). 13 plates. See also CLA V.606a.

313

MANUSCRITS DATES
A project (1953) of the Comité international de paléographie which aims to provide scholars with a corpus of facsimiles of all dated or datable MSS in Latin, country by country, for the period up to A.D. 1600 (and more particularly 800-1500), in a limited continuation of, or, as the case may be, with additions to, the *Codices Latini antiquiores* of E.A. Lowe (**251-63**). Although there are variations from country to country, the facsimiles generally concentrate on evidence of date and location, and the editors provide transcriptions of the passages in question. For a recent survey of the project, see M.-C. Garand, **87** and 'Etat actuel du catalogue des manuscrits médiévaux datés,' *Academie des inscriptions & belles lettres: Comptes*

rendus Nov.-Dec. (1979) 605-10. See also P. Spunar, *CM* 5 (1979) 114-16, for some criticisms.

314

Austria. *Katalog der datierten Handschriften in lateinischer Schrift in Österreich* (Vienna 1969-):

315

I. *Die datierten Handschriften der österreichischen Nationalbibliothek bis zum Jahre 1400,* ed. F. Unterkircher (1969)
Two parts: text; 272 plates, from A.D. 783.

316

II. ――― *von 1401 bis 1450,* ed. F. Unterkircher (1971)
Two parts: text; 517 plates.

317

III. ――― *von 1451 bis 1500,* ed. F. Unterkircher (1974)
Two parts: text; 633 plates.

318

IV. ――― *von 1501 bis 1600,* ed. F. Unterkircher (1976)
Two parts: text; 600 plates: nos. 1-475 (1501-1600), 476-600 (additions for years 1177-1498).

319

VI. *Die datierten Handschriften der Universitätsbibliothek Graz bis zum Jahre 1600,* ed. M. Mairold (1979)
Two parts: text; 385 plates.

320

Belgium. *Manuscrits datés conservés en Belgique,* ed. F. Masai and M. Wittek (Brussels―Ghent 1968-):

321

I. *819-1400,* ed. A. Brounts, P. Cockshaw, et al. (1968)
All Belgian libraries covered. Text, 217 plates.

322

II. *1401-1440: Manuscrits conservés à la Bibliothèque royale Albert Ier, Bruxelles,* ed. A. Brounts, P. Cockshaw, et al. (1972)
Text, 198 plates.

323

III. *1441-1460: Manuscrits conservés à la Bibliothèque royale Albert Ier, Bruxelles,* ed. A. Brounts, P. Cockshaw, et al. (1978)
Text, 280 plates.

324

France. *Catalogue des manuscrits en écriture latine portant des indications de date, de lieu, ou de copiste,* ed. C. Samaran and R. Marichal (Paris 1959-):

325

I. *Musée Condé et bibliothèques parisiennes,* ed. M.-C. Garand, J. Metman, and M.-Th. Vernet (1959)
Two parts: text; 193 plates.

326

II. *Bibliothèque nationale, Fonds latin (nos. 1 à 8000),* ed. M.-Th. d'Alverny, M.-C. Garand, M. Mabille, and J. Metman (1962)
Two parts: text; 210 plates.

327

III. *Bibliothèque nationale, Fonds latin (nos. 8001 à 18613),* ed. M.-Th. d'Alverny, M. Mabille, M.-C. Garand, and D. Escudier (1974)
Two parts: text; 255 plates.

328

IV.1. *Bibliothèque nationale, Fonds latin (supplément): Nouvelles acquisitions latines. Petits fonds divers,* ed. M.-C. Garand, M. Mabille, D. Muzerelle, and M.-Th. d'Alverny (1981)
Two parts: text; 120 plates.

329

V. *Est de la France* [Besançon – Vesoul], ed. M.-C. Garand, M. Mabille, J. Metman, and M.-Th. Vernet (1975)
Two parts: text; 249 plates.

330

VI. *Bourgogne, Centre, Sud-est et Sud-ouest de la France* [Agen – Valence], ed. M.-C. Garand, M. Mabille, and J. Metman (1968)
Two parts: text; 200 plates.

331

Great Britain. [I]. *Catalogue of Dated and Datable Manuscripts c. 700-1600 in the Department of Manuscripts, the British Library,* ed. A.G. Watson (London 1979)
Two parts: text; 915 plates.

332

Holland. *Manuscrits datés conservés dans les Pays-Bas: Catalogue paléographique des manuscrits en écriture latine portant des indications de date,* ed. G.I. Lieftinck (Amsterdam 1964-):

333
I. *Les Manuscrits d'origine étrangère (816-c. 1550)*, ed. G.I. Lieftinck
(1964)
Two parts: text (with valuable pages on the nomenclature of scripts,
pp. XIII-XVII; see also **1101**); 477 plates.
334
Italy. *Catalogo dei manoscritti in scrittura latina datati o databili per
indicazione di anno, di luogo, o di copista* (Turin 1971-):
  335
  I. *Biblioteca Nazionale Centrale di Roma*, ed. V. Jemolo (1971)
  Two parts: text; 215 plates.
336
Sweden. *Katalog der datierten Handschriften in lateinischer Schrift vor
1600 in Schweden* (Stockholm 1977-80):
  337
  I. *Die Handschriften der Universitätsbibliothek Uppsala*, ed. G.
  Hornwall, J.-O. Tjäder, and M. Hedlund (1977)
  Two parts: text; 195 plates.
  338
  II. *Die Handschriften Schwedens ausgenommen UB Uppsala*, ed. M.
  Hedlund (1980)
  Two parts: text; 202 plates.
339
Switzerland. *Katalog der datierten Handschriften in der Schweiz in
lateinischer Schrift vom Anfang des Mittelalters bis 1550* (Zürich 1977-):
  340
  I. *Die Handschriften der Bibliotheken von Aarau, Appenzell, und
  Basel*, ed. B.M. von Scarpatetti (1977)
  Two parts: text (with a 'Biographical catalogue' of scribes at pp.
  249-75); 298 plates.
341
MONUMENTA MUSICAE SACRAE (Macon, etc. 1952-):
  342
  I. *Le Prosaire de la Sainte-Chapelle: Manuscrit du Chapitre de Saint-
  Nicolas de Bari* (Macon 1952)
  Bari, Biblioteca capitolare di S. Nicola, MS. s.n. Latin Gradual and
  proses. Littera textualis, ca. A.D. 1250. 152 folios. CF.

343

III. *Le Prosaire d'Aix-la-Chapelle* (Rouen 1961)
Aachen, Bibliothek des Domkapitels, MS. 13. Early Littera textualis.
Possibly Paris, beginning of the 13th century. 169 folios. PF. 98 plates
of proses.

344

PALEOGRAPHIE MUSICALE: LÈS PRINCIPAUX MANUSCRITS DE CHANT
GREGORIEN, AMBROSIEN, MOZARABE, GALLICAN, PUBLIES EN FAC-
SIMILES PHOTOTYPIQUES PAR LES BENEDICTINS DE SOLESMES, ed. A.
Mocquereau and (from Series One, vol. 14) J. Gajard (Solesmes, etc.
1889-)
Selected volumes only:
   [Series One]
   345

I. *Le Codex 339 de la Bibliothèque de Saint-Gall (Xe siècle): Antiphonale missarum Sancti Gregorii* (Solesmes 1889)
St. Gall, Stiftsbibliothek, MS. 339. Written at St. Gall, 10th-11th
century. 325 folios. PF. 173 plates.

346

IV. *Le Codex 121 de la Bibliothèque d'Einsiedeln (X^e-XIe siècle):
Antiphonale missarum Sancti Gregorii* (Solesmes 1894)
Einsiedeln, Stiftsbibliothek, MS. 121. Written at Einsiedeln shortly
before A.D. 996. 300 folios. PF. 114 plates and 432 illustrations.

347

V-VI. *Antiphonarium Ambrosianum du Musée britannique (XIIe siècle):
Codex Additional 34209.* 2 vols. (Solesmes 1896, 1899)
London, BL, Add. MS. 34209. 12th century. 305 folios. CF.

348

VII-VIII. *Antiphonarium tonale missarum, XIe siècle: Codex H. 159 de
la Bibliothèque de l'Ecole de médecine de Montpellier.* 2 vols.
(Solesmes 1901, 1905)
161 folios. CF.

349

IX. *Antiphonaire monastique, XIIe siècle: Codex 601 de la Bibliothèque
capitulaire de Lucques* (Tournai 1906)
Lucca, Biblioteca capitolare, MS. 601. 12th century. 280 folios. CF.

350

X. *Antiphonale missarum Sancti Gregorii, IXe-Xe siècle: Codex 239 de*

la Bibliothèque de Laon (Tournai 1909)
Laon, Bibliothèque municipale, MS. 239. Mixture of Uncial and
Caroline. Written at Laon, mid-9th century. 88 folios. CF.
351

XI. *Antiphonale missarum S. Gregorii, Xe siècle: Codex 47 de la
Bibliothèque de Chartres* (Tournai 1912)
Chartres, Bibliothèque municipale, MS. 47. End of the 9th or beginning
of the 10th century. 85 folios. CF.
352

XII. *Antiphonaire monastique, XIIIe siècle: Codex F. 160 de la Bibliothèque de la Cathédrale de Worcester* (Tournai 1922)
13th century. 227 folios. CF.
353

XIII. *Le Codex 903 de la Bibliothèque nationale de Paris (XIe siècle):
Graduel de Saint-Yrieix* (Tournai 1925)
Paris, BN, MS. lat. 903. Written at the beginning of the 11th century for
the church of Saint-Yrieix-la-Perche (arr. Limoges). Later belonged to
Saint-Martial, Limoges. 204 folios. PF. 273 plates.
354

XIV. *Le Codex 10 673 de la Bibliothèque Vaticane, fonds latin (XIe
siècle): Graduel bénéventain.* 2 vols. (Tournai 1931, 1936)
Vatican City, BAV, MS. Vat. lat. 10673. Beneventan area, 11th century.
35 folios. CF (with long introduction).
355

XV. *Le Codex VI. 34 de la Bibliothèque capitulaire de Bénévent (XIe-
XIIe siècle): Graduel de Bénévent avec prosaire et tropaire* (Tournai
1937)
PF. 146 plates.
356

XVIII. *Le Codex 123 de la Bibliothèque Angelica de Rome (XIe siècle):
Graduel et tropaire de Bologne* (Solesmes 1969)
Rome, Biblioteca Angelica, MS. 123. Bologna, 11th century. 265 folios.
PF. 266 plates.
357

XIX. *Le Manuscrit 807, Universitätsbibliothek Graz (XIIe siècle):
Graduel de Klosterneuburg* (Berne 1974)
PF. 86 plates.

[Series Two]
358
I. *Antiphonale officii monastici écrit par le B. Hartker* (Solesmes 1924);
2nd ed. as *Antiphonaire de l'Office monastique transcrit par Hartker: MSS. Saint-Gall 390-391 (980-1011)*, ed. J. Froger (Bern 1970)
St. Gall, Stiftsbibliothek, MSS. 390, 391. Written at St. Gall in the late 10th century by Hartker 'reclusus.' 97 and 132 folios. CF.
359
II. *Cantatorium, IXe siècle: No. 359 de la Bibliothèque de Saint-Gall* (Tournai 1924)
St. Gall, Stiftsbibliothek, MS. 359. 162 folios. PF.
360
The Palaeographical Society. *Facsimiles of Manuscripts and Inscriptions* (London 1873-94, with *Indices* 1901): [*First Series*], ed. E.A. Bond and E.M. Thompson, 2 vols. (1873-83), 260 pls.; [*Second Series*], ed. Bond and Thompson with G.F. Warner, 2 vols. (1884-94), 205 pls.
Wide range of subjects. 465 plates in all, with full transcription, running from ca. 600 B.C. to A.D. 1500. This magnificent venture was succeeded by that of **361**.
361
The New Palaeographical Society. *Facsimiles of Ancient Manuscripts* (London 1903-30): *First Series*, ed. E.M. Thompson, G.F. Warner, F.G. Kenyon, and J.P. Gilson, 2 vols. (1903-12, with *Indices* 1914), 250 pls.; *Second Series*, ed. Thompson etc., with J.A. Herbert and H.I. Bell, 2 vols. (1913-30, with *Indices* [by F. Wormald] 1932), 202 pls.
The total 452 plates cover the period 400 B.C.-A.D. 1535, and, again, are fully transcribed. (Note that there is also an index to the two series of the Palaeographical Society and to the first of the New Palaeographical Society in L.R. Dean, *An Index to Facsimiles in the Palaeographical Society Publications, arranged as a Guide for Students in Palaeography* [Princeton 1914].)
362
PLAINSONG AND MEDIAEVAL MUSIC SOCIETY (London; later Burnham, Bucks. 1889-)
Some facsimile volumes only:
363
[a] *Graduale Sarisburiense*, ed. W.H. Frere (1894, repr. 1966)
London, BL, Add. MS. 12194. Late Caroline, beginning of the 13th

century. 236 folios. CF.

364

[b] *Antiphonale Sarisburiense,* ed. W.H. Frere. 4 vols. (1901-27, repr. 1966)
Cambridge University Library, MS. Mm. ii. 9. Salisbury, A.D. 1200-1250. 334 folios. CF.

365

[c] *Pars Antiphonarii,* ed. W.H. Frere (1923)
Durham Cathedral, Chapter Library, MS. B. III. 11. 11th century. 159 folios. PF. 48 plates.

366

THE ROXBURGHE CLUB, LONDON (1814-)
Facsimile volumes only of the publications, in very limited editions, of an unlikely club founded in London in 1812 to commemorate the sale of the Duke of Roxburghe's copy of the Valdarger Boccaccio, 'the first great sale of modern times.' The brilliant series below of facsimiles of decorated MSS only began some sixty years later, and no. 103 is regarded as 'the real precursor of the modern series of manuscript facsimiles': see N. Barker, *The Publications of the Roxburghe Club, 1814-1962* (Cambridge 1964).

367

103. *The Apocalypse of St. John the Divine,* ed. H.O. C [oxe] (London 1876)
Oxford, Bodleian Library, MS. Auct. D. 4. 17. An illustrated Apocalypse. Set textual hand (Littera textualis formata). England, second half of the 13th century. 23 folios. CF.

368

114. *Miracles de Nostre Dame, collected by Jean Miélot, Secretary to Philip the Good, Duke of Burgundy,* ed. G.F. Warner (Westminster 1885)
Oxford, Bodleian Library, MS. Douce 374. Cursive Bastarda. Netherlands, slightly after A.D. 1467. 120 folios. CF, with complete transcription of text.

369

137. *Thirty-Two Miniatures from the Book of Hours of Joan II, Queen of Navarre,* ed. H. Yates Thompson (London 1899)
From the library of Henry Yates Thompson; now Paris, BN, MS. Nouv. acq. lat. 3145. Miniatures include a series of scenes from the life of St. Louis, king of France. Set textual hand, ca. 1330. 191 fols. PF. 32 pls.

370

138. *The Metz Pontifical,* ed. E.S. Dewick (London 1902)
From the library of H. Yates Thompson; now Cambridge, Fitzwilliam
Museum, MS. 298. Many illuminations, several pieces of plain chant.
Fractura. Written for Reinhald von Bar (Renaud de Bar), bishop of
Metz (A.D. 1302-16). 140 folios. PF. 100 plates. Complete transcrip-
tion of text. Another part of this pontifical is in Prague, University
Library, MS. XXIII. C. 120.

371

150. *The Pageants of Richard Beauchamp, Earl of Warwick,* ed. William,
Earl of Carysfort (Oxford 1908)
London, BL, MS. Cotton Julius E. IV. Written in English ca. A.D. 1493,
in Bastarda, with decoration by Flemish artists. 28 folios. CF, with
transcription.

372

155. *The Trinity College Apocalypse,* ed. M.R. James (London 1909)
Cambridge, Trinity College, MS. 950 (R. 16. 2). Written in French in a
set textual hand in England or N. France, A.D. 1242-50. An introduction by James deals with the evolution of illuminated Apocalypses. 32
folios. CF.

373

156. *The Benedictional of St. Aethelwold, Bishop of Winchester 963-
984,* ed. G.F. Warner and H.A. Wilson (Oxford 1910)
Then in the library of the Duke of Devonshire, Chatsworth House; now
London, BL, Add. MS. 49598. Written at Winchester in Caroline for
Aethelwold by the monk Godeman (later abbot of Thorney), ca. 980.
119 folios, 21 miniatures. CF, with transcription.

374

162. *The Treatise of Walter de Milemete, De nobilitatibus, sapientibus,
et prudentiis regum, reproduced in facsimile from the unique manuscript preserved at Christ Church, Oxford, together with a selection of
pages from the companion manuscript of the treatise De secretis secre-
torum Aristotelis preserved in the library of the Earl of Leicester at
Holkham Hall,* ed. M.R. James (Oxford 1913)
Oxford, Christ Church College, MS. 92; Holkham Hall, Wells, Norfolk,
MS. 458 (now London, BL, Add. MS. 47680). Both works written in a
set textual hand and decorated in or about A.D. 1326, shortly after the
composition of the first treatise above. CF of *De nobilitatibus* (82 fols.),

with some transcriptions. Total plates 184, including 28 of *De secretis.*
375
171. *The Chaundler MSS,* ed. M.R. James (London 1916)
Oxford, New College, MS. 228 (*De vita... Willelmi Wykeham*), 73 folios;
Cambridge, Trinity College, MS. 881 (*Liber apologeticus*), 68 folios.
Both works composed in Latin (with some English) by Thomas Chaundler, the humanist (ca. A.D. 1417-90), for his patron Thomas Bekynton,
bishop of Bath and Wells (1443-65), and written by various scribes in an
Italianized running Gothic, probably (at least for the *Liber*) 1457-61.
PF. 20 plates, with transcriptions.
376
172. *Gospels of Mathilda, Countess of Tuscany, 1055-1115,* ed. G.
Warner (Oxford 1917)
New York, Pierpont Morgan Library, MS. M. 492. Written in N. Italy
possibly by 1099, certainly before 1109, in Caroline, with much decoration and illumination of initials. MS probably given by Mathilda to the
monastery of San Benedetto di Polirone, near Mantua, before her death
in 1115; part of the *Liber vitae* of the monastery to 1143 is at the end
of the MS, with many autograph signatures at folio 105r. 106 folios.
PF, with some transcriptions. 31 plates.
377
175. *La Estoire de Seint Aedward le Roi: The Life of St. Edward the
Confessor, reproduced in facsimile from the unique manuscript in the
University Library, Cambridge, MS. Ee. 3. 59, together with some pages
of the manuscript of the Life of St. Alban at Trinity College, Dublin,*
ed. M.R. James (Oxford 1920)
Cambridge, University Library, MS. Ee. iii. 59, 34 folios; Dublin, Trinity
College, MS. 177 (E. I. 40). Written in the mid-13th century, possibly
at St. Albans, in a set textual hand. CF (65 plates), with 10 plates of
the Dublin MS.
378
176. *The Sherborne Missal,* ed. J.A. Herbert (Oxford 1920)
Alnwick Castle, Northumberland, Library of the Duke of Northumberland, MS. 450. Written in a set textual hand for Sherborne Abbey,
Dorset, A.D. 1396-1407, by the monk John Whas, with the Dominican
John Siferwas as chief illuminator. 347 folios. PF. 30 plates.
379
177. *Illustrations of the Book of Genesis: Being a complete reproduction*

in facsimile of the manuscript British Museum, Egerton 894, ed. M.R.
James (Oxford 1921)
London, BL, MS. Egerton 894. Anglo-Norman and French Genesis,
written by two scribes in England in the mid-14th century, mostly in
Littera anglicana, with a systematic series of illustrations. 20 folios. CF
380

178. *A Peterborough Psalter and Bestiary of the Fourteenth Century,*
ed. M.R. James (Oxford 1921)
Cambridge, Corpus Christi College, MS. 53 (E. 12). Sometimes known
as the Stewkley Psalter, after a monk-owner, Hugo de Stewkley, in the
Peterborough community in the 14th century. Set textual hand. Writte
and decorated at Peterborough ca. 1310. 210 folios. PF. 72 plates.
381

180. *The Apocalypse in Latin and French (Bodleian MS. Douce 180),*
ed. M.R. James (Oxford 1922)
Oxford, Bodleian Library, MS. Douce 180. Unfinished MS in Anglo-
Norman (12 fols.) and Latin (51 fols.), probably in one hand. Latin
text in a set Fractura, decorated 'by an artist writing at Canterbury,'
for, probably, King Edward I or his wife Eleanor of Castile, 'a year or
two before his accession to the throne' (A.D. 1272). CF of Latin text.
The introduction provides a general comparative survey of 70 Apocalypses from the Middle Ages.
382

182. *The Herbal of Apuleius Barbarus from the Early Twelfth-Century
Manuscript formerly in the Abbey of Bury St. Edmunds (MS. Bodley
130),* ed. R.T. Gunther (Oxford 1925)
Oxford, Bodleian Library, MS. Bodley 130. The Herbal of Apuleius
and other works, written (in England?) in an uncertain Caroline hand
ca. A.D. 1100. At Bury ca. 1300 (pressmark). 101 folios. CF of Herbal
(67 fols., where all the pictures are numbered in sequence to cxli).
181 plates in all.
383

185. *Two East Anglian Psalters at the Bodleian Library, Oxford,* ed.
S.C. Cockerell and M.R. James (Oxford 1926)
Oxford, Bodleian Library, MS. Douce 366 (the Ormesby Psalter, given
to Norwich Cathedral Priory by William de Ormesby in the mid-14th
century, and written and decorated 'in Norfolk or Suffolk' in the last
years of the 13th century; described by Cockerell); MS. Ashmole 1523

(the Bromholm Psalter, once the property of the Cluniac Priory of St. Andrew, Bromholm, Norfolk, and written and decorated in East Anglia ca. A.D. 1300; described by James). Both psalters are in Litterae tonsae. PF. 42 plates (35 of Ormesby, 7 of Bromholm).
384
186. *A Book of Old Testament Illustrations of the Middle of the Thirteenth Century sent by Cardinal Bernard Maciejowski to Shah Abbas the Great, King of Persia,* ed. S.C. Cockerell, M.R. James, and C.J. Ffoulkes (Cambridge 1927)
New York, Pierpont Morgan Library, MS. M. 638. Written in Italy in a Littera rotunda, and illustrated at Paris ca. A.D. 1250. Presented by Maciejowski, bishop of Cracow, to the Shah in 1604. 43 folios. CF. See also *Old Testament Miniatures: A Medieval Picture Book with 283 Paintings from the Creation to the Story of David* (New York – London 1969), preface by J. Plummer, introduction and legends by S.C. Cockerell (as in the Roxburghe edition).
385
187. *The Guthlac Roll,* ed. G. Warner (Oxford 1928)
London, BL, Harley Roll Y. 6. Long vellum roll, with scenes from the life of St. Guthlac (ca. A.D. 673-714) of Crowland, Lincolnshire, from the end of the 12th century. What little writing there is is late Caroline. Five sheets. CF. 32 plates.
386
190. *The Bestiary: Being a reproduction in full of the manuscript Ii. 4. 26 in the University Library, Cambridge, with supplementary plates from other manuscripts of English origin and a preliminary study of the Latin Bestiary as current in England,* ed. M.R. James (Oxford 1928)
Cambridge, University Library, MS. Ii. iv. 26. Late Caroline. England, end of the 12th century. Imperfect (74 fols.). CF (148 pls.), with 22 plates from Aberdeen University Library, MS. II. 3. 9.
387
191. *De rebus in oriente mirabilibus, The Marvels of the East: A full reproduction of the three known copies,* ed. M.R. James (Oxford 1929)
(1) London, BL, MS. Cotton Vitellius A. XV, fols. 98v-106v (item 2 in the 'Nowell Codex'; see **747**): Anglo-Saxon, ca. A.D. 1000 in Anglo-Caroline script. (2) London, BL, MS. Cotton Tiberius B. V, fols. 78v-87v: Latin and Anglo-Saxon; transcription by editor of Latin text, written in Anglo-Caroline. (3) Oxford, Bodleian Library, MS. Bodley 614, fols.

36r-51v: Latin, in Caroline writing of the early 12th century. 47 plates.
388
192. *The Work of W. de Brailes, an English Illuminator of the Thirteenth Century,* ed. S.C. Cockerell (Cambridge 1930)
20 plates illustrating five of six MSS then known to have been illustrate
by de Brailes (probably at Oxford) ca. 1240-50, chiefly: Oxford, New
College, MS. 322 (a folio psalter); Dyson Perrins Collection, MS. 4, now
London, BL, Add. MS. 49999 (Hours of Sarum with two signed portraits); Dublin, Chester Beatty Library, MS. 38, now Cambridge, Fitzwilliam Museum, MS. 330 (six leaves with one signed portrait); and a
psalter then in Cockerell's possession, now Stockholm, National Museu
MS. B. 2010. The New College and Dyson Perrins MSS are in an uprigh
set textual hand of the Litterae tonsae type. See also **1165.**
389
195. *The Dublin Apocalypse,* ed. M.R. James (Cambridge 1932)
Dublin, Trinity College, MS. 64 (K. 4. 31). Written in a set textual hand
and decorated in East Anglia in the early 14th century. Pictures are
numbered in Roman numerals (III-LXXV; I-II are wanting). 39 folios. CF
390
196. *Le Chanson de Roland,* ed. A. de Laborde and C. Samaran (Paris
1932)
Oxford, Bodleian Library, MS. Digby 23, second part. Written in
squarish Caroline ca. A.D. 1125-50 (in Normandy?). 72 folios. CF.
An 'étude paléographique' by Samaran is on pp. 9-58.
391
200. *The Bohun Manuscripts: A group of five manuscripts executed in
England about 1370 for members of the Bohun family,* ed. M.R. James
and E.G. Millar (Oxford 1936)
Psalters written in Fractura for the family of the seventh Earl of Here-
ford (1342-1419): (1) Oxford, Exeter College, MS. 47: 127 folios, pls.
I-XXII; (2) Oxford, Bodleian Library, MS. Auct. D. 4. 4: 274 folios, pls
XXII-XXXVIII; (3) Vienna, ONB, MS. lat. 1826*: 160 folios, pls.
XXXIX-LVI; (4) Copenhagen, Koneglige Bibliotek, MS. Thott 547 4°:
66 folios, pls. LVII-LXI; (5) Collection of T.H. Rich, Shenley, Hertford
shire ('Psalter of John of Gaunt,' formerly in H. Yates Thompson
collection, now Cambridge, Fitzwilliam Museum, MS. 38 – 1950): 243
folios, pls. LXII-LXVIII.

392

201. *A Picture Book of the Life of St. Anthony the Abbot,* ed. R. Graham (Oxford 1937)

Valetta, Malta, Public Library, MS. s.n. A *Vita* of St. Anthony compiled by John Marcellarii, sacristan of the monastery of St. Anthony in Vienne, at the request of his prior, Guigo Robert of Tullins. Written at Avignon or neighbourhood by Petrus Petri de Istrio (Istres) in A.D. 1426 and illustrated by Magister Robertus Fornerii (Fournier). 102 folios. PF. 66 plates in all. Transcription of colophon.

393

203. *The Rutland Psalter,* ed. E.G. Millar (Oxford 1937)

Belvoir Castle, Leicestershire, Library of the Duke of Rutland, MS. s.n. Written in a set 'liturgical' hand of the early second half of the 13th century, in England. Belonged to Reading Abbey. 198 folios. CF of psalter (fols. 1-168).

394

211. *The St. Trond Lectionary,* ed. E.G. Millar (Oxford 1949)

Collection of E.G. Millar, formerly Phillipps MS. 3535; now New York, Pierpont Morgan Library, MS. M. 883. Written in a late Caroline hand ca. A.D. 1180 in the monastery of St. Trond, prov. Limburg, Belgium. 247 folios. PF. 12 plates.

395

212. *The Liber epistolaris of Richard de Bury,* ed. N. Denholm-Young (Oxford 1950)

Brogyntyn, Oswestry, Shropshire, Library of Lord Harlech, MS. s.n. Whole MS of letters from various sources, compiled in A.D. 1324-5 by Richard de Bury (1287-1345), author or co-author of the *Philobiblon* and later (1333-45) bishop of Durham, and written out by him a little hastily in 'a pure court hand of the best type.' The MS belonged by 1400 to Bury St. Edmunds. 240 folios. Complete transcription of un-published letters. PF. 7 plates.

396

216. *A Thirteenth-Century York Psalter,* ed. E.G. Millar (Oxford 1952)

Collection then of E.G. Millar (from the library of English College, Lisbon, 1943); now London, BL, Add. MS. 54000. Written in a set liturgical hand and decorated (with, e.g., 24 medallions) in the diocese of York ca. A.D. 1250. Belonged at one time (ca. 1300?) to a Nicholas de Dodington, and later to Matthew Parker, archbishop of Canterbury

(1559-75), who, as was his wont, marked various passages in red chalk
193 folios. PF. 12 plates, with transcription of calendar.

397

219. *An Illuminated Manuscript of the Somme le Roy attributed to th*
Parisian Miniaturist Honoré, ed. E.G. Millar (Oxford 1953)
Collection then of E.G. Millar; now London, BL, Add. MS. 54180.
The *Somme* was written in A.D. 1280 for King Philip III (ob. 1285) by
the Dominican Laurens of Orléans, his confessor; and this MS, written
in a 'beautiful minuscule of type used for volumes for the royal family
with miniatures by Honoré or under his direction, is probably only a
few years later than that. 208 folios. PF. 35 plates, 20 of which are of
illustrations by Honoré in MSS. 192 and 368 at the Fitzwilliam
Museum, Cambridge.

398

224. *A Thirteenth Century Bestiary in the Library of Alnwick Castle,*
ed. E.G. Millar (Oxford 1958)
Alnwick Castle, Northumberland, Library of the Duke of Northumberland, MS. s.n. Written ca. A.D. 1250 in England in a set textual hand. 7
folios. PF. 92 plates, including 11 from other MSS.

399

249. *The Will of Aethelgifu: A Tenth Century Anglo-Saxon Manuscrip*
ed. D. Whitelock (Oxford 1968)
A full facsimile, with transcription, translation, and commentary, of
the will (63 lines) in Anglo-Saxon of the lady Aethelgifu, written (see
N.R. Ker, 'On the manuscript,' pp. 45-8) in a 'dully imitative' Anglo-
Insular minuscule of about the last decade of the 10th century. Belonge
to the monastery of St. Albans, where endorsed in the third quarter of
the 12th century. (Now, since 1969, in the Scheide Library, Princeton
University, Princeton, N.J.).

400

250. *The Stonyhurst Gospel of Saint John,* ed. T.J. Brown (Oxford
1969)
Stonyhurst College, Blackburn, Lancashire, MS. 55 (now on loan to
BL, London). A small, almost 'pocket' codex written, as Brown notes,
in 'crisp capitular' or non-elaborate Uncial 'at Wearmouth-Jarrow' by
the scribe who wrote the fragment of a Gospel book now joined to the
Utrecht Psalter, probably at the same time as, or a shade later than, the
Codex Amiatinus (A.D. 689-716). It was enclosed at some time or othe

(as monks of Durham discovered in 1104) in the decorated coffin made at Lindisfarne in 698 for the remains of St. Cuthbert (ob. 687). 94 folios (Gospel itself, 90 fols.). CF. 186 plates, together with 7 of binding (of which there is a technical description by R. Powell and P. Waters).
401

252. *John Scottowe's Alphabet Books,* ed. J. Backhouse (London 1974) 28 plates illustrating various alphabets of the 16th century (e.g. Italic, Roman, Secretary, Court) in two signed MSS of Scottowe: London, BL, MS. Harley 3885 (24 folios of vellum, ca. 1588), and Chicago, Newberry Library, MS. Wing 7 (24 leaves of paper, dated 1592).
402

254. *The Madresfield Hours: A Fourteenth-Century Manuscript in the Library of the Earl of Beauchamp,* ed. J. Backhouse (Oxford 1975) Madresfield Court, Malvern, Worcestershire, Library of the Earl of Beauchamp, MS. s.n. 188 folios, 1-122 of which (the Hours proper) were written in a set textual hand and decorated in England in the early 14th century. The usage in the Hours is that of York (but altered towards the end of the century to that of Sarum). A handlist is appended (pp. 30-33) of 24 Books of Hours made for English owners between ca. 1240 and the middle of the 14th century. PF. 50 plates.
403

255. *The Sobieski Hours: A Manuscript in the Royal Library at Windsor Castle,* ed. E.P. Spencer (New York 1977) Windsor Castle, Berkshire, Royal Library, MS. s.n. Written in Latin and French and decorated at Paris and Rouen between 1420 and 1440. Belonged (1683?) to John III Sobieski, king of Poland (1674-96). 234 folios. PF. 97 plates.
404

256. *An Early Breton Gospel Book: A Ninth-Century Manuscript from the Collection of H. L. Bradfer-Lawrence 1887-1965,* ed. F. Wormald and J. Alexander (Cambridge 1977) Deposited on loan at Fitzwilliam Museum, Cambridge, where MS. BL 1. Decorated copy of the four Gospels with canon tables. Written in the Breton area, in Caroline minuscule, in the late 9th or early 10th century. Migrated to England in the 10th century and acquired some Anglo-Saxon glosses. Introduction by Wormald, with 'A Note on the Breton Gospel Books' by Alexander (pp. 13-23). 154 folios. PF. 48 plates (35 of MS, 13 'comparative plates').

405

UMBRAE CODICUM OCCIDENTALIUM (Amsterdam 1960-):

406

I. *Servii Grammatici in Vergilii Carmina Commentarii,* ed. G.I. Lieftinck (1960)
Leiden, BRU, MS. B.P.L. 52. Maurdramnus-type script. Corbie, ca. A.D. 800-25, with 16 folios ca. 950-60. 105 folios. CF.

407

II. *Notitiae regionum urbis Romae et urbis Constantinopolitanae. Glossarium Latine-Theotiscum,* ed. F. Unterkircher (1960)
Vienna, ONB, MS. lat. 162. Two hands, Caroline of ca. A.D. 800-50. *Notitiae,* Fulda, ca. 840-50; *Glossarium,* Regensburg, ca. 820-30. 50 folios. CF.

408

III. *Registrum autographum priorum Collegii Sorbonae,* ed. R. Marichal (1960)
Paris, BN, MS. lat. 5494A, covering priors from A.D. 1431-85. Hands of various priors. Paper. 105 folios (wanting 85-7). CF.

409

IV. *Saint Dunstan's Classbook from Glastonbury,* ed. R.W. Hunt (1961)
Oxford, Bodleian Library, MS. Auct. F. 4. 32. Various hands: Anglo-Caroline, Glastonbury, 9th century; Anglo-Insular mixed minuscule, second half of the 11th century; Wallico-Insular, first half of the 9th century. 47 folios. CF.

410

V. *Psalterium Graeco-Latinum,* ed. L. Bieler (1960)
Basel, Universitätsbibliothek, MS. A. VII. 3. Two scribes in turn for both Greek text and Latin interlinear version. Greek majuscule of the West; Hiberno-Insular minuscule, probably St. Gall. 9th century (850-80?). 99 folios. CF.

411

VI. *Liber cartularis S. Petri principis apostolorum Monasterii Romanensis,* ed. A. Bruckner (1962)
Lausanne, Bibliothèque cantonale et universitaire, MS. 5011. Whole MS (58 fols.) written by various hands at Romainmôtier, W. Switzerland. Original part (fols. 1-29), here reproduced in facsimile, is in two late Caroline hands, A.D. 1126-41.

412

VII. *Celtic Psalter*, ed. C.P. Finlayson (1962)

Edinburgh, University Library, MS. 56. Latin. Hiberno-Insular minuscule. Ireland, or possibly Scotland, probably 11th century. 143 folios. CF (4 pages to each plate).

413

VIII. *Lectionarium Sancti Lamberti Leodiensis tempore Stephani episcopi paratum (901-920)*, ed. F. Masai and L. Gilissen (1963)

Brussels, Bibliothèque royale, MS. 14650-59. Caroline, probably one scribe. Liège, early 10th century. 167 folios. CF.

414

IX. *Le Recueil epistolaire autographe de Pierre d'Ailly et les notes d'Italie de Jean de Montreuil*, ed. G. Ouy (1966)

Cambrai, Bibliothèque municipale, MS. 940; Vatican City, BAV, MSS. Reg. lat. 689A (d'Ailly), 1653 (de Montreuil). Mostly cursive chancery hand. Late 14th century, early 15th (ca. 1390-1420). 183 plates: CF of Cambrai MS (59 fols., 158 pls.), PF of Reg. lat. 1653 (25 pls.).

415

X. *Aethici Istrici Cosmographia Vergilio Salisburgensi rectius adscripta*, ed. T.A.M. Bishop (1966)

Leiden, BRU, MS. Scaligeranum 69. A copy of the *Cosmographia* (ca. A.D. 770) of Vergil of Salzburg, written in Anglo-Caroline at St. Augustine's, Canterbury, second half of the 10th century. Pp. xix-xx contain an important discussion of Anglo-Caroline script at Canterbury, together with a provisional list of MSS of ca. 950-1000 surviving from St. Augustine's. 87 folios. CF, with 5 plates of other products of the same scriptorium (3 of which are by the scribe of the *Cosmographia*).

General Collections

416

Arndt, W. and M. Tangl. *Schrifttafeln zur Erlernung der lateinischen Palaeographie*. 3 vols. (Berlin, 4th ed. of I-II 1904-7, 2nd ed. of III 1904-6; repr. Berlin 1929, Hildesheim 1976). 107 pls. with transcriptions.

417

Bartoloni, F. *Esempi di scrittura latina dal secolo I avanti Cristo al secolo XV: Appendice agli 'Esempi di scrittura latina' di Ernesto Monaci* (Rome

1934). 40 pls.

For Monaci see **438**.

418

Beer, R. *Monumenta palaeographica vindobonensia: Denkmäler der Schreib kunst aus der Handschriftensammlung des hapsburg-lothringischen Erz-hauses.* 2 vols. (Leipzig 1910, 1913)
46 plates (with 29 others in introductions to vols. I and II) illustrate the following MSS from Vienna (now Nationalbibliothek): vol. I: MS. lat. 2160* (Hilary, *De trinitate* and *Contra Arianos,* papyrus, Semi-uncial, 6th century), 1861 ('Golden' Psalter of Charlemagne, Caroline minuscule, ante 795); vol. II: MS. lat. 16 (Bobbio miscellany, palimpsest in part, 4th-8th century), lat. 958 (*Liber sacramentorum* of Gregory the Great, Uncial, 9th century).

419

Canellas, A. *Exempla scripturarum in usum scholarum.* 2 vols. (Saragossa, 3rd ed. of I 1967, 2nd ed. of II 1974). 157 pls. with full transcriptions
Vol. I (63 pls.) covers scripts in general, II (94 pls.) confines itself to scripts in Hispanic areas from ca. A.D. 44-1594. See also **784**.

420

Chatelain, E. *Paléographie des classiques latins: Collection de fac-similés des principaux manuscrits de Plaute, Térence, Varron, Cicéron, César, Cornélius Népos, Lucrèce, Catulle, Salluste, Virgile, Horace, Tibulle, Properce, Ovide, Tite-Live, Justin, Phèdre, Sénèque, Quinte Curce, Perse, Lucain, Pline l'Ancien, Valerius Flaccus, Stace, Martial, Quintilien, Juvénal, Tacite, Pline le Jeune, Suétone, etc.* 2 vols. (Paris 1884-1900)
210 plates exhibit 304 samples in various scripts from ca. A.D. 400-1500. Each MS is described. Sometimes there are transcriptions, notably of glosses. The plates are numbered I-CXCV and do not take account of 15 plates in fascicule 7 (1892) which are for insertion at various points in the first six fascicules (e.g. IV A).

421

Chroust, A. *Monumenta palaeographica: Denkmäler der Schreibkunst des Mittelalters.* 1st ser. (Munich 1902-6), 2nd ser. (1907-17), 3rd ser. incomplete (Leipzig 1931-40)
Issued in parts, not all of which are possessed by libraries. Includes 690 plates in all, with transcriptions, of MSS in Latin and German.

422

De Boüard, A. *Manuel de diplomatique française et pontificale,* I: *Diploma-*

tique générale. Avec un album de 54 planches en phototypie (Paris 1925), *Transcription et explication des planches de l'album* (1929); II: *L'Acte privé* (1948), *Album* (1949-52) with 34 pls., *Transcription et explication des planches de l'album* (1952)
The plates in vol. I cover A.D. 780-1812; those in II run from 840-1480/81.

423
[Delisle, L.] *Album paléographique ou Recueil de documents importants relatifs à l'histoire et à la littérature nationales, reproduits en héliogravure d'après les originaux des bibliothèques et des archives de la France, avec des notices explicatives, par la Société de l'Ecole des chartes* (Paris 1887)
Includes 50 plates of 67 documents from A.D. 400-1685.

424
De Vries, S. *Album palaeographicum: Tabulae LIV selectae ex cunctis jam editis tomis codicum Graecorum et Latinorum photographice depictorum* (Leiden 1909)
Gives 54 samples from the series Codices Graeci et Latini (**226-42**).

425
Ehrle, F. and P. Liebaert. *Specimina codicum Latinorum Vaticanorum.* Tabulae in usum scholarum [ed. J. Lietzmann] 3 (Berlin–Leipzig 1912, 2nd ed. 1932; repr. Berlin 1968)
Prints 50 plates, with transcriptions, of codices from ca. A.D. 350 to ca. 1497.

426
EXEMPLA SCRIPTURARUM EDITA CONSILIO ET OPERA PROCURATORUM BIBLIOTHECAE ET TABULARII VATICANI:

427
I. *Codices Latini saeculi XIII,* ed. B. Katterbach, A. Pelzer, and C. Silva-Tarouca (Rome 1929)
32 plates, with full or partial transcriptions, of MSS in the Vatican Library and Archives.

428
II. *Epistolae et instrumenta saeculi XIII,* ed. B. Katterbach and C. Silva-Tarouca (Vatican City 1930)
40 plates, with transcriptions, of documents, papal and notarial, in the Vatican Archives.

429
III. *Acta pontificum,* ed. G. Battelli. 2nd ed. (Vatican City 1965)
50 plates, with transcriptions, from holdings of the Vatican Archives,

A.D. 819-1843. For IV, see **486**.
430
Foerster, H. *Mittelalterliche Buch- und Urkundenschriften* (Bern 1946).
50 pls. with transcriptions
Covers diplomatic documents, in the main.
431
————. *Urkundenlehre in Abbildungen* (Bern 1951). 40 pls. with transcriptions
Deals with imperial, papal, and other documents, A.D. 57-1583.
432
[Giry, A.] *Recueil de fac-similés à l'usage de l'Ecole des chartes.* 4 fascs.
(Paris 1880-87)
The 'Giry' *Recueil.* But there is a much larger 'Recueil à l'usage de l'Ecole
des chartes' which was never published as such. Few libraries possess this
complete 'private' set, and fewer still the complete set of transcriptions,
some of which are in typescript.
433
Ihm, M. *Palaeographia Latina: Exempla codicum Latinorum phototypice
expressa scholarum maxime in usum.* 2nd ed. (Leipzig 1931)
Includes 22 plates, without transcriptions, mostly from Wolfenbüttel MSS.
434
Kirchner, J. *Scriptura Latina libraria a saeculo primo usque ad finem medii
aevi.* 2nd ed. (Munich 1970). 77 pls. with transcriptions
One of the best general collections, first published in 1955. For some
adverse comment, see G.I. Lieftinck in *Museum* 62 (1957) 28-33, and
Scriptorium 22 (1968) 66-71.
435
Krzyżanowski, S. *Album palaeographicum.* 3rd ed. by W. Semkowicz and
S. Budkowa. 2 vols. (Cracow 1935, 1936). 31 pls. with transcriptions
Mostly of diplomatic documents relative to Poland, from A.D. 1100/1102
to 1496.
436
Melis, F. *Documenti per la storia economica dei secoli XIII-XVI* (Florence
1972). 200 pls. with transcriptions
Covers a wide range of commercial documents, with a note by E. Cecchi
on 'Commercial palaeography' at pp. 561-75.
437
Merkelbach, R. and H. van Thiel. *Lateinisches Leseheft zur Einführung in*

Paläographie und Textkritik (Göttingen 1969). 111 pls. without transcriptions
Deals with classical texts, often with the same passage of a classical or other author from two or more MSS.

438

Monaci, E. *Esempi di scrittura latina dal sec. I dell'era moderna al XVIII* (Rome 1906). 50 pls. with transcriptions
See also **417**.

439

Monumenta palaeographica sacra: Atlante paleografico-artistico compilato sui manoscritti esposti in Torino alla mostra d'arte sacra nel MDCCCXCVIII, ed. F. Carta, C. Cipolla, and C. Frati (Turin 1899). 120 pls. without transcriptions
Covers a wide range of scripts.

440

Prou, M. *Recueil de fac-similés d'écritures du Ve au XVIIe siècle.* 2 vols. (Paris 1904)
55 plates, with a companion volume of transcriptions, to illustrate texts largely of a documentary nature in Latin, French, and Provençal, for the benefit of those who are 'loin d'un centre universitaire.' Not to be confused with the *Album* accompanying the 4th edition (1924) of Prou's manual **(138)**.

441

Seider, R. *Paläographie der lateinischen Papyri* (Stuttgart 1972-):

442

I. *Urkunden* (1972)
40 plates, with transcriptions, of some 66 separate diplomatic documents up to the time of Pope Leo IV (A.D. 847-55).

443

II. *Literarische Papyri,* 1: *Texte klassischer Autoren* (1978): 40 plates, with transcriptions, of some 68 items, most of which are also available in CLA or ChLA; 2: *Juristische und christliche Texte* (1981): 40 plates, with transcriptions, of some 76 texts.

444

Steffens, F. *Lateinische Paläographie.* 2nd ed. (Trier 1909, repr. Berlin 1929, 1964)
The first edition of this, the best general collection of facsimiles for teaching, was published at Fribourg in 1903 as *Lateinische Paläographie: Hundert*

*Tafeln ... mit einer systematischen Darstellung der Entwicklung der latein-
ischen Schrift.* The second edition (with a French translation, *Paléographie
latine,* by R. Coulon [Trier–Paris 1910]) suppresses some of those plates
and adds some more, bringing the total to 125 plates, all of which have
exhaustive descriptions and transcriptions.

445

Van Thiel, H. *Mittellateinische Texte: Ein Handschriften-Lesebuch*
(Göttingen 1972)

80 plates illustrate some 36 authors and texts, but generally without
transcriptions, from ca. A.D. 800-ca. 1500.

446

Vogels, H.J. *Codicum Novi Testamenti specimina* (Bonn 1929)

Includes 54 plates (51 of MSS) of Greek and Latin versions of the New
Testament, without transcriptions.

Cultural Setting

From its earliest days until the advent of printing, Latin writing was an expression of four Western cultures in turn: Roman, monastic, scholastico-mercantile, and humanist. The forms it took in these successive cultures occupy the core of this book (**516-1305**). The section is prefaced by something on writing as such (**447-75**) and on Greek and other alphabets that have a bearing on its Latin variety (**476-515**).

WRITING IN GENERAL

447
Alfabetismo e cultura scritta nella storia della società italiana. Atti del seminario tenutosi a Perugia il 29-30 marzo 1977 (Perugia 1978)
Contains notable contributions by A. Petrucci (pp. 33-47) and G. Cavallo (119-45).

448
Anderson, D.M. 'Calligraphy' in *Encyclopedia of Library and Informational Services,* ed. A. Kent and H. Lancour (New York 1970) IV, 1-33
Curiously, there is no entry on palaeography as such in this encyclopedia.

449
Audin, M. 'Naissance de l'alphabet' in *Somme typographique,* I: *Les Origines,* ed. M. Audin (Paris 1948) 35-59.

450
Auerbach, E. *Literary Language and its Public in Late Latin Antiquity and in the Middle Ages,* trans. R. Manheim (London – New York 1965).

451
Basso, K.H. 'The Ethnography of Writing' in *Explorations in the Ethnography of Speaking,* ed. R. Bauman and J. Sherzer (London 1974) 425-32.

452

Clanchy, M.T. *From Memory to Written Record: England, 1066-1307* (London–Cambridge, Mass. 1979). 19 pls.

On the growth of practical literacy and of the dependence for daily business on written record instead of the living memory.

453

Classen, P., ed. *Recht und Schrift im Mittelalter* (Sigmaringen 1977)

In spite of the title, the only essay which directly discusses the relationship of writing to law is that of Classen, 'Fortleben und Wandel spätrömischen Urkundenwesens im frühen Mittelalter,' pp. 13-54.

454

Cohen, M. *La Grande Invention de l'écriture et son évolution.* 2 vols. and a portfolio of 95 pls. (Paris 1958).

455

————. 'Les Ecritures latines: Extensions passées et récentes' in **456**, 313-23

With charts and map of the spread of the Latin alphabet (even to China).

456

[Cohen, M., ed.] *L'Ecriture et la psychologie des peuples* (Paris 1963)

Proceedings of a 'semaine de synthèse' at the Centre international de synthèse, Paris, 1960. Contributions range over all peoples and languages, e.g. for Greek and Latin, by M. Cohen (see **455**), A. Dain (**482**), H. Lévy-Bruhl (**468**), and R. Marichal (**124**).

457

Degering, H. *Lettering: A Series of 240 Plates illustrating Modes of Writing in Western Europe from Antiquity to the End of the 18th Century* (London 1954, repr. New York 1965)

A translation of *Die Schrift: Atlas...* (Berlin 1929). One of the most comprehensive works of its kind, ranging from the *Lapis niger* in the Roman Forum (5th century B.C.) to 1798. Includes 240 plates of MSS, letters, monuments, tombs, and early printing, with a brief general introduction.

458

Diringer, D. *Writing.* Ancient Peoples and Places 25 (London 1962). 78 pls., 3 maps.

459

————. *The Alphabet: A Key to the History of Mankind.* 3rd ed. (London 1968). 256 figs.

460

Drogin, M. *Medieval Calligraphy: Its History and Technique* (Montclair, N.J.–London 1980). 142 pls., 42 figs.

Practical instruction on how to write in the principal medieval scripts.

461

Fairbank, A. *A Book of Scripts*. King Penguin Books (Harmondsworth 1949, 2nd ed. 1952)

Includes 64 plates of Latin and vernacular scripts (16 from MSS or inscriptions), many in illustration of modern versions of 'Italic' hand.

462

————. *The Story of Handwriting: Origins and Development* (London 1970). 28 pls.

463

Février, J.G. *Histoire de l'écriture.* 2nd ed. (Paris 1959).

464

Fichtenau, H. *Mensch und Schrift im Mittelalter* (Vienna 1946). 16 pls. with transcriptions

Sees writing as a human expression that reflects time and place, and subjectivity.

465

Higounet, C. *L'Ecriture.* Que sais-je? 653. 3rd ed. (Paris 1964)

Has two good chapters on Latin writing.

466

Jackson, D. *The Story of Writing* (New York 1981)

A well-illustrated volume by a practised calligrapher.

467

Jensen, H. *Sign, Symbol, and Script: An Account of Man's Efforts to Write,* trans. G. Unwin (New York 1969, London 1970). 303 illustrations

A translation of *Die Schrift in Vergangenheit und Gegenwart,* 3rd ed. (Berlin 1969).

468

Lévy-Bruhl, H. 'L'Ecriture et la droite' in **456**, 325-38

On the role of writing in the refinement of law. See also **453**.

469

Lot, F. 'A quelle époque a-t-on cessé de parler Latin?' *Archivum Latinitatis medii aevi* 6 (1931) 97-159

By Latin, the author means 'vulgar' Latin or Latin as commonly spoken. The focus of the article is the period ca. A.D. 600-900.

470

Morison, S. *Politics and Script: Aspects of Authority and Freedom in the Development of Graeco-Latin Script from the Sixth Century B.C. to the Twentieth Century A.D.*, ed. N. Barber (Oxford 1972)
The Lyell Lecture for 1957 at Oxford University. A useful and imaginative survey of the main Western scripts. Includes 187 illustrations.

471

Parkes, M.B. 'The Literacy of the Laity' in *Literature and Western Civilization*, ed. D. Daiches and A.K. Thorlby, II: *The Medieval World* (London 1973) 555-77.

472

Pirenne, H. 'De l'état d'instruction des laïcs à l'époque mérovingienne,' *RB* 46 (1934) 165-77.

473

Tschichold, J. *Treasury of Alphabets and Lettering* (New York 1966)
Includes 175 plates of various letter forms (pp. 49-224) from the Roman period to modern times. A translation of *Meisterbuch der Schrift* (Ravensburg 1961).

474

Visible Language: The Journal for Research on the Visual Media of Language Expression (Cleveland, Ohio 1967-)
Like the parallel *Journal of Typographic Research* (1966-), this is published four times a year from the Cleveland Museum of Art. Both carry valuable bibliographies.

475

Walter, A.J. 'Die Schrift als Kulturobjekt,' *Mitteilungen des Instituts für österreichische Geschichtsforschung* 57 (1949) 375-82
Reflections on Fichtenau **464**.

GREEK AND OTHER WRITING

Greek

476

De Montfaucon, B. *Palaeographia Graeca sive De ortu et progressu literarum Graecarum et de variis omnium saeculorum scriptionis Graecae generibus: Itemque de abbreviationibus et de notis variarum artium ac disciplina-*

rum, additis figuris et schematibus ad fidem manuscriptorum codicum (Paris 1708)

The first use of the term *palaeography*.

477

Barbour, R. 'Greek Palaeography 8th to 16th Centuries A.D.' in *Encyclopedia Britannica* 17 (1966) 123-7.

478

—————. *Greek Literary Hands A.D. 400-1600* (Oxford 1981). 110 facsimiles with transcriptions.

479

Bataille, A. *Pour une terminologie en paléographie grecque* (Paris 1954).

480

Blanchard, A. 'Les Origines lointaines de la minuscule' in **497**, 167-73

Discusses the effect of Latin minuscule on Greek practice.

481

Cavallo, G. *Ricerche sulla maiuscola biblica* (Florence 1967)

Includes a portfolio of 115 plates.

482

Dain, A. 'L'Ecriture grecque du VIIIe siècle avant notre ère à la fin de la civilisation byzantine' in **456**, 167-82.

483

David, M. and B.A. van Groningen. *Papyrological Primer*. 4th ed. (Leiden 1965). 6 pls., 2 maps.

484

Devreesse, R. *Introduction à l'étude des manuscrits grecs* (Paris 1954). 17 pls.

485

—————. *Les Manuscrits grecs de l'Italie méridionale (histoire, classement, paléographie)* (Vatican City 1955). 7 pls.

486

Follieri, E. *Codices Graeci Bibliothecae Vaticanae selecti* (Vatican City 1969). 70 pls. with transcriptions

This is vol. 4 of Exempla scripturarum **426**; for the others see **427-9**.

487

Franchi de' Cavalieri, P. and J. Lietzmann. *Specimina codicum Graecorum Vaticanorum*. Tabulae in usum scholarum 1. 2nd ed. (Berlin–Leipzig 1929). 60 pls. with transcriptions.

488

Gardthausen, V. *Griechische Palaeographie*. 2 vols. (Leipzig 1911, 1913;

repr. Leiden 1979)
First published in 1879 in one volume.
489
Hatch, W.H.P. *Facsimiles and Descriptions of the Minuscule Manuscripts of the New Testament* (Cambridge, Mass. 1951). 100 pls.
490
Hunger, H. *Studien zur griechischen Paläographie* (Vienna 1954).
491
Kern, O. *Inscriptiones Graecae.* Tabulae in usum scholarum 7 (Bonn 1913) 50 facsimiles with some transcriptions.
492
Lake, K. and S. Lake. *Dated Greek Minuscule Scripts to the Year 1200 A.D.* 10 vols. (Boston, Mass. 1934-9), with *Indices* (1945)
A survey of libraries, country by country, with facsimiles of dated MSS.
493
Lefort, L. Th. and J. Cochez. *Palaeographisch Album van gedagteekende grieksche Minuskelhandschriften uit de IXᵉ en Xᵉ eeuw: Album palaeographicum codicum Graecorum minusculis litteris saec. IX et X certo tempore scriptorum* (Louvain [1932]). 100 pls.
494
Metzger, B. *Manuscripts of the Greek Bible: An Introduction to Greek Palaeography* (New York–Oxford 1981). 45 pls. with descriptions and some transcriptions.
495
Mioni, E. *Introduzione alla paleografia greca* (Padua 1973). 30 pls.
496
Norsa, M. *La scrittura letteraria greca dal sec. IV A.C. all' VIII D.C.* (Florence 1939). 19 pls. with transcriptions.
497
La Paléographie grecque et byzantine. Colloques internationaux du Centre national de la recherche scientifique 559 (Paris 1977)
Proceedings of a colloquium held in 1974.
498
Roberts, C.H. *Greek Literary Hands 350 B.C.-A.D. 400* (Oxford 1956)
Includes 24 plates, with a few lines of transcription in each case.
499
Schubart, W. *Griechische Paläographie* (Munich 1925, repr. 1966).

500

————. *Griechische Papyri: Urkunden und Briefe.* 2 vols. (Leipzig 1927). 10 pls.

501

Spatharakis, I. *Corpus of Dated Illuminated Greek Manuscripts to the Year 1453.* 2 vols. (Leiden 1981)
Includes 611 plates, 395 of which show specimens of text.

502

Turner, E.G. *Greek Manuscripts of the Ancient World* (Oxford 1971). 73 facsimiles with partial transcription.

503

Turyn, A. *Codices Graeci Vaticani saeculis XIII et XIV scripti annorumque notis instructi* (Vatican City 1964)
Includes 205 plates, arranged chronologically, with descriptions. This is vol. 28 of the series Codices e Vaticanis selecti (see **192**).

504

————. *Dated Greek Manuscripts of the Thirteenth and Fourteenth Centuries in the Libraries of Italy.* 2 vols. (Urbana, Ill. 1972)
A descriptive catalogue, chronologically arranged, with 265 plates.

505

Van Groningen, B.A. *A Short Manual of Greek Palaeography* (Leiden 1940). 10 pls.

506

Voicu, S.J. and S. D'Alisera. *Index in manuscriptorum Graecorum edita specimina* (Rome 1981)
A complete listing of reproductions of any kind or size from Greek MSS in libraries from the Aigion Library, Kalávrita, Greece, to Zwickau.

507

Wattenbach, W. *Anleitung zur griechischen Palaeographie.* 3rd ed. (Leipzig 1895).

508

————. *Scripturae Graecae specimina in usum scholarum.* 4th ed. (Berlin 1936). 35 pls.

509

Wilson, N. *Medieval Greek Bookhands: Examples selected from Greek Manuscripts in Oxford Libraries.* 2 vols. (Cambridge, Mass. 1972, 1973)
Includes 88 plates, with a few lines of transcription in each case.

510

Wittek, M. *Album de paléographie grecque: Spécimens d'écritures livresques du IIIe siècle av. J.C. au XVIIIe siècle conservés dans des collections belges* (Ghent 1967). 64 pls.

Other Writing

SEMITIC

511

Birnbaum, S.A. *The Hebrew Scripts.* 2 vols. (Leiden 1971)
Vol. II contains 339 plates, without transcriptions (first issued London 1954-7). I covers classification of scripts, etc.

512

Driver, G. *Semitic Writing: From Pictograph to Alphabet,* ed. S.A. Hopkins. 2nd ed. (London 1976). 66 pls.

OLD GOTHIC

513

Codex argenteus Upsaliensis (Uppsala 1930)
Uppsala, Universitetsbiblioteket, MS. s.n. The Gothic or Ulfila Bible.
N. Italy, 6th century. 374 folios. CF. See also **514-15**.

514

Tjäder, J.-O. 'Der Codex argenteus in Uppsala und der Buchmeister Viliaric in Ravenna' in *Studia Gotica* (Stockholm 1972) 144-64.

515

————. 'Studier till "Codex argenteus" historia,' *Nordisk tidskrift Bochoch Biblioteksväsen* 61 (1974) 51-99.

LATIN WRITING (AND VERNACULAR DERIVATIVES)

At a great risk of simplification the following diagram may help students to follow the various stages of development of Latin and vernacular script from some of the earliest datable samples of Latin writing in A.D. 45-54 (various documents from Oxyrhynchus, Egypt) to ca. 1450, the beginning of printing:

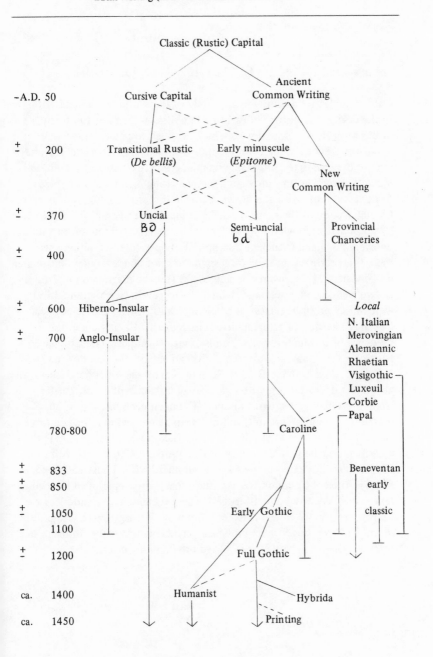

Period of Roman Culture

See in general **7**, 119-24; **148**, 55-94; **152**, 60-81; **159**, 71-100.

Dated samples are essential in any study of the evolution of handwriting. In the case of the history of early Latin writing we are not too fortunate in this respect, but at least we are lucky enough to possess three securely-dated samples of writing from the time of Claudius (A.D. 41-54). These are not the first dated or datable samples (see **516**), but they are interesting in that each in turn provides a sample within one decade, of three distinct styles of writing: a house census in professional cursive Rustic Capital, a copy of the same in a calligraphic Rustic Capital, and a speech (*Oratio Claudii*) in what may be termed a cursive 'common' or 'private' or 'everyday' hand ('Ancient Common Writing'). Interaction between these three scripts (not forgetting some variations on 'everyday' postulated by Cencetti **521-2**) gave rise in due course (see the diagram on p. 75 above) to two well-known bookhands which until recently (see Mallon **535-9**) were presumed to be related as whole is to half: Uncial and Semi-uncial. Uncial is a version of calligraphic or classic Rustic Capital under the influence of certain 'everyday' forms of letters, and, as 'Transitional Rustic Capital,' may be observed at the earliest in a fragment of the *De bellis Macedonicis* (CLA II.207). Semi-uncial, on the other hand, seems to be a direct development, with only a small influence of classic Rustic, from 'everyday' or Ancient Common Writing; it gives us most of our present-day minuscule script, and is first to be noticed in a fragmentary copy of the *Epitome Livii* (CLA II.208). These two scripts dominate the bookhands of the period from ca. A.D. 350 to ca. 800, Uncial with some 600 samples illustrated in the CLA, Semi-uncial with almost 150 (see also **532-3**). Ancient Common Writing, the cursive script employed in documentary as well as everyday writing, gave way, probably in the middle of the fourth century, to 'New' or 'Recent' Common Writing. This became the script of the various Roman provincial chanceries and is the source in one form or other of most of the localized pre-Caroline scripts.

STUDIES

516

Anderson, R.D., P.J. Parsons, and R.G.M. Nisbet. 'Elegiacs by Gallus from Qaṣr Ibrîm,' *Journal of Roman Studies* 69 (1979) 125-55. 3 pls.

The article dates, discusses, and edits a fragment of papyrus roll from, perhaps, the period 50 B.C. to A.D. 25, carrying nine lines by Gaius Cornelius Gallus (ob. 27 or 26 B.C.) and found recently in Egyptian Nubia. The fragment is written in good but not 'canonized' Rustic Capital and may well preserve the earliest datable example of that script.

517

Bischoff, B. 'Die alten Namen der lateinischen Schriftarten' in **32**, I, 1-5.

518

Casamassima, E. and E. Staraz. 'Varianti e cambio grafico nella scrittura dei papiri latini: Note paleografiche,' *SC* 1 (1977) 9-110. 6 pls.

On the development of Roman cursive (common) script.

519

Cau, E. 'Ricerche sui codici in Onciale dell'Italia settentrionale (secoli IV-VI),' *RM* 3 (1968) 1-26. 14 pls.

520

————. 'Fulgenzio e la cultura scritta in Sardegna agli inizi del VI secolo,' *Sandalion* (Sassari) 2 (1979) 5-13

Suggests that some notes written in the Codex Basilicanus of Hilary (**578**) while it was at Cagliari in A.D. 509-10 are perhaps in the hand of Fulgentius, bishop of Ruspe in N. Africa, then in exile in Sardinia.

521

Cencetti, G. 'Vecchi e nuovi orientamenti nello studio della paleografia,' *La Bibliofilia* 50 (1948) 4-23

In reaction to the new 'French' approach of, e.g., Mallon, Marichal, and Perrat (**581**) to Roman writing, Cencetti stresses, as most Italian palaeographers do in his wake, the place of *scrittura usuale* or 'everyday' writing – a writing unfettered by fixed rules – in the development of writing in Roman times. See also **568**.

522

————. 'Ricerche sulla scrittura latina nell'età arcaica, 1: Il filone corsivo,' *BAPI* new ser. 2-3 (1956-7) pt. 1, 175-205. 1 pl., 21 figs.

Introduces the term *scrittura normale* to denote the ensemble of models for *scrittura usuale*.

523

————. 'Note paleografiche sulla scrittura dei papiri latini dal I al III secolo d. C.,' *Accademia delle scienze dell'Istituto di Bologna, Classe di scienze morali: Memorie* 5th ser. (1950) 3-58. 5 pls.

524

Christiansen, J. *De apicibus et I-longis inscriptionum Latinarum* (Husum [= Oberhausen] 1889)

A fundamental study in thesis form of marks over vowels, etc.

525

Cockle, W. 'A new Vergilian Writing Exercise from Oxyrhynchus,' *SC* 3 (1979) 55-75. 11 pls.

Discusses two hexameters from *Aeneid* XI.371-2 written in Rustic Capital script; the papyrus may be dated to the 1st or 2nd century A.D.

526

Collart, P. 'Les Papyrus littéraires latins,' *Revue de philologie, de littérature, et d'histoire anciennes* 3rd ser. 15 (1941) 112-28.

527

Courtois, C., L. Leschi, C. Perrat, and C. Saumagne. *Tablettes Albertini: Actes privés de l'époque vandale (fin du Vᵉ siècle)* (Paris 1952)

Includes an album of 48 plates, introduction (see especially Perrat on the script, pp. 15-62), and transcriptions. The tablets were written A.D. 493-6 in SW Algeria, and are now in the National Museum, Algiers.

528

Green, W.M. 'A Fourth Century Manuscript of Saint Augustine?' *RB* 69 (1959) 191-7

Suggests that Leningrad, Public Library, MS. Lat. Q. V. I. 3, in Uncial, contains the *De doctrina Christiana* in its 'first edition' as it circulated in the years 396-426, and was written early in this period, probably in Hippo.

529

Hammond, C.P. 'A Product of a Fifth-Century Scriptorium preserving Conventions used by Rufinus of Aquileia,' *Journal of Theological Studies* new ser. 29 (1978) 366-91

Discusses citation marks and punctuation in Lyons, Bibliothèque de la ville, MS. 483 (Rufinus' translation of Origen on Romans).

530

Hornshöj-Möller, S. 'Die Beziehung zwischen der älteren und der jüngeren römischen Kursivschrift: Versuch einer kulturhistorischen Deutung,' *Aegyptus* 60 (1980) 1-63

Maintains, among other things, that the hegemony enjoyed by 'Later Roman cursive' from the 4th century onwards may have been due to official action in its favour around A.D. 300. Argues that the script may have been developed in the eastern part of the Empire, perhaps at Alexandria.

531

Kresten, O. 'Diplomatische Auszeichnungsschriften in Spätantike und Frühmittelalter,' *Mitteilungen des Instituts für österreichische Geschichtsforschung* 74 (1966) 1-50

On tall writing (*litterae caelestes*, etc.) in imperial, papal, and Merovingian chanceries.

532

Lowe, E.A. and E.K. Rand. *A Sixth-Century Fragment of the Letters of Pliny the Younger: A Study of Six Leaves of an Uncial Manuscript preserved in the Pierpont Morgan Library New York* (Washington, D.C. 1922)

CF of MS. M. 462 (Uncial ca. A.D. 500, Italy). Includes an important contribution by Lowe (pp. 3-22) on the dating of Uncial MSS of the 5th-8th centuries, reprinted in **60**, I, 103-26 and pls. 8-21.

533

Lowe, E.A. 'A Hand-List of Half-uncial Manuscripts' in **41**, IV, 34-61

The introduction only to this paper of 1924 is reprinted in **60**, I, 139-41.

534

————. 'Greek Symptoms in a Sixth-Century Manuscript of St. Augustine and in a Group of Latin Legal Manuscripts' in **29**, 279-89. 6 pls.; repr. in **60**, II, 466-74 and pls. 108-13

Argues for evidence of a Latin scriptorium at Constantinople in the 6th century A.D. from two 6th-century MSS: Lyons 478 (an Uncial MS which reached Lyons by the 9th century) and the famous copy of the *Digest* of Justinian (see **580**) now in the Biblioteca Laurenziana, Florence (Uncial and Semi-uncial).

535

Mallon, J. 'Remarques sur les diverses formes de la lettre B dans l'écriture latine,' *BEC* 99 (1938) 229-42

One of the first intimations of a completely new approach to writing of the Roman period, which in Mallon's case has its fullest expression in **538**.

536

————. 'Observations sur quelques monuments d'écriture latine calligraphiés dans les cinq premiers siècles de notre ère,' *Arts et métiers graphiques*

66 (1939) 37-41.
537
————. *L'Ecriture de la chancellerie impériale romaine* (Salamanca 1948). 2 pls., 2 tables.
538
————. *Paléographie romaine* (Madrid 1952). 32 pls.
A revolutionary study, giving Roman Rustic a prominence denied it since Mabillon and Square Capital, destroying the sacrosanct relationship of Uncial and Semi-uncial, and emphasizing the importance of *ductus,* or the direction of the hand when writing, over *forma,* the 'look' of a letter. See reviews of C. Higounet, *Revue des études anciennes* 58 (1954) 235-41; A. Dain, *Latomus* 15 (1956) 398-404; and J.-O. Tjäder **565**.
539
————. 'Paléographie des papyrus d'Egypte et des inscriptions du monde romain,' *Museum Helveticum* 10 (1953) 141-60.
540
————. 'Scriptoria épigraphiques,' *Scriptorium* 11 (1957) 177-94
See also **2175-85**.
541
————. 'Paléographie romaine' in **42**, 553-84. 5 pls.
542
————. *Ductus ou la formation de l'alphabet moderne* (Paris 1976)
A witty 16 mm. film, with music and sparkling graphics, summing up in 20 minutes Mallon **538**. For a review see **559**.
543
Marichal, R. 'Paléographie précaroline et papyrologie,' *Scriptorium* 1 (1946-7) 1-5
See further **546**.
544
————. 'De la capitale romaine à la minuscule' in *Somme typographique* I (see **449**) 61-111. 2 pls., 54 figs.
545
————. 'L'Ecriture latine et l'écriture grecque du Ier au VIe siècle,' *L'Antiquité classique* 19 (1950) 113-44. 6 pls.
546
————. 'Paléographie précaroline et papyrologie (1). II: L'Ecriture latine du Ier au VIIe siècle: Les Sources,' *Scriptorium* 4 (1950) 116-42
An important list, with bibliography, of Latin papyri before A.D. 500.

547

————. 'L'Ecriture latine de la chancellerie impériale,' *Aegyptus* 32 (1952) 336-50.

548

————. 'Le *B* "à panse à droite" dans l'ancienne cursive romaine et les origines du *B* minuscule' in *Studi di paleografia, diplomatica, storia, e araldica in onore di Cesare Manaresi* (Milan 1953) 345-63.

549

————. 'Paléographie précaroline et papyrologie, III,' *Scriptorium* 9 (1955) 127-49

A survey of publications 1949-54, with particular reference to Mallon **538** and his theory there of a change of angle of writing in the 3rd or 4th century.

550

————. 'La Date des Graffiti de la Triclia de Saint-Sébastien et leur place dans l'histoire de l'écriture latine,' *Revue des sciences religieuses* 36 (1962) 111-54.

551

Norsa, M. 'Analogie e coincidenze tra scritture greche e latine nei papiri' in **63**, VI, 105-21. 10 pls.

552

Pack, R.A. *The Greek and Latin Literary Texts from Graeco-Roman Egypt.* 2nd ed. (Ann Arbor, Mich. 1965)

A revised and enlarged edition of the work of 1952.

553

Pagnin, B. 'Codice sconosciuto in onciale del VI secolo,' *RM* 10-12 (1975-1977) 3-17. 6 pls.

Discusses 7 folios in the Giustiniani Recanati collection at Venice. Concludes that they are possibly connected with Verona and the circle of Ursicinus (see **220**).

554

Perrat, Ch. 'Paléographie romaine' in **76**, I, 345-84

A well-documented survey of work on Roman palaeography up to 1955.

555

Petronio Nicolaj, G. 'Osservazioni sul canone della capitale libraria romana fra I e III secolo' in **35**, 3-28. 6 pls.

556

Petrucci, A. 'Per la storia della scrittura romana: I graffiti di Condatomagos,'

BAPI 3rd ser. 1 (1962) 85-132. 2 pls.
On the witness of graffiti of the 1st century A.D. in a cave at Condatomagos (La Graufesenque, near Millau, département Aveyron, Auvergne) to
the influence of 'popular' (as distinct from 'private') script on the formation of Roman common cursive.

557
————. 'Nuove osservazioni sulle origini della "b" minuscola nella
scrittura romana,' *BAPI* 3rd ser. 2-3 (1963-4) 55-72.

558
————. 'Per la datazione del "Virgilio Augusteo": Osservazioni e proposte' in **35**, 29-45
Argues for a date between, probably, 495 and 530, against the common
opinion as expressed, e.g., by C. Nordenfalk in his facsimile edition of the
'Augusteus' (**299**), that the codex belongs to the second half of the 4th
century and is contemporaneous with the 'Damasan' inscriptions (A.D.
366-84).

559
Poulle, E. 'Une histoire de l'écriture,' *BEC* 135 (1977) 137-44
On the film (**542**) and writings of Mallon.

560
Pratesi, A. 'Appunti per la datazione del Terenzio Bembino' in **31**, I, 71-84
Contrary to S. Prete (see **583**), dates the Codex Bembinus of Terence to
the end of the 5th century A.D. or beginning of the 6th, arguing from the
scholia (which he shows to have been written before the codex was bound).

561
Raffaelli, R. 'Prologhi, perioche, didascalie nel Terenzio Bembino (e nel
Plauto Ambrosiano),' *SC* 4 (1980) 41-101. 19 pls.
Are these technical aspects of text 'extra-textual'? A discussion of their
value for textual tradition.

562
Rosenthal, E. *The Illuminations of the Vergilius Romanus (Cod. Vat. Lat.
3867): A Stylistic and Iconographical Analysis* (Dietikon–Zürich 1972).
19 pls., 140 figs.
Argues that the origin of the codex is the East or eastern Roman provinces.
For PF see **194**.

563
Schiaparelli, L. *La scrittura latina nell'età romana (Note paleografiche):
Avviamento allo studio della scrittura latina nel medio evo* (Como 1921)

Has 11 plates.
564
Tjäder, J.-O. 'La misteriosa "Scrittura grande" di alcuni papiri ravennati e il suo posto nella storia della corsiva latina e nella diplomatica romana e bizantina dall'Egitto a Ravenna,' *Studi romagnoli* 3 (1952) 173-221.
565
————. 'Die Forschungen Jean Mallons zur römischen Paläographie,' *Mitteilungen des Instituts für österreichische Geschichtsforschung* 61 (1953) 385-96
Disputes Mallon's view (**538**) that minuscule writing was developed in 'bookhand' circles.
566
————. *Die nichtliterarischen lateinischen Papyri Italiens aus der Zeit 445-700*, vol. I, 2 pts. (Lund 1955, 1954)
Part 1 (1955) covers 28 papyri in deposits in Italy, Vatican City, and England, with texts, translation (into German), exhaustive commentary (pp. 81-116: types of writing), and 4 plates. Part 2 (1954) consists of 55 plates of the papyri described in Part 1.
567
————. 'Der Ursprung der Unzialschrift,' *Basler Zeitschrift für Geschichte und Altertumskunde* 74 (1974, = *Festgabe Albert Bruckner zum siebzigsten Geburtstag*) 9-40
Suggests that Uncial script was 'canonized' at Rome, where it became the preferred script for juridical literature from the 2nd century A.D.
568
————. 'Considerazioni e proposte sulla scrittura latina nell'età romana' in **31**, I, 31-62
A re-examination (1979) of the theories of Mallon, Cencetti, and Petrucci on the origins of minuscule. Affirms the 'Italian' view that it developed from 'private' writing.
569
Turner, E.G. and O. Skutsch. 'A Roman Writing-Tablet from London,' *Journal of Roman Studies* 50 (1960) 108-11. 1 pl.
570
Van Haelst, J. *Catalogue des papyrus littéraires juifs et chrétiens* (Paris 1976)
Contains 1230 items.

571

Vattasso, M. *Frammenti d'un Livio del V secolo recentemente scoperti: Codex Vat. lat. 10696* (Rome 1906). 3 pls.

Discusses seven pieces of parchment, forming a leaf and a half, in Uncial of the 4th or 5th century A.D., found in the church of St. John Lateran in Rome in a cypress box made to the order of Pope Leo III (795-816), where used as 'envelopes' to preserve relics from the Holy Land. A good example of fortuitous 'transmission.'

572

Wilmart, A. 'L'Odyssée du manuscrit de San Pietro qui renferme les oeuvres de Saint Hilaire' in **67**, 293-305

A discussion of the fortunes of the 'Codex Basilicanus' of the works of Hilary (**578**). See now **520**.

573

Zelzer, M. 'Palaeographische Bemerkungen zur Vorlage der Wiener Livius-handschrift' in *Antidosis: Festschrift für Walther Kraus zum 70. Geburtstag,* ed. R. Hanslik et al. (Vienna–Cologne–Graz 1972) 487-501

Argues, chiefly from *b-d* confusion, that MS. lat. 15 in Nationalbibliothek in Vienna, an Uncial codex of Livy Bks. 41-5 dating from the first half of the 5th century, was copied from an exemplar in ancient Roman cursive of the 1st century A.D. or the beginning of the 2nd.

FACSIMILES

For facsimiles of MSS of this period in various series see **177, 193** and **213** (Vatican Vergil), **199** (Palatine Vergil), **200** (Vergilius Augusteus), **205** (Cicero, *De re publica*), **232** (Uncial Livy), **242** (*Corpus agrimensorum*), **244** (Jerome), **250** (Constance-Weingarten Uncial fragments), **299** (Vergilius Augusteus). In general see **181** and **183-7** for volumes of ChLA. See also all volumes of CLA (**252-63**), e.g. for Rustic Capital: I.11-12, 19, 30, 70, 72, 74, 99, 101; II.118-19, 212, 223; III.345-6, 363, 385-7, 392; IV.442, 445, 447-8, 501; V.526, 571a; VI.809, 833; VII.974; VIII.1053 [**809], 1054, 1214, 1219-20; IX.1342, 1347, 1423; X.1520, 1539; XI.**212, 1645-66; S.169, 1705, 1709, 1721, 1735, 1766; for Square Capital: I.13; VII.977; VIII.1051 [**13]; X.1569; S.1693; for Early Roman cursive: II.249; VII.885; VIII.1038; S.1673 [**249]; for Later Roman cursive: II.166; VI.832; IX.1349-50; for Uncial: some 600 samples in I-XI and S., esp. vols. I, III, IV, V; for Semi-uncial: about 150 samples, especially vols. III, IV, V. See also **442-3**.

574

Bassi, S. *Monumenta Italiae graphica,* I: *La scrittura greca in Italia nell'età arcaica (VIII-III secolo a.C.)* (Cremona 1956); II: *La scrittura calligrafica Greco-romana* (1957)

This two-part work, in which the pagination is continuous, provides the most complete collection of examples of pre-Roman and Roman writing in Italy. There are 72 plates, illustrating 203 subjects.

575

Chatelain, Ae. [= E.] *Uncialis scriptura codicum Latinorum novis exemplis illustrata* (Paris 1901-2)

Prints 100 plates (nos. 61-100 showing Semi-uncial) of 5th-8th-century examples, with transcriptions.

576

Gaius: *Gai codex rescriptus in Bibliotheca capitulari ecclesiae cathedralis Veronensis,* ed. A. Spagnolo (Leipzig 1909)

Verona, Biblioteca capitolare, MS. XV (13). Palimpsest: Gaius, *Institutionum commentarii IV,* in Uncial of the 5th century A.D. (Constantinople?) under letters of Jerome in Uncial of the 8th century (France?). 127 folios. CF.

577

Gospels: *Codex Bezae Cantabrigiensis.* 2 vols. (Cambridge 1899)

Cambridge, University Library, MS. Nn. ii. 41. Hesitant Semi-uncial of the beginning of the 5th century A.D., possibly in a centre in the Near East. A celebrated MS of the four Gospels and Acts of the Apostles in Greek with parallel Latin translation (see CLA II.140). Presented to the University of Cambridge in 1581 by the Calvinist theologian Theodore Beza (1519-1605), who had acquired it from the loot of a church at Lyons (where it had been since the 9th century) in 1562. 406 folios. CF.

578

Hilary of Poitiers: *S. Hilarii Pictaviensis De Trinitate: Codex Archivi S. Petri in Vaticano no. D 182,* ed. A. Amelli and G. L. Perugi. 2nd ed. (Turin 1930)

Vatican City, BAV, MS. Archivio della Basilica di S. Pietro D. 182. Semi-uncial (fols. 13-27, 34-288) and Uncial (fols. 288-311) of the late 5th or early 6th century A.D., possibly written at Cagliari in Sardinia where the text of the Semi-uncial part was 'corrected' in 509-10 (see **520**). From the time of Tassin and Toustain 74 until recently (see 538) this codex, known as 'Basilicanus,' was in effect the yardstick by which all 'Uncial' and 'Semi-uncial' MSS were measured. 311 folios. CF. See also 572.

579

Jerome: *The Bodleian Manuscript of Jerome's Version of the Chronicle of Eusebius*, ed. J.K. Fotheringham (Oxford 1905)
Oxford, Bodleian Library, MS. Auct. T. 2. 26, fols. 33-144. Uncial, mid-5th century, probably written in Italy. CF.

580

Justiniani Augusti Digestorum seu Pandectarum codex Florentinus olim Pisanus phototypice expressus. 10 pts. (Rome 1902-10)
Florence, Biblioteca Laurenziana, MS. s.n. The famous copy of the *Digest* in Greek and Latin, written in Uncial and Semi-uncial at Constantinople shortly after the promulgation of the Code in A.D. 533 (see 534). At Pisa by the mid-12th century, where seized by Florentines as booty in 1406. Reached the Laurenziana after 1786. 905 folios (now bound in 2 vols.). CF

581

Mallon, J., R. Marichal, and C. Perrat. *L'Ecriture latine de la capitale romaine à la minuscule: 54 planches reproduisant 85 documents originaux* (Paris 1939)
A collection of facsimiles, with diplomatic transcriptions, which set the scene for Mallon 538.

582

Spicilegium palimpsestorum (Beuron—Leipzig 1913-), I: *Codex Sangallensis 193 continens fragmenta plurium prophetarum secundum translationem S. Hieronymi,* ed. A. Mauser (1913)
St. Gall, Stiftsbibliothek, MS. 193. Lower script (Prophets) is Semi-uncial of the 5th century written in, probably, N. Italy; upper script (homilies of Caesarius of Arles, etc.) is Rhaetian and Alemannic minuscule of the 8th-9th century. 152 folios. CF.

583

Terence: *Il codice di Terenzio Vaticano Latino 3226: Saggio critico e riproduzione del manoscritto,* ed. S. Prete. Studi e testi 262 (Vatican City 1970)
Vatican City, BAV, MS. Vat. lat. 3226. *Fabulae* of Terence in Rustic Capital. Dated by CLA (I.12) and Prete to the 4th-5th century A.D. (but see 560). 115 folios. CF. For Vat. lat. 3868 (Terence) see 202.

84
heodosius: *Code Théodosien, livres VI-VIII: Reproduction réduite du
anuscrit en onciale, latin 9643 de la Bibliothèque nationale [ed. H.
mont] (Paris 1909)
'ncial copy of Codex Theodosianus (A.D. 438), probably written at Lyons
the 5th-6th century. 122 folios. CF.

85
'ergil: *Il codice Mediceo di Virgilio,* ed. E. Rostagno. 2 vols. (Rome 1931)
lorence, Biblioteca Laurenziana, MS. Plut. XXXIX, 1. Rustic Capital of
ne 5th century (before A.D. 494), possibly at Rome. 222 folios. CF. For
acsimiles of other celebrated codices of Vergil in Rustic or Square Capital
ee **193** and **213** ('Vaticanus'), **194** ('Romanus'), **199** ('Palatinus'), **200**
'Augusteus').

86
Vessely, C. *Schrifttafeln zur älteren lateinischen Palaeographie* (Leipzig
898)
las 20 plates, almost exclusively of papyri.

87
Zangemeister, K. and W. Wattenbach. *Exempla codicum latinorum litteris
maiusculis scriptorum* (Heidelberg 1876), with *Supplementum* (1879).
56 pls. with transcriptions.

Period of Monastic Culture (ca. A.D. 500-1200)

Although the production of books and documents (*instrumenta*) was not
at all confined to monastic circles in the period, the long stretch from the
collapse of the Roman Empire (A.D. 476) to the renaissance of the twelfth
century may usefully be described in the present context of writing as the
period of monastic culture.

All the same, the period is not uniformly monastic. During and after the
Gregorian Reform (ca. 1050-1100), there was a shift away from monastic
centres which gradually led to their almost complete eclipse as centres of
writing towards the end of the twelfth century. This was mainly because of
the renaissance of learning (theological, legal, philosophical, grammatical,
classical, and biblical) in cathedral and other schools in France and Italy,
and because the rise of the communes and of commerce created a demand
for writers (notaries) who were versed in the writing of commune business

and commercial contracts.

In the present bibliography the high period of monastic culture (ca. A.]
500-1100) falls on either side of the emergence of Caroline writing ca. 80(
The division of the period as a whole into pre-Carolingian and post-Caroliı
gian works well for areas which adopted Caroline writing at once around
or after that year, but not so well for those such as England and Spain in
which the influence of Caroline writing was not felt until much later. The
pre-Carolingian period, from which about 1800 MSS (see **588**) and a good
ly number of *instrumenta* (see **178-91**) survive, has received more attentio.
from scholars than has the post-Carolingian period, mainly because of the
fascination of centres of transmission such as Luxeuil, Bobbio, or Corbie,
and of the presence of the so-called 'national' hands (Insular, Visigothic,
Merovingian, and Beneventan). Hence the bibliography for the pre-Carolin
gian period is larger than that for the post-Carolingian period, although
one should note that many of the sources cited under pre-Carolingian
often straddle both periods. It is hard, too, to separate the latter part of
the post-Carolingian period (after the Gregorian Reform, that is) from the
beginnings of the period of scholastico-mercantile culture, and hence from
the beginnings of Gothic handwriting. So one has to allow for a certain
amount of overlapping.

Here, in the pre-Carolingian period the areas of the British Isles, Spain,
and S. Italy are treated first, in order to keep those areas in which Carolin
writing was devised or was adopted at once (France, Germany, Switzerland, Italy) as close as possible to the Carolingian divide.

GENERAL STUDIES

588
Bischoff, B. 'Scriptoria e manoscritti mediatori di civiltà dal sesto secolo
alla riforma di Carlo Magno' in *Centri e vie di irradiazione della civiltà
nell'alto medio evo*. Settimane di studio 11 (Spoleto 1964) 479-504; repr.
in **589**, 29-47, and (in German) in **32**, II, 312-27.
589
Cavallo, G., ed. *Libri e lettori nel medioevo: Guida storica e critica*
(Rome – Bari 1977). 24 pls.
Reprints, in Italian, various studies by Bischoff (**588, 916**), Cavallo (**832**),
Cencetti (**590**), Fink-Errera (**1755**).

590
Cencetti, G. 'Scriptoria e scritture nel monachesimo benedettino' in *Il monachesimo nell'alto medioevo e la formazione della civiltà occidentale.* Settimane di studio 4 (Spoleto 1957) 187-219; repr. in **589**, 75-97.

591
Jones, L.W. 'The Influence of Cassiodorus on Mediaeval Culture,' *Speculum* 20 (1945) 433-42
See also **597**.

592
Laistner, M.L.W. *Thought and Letters in Western Europe A.D. 500-900.* 2nd ed. (London 1957).

593
————. *The Intellectual Heritage of the Early Middle Ages* (Ithaca, N.Y. 1957).

594
Lesne, E. *Histoire de la propriété ecclésiastique en France,* IV: *Les Livres, 'scriptoria,' et bibliothèques du commencement du VIIIe à la fin du XIe siècle* (Lille 1938)
A valuable survey of church inventories, libraries, and treasuries of the period.

595
Lindsay, W.M. 'The Letters in Early Latin Minuscule (till c. 850)' in **49**, 1 (1922) 7-61. 1 pl.
A discussion from A-Z of the letter-forms practised in Uncial, Semi-uncial, Insular, Merovingian, Caroline, and other scripts.

596
McGurk, P. *Latin Gospel Books from A.D. 400 to A.D. 800* (Paris – Brussels 1961)
A catalogue of MSS (mostly of Insular origin), with a list of incipits and a discussion of format and script. For a review see D.H. Wright, *Speculum* 37 (1962) 637-43.

597
Momigliano, A.D. 'Cassiodorus and the Italian Culture of his Time' in *PBA* 41 (1955) 207-45; repr. in his *Studies in Historiography* (London 1966) 181-210.

598
Riché, P. *Education and Culture in the Barbarian West: From the Sixth through the Eighth Century,* trans. from 3rd French ed. (1973) by J.J.

Contreni (Columbia, S.C. 1976).
599
Zimmermann, E.H. *Vorkarolingische Miniaturen* (Berlin 1916)
Four portfolios of samples of pre-Carolingian miniatures, with commenta

PRE-CAROLINGIAN

Insular

Very, very little evidence of writing survives from the period of the Rom.
occupation of Britain (see **569**). The Romans never occupied Ireland, but
not long after they had definitively withdrawn from Britain at the beginning of the fifth century A.D., Latin writing and some Roman culture
reached Ireland through the mission of St. Patrick in A.D. 432. What
scripts the books owned by the missionaries were written in we do not
know, but the chances are good that they were in Uncial and Semi-uncial
since the 'Insular' form of Latin writing which was in use in Ireland by 6(
and which was taken to Scotland, Britain, and continental Europe by Iris.
missionaries from the second half of the sixth century onwards, does not
show any manifest influence of cursive on its ductus and letter-forms. In
general this Insular script is the result of an artificial blending of Semi-
uncial and Uncial forms. The earliest datable (or approximately datable)
example of the script is the Psalter known as the 'Cathach' of St. Columb
(CLA II.266), which if it is not to be dated before 597 (the death of
Columba on Iona), probably is not many years after that. About the time
that the Cathach was written, the Uncial form of Latin writing obtained a
foothold in Britain when Augustine and his small band of missionaries
from Rome reached the south of England in the summer of 597. Later it
spread northwards, providing a model for a goodly series of codices in
'English Uncial' (see **717**), notably the massive Codex Amiatinus (CLA II
299) at the beginning of the eighth century. Some forty years after the
introduction of Uncial to S. England, the new Insular script from Ireland
established itself firmly in the north, when missionaries from Columba's
foundation on Iona were invited into Northumbria in 635 and set up an
influential monastery at Lindisfarne. By the time of Bede's death in 735,
the Insular script as practised at Lindisfarne and later Northumbrian
centres such as Wearmouth and Jarrow, had become a distinctive form to
which one may not unreasonably give the name Anglo-Insular. Before the

rst quarter of the eighth century it is not easy to distinguish between the
ative Irish brand of Insular and its Northumbrian derivative. After that
ie two versions go their own distinctive ways, whether at home or abroad,
nd whether employed for Latin texts or for those in the respective verna-
ulars. The original Insular script (Hiberno-Insular, if you will) endured
iore or less unchanged until the present day; Anglo-Insular, while success-
illy surviving a strong challenge from Caroline in S. England in the second
alf of the tenth century, faded away in the wake of the Norman Conquest
f 1066. The early Insular period (ca. 600-800) produced some exquisitely
lustrated bibles and liturgical books (see, e.g., **651, 671-2, 755-6**). The
omeland of this great moment in the history of Insular book-production
s still a matter of much debate (see, e.g., **704-5**).

HIBERNO-INSULAR (TO ca. A.D. 1600)

See 7, 124-8; **148**, 170-85; **152**, 86-93; **159**, 107-13; CLA II (**253**),
1972 ed., especially pp. xv-xx.

General

600
Bieler, L. 'The Classics in Celtic Ireland' in **1871**, 45-9.
601
————. *Ireland, Harbinger of the Middle Ages* (London—New York
1963)
First published in German and translated, with slight revisions, by the
author.
602
————. 'Ireland's Contribution to the Culture of Northumbria' in
*Famulus Christi: Essays in Commemoration of the Thirteenth Centenary
of the Birth of the Venerable Bede,* ed. G. Bonner (London 1976)
210-28.
603
Bischoff, B. 'Il monachesimo irlandese nei suoi rapporti col continente'
in *Il monachesimo nell'alto medioevo e la formazione della civiltà
occidentale.* Settimane di studio 4 (Spoleto 1957) 121-38; repr. in **32**,
I, 195-205.

604
Boyer, B.B. 'Insular Contributions to Medieval Literary Tradition on the Continent,' *Classical Philology* 42 (1947) 209-22; 43 (1948) 31-9.
605
Coccia, E. 'La cultura irlandese precarolingia: Miracolo o mito?' *SM* 3rd ser. 8 (1967) 257-420
A myth, to his way of thinking: 'tanto dubbia e incerta quanto mediocre e di scarsissimo valore.'
606
Duft, J. 'Irische Einflüsse auf St. Gallen und Alemannien' in *Mönchtum Episkopat, und Adel zur Gründungszeit des Klosters Reichenau,* ed. A. Borst (Sigmaringen 1974) 9-35.
607
Gougaud, L. *Celtic Christianity* (London 1932)
A translation, with revisions, of *Les Chrétientés celtiques* (Paris 1911).
608
Hayes, R.J. *Manuscript Sources for the History of Irish Civilization.* 11 vols. (Boston 1965)
A survey of libraries, archives, and private collections in some 30 countries. Supplements **611** for the medieval period.
609
Hillgarth, J.N. 'Visigothic Spain and Early Christian Ireland,' *PRIA* 62C (1962) 167-94. 1 pl.
610
Hughes, K. *Early Christian Ireland: Introduction to the Sources* (Ithaca, N.Y. 1972)
Has good chapters on secular literature, ecclesiastical learning, hagiography, art, and architecture.
611
Kenney, J.F. *The Sources for the Early History of Ireland,* I: *Ecclesiastical. An Introduction and Guide* (New York 1929; repr. New York–Shannon 1966, with brief addenda and corrigenda by L. Bieler)
This very comprehensive work is especially valuable for its survey (pp. 622-744) of surviving works of 'religious, literary and ecclesiastical culture' from the 7th-12th centuries.
612
O'Grady, S. and R. Flower. *Catalogue of Irish Manuscripts in the British Museum.* 3 vols. (London 1926-53)

A general introduction to vols. I (ed. O'Grady) and II (ed. Flower) is in III, together with *initia* of MSS and 25 plates of MSS (all in Irish) from A.D. 1138 to 1803-4.

613

Traube, L. *Perrona Scottorum, ein Beitrag zur Ueberlieferungsgeschichte und zur Palaeographie des Mittelalters* (Munich 1900); repr. in **70**, III, 95-119

A pioneer work. The first general study of 'Insular Writing' (a coinage of Traube's to cover Irish and Anglo-Saxon writing) and its influence on the continent of Europe, especially as seen in the literary history of Perrona Scottorum (Péronne, some 40 km. west of Amiens), one of the few Irish settlements abroad to keep in regular touch with Ireland.

Script and Scriptoria

614

Beeson, C.H. 'Insular Symptoms in the Commentaries on Vergil,' *SM* new ser. 5 (1932) 81-100.

615

Best, R.I. 'Notes on the Script of the *Lebor na hUidre*,' *Ériu* 6 (1912) 161-74

Discusses the 'Book of the Dun (Cow),' a compendium of prose and verse written ca. A.D. 1100 by three scribes, probably at Clonmacnoise, Co. Offaly.

616

Bieler, L. 'The Irish Book of Hymns: A Palaeographical Study,' *Scriptorium* 2 (1948) 177-94. 3 pls. (nn. 25-7)

Examines Dublin, Trinity College, MS. 1441 (E.4.2) and Dublin, Franciscan Library (now Dun Mhuire, Killiney, Co. Dublin), MS. A.2, both from the 11th century.

617

————. 'Insular Palaeography: Present State and Problems,' *Scriptorium* 3 (1949) 267-94

A good general survey, with bibliography, for the period 1918-49.

618

————. 'The *Notulae* in the Book of Armagh,' *Scriptorium* 8 (1954) 89-97

Discusses the problem of whether these *notulae* (Dublin, Trinity College,

MS. 52, fols. 18v-19r) were copied from a late 7th-century source, Tírechán perhaps, or were an original compilation of Ferdomnach, the scribe of the Book of Armagh (A.D. 895-901). He argues for the former

619

————. 'The Palaeography of the Book of Durrow' in **672**, 89-97.

620

————. 'A Gallican Psalter in Irish Script: Vaticanus Lat. 12910' in **52**, 7-15. 2 pls.

Vatican City, BAV, MS. Vat. lat. 12910. A codex of the 11th century which was written in Ireland and in medieval times was in the church of S. Angelo in Spata, Viterbo.

621

Bischoff, B. 'Irische Schreiber im Karolingerreich' in *Jean Scot Erigène et l'histoire de la philosophie*. Colloques internationaux du Centre de la recherche scientifique 561 (Paris 1977) 47-58; repr. in **32**, III, 39-54 Notes especially Caroline letter-forms which influenced Irish scribes writing on the continent. See also **623**.

622

Byrne, F.J. *A Thousand Years of Irish Script* (Oxford 1979) A catalogue, without reproductions, of an exhibition in 1979 at the Bodleian Library, Oxford.

623

Contreni, J.J. 'The Irish Colony at Laon during the Time of John Scotus' in *Jean Scot Erigène* (see **621**) 59-67.

624

Dold, A. and J. Duft. *Die älteste irische Handschriften-Reliquie der Stiftsbibliothek St. Gallen mit Texten aus Isidors Etymologien* (Beuron 1955) On St. Gall, Stiftsbibliothek, MS. 1399 a.1: fragments in 'Irish cursive minuscule' of the 7th century, representing one of the earliest Hiberno-Insular MSS extant. See also **609**, 182-5.

625

Dold, A., L. Eizenhöfer, and D.H. Wright. *Das irische Palimpsestsakramentar im CLM 14429 der Staatsbibliothek München* (Beuron 1964). 8 pls. A study of a Gallican sacramentary written in Hiberno-Insular majuscule in Ireland in the mid-7th century and palimpsested by an Irish scribe in the 9th century, probably at Reichenau. See CLA IX.1298.

626

Draak, M. 'A Leyden Boethius-Fragment with Old-Irish Glosses,' *Mededelingen der Koninklijke Nederlandsche Akademie van Wetenschappen*, Afdeling Letterkunde, new ser. 11 (1948) 115-27. 2 pls.

On Leiden, BRU, MS. B.P.L. 2391a: one leaf written in the second quarter of the 9th century in Anglo-Insular minuscule, with glosses in Hiberno-Insular minuscule.

627

————. 'Construe Marks in Hiberno-Latin Manuscripts,' *Mededelingen* (see **626**) 20 (1957) 261-82. 4 pls.

628

————. 'The Higher Teaching of Latin Grammar in Ireland during the Ninth Century,' *Mededelingen* (see **626**) 30 (1967) 109-44. 1 pl.

629

Duft, J. and P. Meyer. *Die irischen Miniaturen der Stiftsbibliothek St. Gallen* (Olten – Berne – Lausanne 1953). 43 pls.

The introduction gives a complete list of Irish books at St. Gall, including a 9th-century catalogue of 32 books 'scottice scripti.' There is an English translation: *The Irish Miniatures in the Abbey of St. Gall* (Olten – Lausanne – Fribourg 1954).

630

Eizenhöfer, L. 'Zu dem irischen Palimpsestsakramentar im Clm 14429,' *Sacris erudiri* 17 (1966) 355-64

See also **625**.

631

Friend, A.M., Jr. 'The Canon Tables of the Book of Kells' in *Medieval Studies in Memory of A. Kingsley Porter*, ed. W.R.W. Koehler. 2 vols. (Cambridge, Mass. 1939) II, 611-66. 24 pls.

Friend argues that the tables and portraits derive from a codex made in the Palace School of Charlemagne ca. A.D. 800 — an egregious view, in the opinion of A. Boeckler, 'Die Evangelistenbilder der Adagruppe,' *Münchener Jahrbuch der bildenden Kunst* 3rd ser. 3-4 (1952-3) 121-44.

632

Gougaud, L. 'Les Scribes monastiques d'Irlande au travail,' *RHE* 27 (1931) 293-306.

633

————. 'The Remnants of Ancient Irish Monastic Libraries' in *Féil-Sgríbhinn Eóin Mhic Néill*, ed. J. Ryan (Dublin 1940) 319-44.

634

Gwynn, A. 'The Irish Missal of Corpus Christi College, Oxford' in *Studies in Church History,* I, ed. C.W. Dugmore and C. Duggan (London 1964) 47-68

Oxford, Corpus Christi College, MS. 282. Beginning of the 11th century

635

Haseloff, G. 'Fragments of a Hanging-Bowl from Bekesbourne, Kent, and some Ornamental Problems,' *Medieval Archeology* 2 (1958) 72-103

Translated from German (by L. de Paor). Considers interlacing on the bowl in terms of Irish MS ornamentation and of the continuity between Irish ornamentation in MSS and enamelling and millefiori-working of bowls in Ireland from the 5th century A.D.

636

Hennessey B.J. 'The Early Insular Script,' *Harvard Studies in Classical Philology* 77 (1973) 250-52

Argues that classification by region is better than old majuscule/minuscule distinction, and that none of Lowe's criteria in CLA II is useful.

637

Henry, F. 'Irish Culture in the Seventh Century,' *Studies* (Dublin) 37 (1948) 267-79; followed by S.P. Ó Riordáin, 'A Note on the Archeological Evidence,' 279-82

Against Masai **651**.

638

————. 'Les Débuts de la miniature irlandaise,' *Gazette des beaux-arts* 6th ser. 37 (1950) 5-34

Masai **651** again.

639

————. 'An Irish Manuscript in the British Museum (Add. 40.618),' *Journal of the Royal Society of Antiquaries of Ireland* 87 (1958) 147-66 with figs. and illustrations

An example of gospels of small form in Ireland at the end of the 8th and beginning of the 9th century. See also **653**.

640

———— . 'Remarks on the Decoration of Three Irish Psalters,' *PRIA* 61C (1960) 24-40. 19 pls.

The psalters: London, BL, MS. Cotton Vitellius F. XI; Cambridge, St. John's College, MS. 59; Rouen, Bibliothèque municipale, MS. 24. Argues that the type of decoration here was standard in Irish scriptoria

in the first half of the 11th century, and was imitated in Wales at Llanbadarn, e.g. in the psalter of Ricemarch (see **310**).

641

————. *Irish Art in the Early Christian Period (to 800 A.D.)*. 2nd ed.
(London 1965). 80 pls.

An enlarged edition of a publication of 1940.

642

————. *Irish Art during the Viking Invasions 800-1200 A.D.*
(London 1967). 70 pls.

643

————. *Irish Art in the Romanesque Period 1020-1170 A.D.* (London
1970). 134 pls.

644

————. *The Book of Kells: Reproductions from the Manuscript in
Trinity College, Dublin, with a Study of the Manuscript* (London—
New York 1974). 126 colour, 75 monochrome pls.

645

Henry, F. and G.L. Marsh-Micheli. 'A Century of Irish Illumination
(1070-1170),' *PRIA* 62C (1962) 101-66. 44 pls.

Covers various MSS illuminated in Ireland or by Irish monks elsewhere
(e.g. Vatican City, BAV, MS. Pal. lat. 830: the chronicle of Marianus
Scotus of Mainz — 'Moel Brigte,' more properly — copied in part by an
Irish scribe in Hiberno-Insular minuscule for the author at Mainz in A.D.
1072-3 and in part by the author himself).

646

Hughes, K. 'The Distribution of Irish Scriptoria and Centres of Learning
from 730 to 1111' in *Studies in the Early British Church,* ed. N.K.
Chadwick (Cambridge 1958) 243-72.

647

Lawlor, H.J. and W.M. Lindsay. 'The Cathach of St. Columba,' *PRIA*
33C (1916) 241-443. 5 pls.

On Dublin, Royal Irish Academy, MS. s.n., 58 folios: an early Irish
majuscule codex (psalter) traditionally associated with St. Columba
(ob. 597, Iona). See also CLA II. 266.

648

Lewis, S. 'Sacred Calligraphy: The Chi Rho Page in the Book of Kells,'
Traditio 36 (1980) 139-59. 14 pls.

649

Lindsay, W.M. *Early Irish Minuscule Script* (Oxford 1910). 12 pls.
A pioneer work (see also **613**).

650

MacNiocaill, G. 'Fragments d'un coutumier monastique irlandais du
VIIIe-IXe siècle,' *Scriptorium* 15 (1961) 228-33
On Karlsruhe, Badische Landesbibliothek, MS. Frag. Augiense 20: one
parchment leaf (CLA VIII.1118), here edited. Suggests that the Stowe
Missal (**308**) may be from Terryglass, not Tallaght (see CLA II. 268).

651

Masai, F. *Essai sur les origines de la miniature dite irlandaise* (Brussels–
Antwerp 1947). 64 pls. (46 illustrating MSS, 18 various artifacts)
Maintains that while Insular minuscule writing is indeed a creation of
the Irish, one must turn to Northumbria for the origins of the so-called
'Irish majuscule' form. Argues that Northumbria is also the cradle of
Insular illumination (against Micheli **654**); the Book of Kells (**671**)
belongs there, or at least to a 'Northumbrian area' such as Iona (see als
705). For reactions, often sharp, see Nordenfalk **657**, Henry **637-8**;
L. Bieler, *Speculum* 23 (1948) 495-502; M. Shapiro, *Gazette des beaux
arts* 37 (1950) 134-8.

652

McCormick, M. 'Un fragment inédit de lectionnaire du VIIIe siècle,'
RB 86 (1976) 75-82. 1 pl.
On one leaf (Bibliothèque centrale de l'Université catholique de Louva
MS. Omont 1) from the beginning of the 8th century in an Insular scrip
midway between majuscule and minuscule.

653

McGurk, P. 'The Irish Pocket Gospel Book,' *Sacris erudiri* 8 (1956)
249-70
Remarks on the character of pocket Gospel Books, with reference to
Irish survivals from the 8th and 9th centuries, notably the books know
as 'Moling,' 'Dimma,' 'Cadmug,' and 'McDurnan.'

654

Micheli, G.L. *L'Enluminure du haut moyen âge et les influences
irlandaises* (Brussels 1939). 280 pls.
Covers the period to the 10th century. See **651**.

655

Natale, A.R. *Studi paleografici: Arte e imitazione della scrittura insulare in codici bobbiesi* (Milan 1950).

656

————. 'Esercizi di calligrafia insulare in codici del sec. VIII: Nota paleografica,' *Archivio storico italiano* 116 (1958) 54-74. 5 pls.

657

Nordenfalk, C. 'Before the Book of Durrow,' *Acta archaeologica* 18 (1947) 141-74

A first attempt, in reaction to Masai **651**, at a study of the history of Insular illumination prior to the Book of Durrow (**672**), and particularly in the second half of the 6th century and first of the 7th. Notes a connection between initials in the Cathach of St. Columba (see CLA II. 266) and Italian initials of the 6th and 7th centuries, especially those of 'Roman' Uncial codices (see **817**).

658

————. *Celtic and Anglo-Saxon Painting: Book Illumination in the British Isles 600-800* (London 1977)

Has 48 plates, with introduction and commentary, of the Books of Durrow (**672**), Kells (**671**), and Mulling (see **653**), and of undoubted Anglo-Insular products such as the Book of Lindisfarne (**756**), the Gospels of St. Willibrord (Paris, BN, MS. lat. 9389), the Codex aureus from Canterbury in Uncial (now in Stockholm: see CLA XI.1642), and the Durham Cassiodorus (CLA II.152).

659

O'Sullivan, W. 'Notes on the Scripts and Make-up of the Book of Leinster,' *Celtica* 7 (1966) 1-31

On Dublin, Trinity College, MS. 1339 (H.2.18), incomplete (197 fols.). A miscellany in Irish put together by several scribes from ca. A.D. 1152 to post-1201, with Aed, abbot of Terryglass, Co. Tipperary, as the chief contributor.

660

Plummer, C. 'On the Colophons and Marginalia of Irish Scribes,' *PBA* 12 (1926) 11-44

A famous and lively lecture.

661

Powell, R. 'The Book of Kells, The Book of Durrow: Comments on the Vellum, the Make-up, and Other Aspects,' *Scriptorium* 10 (1956) 3-21.

662

Schauman, B.T. 'The Irish Script of the MS Milan, Biblioteca Ambrosiana,

S. 45 sup. (ante ca. 625),' *Scriptorium* 32 (1978) 3-18. 2 pls.
On two unnoticed early 7th-century Irish hands. See also CLA III.365.
663
Schiaparelli, L. 'Note paleografiche: Intorno all'origine e ad alcuni
caratteri della scrittura e del sistema abbreviativo irlandese,' *Archivio
storico italiano* 74/2 (1916) 3-126. 2 pls.; repr. in **68**, 189-314.
664
Waterer, J.W. 'Irish Book-Satchels or Budgets,' *Medieval Archeology*
12 (1968) 70-82. 4 pls., 4 figs.
665
Wright, D. 'The Tablets from the Springmount Bog: A Key to Early
Irish Palaeography,' *American Journal of Archaeology* 67 (1963) 219
Discusses six wooden tablets (see CLA S.1684) in early Irish minuscule
of the 7th century, now in the National Museum, Dublin.

Facsimiles

For the Antiphonary of Bangor see **306**, for the Stowe Missal **308**, for
various psalters **410, 412**; and, in general, CLA **(252-63)** as follows:
I.87; II.132-3, 144, 147, 148b, 149, 179, 218, 231 (MacRegol Gospels)
232, 256, 266 (Cathach of Columba), 267, 268 (Stowe Missal), 269
(MS of 'Domnach Airgid'), 270 (Book of Armagh), 271, 272 ('Garland
of Howth'), 273 (Book of Durrow), 274 (Book of Kells), 275 (Book of
Dimma), 276 (Book of Mulling), 277; III.299 [**5b], 311 (Antiphonary of Bangor), 312, 326-9, 336-7, 339-40, 344b, 350-55, 361, 391,
394, 397b, 400; IV.441, 452-4, 457; V.581-3, 610, 642; VI.757,
828; VII.847, 901-2, 979-80, 988-91, 995, 998-1001, 1008, 1010,
1012; VIII.1083-5, 1088-92, 1116, 1117-18, 1135, 1169, 1172, 1185,
1227; IX.1298, 1368, 1398-9, 1403, 1415-17; X.1492, 1511, 1557,
1574; XI.p. 22 (**1185, **144); S.1684, 1734, 1741, 1797.

666
The Annals of Inisfallen, ed. R.I. Best and E. MacNeill (Dublin –
London 1933)
Oxford, Bodleian Library, MS. Rawlinson B 503. Hiberno-Insular
minuscule (with some Gothic later). Written by about 38 hands from
shortly before A.D. 1092 to the 14th century. Begun at Emly, Co.
Tipperary, continued at Lismore, Co. Waterford, completed at Inis-

fallen Island (Killarney), Co. Kerry. 57 folios. CF.

667

The Book of Ballymote, ed. R. Atkinson (Dublin 1887)
Dublin, Royal Irish Academy, MS. 25. Collection of literary pieces in
Irish written ca. 1400 at Ballymote, Co. Sligo, in Hiberno-Insular minus-
cule. 251 folios. CF.

668

Der Codex Boernerianus der Briefe des Apostels Paulus. ed. A. Reichardt
(Leipzig 1909)
Dresden, Sächsische Landesbibliothek, MS. Bibl. Misc. A 145b (see CLA
VIII.**1181). Greek, with interlinear Latin written at St. Gall (?) in
Hiberno-Insular minuscule by two hands. Some marginal quatrains in
Old Irish. 111 folios. CF.

669

*The Commentary on the Psalms with Glosses in Old-Irish preserved in
the Ambrosiana Library,* ed. R.I. Best (Dublin 1936)
Milan, Biblioteca Ambrosiana, MS. C 301 inf. (see CLA III.326). Text
of the *Commentarius* (of pseudo-Theodore of Mopsuestia, etc.) written
in Hiberno-Insular minuscule by the scribe Diarmait in Ireland, 8th-9th
century, probably at Bangor. At Bobbio by the 15th century. Contains
a large number of marginal and interlinear glosses in Old Irish. 146 folios.
CF.

670

*Epistolae Beati Pauli glosate glosa interlineali: Irisch-lateinischer Codex
der Würzburger Universitätsbibliothek,* ed. L.C. Stern (Halle 1910)
Würzburg, Universitätsbibliothek, MS. M. p. th. f. 12 (see CLA IX.
1403). Written in Ireland in Hiberno-Insular minuscule, and possibly
taken to Würzburg by Clemens Scottus, who died there in A.D. 826.
36 folios. CF.

671

Evangeliorum quattuor codex Cenannensis, ed. E.H. Alton and P. Meyer.
3 vols. (Berne 1950-51)
The 'Book of Kells.' Dublin, Trinity College, MS. 58 (A. I. 6). Hiberno-
Insular majuscule from, perhaps, A.D. 795-807. Begun, seemingly, at
Iona in Scotland, and completed at Kells, Co. Meath (but see **651, 661,
705**). 340 folios. CF. See also **644** for reproductions, and CLA II.274.

672

Evangeliorum quattuor codex Durmachensis, ed. A.A. Luce. 2 vols.

(Olten—Lausanne 1960)

With notes by L. Bieler (**619**), R. Powell (see also **661**), etc. The 'Book of Durrow.' Dublin, Trinity College, MS. 57 (A. IV. 5). Hiberno-Insular majuscule written, according to the editor, in Ireland ca. A.D. 650 in Durrow Abbey, Co. Offaly, one of the earliest of St. Columba's foundations (but see CLA II.273: 'Written in Northumbria in a hand trained in the Irish manner, and copied from an exemplar in the hand of St. Columba, the founder of Durrow, to judge by the two inscriptions on fol. 12^V...'). 248 folios. CF. See also **657**.

673

FACSIMILES IN COLLOTYPE OF IRISH MANUSCRIPTS (Irish Manuscripts Commission, Dublin, 1931-):

> **674**
>
> I. *The Oldest Fragments of the Senchus Már from MS. H. 2. 15 in the Library of Trinity College,* ed. R.I. Best and R. Thurneysen (1931)
>
> Dublin, Trinity College, MS. 1316 (H. 2. 15), fols. 11r-66v. A 14th-century copy of the 'Brehon laws.'
>
> **675**
>
> II. *The Book of Lecan: Leabhar Mór Mhic Fhir Bhisigh Leacain,* ed. K. Mulchrone (1939)
>
> Dublin, Royal Irish Academy, MS. 535 (23. P. 2). Compiled in Irish at Lecan, Co. Mayo, ca. A.D. 1417, by Gilla lsu Mac Fir Bhisigh and his scribe-pupils.
>
> **676**
>
> III. *Book of Armagh, the Patrician Documents,* ed. E. Gwynn (1937)
>
> Dublin, Trinity College, MS. 52 ('Liber Armachanus'). New Testament, Patrician documents, etc. Hiberno-Insular minuscule ca. A.D. 807 at Armagh. 215 folios. PF (fols. 2-24). See **618**.
>
> **677**
>
> IV. *The Book of Uí Maine, otherwise called 'The Book of the O'Kelly's,'* ed. R.A.S. Macalister (1942)
>
> Dublin, Royal Irish Academy, MS. 1225 (D. ii. 1). Written in Irish by scribe Faelan mac a' Gabann for Muircertach ua Ceallaigh, bishop of Clonfert, A.D. 1378-94.
>
> **678**
>
> V. *The Book of Mac Carthaigh Riabhach, otherwise The Book of Lismore,* ed. R.A.S. Macalister (1950)

Chatsworth House, Derbyshire, Library of the Duke of Devonshire, MS. s.n. A collection in Irish of lives of Irish saints, written A.D. 1090-1113 in Hiberno-Insular minuscule by several scribes, one of whom, Aongus Ó Callanáin, is named. 203 folios. CF.

679

VI. *MS. 23 N 10 (formerly Betham 145) in the Library of the Royal Irish Academy,* ed. R.I. Best (1954)

A collection of medieval literary pieces copied in A.D. 1575 at Ballycumin, Co. Roscommon, by three scribes in the house of John O'Mulconry. Now MS. 967. A good example of the continuity of Hiberno-Insular minuscule. 75 folios (14 of vellum). CF.

680

FACSIMILES OF NATIONAL MSS OF IRELAND, ed. J.T. Gilbert. 5 vols. (Dublin, later London, 1874-84)

A selection in photozincograph from MSS and documents ca. A.D. 600-1750. Each facsimile is accompanied by a transcription, and in the case of MSS and documents in Irish, by a translation. Although the selection is confined to repositories in the British Isles, it is the only general collection to date of samples of Hiberno-Insular and other scripts from medieval Ireland:

681

I. (Dublin 1874)

45 plates from MSS between ca. A.D. 600 and ca. 1150 (including samples from the Cathach of St. Columba; the Books of Kells, Armagh, Mulling, and Dimma; and the Gospels of MacRegol).

682

II. (London 1878)

46 plates (numbered XLVI-XCI) from MSS and charters between ca. 1150 and the end of the 13th century (including Saltair na Rann, the Book of Leinster, and the *Topographia* of Giraldus Cambrensis). An appendix presents 2 plates of the 'Psalter of Rhyddmarch' (see **310**).

683

III. (London 1879)

87 plates of MSS, charters, and other documents from ca. 1300 to ca. 1550 (including the Yellow Book of Lecan, the Leabhar Breac, the Book of Ballymote, and the Book of Lismore).

684

IV.1. (London 1882)

40 plates of documents from ca. 1550-ca. 1600, with 4 further
plates of an earlier period, notably the Psalter of Holy Trinity
(Christchurch), Dublin, from the 14th century.
685
IV.2. (London 1884)
60 plates (numbered XLI-C) of material ca. 1600-ca. 1750, with 5
plates (nos. 21-5 in appendix) from medieval MSS, e.g. the Book of
Hymns in the Franciscan Library, Dublin (but see **616**), from the
11th century, and the Red Book of Ossory (with poems by Bishop
Ledrede) and the Waterford illustrated charter roll from the 14th.

WELSH AND BRETON SCRIPTORIA

See in general **151**, pls. 7 and 16-19; **159**, 114-15; CLA II.157 and 159
(Welsh), V.684 (Breton) (**253, 256**); **310** (Psalter of Ricemarch); **404**
(Breton pocket Gospel book); **409** (Dunstan's Classbook, fols. 37r-
46v: a copy in Wallico-Insular minuscule of Ovid's *Ars amatoria,* first
half of the 9th century); **694**.

686
Davies, W. *An Early Welsh Microcosm: Studies in the Llandaff Charters*
(London 1978)
Examines 158 charters in the *Liber Landavensis* (**689**) purporting to be
from between the 6th and 11th centuries A.D.
687
————. *The Llandaff Charters* (Aberystwyth 1979)
A description, with one plate, of the contents of the *Liber Landavensis*
(**689**). Includes a diplomatic analysis.
688
Dumville, D.N. 'Palaeographical Considerations in the Dating of Early
Welsh Verse,' *Bulletin of the Board of Celtic Studies* 27 (1977) 246-51
Concludes that, in spite of a postulated 9th-century copy in Insular
script, early Welsh verse (the B text of *Gododdin*) is not before 1100.
689
Evans, J.G. and J. Rhys. *The Text of the Book of Llan Dâv reproduced
from the Gwysaney Manuscript* (Oxford 1893, repr. Aberystwyth
1979). 10 pls.
Now Aberystwyth, National Library of Wales, MS. 17110 E. 84 folios.

Original part (*Liber Landavensis* proper) is in one late Caroline hand ca. 1125-50.

690

Lindsay, W.M. *Early Welsh Script* (Oxford 1912). 17 pls. with transcriptions.

691

—————. 'Breton Scriptoria: Their Latin Abbreviation-Symbols,' *Zentralblatt für Bibliothekswesen* 29 (1912) 264-72

Holds that immigrants from Cornwall to Brittany retained the Insular abbreviation system long after they had abandoned Insular script for Caroline.

692

Peden, A. 'Science and Philosophy in Wales at the Time of the Norman Conquest: A Macrobius Manuscript from Llanbadarn,' *Cambridge Medieval Celtic Studies* 2 (Winter 1981) 21-46. 6 pls.

On London, BL, MS. Cotton Faustina C. I, pt. 2 (fols. 66-93): a MS of the early 12th century, but probably reflecting the time of Sulien, bishop of St. David's (A.D. 1073-8, 1080-85), since it carries poetry of his son Rhygyfarch or 'Ricemarch' (see **310**).

ANGLO-INSULAR (TO ca. A.D. 800)

See **7**, 124-8; **148**, 170-85; **152**, 86-93; **159**, 115-22; and CLA II, intro. (**253**).

General

693

Bolton, W.F. *A History of Anglo-Saxon Literature, 597-1066,* I: *597-740* (Princeton 1967)

Useful for an extensive bibliography, pp. 229-93.

694

Brown, T.J. 'An Historical Introduction to the Use of Classical Latin Authors in the British Isles from the Fifth to the Eleventh Century' in **1872**, II, 237-93

A wide-ranging article, with a valuable bibliography, on Irish, Anglo-Saxon, and Welsh writers and centres of writing, including (pp. 281-9, 293) some observations on 'Insular symptoms' in the traditions of

patristic and classical texts. See also **600**.
695
Bullough, D. 'Alcuino e la tradizione culturale insulare' in *I problemi dell'Occidente nel secolo VIII*. Settimane di studio 20 (Spoleto 1973) II, 571-600
On Alcuin's debt to his education at York (ca. A.D. 760), in particular.
696
Farmer, H. 'The Studies of Anglo-Saxon Monks (A.D. 600-800)' in *Los monjes y los estudios: IV semana de estudios monasticos* (Poblet 1963) 87-103.
697
Gneuss, H. 'A Preliminary List of Manuscripts Written or Owned in England up to 1100,' *ASE* 9 (1981) 1-60
Lists some 947 items from British, European, and American libraries.
698
Ker, N.R. *Catalogue of Manuscripts Containing Anglo-Saxon* (Oxford 1957), and 'A Supplement to *Catalogue of Manuscripts Containing Anglo-Saxon*,' *ASE* 5 (1976) 121-31
Provides valuable notes at pp. xxiii-lxii of the *Catalogue* on the palaeography and history of the principal MSS.
699
Levison, W. *England and the Continent in the Eighth Century* (Oxford 1946).
700
Sawyer, P.H. *Anglo-Saxon Charters: An Annotated List and Bibliography*(London 1968)
A list of 1875 charters, granting land or secular rights over land, that purport to have been issued in England before the Conquest.

Script and Scriptoria

701
Alexander, J.J.G. *Anglo-Saxon Illumination in Oxford Libraries* (Oxford 1970)
A pamphlet, with 36 plates. See also **728**.
702
Bieler, L. 'Some Recent Studies in English Palaeography,' *Scriptorium* 16 (1962) 333-6

For current bibliography see *ASE* (see **13**).

703

Brooks, N. 'Anglo-Saxon Charters: The Work of the last Twenty Years,' *ASE* 3 (1974) 211-31.

704

Brown, T.J. 'The Lindisfarne Scriptorium' in **756**, 89-110
Concludes that Echternach (CLA V.578; **756**, pls. 3, 5, 7, 9, 12-14) and Durham (CLA II.149; CF in **755**) Gospels are by one hand, and that the Lindisfarne scriptorium produced the Lindisfarne Gospels shortly before these two, ca. A.D. 696-8. For a critical evaluation of this conclusion see F. Henry, *Antiquity* 37 (1963) 100-10.

705

————. 'Northumbria and the Book of Kells,' *ASE* 1 (1972) 219-43, 245-6, with appendix by C.D. Verey. 18 pls.
Discusses the traditional attribution of the Book of Kells to Ireland and Masai's Northumbrian theory (**651**). Argues tentatively for 'a great insular centre ... subject to Northumbrian influence ... in eastern Scotland' probably in the middle years of the 8th century (see also CLA II. 274).

706

Bruce-Mitford, R.L.S. 'The Art of the Codex Amiatinus. Jarrow Lecture 1967,' *Journal of the Archaeological Association* 3rd ser. 32 (1969) 1-25. 22 pls.
See also **717, 726**.

707

Chaplais, P. 'The Origin and Authenticity of the Royal Anglo-Saxon Diploma,' *Journal of the Society of Archivists* 3 (1965-9) 48-61
Discusses evidence for the presence of written charters in England before the arrival of Theodore of Tarsus (to whom the introduction of charters usually is credited) from Italy in A.D. 669.

708

————. 'Who Introduced Charters into England? The Case for Augustine,' *Journal of the Society of Archivists* 3 (1965-9) 526-42
Argues that the case is not conclusive, yet not wholly improbable.

709

————. 'The Letter of Bishop Wealdhere of London to Archbishop Brihtwold of Canterbury: The Earliest Original "letter close" extant in the West' in **46**, 3-23. 6 pls.

On London, BL, MS. Cotton Aug. II. 18, written in A.D. 704-5 to
Brihtwold (Beorhtweald).

710

Keller, W. *Angelsächsische Palaeographie: Die Schrift der Angelsachsen
mit besonderer Rücksicht auf die Denkmäler in der Volkssprache.* 2
vols. (Berlin—Leipzig 1906, repr. New York 1970-71). 13 pls. with
transcriptions
Deals primarily with MSS in the vernacular, but also has sections on the
script of early Latin charters and codices in England.

711

————. *Über die Akzente in den angelsächsischen Handschriften*
(Prague 1908).

712

Kuhn, S.M. 'The Vespasian Psalter and the Old English Charter Hands,'
Speculum 8 (1943) 458-83
For a CF of the Vespasian Psalter see **749**.

713

Laistner, M.L.W. 'Source-Marks in Bede Manuscripts,' *Journal of
Theological Studies* 34 (1933) 350-54.

714

————. 'The Library of the Venerable Bede' in **593**, 117-49.

715

Lowe, E.A. 'An Autograph of the Venerable Bede?' *RB* 68 (1958)
200-02
Suggests that 'Beda famulus Christi indignus' on fol. 161 of the Leningrad Bede (**737**) is perhaps an autograph. But see D.H. Wright, *RB* 71
(1961) 265-73, and Meyvaert **720**.

716

————. 'A Key to Bede's Scriptorium: Some Observations on the
Leningrad Manuscript of the *Historia ecclesiastica gentis Anglorum*,'
Scriptorium 12 (1958) 182-90. 6 pls.; repr. in **60**, II, 441-9
Argues that the Leningrad Bede was written at Jarrow in A.D. 746.

717

————. *English Uncial* (Oxford 1960). 40 pls.
A complete survey of English Uncial and its beginnings in the late 7th
century. For a review see D.H. Wright, *Speculum* 36 (1961) 63-7; see
also **726**.

718

————. 'A Sixth-Century Italian Uncial Fragment of Maccabees and its Eighth-Century Northumbrian Copy,' *Scriptorium* 16 (1962) 84-5; repr. in **60**, II, 475-6

A note on CLA II.153 (Durham, Cathedral Library, MS. B. IV. 6), an Italian Uncial MS, and on its role as a model for Northumbrian scribes.

719

McGurk, P.M.J. 'An Anglo-Saxon Bible Fragment from the Late 8th Century: Royal 1. E. VI,' *Journal of the Warburg and Courtauld Institutes* 30 (1962) 18-34. 2 pls.

See also CLA II.214.

720

Meyvaert, P. 'The Bede "signature" in the Leningrad Bede,' *RB* 71 (1961) 274-86

Argues that it is very probably a medieval forgery. See **715**.

721

Parkes, M.B. 'The Handwriting of St. Boniface: A Reassessment of the Evidence,' *Beiträge zur Geschichte der deutschen Sprache* 98 (1976) 161-79

Concludes that Glossator A in some margins of the Codex Fuldensis of the New Testament (Fulda, Landesbibliothek, MS. Bonifatianus I, fols. 435v-441v; CLA VIII.1196) is, on the internal evidence of the glosses, Boniface himself.

722

Petersohn, J. 'Neue Bedafragmente in Northumbrischer Unziale saec. VIII,' *Scriptorium* 20 (1966) 215-47. 2 pls.

Darmstadt, Hessische Landes- und Hochschulbibliothek, MS. 4262 (see CLA IX.1233; S. pp. 4 and [63]).

723

Shapiro, M. 'The Decoration of the Leningrad MS of Bede,' *Scriptorium* 12 (1958) 191-207

Notes that ornamentation confirms Northumbrian origin. See also **715-16, 720, 737.**

724

Werckmeister, O.K. 'Three Problems of Tradition in Pre-Carolingian Figure Style: From Visigothic to Insular Illumination,' *PRIA* 63C (1963) 167-89. 14 pls.

Argues that stylized figure-type in MSS illustrated in the British Isles

was imported ready-made from somewhere else, probably from Spain.
725
————. *Irisch-Northumbrische Buchmalerei des 8. Jahrhunderts und monastische Spiritualität* (Berlin 1967). 48 pls.
A study of the religious symbolism of four illuminations, one each from the Echternach and Durham Gospels, two from the Book of Kells. For very critical reviews see A. Grabar, *Cahiers archéologiques* 18 (1968) 254-6; P. Meyvaert, *Speculum* 46 (1971) 408-11.
726
Wright, D.H. 'Some Notes on English Uncial,' *Traditio* 17 (1961) 441-456. 4 pls.
Argues that the Codex Amiatinus (Florence, Biblioteca Laurenziana, MS. Amiatino 1; CLA III.299), written before A.D. 716, was the work of seven Northumbrian scribes, all but one of whom were learning how to write Uncial as they went along. See also **706**.

Facsimiles

In general see CLA **(252-63)** as follows: I. nos. 4, 63, 78, 83, 90, 95, 97; II. passim; V.559, 577-8, 584-6, 588, 590, 595-6, 598, 605, 606a, 606b (mostly Anglo-Insular from Echternach), 648, 651; VI.714, 737-8, 740, 750, 760, 787, 820, 826; VII.842-6, 848-9, 851, 853, 869, 976, 982-3, 1009; VIII. passim; IX. passim, especially 1397, 1400-01, 1404-7, 1409-12, 1414, 1418, 1424-6, 1432-9, 1441-2 (MSS written in Anglo-Insular possibly at Würzburg); X.1443, 1451-3, 1459, (**1124), 1500, 1514-15, 1549-51, 1558, 1567, 1578; XI.1589, 1591, 1599-1600, 1605, 1618, 1621-2, 1655, 1661-2; S.1674-6, 1685-91, 1698, p. 10 (**220, **1229), 1703, 1730-33, p. 21 (**1400), 1746-7, 1749, 1760, 1768, 1777-8, 1786-8, 1792, 1798, 1803, 1806. See also ChLA **(181-2)** III.179-80, 182-97, 220-23; IV.235-6, 274 (complete facsimiles and diplomatic transcriptions of charters from A.D. 679-799, with a diplomatic analysis in IV. pp. XIII-XXIII). For the Vercelli Book see **218** and **754**; for Comes Romanus, **276**, and for the Stonyhurst Gospel, **400**.

727
Alexander, J.J.G., ed. *A Survey of Manuscripts Illuminated in the British Isles* (London—Oxford—New York 1975-):

728

1. Alexander, J.J.G. *Insular Manuscripts 6th to the 9th Century* (1978). 380 illustrations.

729

2. Temple, E. *Anglo-Saxon Manuscripts 900-1066* (1976). 370 illustrations

For a review see **1051.**

730

3. Kauffmann, C.M. *Romanesque Manuscripts 1066-1190* (1975). 350 illustrations.

731

4. Morgan, N. *Early Gothic Manuscripts [I] 1190-1250* (1982). 330 illustrations; *Early Gothic Manuscripts [II] 1250-1285* (forthcoming).

732

5. Sandler, L.F. *Gothic Manuscripts, 1285-1400* (forthcoming).

733

6. Scott, K. *Later Gothic Manuscripts* (forthcoming).

734

Backhouse, J. *Lindisfarne Gospels* (London 1981). 36 pls. with commentary.

735

Bond, E.A. *Facsimiles of Ancient Charters in the British Museum.* 4 vols. (London 1873-8). 111 pls. with transcriptions

Covers charters in Latin and Anglo-Saxon (and four 'foreign' documents) from ca. A.D. 624-1017/23. For a continuation see **1090.**

736

EARLY ENGLISH MANUSCRIPTS IN FACSIMILE (Copenhagen and Baltimore 1951-)

Since most volumes carry palaeographical and codicological introductions, all (excepting the first, *The Thorkelin Transcripts of Beowulf*) are listed here.

737

II. *The Leningrad Bede,* ed. O. Arngart (1952)

Leningrad, Public Library, MS. Lat. Q. V. I. 18. Bede, *Historia ecclesiastica gentis Anglorum.* Anglo-Insular minuscule, ca. A.D. 746. 162 folios. CF. See also **715-16, 720.**

738

III. *The Tollemache Orosius,* ed. A. Campbell (1953)

London, BL, Add. MS. 47967 (formerly owned by the Earl of
Tollemache, Holkham Hall). Paulus Orosius, *Historiae.* Old English
(West Saxon). Anglo-Insular 'charter hand' of ca. 900-25 (Winchester?). 80 folios (but 27-30 blank). CF.
739

IV. *The Peterborough Chronicle,* ed. D. Whitelock and C. Clark
(1954)
Oxford, Bodleian Library, MS. Laud misc. 636. Old English and
Latin. Anglo-Caroline hand of ca. 1100-30. 91 folios. CF.
740

V. *Bald's Leechbook,* ed. C.E. Wright and R. Quirk (1955)
London, BL, MS. Royal 12 D XVII. Medical tract. Old English.
Anglo-Insular, mid-10th century. 128 folios. CF.
741

VI. *The Pastoral Care: King Alfred's Translation of St. Gregory's
Regula pastoralis,* ed. N.R. Ker (1956)
Oxford, Bodleian Library, MS. Hatton 20. Old English (West Saxon).
Anglo-Insular 'charter hand' ca. 900. 97 folios. CF. 198 plates, with
6 plates of fragments in London, BL, MS. Cotton Tiberius B. XI
and Kassel, Hessische Landesbibliothek, MS. Anhang 19.
742

VII. *Textus Roffensis* [1], ed. P. Sawyer (1957)
Rochester, Cathedral Library, MS. A. 3. 5. This part is a collection
of legal texts in Old English. Rochester, Anglo-Insular hand of the
early 12th century, possibly 1122/3. 235 folios. PF. 224 plates. For
second part, see **746.**
743

VIII. *The Paris Psalter,* ed. B. Colgrave (1958) with contributions by
J. Bromwich, N.R. Ker (palaeography), F. Wormald, C. Sisam, and
K. Sisam
Paris, BN, MS. lat. 8824. Latin and Old English psalter. Anglo-Insular. England, 1050-1100. 186 folios. CF.
744

IX. *The Moore Bede,* ed. P.H. Blair [and R.A.B. Mynors] (1959)
Cambridge, University Library, MS. Kk. v. 16. Bede, *Historia ecclesiastica.* Anglo-Insular minuscule. Northumbria, 734-7 (?). 128 folios.
CF.

745

X. *The Blickling Homilies,* ed. R. Willard (1960)
Titusville, Penn. (as in subtitle, but now Princeton, N.J., John H.
Scheide Library). Part Three only of a composite codex which, until
1928, was owned by the marquises of Lothian at Blickling Hall,
Norfolk. Homilies. Old English. England, early 11th century. 139
folios. CF.

746

XI. *Textus Roffensis* [2], ed. P. Sawyer (1962)
Rochester, Cathedral Library, MS. A. 3. 5, pt. 2 (for pt. 1 see **742**).
Chartulary of the cathedral church of St. Andrew, Rochester, mostly
in Latin. Anglo-Caroline, by the scribe of pt. 1. Early 12th century,
probably before 1125. 117 folios. CF.

747

XII. *The Nowell Codex,* ed. K. Malone (1963)
London, BL, MS. Cotton Vitellius A. XV, 2nd item only (fols. 94-
209: a separate codex, in fact, carrying chiefly the only surviving
text of *Beowulf* on fols. 132-201). Old English. Two hands: Anglo-
Caroline and late Anglo-Insular, ca. A.D. 1000. 116 folios. CF. See
also **1724.**

748

XIII. *Aelfric's First Series of Catholic Homilies,* ed. N. Eliason and
P. Clemoes (1966)
London, BL, MS. Royal 7 C XII, fols. 4-218. Old English. Anglo-
Insular script, written in A.D. 900 at Cerne Abbas, Dorset. 215
folios. CF.

749

XIV. *The Vespasian Psalter,* ed. D.H. Wright and A. Campbell (1967)
London, BL, MS. Cotton Vespasian A. I. Latin, with Old English
interlinear glosses. Uncial. Canterbury, 8th century. 159 folios. CF.

750

XV. *The Rule of St. Benedict,* ed. D.H. Farmer (1968)
Oxford, Bodleian Library, MS. Hatton 48. Codex *O* of the tradition
of the *Regula.* Uncial, 7th-8th century. 76 folios. CF.

751

XVI. *The Durham Ritual: A Southern English Collectar of the Tenth
Century with Northumbrian Additions,* ed. T.J. Brown (1969) with
contributions by F. Wormald, A.S.C. Ross, E.G. Stanley

Durham, Cathedral Library, MS. A. IV. 19. Latin, with Old English interlinear glosses. 89 folios (1-65: Anglo-Insular hand, early 10th century; 66-89: Caroline, 10th-11th century). CF.
752

XVII. *A Wulfstan Manuscript, containing Institutes, Laws, Homilies,* ed. H.R. Loyn (1971)

London, BL, MS. Cotton Nero A. 1. Latin and Old English. Two parts: folios 3-57, Anglo-Insular hand, mid-11th century; 70-177, Anglo-Insular hand, early 11th century. CF. 185 plates and 339 illustrations.
753

XVIII. *The Old English Illustrated Hexateuch,* ed. C.R. Dodwell and P. Clemoes (1974)

London, BL, MS. Cotton Claudius B. IV. Old English. Anglo-Insular hand, second quarter of the 11th century. Probably written at St. Augustine's, Canterbury. 156 folios. CF (including fols. 74 and 147, which belong to the 12th century).
754

XIX. *The Vercelli Book,* ed. C. Sisam (1976)

Vercelli, Biblioteca capitolare, MS. 117. A private collection of homilies and religious verse in Old English. Written in England towards the end of the 10th century in a good Anglo-Insular minuscule which the editor notes as 'elegant, individual, old-fashioned.' The MS reached Vercelli in some way or other by the late 11th century. 136 folios. CF. For another facsimile see **218**.
755

XX. *The Durham Gospels, together with Fragments of a Gospel Book in Uncial: Durham, Cathedral Library, MS. A. II. 17,* ed. C.D. Verey, T.J. Brown, E. Coatsworth, and R. Powell (1980)

A composite MS containing the remains of two Latin Gospel Books: one (fols. 2-102) is, according to Brown (palaeographical introduction), in 'insular half-uncial' and richly decorated at, probably, Lindisfarne, in the late 7th century; the other (fols. 103-11) is in Uncial of the end of the 7th or beginning of the 8th century (and possibly reached Lindisfarne soon after). Both Gospels were possessed by Durham Cathedral Chapter by the mid-10th century. CF. See also **704**.

756

Evangeliorum quattuor codex Lindisfarnensis, ed. T.D. Kendrick. 2 vols. (Olten–Lausanne 1956-60) with notes by T.J. Brown (see **704**), R.L.S. Bruce-Mitford, A.S.C. Ross, E.G. Stanley

London, BL, MS. Cotton Nero D. IV. Anglo-Insular majuscule. According to Brown, written and illuminated at Lindisfarne, Northumbria, between A.D. 687 and 698 (and probably ca. 696-8) by Eadfrith, later bishop of Lindisfarne (698-720). 258 folios. CF. See also for reproductions **734, 758**.

757

Lowe, E.A. *Regula S. Benedicti: Specimina selecta e codice antiquissimo Oxoniensi* (Oxford 1929)

8 plates from Oxford, Bodleian Library, MS. Hatton 48. For CF see **750**.

758

Millar, E.G. *The Lindisfarne Gospels* (London 1923)

39 plates from London, BL, MS. Cotton Nero D. IV, and related MSS.

759

Mynors, R.A.B. *Durham Cathedral Manuscripts to the End of the Twelfth Century* (Oxford 1939)

A description of the MSS, with 57 plates illustrating MSS from the 6th century.

Visigothic (to ca. A.D. 1080)

See in general 7, 48-61, 139-46, 320-59; **148**, 144-54; **152**, 134-8; **159**, 122-9; and, more specifically, **140, 142, 145**.

The Visigothic assimilation of Hispano-Roman culture began about A.D. 469-78, lasting until the conquest of Spain by the Arabs, 711-14. Few examples survive of the script current in this period (see CLA IV.727a, 728), and in fact the name Visigothic is generally applied to scripts which belong to the period after the conquest:

a. Visigothic (Leonese) cursive: an irregular, documentary script practised in a small Hispano-Visigothic enclave (the kingdom of Asturias, with Oviedo as capital) which survived in N. Spain behind the Cantibirian mountains. When in A.D. 910 the Asturians captured from the Arabs the area with León as centre, to form the kingdom of León, the script continued as the documentary script of the new kingdom and hence may also be termed

Leonese (a name that is also often applied to the pre-León period). See
further **765**.
b. Visigothic (Mozarabic) bookhand: a literary script which was developed
in the Caliphate of Córdoba. Since all business in the conquered area was
in Arabic it has no documentary counterpart. Usually the script is labelled
Visigothic, but more accurately it could be termed Mozarabic, as it was on
occasion in the thirteenth century. It endured until about A.D. 1080, when
the Mozarabic liturgy was banned by Rome and writing in Caroline became
the norm, and had a great calligraphic period from about 940, mostly in
the Toledo area (hence the term *littera Toletana*): see, for example, **785**.
In 785-801, when Catalonia was wrested from the Arabs by Charlemagne,
the Visigothic script in the new Spanish March soon took on some of the
characteristics of Caroline writing. The great monastic centre of the March
was Ripoll, which used Caroline exclusively and whose scriptorium was
especially active from about 1008 to 1046: see **761**.

GENERAL

760
Beer, R. *Handschriftenschätze Spaniens: Bericht über eine in den
Jahren 1886-1888 durchgeführte Forschungsreise* (Vienna 1894, repr.
Amsterdam 1970)
A review of some 616 MSS from Spanish libraries and archives.
761
————. *Die Handschriften des Klosters S. Maria de Ripoll.* 2 vols.
(Vienna 1907, 1908). 5 pls.
762
Díaz y Díaz, M.C. 'La Circulation des manuscrits dans la Péninsule
ibérique du VIIIe au XIe siècle,' *Cahiers de civilisation médiévale* 12
(1969) 219-41, 383-92. 4 pls.
763
Domínguez-Bordona, L.J. *Die spanische Buchmalerei vom 7. bis 17.
Jahrhundert.* 2 vols. (Munich–Florence 1930). 100 pls.
764
————. *Manuscritos con pinturas: Notas para un inventario de los
conservados en colecciones publicas y particulares de España* (Madrid
1933). 2 pls.

765

Floriano Cumbreño, A.C. *Diplomática española del periodo Astur: Estudio de las fuentes documentales del Reino de Asturias (718-910)* (Oviedo 1949).

SCRIPTS AND SCRIPTORIA

766

Delcor, M. 'Le Scriptorium de Ripoll et son rayonnement culturel: Etat de la question,' *Cahiers de Saint Michel de Cuxa* 5 (1974) 45-64.

767

Díaz y Díaz, M.C. *Libros y librerías en la Ríoja altomedieval* (Longroño 1979). 32 facs.
On the scriptoria of Nájera, Albelda, Valvanera, and especially San Millán in the 10th and 11th centuries.

768

Loew [= Lowe], E.A. *Studia palaeographica: A Contribution to the History of Early Latin Minuscule and to the Dating of Visigothic Manuscripts* (Munich 1910). 7 pls.; repr. in **60**, I, 2-65 and pls. 1-7. See also **773, 779**.

769

Lowe, E.A. 'An Unedited Fragment of Irish Exegesis in Visigothic Script,' *Celtica* 5 (1960) 1-7. 5 pls.; repr. in **60**, II, 459-65 and pls. 103-7
On two flyleaves in Paris, BN, MS. lat. 536 (12th century), both of the 9th century.

770

Marazuela, T.A. 'Un scriptorium español desconocido,' *Scriptorium* 2 (1948) 3-27
On an episcopal scriptorium at Calahorra in the early 12th century.

771

Millares Carlo, A. *Contribución al 'Corpus' de códices visigóticos* (Madrid 1931). 53 pls.

772

————. *Nuevos estudios de paleografía española* (Mexico City 1941).

773

————. *Manuscritos visigóticos: Notas bibliográficas* (Barcelona—Madrid 1963). 16 facs.
A critical revision of previous lists, e.g. **768**; see also **779**.

774

――――. *Consideraciones sobre la escritura visigótica cursiva* (León 1973). 41 pls. with transcriptions.

775

Mundó, A.M. 'Códices Isidorianos de Ripoll' in *Isidoriana* (León 1961) 389-401.

776

――――. 'La datación de los códices litúrgicos visigóticos toledanos,' *Hispania sacra* 18 (1965) 1-25. 16 pls.

777

Robinson, R.P. *Manuscripts 27 (S. 29) and 107 (S. 129) of the Municipal Library of Autun: A Study of Spanish Half-Uncial and Early Visigothic Minuscule and Cursive Scripts* (New York 1939). 73 pls. with transcriptions.

778

Schiaparelli, L. 'Note paleografiche: Intorno all'origine della scrittura visigotica,' *Archivio storico italiano* 7th ser. 12 (1929) 165-207. 1 pl.; repr. in **68**, 465-510.

779

Shailor, B. 'Corrections and Additions to the Catalogue of Visigothic Manuscripts,' *Scriptorium* 32 (1978) 310-12

Deals with some isolated leaves.

780

――――. 'The Scriptorium of San Pedro de Cardeñas,' *Bulletin of the John Rylands Library* 61 (1979) 441-73

Notes that the monastery, founded in A.D. 899 near Burgos, had a flourishing scriptorium in the first half of the 10th century.

781

Williams, J. *Early Spanish Manuscript Illumination* (London 1977)

Includes 40 plates of MSS from the 7th-11th centuries.

FACSIMILES

For Visigothic and other Spanish MSS see CLA (**252-63**) as follows: I.111; II.195, 263; IV.432, 515; V.587, 592, 640, 677-8; VI.705, 727a, 728-9, 774c; VII.856, 918; IX.1286ab; X. p. 2 (**1286ab); XI.1628b, 1630-32, 1635-7 (and p. 17), 1638, 1654; S.1785. For a facsimile of the Codex Toletanus of Isidore see **234**; and for plates in collections of facsimiles see **140, 142, 145, 1221, 1224.**

782
Antifonario visigotico mozarabe de la Catedral de León: Edición facsimil
(Madrid – Barcelona – León 1953)
León, Archivo Catedral, MS. 8. A complete antiphonary (A.D. 1066) in
Visigothic script with musical notation. 306 folios. PF (fols. 29-306).
783
Beatus a Liebana. *Sancti Beati a Liebana In apocalypsim codex Gerun-
densis,* ed. J.M. Casanovas, C.E. Dubler, W. Neuss (Olten – Lausanne
1962)
Gerona, Biblioteca capitular, MS. 7. Written in A.D. 975 at the monas-
tery of San Salvador, Zamora, by the priest Senior at the request of
Abbot Dominicus. Decorated (with 114 full-page miniatures) by the
monk Emeterius and the lady En. 248 folios. CF.
784
Canellas, A. *Exempla scripturarum Latinarum in usum scholarum: Pars
altera.* 2nd ed. (Saragossa 1974)
This second volume of Canellas' *Exempla* **(419)** draws exclusively on
Spanish deposits of MSS and provides the best general coverage of
Spanish scripts (ca. A.D. 44-1594). Includes 94 plates (19 of Visigothic,
15 of Hispano-Caroline, 33 of Spanish Gothic), with transcriptions.
785
Clark, C.U. *Collectanea Hispanica* (Paris 1920). 70 pls. of Spanish scripts.
786
Ewald, P. and G. Loewe. *Exempla scripturae Visigoticae* (Heidelberg
1883). 40 pls. with transcriptions.
787
Mateu Ibars, J. and M.D. Mateu Ibars. *Colectanea paleográfica de
la Corona de Aragón, siglos IX-XVIII.* 2 vols. (Barcelona 1980)
Vol. II has a series of 414 plates (nos. 1-267 covering A.D. 815-1500)
of documents from various archives in Spain and Italy. A table of scripts
is at pp. 61-4.

Near East

788

Lowe, E.A. 'An Unknown Latin Psalter on Mount Sinai,' *Scriptorium* 9
(1955) 177-99. 6 pls.; repr. in **60**, II, 417-40 and pls. 89-94
Mount Sinai, Monastery of St. Catherine, Slavonic MS. 5. 'Exotic minuscule,' not later than A.D. 900. For a facsimile see **791**.

789

————. 'Two New Latin Liturgical Fragments on Mount Sinai,' *RB* 74
(1964) 252-83. 4 pls.; repr. in **60**, II, 520-45 and pls. 120-23
Fragments of an epistolary, 9th-10th century, and of an antiphonary, end
of the 10th century.

790

————. 'Two Other Unknown Latin Liturgical Fragments on Mount
Sinai,' *Scriptorium* 19 (1965) 3-29. 7 pls.; repr. in **60**, II, 546-74 and pls.
124-30
An analysis of the epistolary and antiphonary above. The MSS discussed
in these three articles may come from 'the same remote centre manifestly
exposed to Oriental influences but yet a centre where Latin traditions ...
somehow survived ...' (p. 569); the scriptorium in question shows acquaintance with Visigothic scribal practices but also with Greek, Syriac, and
Arabic as well. See now Bischoff **159**, 124-6, on 'die Sinai-Schrift' and its
relations with Visigothic.

791

*Psalterium Latinum Hierosolymitanum: Eine frühmittelalterliche latein-
ische Handschrift Sin. MS. no. 5,* ed. M. Altbauer (Vienna–Graz–Cologne
1979)
112 folios. CF. See **788**.

Italy (chiefly North)

See **7**, 134-7; **148**, 119-22; **152**, 107-24; **159**, 129-32.

GENERAL

792

Angrisani, M. 'Materiali per uno studio della produzione libraria latina
antica e medievale in Italia,' *Bollettino del Comitato per la preparazion*

dell'Edizione Nazionale dei classici greci e latini new ser. 24 (1976) 87-112; 26 (1978) 113-37; 27 (1979) 139-51
The period covered is to the 8th century A.D.
793
Avril, F. and Y. Załuska. *Manuscrits enluminés d'origine italienne*, I: *VIe-XIIe siècles* (Paris 1980). 56 pls.
The MSS covered are in the Bibliothèque nationale, Paris.
794
Bartoloni, F. 'Semicorsiva o precarolina?' *BAPI* 1st ser. 12 (1943) 2-22.
795
Beer, R. 'Bemerkungen über den ältesten Handschriftenbestand des Klosters Bobbio,' *Anzeiger der phil.-hist. Klasse der kais. Akademie der Wissenschaften* 48 (1911) 78-104
His theory here that many MSS from Vivarium migrated to Bobbio in the North was refuted by Mercati **205** and by Lowe, CLA IV, pp. xx-xxvii.
796
Bertelli, C. 'Stato dello studio sulla miniatura fra il VII e il IX secolo in Italia,' *SM* 9/1 (1968) 379-421.
797
Cau, E. 'Scrittura e cultura a Novara (secoli VIII-IX),' *RM* 6-9 (1971-4) 1-87. 26 pls.
798
Delogu, P. 'I Lombardi e la scrittura' in *Studi in onore di Ottorino Bertolini* (Pisa 1972) 313-24.
799
Lowe, E.A. 'Codices rescripti: A List of the Oldest Latin Palimpsests with stray Observations on their Origin' in **69**, V, 67-112. 6 pls.; repr. in **60**, II, 480-519 and pls. 114-19
Discusses Italy (Bobbio in particular) as a centre of palimpsesting.
800
Petrucci, A. 'Scrittura e libro nell'Italia altomedievale,' *SM* 3rd ser. 10 (1969) 157-213; 14 (1973) 961-1002
On the replacement of lay centres of book production by ecclesiastical from the 6th century A.D. onwards.
801
———. 'Libro, scrittura, e scuola' in *La scuola nell'occidente latino dell'alto medioevo.* Settimane di studio 19 (Spoleto 1972) I, 313-37. 6 pls.

802

————. 'Scrittura e libro nella Tuscia altomedievale (sec. VIII-IX)'
Atti del 5° Congresso internazionale di studi sull'alto medioevo (Spo
1973) 627-43. 12 pls.

SCRIPTS AND SCRIPTORIA

803
Beeson, C.H. 'The Palimpsests of Bobbio' in **63**, VI, 162-84
A fundamental study. See also **799**.
804
Cavallo, G. 'Interazione tra scrittura greca e scrittura latina a Roma t
VIII e IX secolo' in **62**, I, 23-9. 2 pls.
805
Cipolla, C. *Codici Bobbiesi della Biblioteca universitaria di Torino.* 2
vols. (Milan 1907, repr. 1963). 90 pls. with transcriptions.
806
Collura, P. *Studi paleografici: La precarolina e la carolina a Bobbio*
(Florence 1965). 48 pls.
First published in 1943, here reprinted with appendix (pp. 247-66) o
Bobbio studies 1943-55.
807
Engelbert, P. 'Zur frühgeschichte des Bobbieser Skriptoriums,' *RB* 78
(1968) 220-60
Discusses Bobbio 'Half'-uncial, the Irish presence at Bobbio, and the
introduction of Caroline minuscule there in the 9th century.
808
Ferrari, M. 'Nuovi frammenti documentari bobbiesi,' *IMU* 10 (1967)
1-23
On some 8th-century Bobbio documents used as folders or as backing
for gatherings.
809
————. 'Le scoperte a Bobbio nel 1493: Vicenda e fortuna di testi,
IMU 13 (1970) 139-80
On the aftermath of reforms of 1461 and of the compilation of a full
catalogue of the library at Bobbio.
810
————. 'Spigolature bobbiesi,' *IMU* 16 (1973) 1-13

Lists various additions to CLA IV with respect to Bobbio MSS.

811

Levine, P. 'Historical Evidence for Calligraphic Activity in Vercelli from St. Eusebius to Atto,' *Speculum* 30 (1955) 561-81

A survey from the mid-4th to the mid-10th century. Also in Italian as *Lo 'scriptorium' Vercellese da S. Eusebio ad Attone* (Vercelli 1958).

812

Natale, A.R. 'Influenze merovingiche e studi calligrafici nello scriptorium di Bobbio (secoli VII-IX)' in *Miscellanea Giovanni Galbiati* (Milan 1951) II, 1-44. 19 pls.

813

Pagnin, B. 'Studio sulla formazione della precarolina italiana' in **44**, 19-46

Has interesting pages (39-45) on abbreviations.

814

————. 'Espressioni scrittorie dell'ambiente culturale veronese dal V al VII secolo,' *RM* 13-14 (1978-80) 5-18. 4 pls.

Argues that New Roman cursive certainly was in use, with Uncial and Semi-uncial, in the Schola sacerdotum at Verona, paving the way for pre-Caroline Veronese cursive of the 8th century.

815

Palma, M. 'Nonantola e il Sud: Contributo alla storia della scrittura libraria nell'Italia dell'ottavo secolo,' *SC* 3 (1979) 77-88. 5 pls.

Argues that Nonantola script may have been influenced by S. Italian minuscule and not vice-versa, as sometimes supposed. See also **1030**.

816

Paredi, A. and L. Santucci. *Miniature altomedievali lombarde* (Milan 1978). 54 pls.

817

Petrucci, A. 'L'onciale romana: Origini, sviluppo e diffusione di una stilizzazione grafica altomedievale (sec. VI-IX),' *SM* 3rd ser. 12 (1971) 75-134. 19 pls.

On a Roman centre of Uncial, probably at the Lateran church, with influence on Anglo-Insular Uncial at Wearmouth-Jarrow (pp. 121-7) and on Carolingian Uncial. See also **1034**.

818

————. 'Il codice n. 490 della Biblioteca capitolare di Lucca: Un problema di storia della cultura medievale ancora da risolvere,' *Actum*

Luce 2 (1973) 159-75
See **219, 820**.
819
Rabikauskas, P. *Die römische Kuriale in der päpstlichen Kanzlei* (Rome
1958). 37 figs.
Argues that a special style of writing in the papal chancery evolved in
the 7th century from Roman minuscule and from hands in use in episcopal and imperial chanceries, and endured until the early 12th century.
See also **824**.
820
Schiaparelli, L. *Il codice 490 della Biblioteca capitolare di Lucca e la
scuola scrittoria lucchese (sec. VIII-IX).* Studi e testi 36 (Rome 1924).
3 pls.
A separate publication, under a different title, of Schiaparelli's 'Introd-
zione' to the PF **219** of MS. Lucca, Biblioteca capitolare, 490. This
celebrated codex (see CLA III.303 a-f; **818**) is a collection of various
pieces, e.g. *Liber pontificalis* (fols. 137r-210r), 'Hispana' canonical collection (288r-309v), written at various times in the 8th-9th century A.D.
probably at Lucca, by some 24 different hands in a variety of scripts
(notably Uncial, Visigothic, pre-Caroline minuscule).
821
————. 'Note paleografiche: Intorno all'origine della scrittura curiale
romana,' *Archivio storico italiano* 7th ser. 6 (1926) 165-97. 4 pls.; repr.
in **68**, 371-404. See also **819, 824**.
822
————. *Influenze straniere nella scrittura italiana dei secoli VIII e IX.
Note paleografiche* (Rome 1927).
823
Segre Montel, C. *I manoscritti miniati della Biblioteca nazionale di
Torino,* I: *I manoscritti latini dal VII alla metà del XIII secolo* (Turin
1980)
Includes a volume of 176 plates of MSS (from Bobbio, etc.).
824
Tjäder, J.-O. 'Le origini della scrittura curiale romana,' *BAPI* 3rd ser.
2-3 (1963-4) 7-54 with numerous figs.
Against Schiaparelli **821** and Rabikauskas **819**, who highlight the influence of literary scripts such as Uncial and Semi-uncial on the script of
the papal chancery during its formative period (A.D. 600-800), Tjäder

shows from papyri from Ravenna and elsewhere that the only 'matrix' of curial writing was later or 'new' Roman cursive.

825

Wormald, F. *The Miniatures in the Gospels of St. Augustine: Corpus Christi College, MS. 286* (Cambridge 1954). 16 pls.

A codex of 265 folios written in Uncial in Italy in the 6th century (see CLA II.127), and, according to Wormald, probably taken to England by early missionaries from Italy (perhaps by Augustine's group in 596); certainly in England by the end of the 7th or beginning of the 8th century and at Canterbury by the first half of the 10th.

FACSIMILES

See also **161, 163, 167, 220, 224, 566**. For pre-Caroline scripts in general see CLA III-IV (**254-5**) passim. For scripts or MSS from or associated with various localities see CLA (**252-63**) as follows: for Bobbio (including palimpsests): I. 26-49; III. 296, 307, 309, 311-12, 314-23b, 326-8, 330, 333-4, 336-40, 342-3, 344b, 346, 348, 350-53, 361-2, 364-5, 388, 391, 394, 397a-b, 403; IV. 438-45, 447-66; V. 654; IX. 1374; X. 1492-1493; S. 1734, 1810; for Chieti: I. 13 (?); for Lucca: III. 303a-f; for Nonantola: II. 180; III. 369; IV. 420b, 422, 425, 427-8; for Novara: III. 406; for Ravenna: IV. 414, 474; VI. 840; for Vercelli: III. 322; IV. 469; IX. 1386 (?); for Verona or neighbourhood: I. 8; II. 186; III. 318-319; IV. 475, 477 (?), 478, 482, 484, 486 (?), 490-92, 494-5, 503-4, 506-7, 512, 516.

826

Bonelli, G. *Codice paleografico lombardo: Riproduzione in eliotipia e trascrizione diplomatica di tutti i documenti anteriori al 1000 esistenti in Lombardia*, I: *Secolo VIII* (Milan 1908). 23 pls.

827

Natale, A. R. *Il museo diplomatico dell'Archivio di Stato di Milano*, I, 2 vols. (Milan 1971)

A magnificent collection of 163 plates, with diplomatic transcriptions and bibliography, of documents in an archives at Milan formed after 1787 from archives of suppressed ecclesiastical institutions in Lombardy. The period covered by the plates runs from the 6th century to A.D. 900, but some documents are copies from a later period. The plates provide a

great sample of cursive scripts of the period, some of which clearly
caused some difficulty to medieval users of the documents (e.g., the
document from A.D. 777 in pl. 25 carries an interlinear transcription
in a hand of the 12th or 13th century).

828

Salmasianus. *Anthologie de poètes latine, dite de Saumaise,* ed. H.
Omont (Paris 1903)
Paris, BN, MS. lat. 10318: 'Codex Salmasianus.' A poetic anthology
(e.g. *Pervigilium Veneris*) in Uncial of the late 8th century. Written
probably in N. Italy (S. France?). 290 folios. CF (reduced reproduction)

829

Turrini, G. *Millenium scriptorii Veronensis dal IV° al XV° secolo:
Esempi di scrittura veronese scelti dai preziosi tesori della Biblioteca
capitolare di Verona* (Verona 1967). 30 pls.

Italy, South (chiefly Beneventan, to A.D. 1200)

See **7**, 137-9; **148**, 123-43; **152**, 125-34; **159**, 140-43.

S. Italy is largely dominated to A.D. 1200 by the Beneventan script, the
chief authority on which is Lowe **854**. Although only marginally a pre-
Caroline script, Beneventan writing is so closely associated with the history
of Monte Cassino that it is covered here with the main pre-Caroline scripts.
Founded by St. Benedict in 529, Monte Cassino does not fully emerge as
a centre of study, learning, and writing until the mid- or late 8th century.
There is some evidence of a Cassino or Beneventan strain of script in the
century before 833, in which year the monks were forced because of
Saracen incursions to move to Teano and then Capua, where they stayed
until their return to Cassino in 949; but the distinctive 'Beneventan' script
(as it is called in a papal inventory of 1295) appears to have had its beginnings during the Capuan period, reaching calligraphic perfection during
the abbacy of Desiderius, 1058-87. By 1200 it was in decline, though it
lingered on in various Benedictine pockets for another three hundred years
or so. At its highest point it was in use not only in the Duchy of Benevento
(whence its name; that used by Poggio — Lombardic — and taken up by
Mabillon, is, at best, a misnomer) but also all over S. Italy, the most celebrated centre of the script outside Cassino being Bari, where a local version
(853, 862) was used, for example, for some famous Exultet rolls: see **844-5**

and **864**. The script also spread from the Adriatic coast of S. Italy via the Trémiti Islands to Dalmatia. Two dozen and more Beneventan MSS from Dalmatia are extant, notably those now in the Dominican house at Dubrovnik: see **1510**.

GENERAL

830
Bloch, H. 'Monte Cassino, Byzantium, and the West in the Earlier Middle Ages,' *Dumbarton Oaks Papers* 3 (1946) 163-224. 42 pls.
831
————. 'Monte Cassino's Teachers and Library in the High Middle Ages' in *La scuola nell'Occidente latino dell'alto medioevo*. Settimane di studio 19 (Spoleto 1972) II, 563-605.
832
Cavallo, G. 'Aspetti della produzione libraria nell'Italia meridionale longobarda' in **589**, 101-29 with notes at 270-84
A general survey.
833
Petrucci, A. *Scrittura e cultura nella Puglia altomedievale* (Foggia 1968).
834
Salviati, C. 'Le scritture altomedievali dell'Italia meridionale nella tradizione paleografica,' *Rassegna degli Archivi di Stato* 33 (1973) 292-309.
835
Toubert, H. ' "Rome et le Mont-Cassin": Nouvelles remarques sur les fresques de l'église inférieure de Saint-Clément de Rome,' *Dumbarton Oaks Papers* 30 (1976) 2-33
Plates from 10 Beneventan MSS suggest, she argues, that models for these frescoes came from Monte Cassino.

SCRIPTS AND SCRIPTORIA

836
Avarucci, G. et al. 'Nuove testimonianze di scrittura beneventana,' *SM* 3rd ser. 21 (1980) 423-51
Continues De Luca **847** and Di Franco **848**.

837

Babudri, F. 'L'Exultet di Bari del sec. XI,' *Archivio storico pugliese* 10 (1957) 8-169. 25 pls.
On Bari, Archivio del Duomo, MS. s.n. The roll was compiled before A.D. 1067.

838

Battelli, G. 'L'orazionale di Trani,' *Benedictina* 9 (1972) 271-87. 2 pls.; repr. in **30**, 509-27
Publishes notes on a mutilated MS, then lost (but now Canosa di Puglia, Tesoro della Cattedrale, MS. s.n. – see **854**), which until 1934 was in the Duomo at Trani. The MS is from the mid-12th century and is in a mixture of Beneventan and 'Bari' scripts.

839

Belting, H. *Studien zur beneventanischen Malerei* (Wiesbaden 1968). 104 leaves of pls.

840

Bertelli, C. 'L'illustrazione di testi classici nell'area beneventana dal IX all' XI secolo' in *La cultura antica nell'Occidente latino dal VII all'XI secolo.* Settimane di studio 22 (Spoleto 1975) II, 899-926.

841

Brown, V. 'A Second New List of Beneventan Manuscripts, I,' *Mediaeval Studies* 40 (1978) 239-89
Continues Lowe **856**.

842

Cau, E. 'Frammenti cremonesi in scrittura beneventana,' *RM* 4-5 (1969-70) 21-38.

843

Cavallo, G. 'Struttura e articolazione della minuscola beneventana libraria tra i secoli X-XII,' *SM* 3rd ser. 11/1 (1970) 343-68
See also **1035**.

844

————. 'La genesi dei rotoli liturgici beneventani alla luce del fenomeno storico-librario in Occidente ed Oriente' in **35**, 213-29. 4 pls.
See also **863**.

845

————. *I Rotoli di Exultet dell'Italia meridionale* (Bari 1973). 62 pls.
See also **864**.

846

De Luca, A. 'Frammenti di codici in Beneventana nelle Marche' in **35**, 101-40. 16 pls.

847

De Luca, A. et al. 'Nuove testimonianze di scrittura beneventana,' *SM* 3rd ser. 18/1 (1977) 353-400. 16 pls.

A study of MSS of the 9th-12th centuries from some areas usually considered as non-Beneventan (the Marche, Fabriano, Salerno, Perugia, and the Biblioteca Laurenziana are covered in turn by De Luca, C. Tristano, F. Troncarelli, M. Roncetti and M. Pecugi Fop, and again C. Tristano). See **836, 848**.

848

Di Franco, M.C., V. Jemolo, and R. Avesani. 'Nuove testimonianze di scrittura beneventana in biblioteche romane,' *SM* 3rd ser. 8 (1967) 857-81.

849

Falconi, E. 'Frammenti di codici in Beneventana nell'Archivio di Stato di Parma,' *BAPI* 3rd ser. 2-3 (1962) 73-104. 8 pls.

850

Girgensohn, D. 'Documenti Beneventani inediti del secolo XII,' *Samnium* 40 (1967) 262-317.

851

Holtz, L. 'Le Parisinus Latinus 7530, synthèse cassinienne des arts libéraux,' *SM* 3rd ser. 16/1 (1975) 97-152. 2 pls.

A palaeographical and codicological investigation of the formation of this grammatical miscellany at Monte Cassino between A.D. 779 and 796.

852

Inguanez, M. 'La scrittura beneventana in codici e documenti dei secoli XIV e XV' in **44**, 307-14. 9 pls.

853

Levy, B.E. 'The Bari Type of Beneventan Script: Manuscripts from Apulia,' *Harvard Studies in Classical Philology* 66 (1962) 262-5.

854

Loew [= Lowe], E.A. *The Beneventan Script: A History of the South Italian Minuscule,* ed. V. Brown. 2 vols. Sussidi eruditi 33-4 (Rome 1980). 8 pls.

In this new edition of Lowe's celebrated work, originally published in Oxford in 1914, vol. I is a photographic reproduction to p. 333 of the original work, together with a section of 'Addenda et corrigenda' and new indexes of manuscripts and authorities; vol. II is a revision and expansion of the 'Hand List of Beneventan MSS' at the end of the first edition, and includes a meticulous bibliography (generally of the years 1915-76) for each MS in turn.

855
Lowe, E.A. 'Virgil in South Italy: Facsimiles of Eight Manuscripts of Virgil in Beneventan Script,' *SM* new ser. 5 (1932) 43-51. 8 pls.; repr. in **60**, I, 326-34 and pls. 47-54.

856
————. 'A New List of Beneventan Manuscripts' in **28**, II, 211-44. 6 pls.
The introduction only (pp. 211-14) is reprinted in **60**, II, 477-9.

857
Murjanoff, M. and R. Quadri. 'Zum beneventanischen Schrifttum und Initialornamentik,' *IMU* 8 (1965) 309-21. 4 pls. with transcriptions.

858
Newton, F. 'Beneventan Scribes and Subscriptions, with a List of those Known at the Present Time,' *The Bookmark* (Friends of the University of North Carolina Library, Chapel Hill) 43 (1973) 1-35.

859
————. 'The Desiderian Scriptorium at Monte Cassino,' *Dumbarton Oaks Papers* 30 (1976) 35-54. 4 pls.
On the scriptorium from A.D. 1022, and MSS written under Abbot Desiderius (1058-87).

860
Novak, V. *Scriptura Beneventana ... Palaeografijska studija* (Zagreb 1920). 18 pls.
A study of 'Dalmatian' Beneventan.

861
————. 'Something New from the Dalmatian Beneventana,' *Medievalia et humanistica* 14 (1962) 76-85. 3 pls.
A discussion of a 12th-century MS at Zadar, Convent of St. Mary, containing Gregory the Great's *Moralia in Job*.

862
Petrucci, A. 'Note ed ipotesi sulla origine della scrittura barese,' *BAPI* new ser. [ser. 2] 4-5 (1958-9) 101-14. 9 pls.

863
Wurfbain, M.L. 'The Liturgical Rolls of South Italy and their possible Origin' in **54**, 9-15
See also **844-5**.

FACSIMILES

See for plates of early Beneventan: CLA III.284, 381 (oldest extant witness), V.569, VIII.1029; for plates of diplomata from Beneventan area: **175**; for various facsimiles: **210** (Exultet roll), **230** (Tacitus), **237** (Cicero, Codex Heinsianus).

864
Avery, M. *The Exultet Rolls of South Italy*, I, 2 vols. (Princeton 1936). 206 pls.
865
Gilson, J.P., ed. *An Exultet Roll Illuminated in the 11th Century at the Abbey of Monte Cassino* (London 1929)
London, BL, Add. MS. 30337. Beneventan script. Monte Cassino, ca. 1058-87. Vellum, 22 feet. CF. 19 plates.
866
Inguanez, M., ed. *Sexti Julii Frontini De aquaeductu urbis Romae....*
Adiciuntur Varronis De lingua latina fragmentum Petri Diaconi operum catalogus ex eodem codice (Monte Cassino 1930)
Monte Cassino, Archivio della Badia, MS. 361, fols. 43-65, 65-7. Monte Cassino, 12th century. Written, as is the whole codex, by Peter the Deacon in Caroline, with some slight influence of Beneventan. CF.
867
Lowe, E.A. *Scriptura Beneventana: Facsimiles of South Italian and Dalmatian Manuscripts from the Eighth to the Fourteenth Century.*
2 vols. (Oxford 1929)
Provides 100 plates with transcriptions, as a companion to **854**.

Austria, Germany, Switzerland

See 7, 133-4; **148**, 166-9; **152**, 105-7; **159**, 150-51.

SCRIPTS AND SCRIPTORIA

868
Autenrieth, J. 'Insulare Spurien in Handschriften aus dem Bodensee-
gebiet bis zur Mitte des 9. Jahrhunderts' in **66a**, 143-57. 5 pls.
Pp. 156-7 contain a list of MSS in Hiberno- or Anglo-Insular script
which have survived from the libraries of St. Gall and Reichenau.
869
Bischoff, B. *Die südostdeutschen Schreibschulen und Bibliotheken in
der Karolingerzeit*, I: *Die bayrischen Diözesen* (Leipzig 1940; 3rd ed.
Wiesbaden 1974), II: *Die vorwiegend österreichischen Diözesen*
(Wiesbaden 1980)
Vol. I includes 8 plates; II has 25 plates, additions to I, an appendix on
MSS in Caroline in libraries in Czechoslovakia, a survey (pp. 263-72) of
the presence of Caroline minuscule in S. Germany, and a concordance
for both volumes to new Clm call-numbers in the Bayerische Staatsbibliothek, Munich. Although the bulk of the information gathered here
so impressively concerns Caroline writing as such, the volumes are in-
valuable also with respect to centres of pre-Caroline production.
870
Bischoff, B. and J. Hofmann. *Libri Sancti Kyliani: Die Würzburger
Schreibschule und die Dombibliothek im VIII. und IX. Jahrhundert*
(Würzburg 1952). 20 pls.
871
Lindsay, W.M. 'The (Early) Lorsch Scriptorium' in **49**, 3 (1924) 6-48.
12 pls.
Notes on 8th-century MSS and MSS of the Lorsch library in Anglo-
Insular script, and on Lorsch 9th-century abbreviation symbols.
872
Lindsay, W.M. and P. Lehmann. 'The Early Mayence Scriptorium' in
49, 4 (1925) 15-39. 6 pls.
873
Löffler, K. 'Die Sankt Galler Schreibschule in der 2. Hälfte des 8.
Jahrhunderts' in **49**, 6 (1929) 5-66. 10 pls.

874

Steffens, F. 'Die Abkürzungen in den lateinischen Handschriften des 8.
und 9. Jahrhunderts in St. Gallen,' *Zentralblatt für Bibliothekswesen*
30 (1913) 477-88
See also **1784.**

FACSIMILES

For scripts used in documents of this period see ChLA I-II (especially
II for St. Gall deposits and for A. Bruckner's introduction). For bookhands in general see CLA VII (Switzerland), VIII-IX (Germany), X. p. 2
and nos. 1443-1539 (Austria); for bookhands in Swiss repositories,
Bruckner's *Scriptoria* **875-89.** For examples of Alemannic writing (St.
Gall–Reichenau or Bodensee area) see CLA VII.888, 893a-b, 895, 896-9,
906, 908-12, 915, 920-21, 925-6, 928, 931, 933, 935, 937-8, 940, 944,
1002, 1022; VIII.1078-9, 1081, 1087, 1093-4, 1097; IX.1355, 1357-8;
X.1480; for Rhaetian writing (Chur area) see CLA VII.863, 873, 875-6,
878, 882, 889-92, 915, 936, 939, 943, 946, 948, 1004, 1006-7, 1011,
1013-14, 1020, 1023; VIII.1179; IX.1360, 1362; XI.1663; S.1672;
for pre-Caroline minuscule see (for Switzerland) CLA V.561; VII.872,
879, 881, 884, 887, 893a (St. Gall: scribe Winithar), 894 (SG: W), 895,
896 (SG: W), 900, 903 (SG: W), 905, 906 (SG: W), 917, 922, 927, 932,
934 (SG: W), 950, 952 (SG: W), 994, 996 (SG: W), 997, 1003, 1017,
1019, 1021; (for Germany, Austria) CLA IX.1239, 1241-3 (all Benediktbeuern); II.238 (Cologne); II.168; VIII.1228; IX.1251-4, 1263, 1265,
1268-9, 1270, 1272, 1275, 1278-9, 1283, 1314 (Freising); VII.842-9 (?),
853; IX.1234, 1306, 1381 (Fulda); VIII.1144, 1225 (Hersfeld); I.82,
88, 98; VIII.1080, 1173; IX.1406; X.1505, 1506 (Lorsch); VI.795;
IX.1318, 1347; X.1487, 1513 (Mondsee); II.222, 242-3; VI.731, 749,
753, 755-6; VIII.1193; IX.1442 (Murbach); IX.1289a-b, 1291-2,
1297 (Regensburg); IX.1413; X. pl. Ia, Ib facing p. xiv, 1462, 1475-6,
1490 (Salzburg); IX.1317 (Tegernsee).

875

SCRIPTORIA MEDII AEVI HELVETICA: DENKMÄLER SCHWEIZERISCHER
SCHREIBKUNST DES MITTELALTERS, ed. A. Bruckner. 14 vols. (Geneva
1935-78)
A comprehensive series of plates with transcriptions, covering all of the

Middle Ages:
876
I. *Schreibschulen der Diözese Chur* (1935).
877
II. *Schreibschulen der Diözese Konstanz: St. Gallen I* (1936).
878
III. *Schreibschulen der Diözese Konstanz: St. Gallen II* (1938).
879
IV. *Schreibschulen der Diözese Konstanz: Stadt und Landschaft Zürich* (1940).
880
V. *Schreibschulen der Diözese Konstanz: Stift Einsiedeln. Kirchen und Klöster der Kantone Uri, Schwyz, Glarus, Zug* (1943).
881
VI. *Schreibschulen der Diözese Konstanz: Kloster Allerheiligen in Schaffhausen* (1952).
882
VII. *Schreibschulen der Diözese Konstanz: Aargauische Gottes-häuser* (1955).
883
VIII. *Schreibschulen der Diözese Konstanz: Stift Engelberg* (1950).
884
IX. *Schreibschulen der Diözese Konstanz: Stadt und Landschaft Luzern* (1964).
885
X. *Schreibschulen der Diözese Konstanz: Thurgau, Solothurn, Klein-Basel, Bern* (1964).
886
XI. *Schreibschulen der Diözese Lausanne* (1967).
887
XII. *Das alte Bistum Basel* (1971).
888
XIII. *Schreibstätten der Diözese Sitten* (1973).
889
XIV. *Indices* (1978)
Includes some 20 plates of MSS of presumed Swiss origin outside of Switzerland. In all, there are 708 plates for the 14 volumes. Each volume has its own index of plates, and there is a cumulative index

for vols. I-XII here at pp. 190-205, library by library.

France (to ca. A:D. 800)

See **7**, 129-33; **148**, 156-66; **152**, 93-104; **159**, 132-9; **588**.

MEROVINGIAN WRITING

890
Gasnault, P. and J. Vezin. *Documents comptables de Saint-Martin de Tours à l'époque mérovingienne* (Paris 1975)
An edition by Gasnault, with a palaeographical study by Vezin (pp. 159-191), of fragments of accounts from the end of the 7th century or beginning of the 8th which were used in the second half of the 15th century for covers of a commentary on Job. Vezin argues that the basis of the Merovingian script in these accounts was the elongated form of Later Roman cursive used in provincial chanceries.

891
Tessier, G. *Diplomatique royale française* (Paris 1962). 23 pls.
Good chapters on Merovingian, Carolingian, and Capetian chanceries.
See also **913**.

892
Tjäder, J.-O. 'L'origine della "b" merovingica' in **35**, 47-79. 2 pls.
Notes that the distinctive mark of Merovingian cursive is *b* with a stroke sticking out of the hast, allowing for easy ligature; this was created in the second half of the 6th century, but Merovingian writing did not acquire characteristic lengthening and lateral compression until the first half of the 7th.

893
Vezin, J. 'Le *b* en ligature à droite dans les écritures du VIIe et du VIIIe siècles,' *Journal des Savants* (1971) 261-86.

CORBIE SCRIPTS

894
Bishop, T.A.M. 'The Prototype of *Liber glossarum*' in **46**, 69-84
Argues that the prototype of this dictionary-encyclopedia was put together in a-b script by an independent scriptorium of nuns at Corbie;

from this monks of Corbie copied exemplars in Caroline such as CLA
V.611 (Paris, BN, MSS. lat. 11529 and 11530) and VI.743.
895
————. 'The Script of Corbie: A Criterion' in **51**, 9-16
Argues that Corbie MSS are recognizable from the fact that flesh side
normally appears on the outside of quires; further, the ruling generally
is direct onto flesh side.
896
Dobiaš-Roždestvenskaja, O. *Histoire de l'atelier graphique de Corbie de
651 à 830 refletée dans les Corbeienses Leninopolitani* (Leningrad
1934)
A study of 25 MSS in Uncial, Semi-uncial, Anglo-Insular, and Caroline
which were stolen at Paris in 1791 during the Revolution and in 1805
passed to the Imperial Library at Leningrad (then Petrograd) from the
collection of the bibliophile Peter Dubrowsky. See CLA V. p. 4 and nos.
1597-1614, 1616-25; **898, 1495.**
897
Gasparri, F. 'Le Scriptorium de Corbie à la fin du VIIIe siècle et le
problème de l'écriture a-b,' *Scriptorium* 20 (1966) 265-72
Gives a list of extant MSS of a-b writing, the last of the pre-Caroline
Corbie scripts.
898
Jones, L.W. 'The Scriptorium at Corbie, I: The Library,' *Speculum* 22
(1947) 191-204; 'The Scriptorium at Corbie, II: The Script and the
Problems,' *ibid.* 375-94. 4 pls.
The history of a celebrated library (see **896**), with a partial list of the
surviving MSS and of MSS of the various 'Corbie' scripts.
899
Liebaert, P. 'Some Early Scripts of the Corbie Scriptorium' in **49**, 1
(1922) 62-6. 4 pls.
900
Lindsay, W.M. 'The Old Script of Corbie: Its Abbreviation Symbols,'
Revue des bibliothèques 16 (1912) 405-29.
901
Lowe, E.A. 'A Note on the Codex Corbeiensis of the *Historia Francorum* and its Connection with Luxeuil,' *Scriptorium* 6 (1952) 284-6.
1 pl.; repr. in **60**, II, 381-4 and pl. 71.
A note to CLA V.671 (Paris, BN, MS. lat. 17655, end of the 7th cen-

tury): on the presence of 'Insular symptoms,' especially of the *autem* symbol.

902

Mundó, A. 'Sur l'origine de l'écriture dite "eNa" de Corbie: A propos de l'édition diplomatique du Paris lat. 12205,' *Scriptorium* 11 (1957) 258-60

Argues that the 'eNa' script, as witnessed by a tentative form of it in the above MS of the *Regula magistri* (for which see **2058**), may have been imported from an Italian centre (the Roman curia?) to Corbie, perhaps at the beginning of the 8th century.

903

Ooghe, G. 'L'Ecriture de Corbie' in *Corbie, abbaye royale: Volume du XIIIe centenaire* (Lille 1963) 263-82

A general survey.

LYONS

904

Lowe, E. A. *Codices Lugdunenses antiquissimi: Le Scriptorium de Lyon, la plus ancienne école calligraphique de France* (Lyons 1924). 39 pls.

According to Lowe, of the many MSS surviving from before A.D. 800 from the cathedral library at Lyons, not one is indubitably a pro-duct of Lyons; not until the time of Bishop Leidrad (798-814) can one be sure that the origin of a given codex is a scriptorium there. On the best of grounds, however, Lowe accepts 28 'codices antiquissimi' (mostly Uncial and Semi-uncial MSS of the 5th-8th centuries transmitting biblical, patristic, and juridical texts) as genuine local products.

905

Tafel, S. 'The Lyons Scriptorium' in **49**, 2 (1923) 66-73; 4 (1925) 40-70

A preliminary (and pioneer) study of Lyons (see **904**). Points to the presence in many codices of Visigothic emigrant scribes.

LUXEUIL

906

Lowe, E.A. 'The "Script of Luxeuil": A Title Vindicated,' *RB* 63 (1953) 132-42. 6 pls.; repr. in **60**, II, 389-98 and pls. 74-9

Argues that the display capitals on fol. 1v of MS. 334, Pierpont Morgan Library, New York, a codex written in Uncial at Luxeuil in A.D. 669, prove that Traube was correct in labelling a distinctive minuscule script in some 20 MSS of the Merovingian period as 'Luxeuil.' See also **914**.

907
Putnam, M.C.J. 'Evidence for the Origin of the "Script of Luxeuil",' *Speculum* 38 (1963) 256-66
Doubts localization of 'Luxeuil script' at Luxeuil. Suggests N. Italy (perhaps Bobbio) instead. But see **892**.

908
Salmon, P. *Le Lectionnaire de Luxeuil.* 2 vols. (Rome 1944, 1953). 27 pls.
An edition of Paris, BN, MS. lat. 9427, in Luxeuil minuscule of the 7th-8th century.

909
Tribout de Morembert, H. 'Le Plus Ancien Manuscrit de Luxeuil (VIIème s.): Les Fragments de Metz et de Yale,' *Mémoires de l'Académie nationale de Metz* 14 (1972) 87-98. 1 pl.
Metz, Archives de la ville 164, pièce 1; Yale, University Library, MS. 481. Argues that these two fragments are in the same Semi-uncial hand, and may date from ca. A.D. 615.

NUNS' MINUSCULE

910
Bischoff, B. 'Die Kölner Nonnenhandschriften und das Skriptorium von Chelles' in *Karolingische und ottonische Kunst: Werden, Wesen, Wirkung* (Wiesbaden 1957) 395-411; repr. in **32**, I, 16-34
Shows that three codices in Cologne (Dombibliothek, MSS. 63, 65, 67– CLA VIII.1152) which were written for Archbishop Hildebald of Cologne (A.D. 785-819) by nine nuns, each one of whom signs her name as she ends a quire (e.g. Girbalda, Agleberta, Vera, Agnes), are products of the royal convent of Chelles, north of Paris on the Marne. Identifies 13 MSS in all from this scriptorium in what Lowe (CLA VI. p. xxii) terms 'Nuns' minuscule.' See also **257, 259**.

TOURS

911

Rand, E.K. and L.W. Jones. *The Earliest Book of Tours, with Supplementary Descriptions of Other Manuscripts of Tours.* Studies in the Script of Tours 2 (Cambridge, Mass. 1934). 60 pls.
A study of Paris, BN, MS. Nouv. acq. lat. 1575 (Eugippius, *Excerpta ex operibus Augustini*), a codex of the first part of the 8th century in Uncial, Semi-uncial, and minuscule. See also **965**.

FACSIMILES

See in general CLA V and VI (and the latter for a survey of scriptoria); and for some scriptoria: Luxeuil (or Luxeuil school): CLA I.92, 106, 110, 117; II.163, 173; III.300; IV.497; V.548, 579, 671, 702; VI.841; VIII.1197; IX.1328, 1337, 1376-7, 1383, 1396, 1419-21; X.1454-6, 1518; XI.1617, 1658-9; S.1739, 1745, 1807-8; Corbie: I.105; II.124, 182, 200-01; IV.446; V.551, 554, 570, 574, 611-13, 615, 621-3, 631, 636-7 (Maurdramnus), 641 (Maur.), 643 (Maur.), 650, 662, 669, 672, 688, 694-5; VI.707, 709-10, 712 (all Maur.), 743, 767, 792, 822; VIII.1026, 1047, 1066 (Maur.), 1067b, 1130, 1156, 1168, 1178, 1183; IX.1301; X.1554; XI.1598, 1601-2, 1606-7, 1609 (Maur.), 1611, 1619 (Maur.), 1620, 1623-5; S.1752; NE France (Chelles?): II.238-9, 252; V.529, 639, 674; VI.791; VIII.1152, 1170, 1194; IX.1331, 1352; Laon (or area): II.128, 174; V.539, 630; VI.752, 765, 766; VII.852; VIII.1182; Fleury: V.564a, 568, 687; VI.802 (?), 808, 812; Tours: II.196a-b; III.297a; V.530, 536, 682, 683; VI.762, 837; VII.992; IX.1394.

912

Gregory of Tours. *Histoire des Francs de Grégoire de Tours: Ms. de Beauvais,* ed. H. Omont (Paris 1906)
Paris, BN, MS. lat. 17654. The *Historia Francorum* of Gregory of Tours (ob. 594). Uncial. E. France, beginning of the 8th century. Belonged to St. Pierre of Beauvais in the 13th century. 109 folios. CF. See CLA V.670.

913

Lauer, P. and C. Samaran. *Les Diplômes originaux des Mérovingiens: Facsimilés phototypiques avec notices et transcriptions* (Paris 1908)

Provides 48 plates of documents to A.D. 987. See also **191** (for a concordance to **913**) and **973-5**.

914

Mohlberg, L.C. *Missale Gallicanum vetus (Cod. Vat. Palat. lat. 493)* (Rome 1958). 6 pls.

Vatican City, BAV, MS. Pal. lat. 493. A composite codex (106 fols.) of three fragmentary booklets, the first two of which (1-18, 19-99) are sacramentaries written in Uncial in the 8th century, probably in France (see CLA I.92-3).

915

Ruess, F. *Die Kassler Handschrift der Tironischen Noten samt Ergänzungen aus der Wolfenbüttler Handschrift* (Leipzig—Berlin 1914)

Kassel, Hessische Landesbibliothek, MS. Philol. fol. 2. 9th century. Written N or NE France (see CLA VIII.1132, but Ruess suggests Fulda). 147 folios. CF (with 5 pls. of Wolfenbüttel pieces).

CAROLINGIAN AND AFTER (TO ca. A.D. 1200)

See **7**, 146-50; **148**, 186-212; **159**, 139, 143-62; and especially Cencetti **152**, 166-205, for theories, including his own (pp. 182-90 and **938** below), on the origins of Caroline minuscule.

The forty-three years of Charlemagne's reign as sole ruler (A.D. 771-814) were decisive within his empire for the history of writing and for that of book-production. Side by side with administrative measures that gave consistency and uniformity to his government, Charlemagne initiated basic educational reforms in decrees such as that of 789 which ordered that when copies of gospels, psalters, or missals had to be made, they should be 'done with all diligence by men of mature age.' Whether or not Charlemagne had anything directly to do with the movement that resulted in the 'sweet' Caroline script, there is no doubt that by 800 most of the array of cursive bookhands that characterize much of the pre-Caroline period had been swept aside by one form or other of Caroline writing in his territories, and that the passion for an uncluttered, legible minuscule was matched by a high if not spectacular standard of book-production (see **921**, **923-9**, etc.). There had been, of course, some local attempts before Charlemagne's time to achieve some form of unambiguous minuscule from cursive scripts (notably at Luxeuil a century beforehand, at Tours ca. 730, and to some

extent at St. Gall a little later), but the first studied approach to the problem of legibility is probably that of the scriptorium at Corbie in the second
half of the eighth century, particularly in the time of Abbot Maurdramnus
(772-81). Though the matter of the precise model for Caroline minuscule is
much debated (see **937-44**), a reasonable case may be made that in the long
run the Caroline script is nothing more than a straight return (possibly with
Corbie in the vanguard) to the old and very serviceable Semi-uncial, a good
acquaintance with which is attested at Corbie ca. 765, when the scribe
Ingreus deployed it nicely while penning a copy of St. Ambrose on the
Gospel of St. Luke at the request of Abbot Leutchar, the immediate pre-
decessor of Maurdramnus. At all events, the Caroline hand was well and
truly established as the preferred literary script (though for luxury volumes
Uncial also was in demand) by the time Alcuin, at the request of Charlemagne, set up a school and library at Tours in 796, and a scriptorium that
soon began to produce elegant examples of Caroline (see **965**). By 850 the
Caroline alphabet in its standard form was in use generally in the scriptoria
of present-day France, the Rhineland, and N. Italy. In Switzerland the local
Rhaetian script was not abandoned overnight, but centres such as Reichenau,
Chur, and St. Gall soon became wholehearted practitioners of the new
minuscule. N. Italy took to Caroline at an early date, but in central Italy
the papal chancery did not begin to employ it as a rule until about 1118.
In other areas the progress of Caroline was almost as slow as this latter (see
922). England did not begin to use Caroline until the second half of the
tenth century, when monks imported from Corbie, Fleury, and Ghent to
stimulate monastic reforms introduced it into S. England (see **1074**). The
north-east of Spain, as noted earlier, became acquainted with Caroline when
Charlemagne set up the Spanish March, but Spain as a whole did not come
under the influence of Caroline until the end of the eleventh century.

General Studies

916

Bischoff, B. 'Panorama der Handschriftenüberlieferung aus der Zeit Karls
des Grossen' in **926**, 233-54; repr. in **32**, III, 5-39, and (in Italian) in **589**,
47-72
A survey, according to a concept of *Schriftprovinz* or 'writing-province'
('Austrasiana,' NE France, etc.), of all Latin MSS surviving for the period
ca. A.D. 770-850, with a note on place of origin, where possible.

917

————. 'Die Hofbibliothek Karls des Grossen' in **926**, 42-62. 6 pls.;
repr. in **32**, III, 149-70 and pls. V-X.

918

————. 'Frühkarolingische Handschriften und ihre Heimat,' *Scriptorium*
12 (1968) 306-14
Lists the original homes of ca. 400 MSS surviving from the early Carolingian period.

919

————. 'Die Hofbibliothek unter Ludwig dem Frommen' in **45**, 3-22.
2 pls.; repr. in **32**, III, 171-87 and pls. XI-XII
The period is A.D. 813-40.

920

Bullough, D.A. 'Roman Books and Carolingian *renovatio*' in *Renaissance
and Renewal in Christian History,* ed. D. Baker. Studies in Church History
14 (London 1977) 23-50
Argues that the influence of 'profane' literature was not as marked as that
of religious literature.

921

Dodwell, C.R. *Painting in Europe 800-1200.* Pelican History of Art
(Harmondsworth 1971). 240 pls.
Provides excellent coverage of MS illumination in the Carolingian and
Ottonian renaissance, and in Spain (Beatus codices) and Italy (Exultet rolls),
especially pls. 10-91, 96-114, 118-31, 142-5, 160-67, 172-81, 186-99,
202-11, 237-40.

922

Hessel, A. 'Studien zur Ausbreitung der karolingischen Minuskel, I:
Spanien,' *Archiv für Urkundenforschung* 7 (1921) 197-202; 'Studien ... II:
Grossbritannien und Italien,' *ibid.* 8 (1922) 16-25. 1 pl.
On the spread of Caroline minuscule to these countries.

923

Karl der Grosse: Werk und Wirkung (Aachen 1965), trans. as *Charlemagne:
Ouevre, Rayonnement, et Survivances* (ibid. 1965)
The catalogue of the great Charlemagne exhibition at Aachen in 1965
under the auspices of the Council of Europe. Contributions, with a galaxy
of illustrations, by B. Bischoff **(937)**, C. Nordenfalk **(933)**, etc. 158 plates
illustrate 778 exhibits, each one amply described. Exhibits 331-40b cover
diplomas and seals; 341-65 (pls. 33-5, 37), presented by Bischoff, treat of

intellectual life (e.g. *Libri Carolini*) and scriptoria of pre-Carolingian and Carolingian periods; 366-85a (pl. 36), presented by Bischoff (see **937**), deal with reform of writing; 386-498 (pls. 38-85, 96-7), presented by Nordenfalk (see **933**), illustrate, first, miniatures in various pre-Carolingian MSS (386-411, pls. 38-52), then (412-98, pls. 53-85, 96-7) miniatures (and bindings) of MSS of the Carolingian 'Court circle' (Ada Gospels, Dagulf Psalter, etc.) and of MSS outside that circle which reflect its influence.

924
Karl der Grosse: Lebenswerk und Nachleben, ed. W. Braunfels. 4 vols. (Düsseldorf 1965-7)
Four volumes, each with separate editors and an array of contributors and illustrations:
   925
   I. *Persönlichkeit und Geschichte*, ed. H. Beumann (1965).
   926
   II. *Das geistige Leben*, ed. B. Bischoff (1965). 6 pls.
   See **916-17**.
   927
   III. *Karolingische Kunst*, ed. W. Braunfels and H. Schnitzler (1966). 30
   pls. of MSS in colour
   See **931, 934, 994**.
   928
   IV. *Das Nachleben*, ed. W. Braunfels and P.E. Schramm (1967).

929
Köhler, W. *Die karolingischen Miniaturen*. 4 vols. [IV with F. Mütherich] (Berlin 1930-71)
Amply illustrated.

930
Lasko, P. *Ars sacra 800-1200*. Pelican History of Art (Harmondsworth 1972)
Has 297 plates, many of which are reproductions of book-covers, e.g. pls. 2, 25-6, 28-30, 32, 37-9, 40-41, 55, 59, 62, 64, 74, 76-7, 84, 92, 103, 105, 122-4, 132, 141, 168, 170-72, 220, 222-3, and, in colour, the frontispiece.

931
Mütherich, F. 'Die Buchmalerei am Hofe Karls des Grossen' in **927**, 9-53. 20 pls. (12 colour).

932
Mütherich, F. and J.E. Gaehde. *Karolingische Buchmalerei* (Munich 1976),

trans. as *Carolingian Painting* (New York 1976)
Prints 48 plates, all in colour, of the main illuminated MSS.
933
Nordenfalk, C. 'Les Miniatures' in **923**, 220-26. 1 pl.
934
Porcher, J. 'La Peinture provinciale (régions occidentales)' in **927**, 54-73.
24 pls.
935
Schramm, P.E. and F. Mütherich. *Denkmale der deutschen Könige und Kaiser: Ein Beitrag zur Herrschergeschichte von Karl dem Grossen bis Friedrich II. 768-1250* (Munich 1962). 215 pls.
Many plates are of MSS, privileges, and charters.
936
Wallach, L. *Alcuin and Charlemagne* (New York 1959)
See especially pp. 198-226, which print and analyze the mandate (A.D. 794-800) of Charlemagne to Baugulf, abbot of Fulda, in which he sets out his aims for education.

Origins of Caroline Script

937
Bischoff, B. 'Die karolingische Minuskel' in **923**, 207-10; repr. in **32**, III, 1-5
The French version (in *Charlemagne: Ouevre* **923**, 204-7) has been re-placed by Bischoff's 'La Minuscule caroline et le renouveau culturel sous Charlemagne,' *BIRHT* 15 (1967-8) 333-6. He maintains that Caroline minuscule was a gradual development which cannot be pinned down to any one place, though clearly the Maurdramnus minuscule at Corbie was a preliminary stage of importance.
938
Cencetti, G. 'Postilla nuova a un problema paleografico vecchio: L'origine della minuscola carolina,' *Nuova historia* (Verona) 7 (1955) 9-32
Suggests that the model for Caroline minuscule was a Roman minuscule script (mainly primitive minuscule).
939
De Boüard, A. 'La Question des origines de la minuscule caroline' in **49**, 4 (1925) 71-82
Takes up, and to some extent misunderstands, a passing reference of

Schiaparelli (**820**, 108-13) to the possible dependence of Caroline minuscule upon pre-Caroline minuscule rather than upon Semi-uncial.

940
Delisle, L. 'Mémoire sur l'école calligraphique de Tours au IXe siècle,'
Mémoires de l'Académie des inscriptions & belles lettres 32/1 (1885) 29-56
Argues that Caroline minuscule was born at Tours under Alcuin from a re-working of ancient Semi-uncial and Semi-cursive scripts inspired by Alcuin, who was abbot there A.D. 796-804.

941
Hessel, A. 'Zur Entstehung der karolingischen Minuskel,' *Archiv für Urkundenforschung* 8 (1922) 200-14
Considers Caroline minuscule to be the result of a synthesis of the 'Maurdramnus script' at Corbie and pre-Caroline minuscule, which came about in the palace school of Charlemagne.

942
Higounet, C. *La Création de l'écriture caroline: Problème de paléographie et de civilisation* (Paris 1958)
Argues that the scriptorium at Corbie played an essential role in the first stage of the search for 'normal' writing which took place in scriptoria between the Rhine and the Loire in the reign of Charlemagne.

943
Lauer, P. 'La Réforme carolingienne de l'écriture latine et l'école calligraphique de Corbie,' *Mémoires présentés par divers savants à l'Académie des inscriptions et belles lettres* 13 (1924) 417-40. 4 pls.
Argues that Corbie was at the centre of the reform, and that there was much experimentation, finally leading to the Bible of Maurdramnus. This is the oldest example of Caroline minuscule − a minuscule which is really a Semi-cursive written in a set hand under the influence of the small Semi-uncial of the 8th century.

944
Steinacker, H. 'Zum *Liber diurnus* und zur Frage nach dem Ursprung der Frühminuskel' in **41**, IV, 105-76
Proposes a poligenetic origin for Caroline minuscule: it resulted from a general movement in scriptoria of the late 8th century to develop a readable and unligatured minuscule from either Semi-uncial or cursive (or a combination of both); the form practised at the 'Imperial court' won the day. See also **1030, 1032**.

France, Belgium

SCRIPTS AND SCRIPTORIA

945
Alexander, J.J.G. *Norman Illumination at Mont St. Michel 966-1100* (Oxford 1970). 55 pls.
Pls. 2-6 provide a good view of writing in N. France in the period. At pp. 214-32 there is a list of MSS of Mont St. Michel surviving from those years, and at pp. 237-9 a list of Anglo-Saxon MSS in Normandy before the Conquest.

946
Baldwin, C.R. 'The Scriptorium of the Sacramentary of Gellone,' *Scriptorium* 25 (1971) 3-17
Concludes that the Sacramentary (Paris, BN, MS. lat. 12048: CLA V. 618) was written in mixed minuscule at Meaux towards the end of the 8th century by David, a monk of Holy Cross, and Madalberta, a nun, and migrated from there by 812 to 'Gellone' (St. Guilhem-le-Désert, NW of Montpellier).

947
Carey, F.M. 'The Scriptorium at Reims during the Archbishopric of Hincmar (845-882 A.D.)' in **67**, 41-60. 2 pls.

948
Contreni, J.J. *The Cathedral School of Laon from 850 to 930: Its Manuscripts and Masters* (Munich 1978). 4 pls.
An evaluation of 125 MSS in or written at Laon in this period. Establishes a list of some 371 works in the library, and provides the names of four Irish masters, notably Martinus Hibernensis (A.D. 819-75), who collected, wrote, and annotated books or supervised their writing (and to whom two chapters are devoted).

949
De Mérindol, C. *La Production des livres peints à l'abbaye de Corbie au XIIᵉ siècle: Etude historique et archéologique.* 2 vols. (Lille 1976)
A thesis from the University of Lille III.

950
Dufour, J. *La Bibliothèque et le scriptorium de Moissac* (Geneva–Paris 1972). 14 pls.
The period covered is 11th-12th centuries.

951

Gaborit-Chopin, D. *La Décoration des manuscrits à Saint-Martial de Limoges et en Limousin du IXe au XIIe siècle* (Paris–Geneva 1969). 128 pls.

952

Garand, M.-C. 'Le Scriptorium de Guibert de Nogent,' *Scriptorium* 31 (1977) 3-29. 3 pls.

Demonstrates the existence of a small scriptorium at Nogent-sous-Coucy, north of Soissons, at the beginning of the 12th century, with Gilbert as the leading figure.

953

————. 'Le Scriptorium de Cluny, carrefour d'influences au XIe siècle: Le Manuscrit Paris, B.N., Nouv. acq. lat. 1548,' *Journal des Savants* (1977) 257-83

Dates the MS as A.D. 1065-8 and notes that six of its Cluny scribes were also writers of documents.

954

————. 'Copistes de Cluny au temps de Saint Maieul (948-994),' *BEC* 136 (1978) 5-36. 6 pls.

Discusses the first scriptorium at Cluny.

955

Gariépy, R.J. 'Lupus of Ferrières: Carolingian Scribe and Text Critic,' *Mediaeval Studies* 30 (1968) 90-105

Useful for a list of genuine and possible Lupus MSS, but not as thorough as Pellegrin **962**.

956

Gilissen, L. 'Observations codicologiques sur le codex *Sangallensis* 914' in **62**, I, 51-70. 15 figs.

A codicological examination of a copy of the Rule of St. Benedict (St. Gall, Stiftsbibliothek, MS. 914) supposedly made ca. A.D. 800 from a copy, no longer extant, at Aachen, which in turn is reputed to have been copied from the autograph of Benedict destroyed at Teano ca. 886. Sees no codicological reason to dismiss the 'legend.'

957

Homburger, O. *Die illustrierten Handschriften der Bürgerbibliothek Bern: Die vorkarolingischen und karolingischen Handschriften* (Bern 1962)

Includes 158 plates of 55 illustrated MSS from A.D. 699 to the 10th century, but mostly from the 8th and 9th centuries, and then chiefly from the Loire area (Fleury above all). The bulk of the MSS comes from the collection of Jacques Bongars, the French scholar and diplomat (ob. 1612).

958
Jones, L.W. 'The Library of St. Aubin's at Angers in the Twelfth Century' in **67**, 143-61.

959
————. 'The Script of Tours in the Tenth Century,' *Speculum* 14 (1939) 179-98. 4 pls.

960
————. 'The Art of Writing at Tours from 1000 to 1200 A.D.,' *Speculum* 15 (1940) 286-98. 3 pls.

961
Lowe, E.A. 'A Manuscript of Alcuin in the Script of Tours' in **67**, 191-193. 1 pl.; repr. in **60**, I, 342-4 and pl. 58
On Salisbury, Cathedral Library, MS. 133: a not very accurate text of Alcuin's commentary on Ecclesiastes, copied only a few years after his death.

962
Pellegrin, E. 'Les Manuscrits de Loup de Ferrières,' *BEC* 115 (1957) 5-31. 1 pl.
On books owned, annotated, or corrected by Lupus. See also **955**.

963
————. 'Membra disiecta Floriacensia,' *BEC* 117 (1959) 5-56. 1 pl.
On some MSS of the 10th and 11th centuries from Fleury, now in various libraries.

964
————. 'Membra disiecta Floriacensia (II)' in **62**, I, 83-103. 1 pl.
Lists more fragments, now in libraries at Orléans, Paris, Bern, Leiden, and the Vatican.

965
Rand, E.K. *A Survey of the Manuscripts of Tours*. Studies in the Script of Tours 1 (Cambridge, Mass. 1929)
Includes an album of 200 plates. 231 MSS from the 6th-12th centuries are listed and described, the bulk coming from the 9th century.

966
Shapiro, M. *The Parma Ildefonsus, a Romanesque Illuminated Manu-*

script from Cluny, and Related Works (New York 1964). 38 pls.
See the review by J. Vezin, *Scriptorium* 21 (1967) 312-20, who provides
a survey of Cluny MSS to the mid-12th century.

967

Stiennon, J. 'Le Scriptorium et le domaine de l'abbaye de Malmédy du
X^e au début du XIIIe siècle, d'après les manuscrits de la Bibliothèque
Vaticane,' *Bulletin de l'Institut historique belge à Rome* 26 (1950-51)
5-22.

968

Vezin, J. *Les Scriptoria d'Angers au XIe siècle* (Paris 1974). 53 pls.
Argues that, of the 53 MSS of the 11th century known to be extant
from Angers, all but six are products of the scriptoria of Saint-Aubin
(26) and Saint-Serge (21), and that the script is a brave imitation of 9th-
century Caroline models.

969

————. 'Leofnoth: Un scribe anglais à Saint-Benoît-sur-Loire,' *CM* 3
(1977) 109-20. 4 pls.
On England's connection with Fleury, from which it imported both
monastic reform and the Caroline script, in the 10th century.

970

Verhulst, A. 'L'Activité et la calligraphie du scriptorium de l'abbaye
Saint-Pierre-au-Mont-Blandin,' *Scriptorium* 11 (1957) 37-49. 6 pls.
On writing at St. Peter's, Ghent, in 'Gothic' ca. A.D. 1000-60 (particu-
larly under Provost Wichard, 1034-58).

FACSIMILES

For various complete or partial facsimiles see **229** (Tours Tacitus), **231**
(Terence), **233** (Lucretius), **236, 238** (Lucretius), **239, 245, 246** (Ademar of Chabenais), **248, 281, 283** (Metz sacramentary), **284** (Otfried),
291 (canons), **292** ('Court' catalogue, etc.), **295** (Tours, ca. 800), **296**
(Drogo sacramentary), **297, 303** (Dagulf psalter), **350, 351, 353 , 390**
(Roland), **394** (St. Trond), **406** (Servius), **413**. For some early Carolingian MSS, mostly in Caroline, see CLA: for the Rhineland—Moselle
stretch (including 'Court scriptorium,' Wissembourg, Lorsch, Metz, and
Cologne): II.198 (Codex aureus); V.517, 533, 538, 540, 644b, 652,
681 (Godescalc Gospels); VIII.1044, 1051, 1071, 1080; 1147, 1150-52,
1154, 1158 (Cologne); IX.1366 (Ada Gospels), 1384-5, 1389-90, 1393,

1406; X.1469 (Coronation Gospels), 1477, 1504 (Dagulf psalter), 1505; XI.1592; for Corbie: I.86; V.672; VI.707 (Maurdramnus Bible; for other Maurdramnus products see Pre-Carolingian France, above); for Amiens: VIII.1030; X.1579; for Saint-Amand: V.544; VI.758, 839; VIII.1146; IX.1237, 1354; X.1463, 1478-9, 1486, 1489, 1494, 1496 (all possibly by scribes of St. Amand at Salzburg); for St. Denis: V.665, 668; for St. Germain-des-Prés: IX.1240 (?); for Tours: I.109; III.297b; V.525, 528; VII.854, 904; for Orléans – Fleury: V.576; for Burgundy: V.555, 702; for Lyons: IV.417; VI. 774c; for S. France: IX.1295, 1308.

971
Die Bibel von Moutier-Grandval, ed. J. Duft (Bern 1971) with contrib tions by B. Fischer, A. Bruckner, E.J. Beer, A.A. Schmid, E. Irblich, H.J. Frede
London, BL, Add. MS. 10546. Written in Caroline at Tours in A.D. 834-5. Belonged to the monastery of Moutier-Grandval, Switzerland. 449 folios. PF. 239 plates (42 in colour). The editors note, among oth things, that a bible of standard size would require vellum from 210 to 225 sheep, given that a full-grown sheep provides 100 x 55 cm. of vellum, and a smaller sheep a strip of 84 x 45 cm.

972
Der Codex aureus der Bayerischen Staatsbibliothek in München, ed. G Leidinger. 6 vols. (Munich 1921-31)
Munich, Bayerische Staatsbibliothek, MS. Clm 14000. An illustrated L Gospel book, written in A.D. 870 by the priests Beringer and Liuthart at, probably, St. Denis in Paris (the 'Court School'), by commission of Charles the Bald. Given to St. Emmeram, Regensburg, ca. 893 by the emperor Arnulf (hence known as 'Gospels of St. Emmeram'). 126 foli CF.

973
Diplomata Belgica ante annum millesimum centesimum scripta, ed. M. Gysseling and A.C.F. Koch. 2 vols. (Brussels 1950)
A volume of 236 texts before A.D. 1000, with an album of 88 plates illustrating some of these texts. One of the best collections of plates o diplomata.

974
Diplomata Karolinorum: Recueil de reproductions en fac-similé des

actes originaux des souverains carolingiens conservés dans les archives et bibliothèques de France, ed. F. Lot and P. Lauer. 9 vols. (Toulouse — Paris 1936-49)
Provides 273 large reproductions, without transcriptions, of acts from the 8th (A.D. 753) to the 10th century (vols. I-V cover the 8th and 9th, VI-IX the 10th century).

975
Diplomata Karolinorum: Faksimile-Ausgabe der in der Schweiz liegenden originalen Karolinger und Rudolfinger Diplome, ed. A. Bruckner. 5 vols. (Basel 1974)
The volumes comprise four large portfolios, which carry 130 plates from A.D. 776-81 to 1029, and a small volume of brief descriptions.

976
Lamberti S. Audomari canonici Liber Floridus, ed. Ae. I. Strubbe and A. Derolez (Ghent 1968)
An edition, with 123 plates, of an autograph copy (now Ghent, Bibliothèque centrale de l'Université, MS. 1125) of a vast illustrated encyclopedia written ca. A.D. 1100-20 by Lambert, canon of the Chapter of Saint-Omer. Illuminations are generally attributed to Petrus Pictor. For commentaries on this codex, which was copied repeatedly until the 16th century, see **977**.

977
Liber Floridus Colloquium, ed. A. Derolez (Ghent 1973). 35 pls.
Contains commentaries by J.P. Gumbert, Y. Lefèvre, G.I. Lieftinck, H. Swarzenski, F. Wormald.

978
Das Lorsch Evangeliar, ed. W. Braunfels (Munich 1967); also publ. as *The Lorsch Gospels* (New York 1967) with Braunfels' intro. in English Part I (fols. 1-111: Matthew, Mark): Alba Julia, Roumania, Batthyaneum Library, MS. s.n.; part II (fols. 112-239: Luke, John): Vatican City, BAV, MS. Pal. lat. 50; front cover ('Madonna'; 5 panels in ivory): London, Victoria and Albert Museum; back cover ('Christ'; 5 panels in ivory): Vatican City, Museo sacro. This codex of the four Gospels was written at a Court school (Aachen?) ca. A.D. 810 in Uncial, with many illustrations, and given to Lorsch Abbey, near Worms, ca. 820. It was divided into two volumes by 1479, taken from Lorsch before 1563 and placed with MSS in Heidelberg 'Palatina' library, whence, with other Palatine MSS, it passed to the Vatican Library in 1623. When the two volumes

were separated from each other is not clear. Part I was at Alba Julia ('Karlsburg') in Transylvania, in the bishop's library (Batthyaneum), from ca. 1783. The 'Madonna' cover has been in London since 1866. After centuries of separation, the whole codex (pts. I, II, and the two covers) was brought together at Aachen in 1965 for the Council of Europe 'Charlemagne Exhibition' (see **923**), when it was photographed as a whole. 239 folios. CF (including covers, which are reproduced in the slip-booklet accompanying the facsimile).

979

Lupus of Ferrières: *Lupus of Ferrières as Scribe and Text Critic: A Study of his Autograph Copy of Cicero's De oratore, with a Facsimile of the Manuscript,* by C.H. Beeson (Cambridge, Mass. 1930)

London, BL, MS. Harley 2736. Hastily written in a personal Caroline hand, ca. A.D. 836, possibly from a codex in the possession of Einhard the biographer of Charlemagne, then living at Sélestat. Present MS belonged at one time to Cormery Abbey, near Ferrières. 109 folios. CF See also **955, 962**.

980

Norman Anonymous. *Der Codex 415 des Corpus Christi College, Cambridge: Faksimile-Ausgabe der Textüberlieferung des Normannischen Anonymous,* ed. R. Nineham and K. Pellens (Wiesbaden 1977)

30 polemical tracts against hierocratic theories of papal power. Believed by some to be the work of Archbishop Gerard of York (A.D. 1100-08) but more generally attributed to a Norman of Rouen ca. 1100. 154 folios. CF.

981

Orderici Vitalis (Angligenae Cenobii Uticensis monachi) Historiae ecclesiasticae libri VII et VIII (Paris—Rome 1902)

Vatican City, BAV, MS. Reg. lat. 703B (formerly 703A, as in this facsimile). A mid-12th-century copy of Books VII-VIII of the *Historia* of Ordericus (A.D. 1075-1142), based, probably, on the lost third volume the original work, all of which was put together by Ordericus at Saint-Evroul, Normandy, where he was a monk from 1085 to 1142. Written in late Caroline. 52 folios. CF (published to honour Léopold Delisle, by his pupils).

982

Physiologus Bernensis, ed. O. Homburger and C. von Steiger (Basel 1964)

Bern, Bürgerbibliothek, MS. 318, fols. 7-22. Written in Caroline in the mid-9th century by the scribe Haecpertus. CF.

983

Rouleau mortuaire du B. Vital, abbé de Savigni: Edition phototypique, ed. L. Delisle (Paris 1909)
During the year following the death of Abbot Vitalis (A.D. 1122-3), this roll, now Paris, Musée des Archives nationales, no. 138, visited some 207 monasteries in Normandy and England and accumulated some 70 specimens of English, Anglo-Norman, and French hands as it made the rounds. 15 folios. CF (49 pls.). See also **1620**.

984

Der Stuttgarter Bilderpsalter, ed. B. Bischoff. 2 vols. (Stuttgart 1965)
Stuttgart, Würtembergische Landesbibliothek, MS. bibl. fol. 23. A Gallican version of the psalter in two hands, written in Caroline ca. A.D. 820-30 at St. Germain-des-Prés (on the scriptorium of which there is an introduction by Bischoff). The illustrations were influenced by Italo-Byzantine art of the 5th-6th century. 168 folios. CF.

985

Die Trierer Ada-Handschrift, ed. K. Menzel et al. (Leipzig 1889)
Trier, Stadtbibliothek, MS. 22. Written in the 'Palace School' in Caroline minuscule ca. A.D. 800 at the order of an unidentified Ada. The codex was in the monastery of St. Maximin at Trier by the 12th century. 172 folios. PF. 15 plates. For the 'Ada Group' of MSS see CLA II.198, V.681, VI.704, IX.1366.

Austria, Germany, Switzerland

SCRIPTS AND SCRIPTORIA

See especially Bischoff **869**.

986

Bischoff, B. 'Die Entstehung des Sankt Galler Klosterplanes in paläographischer Sicht,' *Mitteilungen zur vaterländischen Geschichte* 42 (St. Gall 1962) 67-78. 2 pls.; repr. in **32**, I, 41-9 and pls. III-IV
Discusses two hands in the text of the plan: one chief, writing elegant Caroline, a second writing Alemannic minuscule; both probably from the time when Reginbert (ob. 846) was librarian at Reichenau.

987

————. 'Lorsch im Spiegel seiner Handschriften' in **996**, II, 7-128. 14 pls.

Also published separately, and seemingly earlier, as *Lorsch im Spiegel seiner Handschriften* (Munich 1974), with the same pagination. At pp 93-121 there is a list of extant MSS from Lorsch library, with a note ‹ origin in each case.

988

Clark, J.M. *The Abbey of St. Gall as a Centre of Literature and Art* (Cambridge 1926). 7 pls. (4 of MSS)

At pp. 298-302 is a list of Insular MSS now in the St. Gall library; at pp. 91-124, a useful chapter on the school.

989

Dengler-Schreiber, K. *Scriptorium und Bibliothek des Klosters Michel* berg in Bamberg von den Anfängen bis 1150 (Graz 1978). 24 pls.

The period covered is 1050-1150.

990

De Rijk, L.M. 'On the Curriculum of the Arts of the Trivium at St. G. from c. 850 - c. 1000,' *Vivarium* 1 (1963) 35-86.

991

Dodwell, C.R. and D.H. Turner. *Reichenau Reconsidered: A Re-asses ment of the Place of Reichenau in Ottonian Art* (London 1965). 12 p of MSS

Argues that, contrary to accepted opinion, Reichenau was a small arti tic outpost; with only one exception (and this itself not a Reichenau product), none of the many masterpieces of the 'Reichenau school' w ever in use there. Many of the illuminated MSS supposed to have bee‹ made at Reichenau are really to be ascribed to schools at Lorsch and Trier. See also **1001, 1007, 1010-11.**

992

Eder [Ineichen-], C.E. *Die Schule des Klosters Tegernsee im frühen Mittelalter im Spiegel der Tegernseer Handschriften* (Munich 1972).

993

————. 'Candidus-Brun von Fulda: Maler, Lehrer, und Schriftstelle in *Hrabanus Maurus und seine Schule: Festschrift der Rabanus-Mauru; Schule,* ed. W. Böhne (Fulda 1980) 182-92

Provides 6 plates of MSS, including 4 of a copy of the Rule of St. Ben dict (Würzburg, Universitätsbibliothek, MS. M. p. th. qu. 22) written a

the beginning of the 9th century in a fine Anglo-Insular minuscule by
Brun (Candidus), a monk of Fulda (ob. 845).

994

Holter, K. 'Der Buchschmuck in Süddeutschland und Oberitalien'
in **927**, 74-114. 18 pls.
Covers Murbach, Wissembourg, Lorsch, etc., Reichenau, St. Gall and
Chur, Verona, Bobbio, and Monza.

995

Houben, H. *St. Blasianer Handschriften des 11. und 12. Jahrhunderts,
unter besonderer Berücksichtigung der Ochsenhauser Klosterbibliothek*
(Munich 1979). 13 pls.
A study, based on codices in Austria and Czechoslovakia, of the scriptorium of this centre of reform in the Black Forest.

996

Knöpp, F., ed. *Die Reichsabtei Lorsch: Festschrift zum Gedenken an
ihre Stiftung 764.* 2 vols. (Darmstadt 1973, 1977)
There is a comprehensive bibliography in vol. II, at pp. 361-489, and 19
plates of MSS. See also **987**.

997

*Kunst und Kultur im Weserraum 800-1600: Austellung des Landes
Nordrhein-Westfalen Corvey 1966.* 2 vols. 3rd ed. (Münster in Westfalen
1966)
The catalogue of the exhibition in vol. II has sections on MSS and illumination, pp. 464-515 (with 45 pls.), and on the MSS of Bishop Sigebert
of Minden (A.D. 1022-36), pp. 516-24 (with 6 pls.).

998

Lieftinck, G.I. 'Le MS. d'Aulu-Gelle à Leeuwarden exécuté à Fulda en
836,' *BAPI* new ser. 1 (1955) 11-17. 11 pls.
On Leeuwarden, Provinciale Bibliotheek van Friesland, MS. 55.

999

Merton, A. *Die Buchmalerei in St. Gallen vom neunten bis zum elften
Jahrhundert.* 2nd ed. (Leipzig 1923). 104 pls.

1000

Pfaff, C. *Scriptorium und Bibliothek des Klosters Mondsee im hohen
Mittelalter* (Vienna 1967). 24 pls.

1001

Powell, K.B. 'Observations on a Number of Liuthar Manuscripts,'
Journal of the Warburg and Courtauld Institutes 34 (1971) 1-11

Argues that the 'Liuthar' school of MS illustration of the late 10th and early 11th centuries (two Gospel books of Otto III, the Bamberg Apocalypse, etc.) should be placed not at Reichenau, as is usual, but within the ecclesiastical complex at Trier. See also **991**.

1002

Schroeder, J. 'Bibliothek und Schule der Abtei Echternach um die Jahrtausendwende,' *Publications de la section historique de l'Institut grand-ducal de Luxembourg* 91 (1977) 201-378. 11 pls.
A palaeographical analysis of 15 MSS from Echternach, all probably written by the same anonymous scribe ca. A.D. 1000.

1003

Spang, P. *Handschriften und ihre Schreiber: Ein Blick in das Scriptoriu der Abtei Echternach* (Luxembourg 1967).
On the scriptorium in the 11th and later centuries. Has 70 pages of illustrations. See also **991, 1002**.

FACSIMILES

For some complete or partial facsimiles see **202** (Corvey), **248** (Metz), **269** (*Codex epistolaris*), **271, 274** (Reichenau), **277** (Salzburg), **278, 280** (letters of Boniface), **284** (Otfried), **285** (Reichenau), **287** (Mainz-Fulda), **293** (*Codex millenarius*), **298** (Salzburg), **301** (Werden), **345** (St. Gall), **346** (Einsiedeln), **358** (St. Gall), **407, 410-11, 582** (St. Gall) For some early Carolingian MSS in Caroline writing see CLA as follows for Benediktbeuern: IX.1241, 1246, 1277; for Freising: IX.1252-3, 1257, 1259-63, 1265, 1267, 1269, 1271, 1273, 1280, 1284-5; for Mondsee: IX.1318; for Murbach: VIII.1193; IX.1290, 1296; for Regensburg: IX.1287-8, 1293, 1299, 1304, 1338; for Salzburg: VIII. 1146, 1180; IX.1247, 1294, 1313, 1413; X.1445, 1448, 1460, 1462, 1464-5, 1468, 1478, 1489-90, 1497, 1501, 1508-10, 1517; for Tegern see: VIII.1216; IX.1315-16, 1321-2; for Reichenau: VIII.1079, 1093-4, 1096; for St. Gall: VII.926. For Switzerland in general see the flood of facsimiles in **875-89**.

1004

Capitulare de villis, ed. C. Brühl. 2 vols. (Stuttgart 1971)
Wolfenbüttel, Herzog August Bibliothek, MS. Helmst. 254: fols. 1r-8v: 10 letters of Leo III to Charlemagne (A.D. 808-13); 9r-12r: 'Brevium

exempla'; 12v-16r: 'Capitulare de villis.' Caroline, A.D. 830-50. 16 folios.
CF (replica form).

1005

*Die Bamberger Apokalypse: Eine Reichenau Bilderhandschrift vom
Jahre '1000,'* ed. H. Wölfflin. 2nd ed. (Munich 1921)
Bamberg, Staatliche Bibliothek, MS. Bibl. 140. Latin Apocalypse (ca.
A.D. 1001-02) and Gospel book (ca. 1107) written at Reichenau in
Caroline, with 57 miniatures. 106 folios. PF (of Apocalypse). 65 plates.
See also **991, 1001** for Trier instead of Reichenau.

1006

Codex Albensis: Ein Antiphonar aus dem 12. Jahrhundert, ed. Z. Falvy
and L. Mezey (Graz—Budapest 1963)
Graz, Universitätsbibliothek, MS. 211. Written in late Caroline in the
first half of the 12th century at Alba Regia (Székeszfehérvar, German
Stuhlweissenburg), Hungary. 159 folios. CF.

1007

*Codex Caesareus Upsaliensis: An Echternach Gospel-Book of the
Eleventh Century,* ed. C. Nordenfalk (Stockholm 1971)
Uppsala, Universitetsbiblioteket, MS. C 93. The 'Goslar' Gospels, written
in Caroline and illustrated at Echternach in A.D. 1050 for Henry III as
a present for Goslar Cathedral, Lower Saxony, on its dedication in that
year. Seized by Swedish troops from the Jesuits of Goslar in 1632.
159 folios. CF. See also **991, 1010-11.**

1008

Codex Egberti der Stadtbibliothek Trier, ed. H. Schiel. 2 vols. (Basel
1960)
Trier, Stadtbibliothek, MS. 24. Latin Gospel book written in Caroline at
Trier to the order of Archbishop Egbert (A.D. 977-93) by monks
Keraldus and Heribertus (both, probably, from Reichenau), and partly
illustrated by the so-called 'Gregory Master' (a list of MSS attributed to
whom is at I, 81). 165 folios. CF.

1009

Der Codex Wittekindius, ed. A. Boeckler (Leipzig 1938)
Berlin, Deutsche Staatsbibliothek, MS. theol. lat. fol. 1. The 'Widukind
Gospels.' Written in Caroline and illuminated at Fulda ca. 975, and
regarded as the masterpiece of the Fulda school. 128 folios. CF.

1010

Das Evangelistar Kaiser Heinrichs III, ed. G. Knoll, J. Plotzek, H. Roosen-

Runge, and P. Spang. 2 vols. (Wiesbaden 1980)
Bremen, Universitätsbibliothek, MS. b. 21. Written in Caroline and illustrated at Echternach (whose scriptorium is pictured in one illustration, fol. 124v), and dedicated to Henry III as king (1039-46) and Gisela, his mother. Probable date is 1039-40. 127 folios. CF. See also **991, 1007.**

1011

Das goldene Evangelienbuch Heinrichs III, ed. A. Boeckler (Berlin 1933)
El Escorial, Real Biblioteca de San Lorenzo, MS. Vitr. 17. Written in Caroline and illustrated at Echternach in A.D. 1043-6 for Henry III as a gift for Speyer. 170 folios. PF. 144 plates. See also **991, 1001, 1007,** and **1010.**

1012

Das goldene Evangelienbuch von Echternach im Germanischen National-Museum zu Nürnberg (Munich 1956); trans. as *The Golden Gospels of Echternach* (London 1957)
Nuremberg, Germanisches National-Museum, MS. 2° 156142. Gospels written in gold and illustrated at Trier, A.D. 985-91, and bound in gold covers with precious stones at Echternach, 1035-40. 136 folios. PF. 109 plates.

1013

Jones, L.W. *The Script of Cologne from Hildebald to Hermann* (Cambridge, Mass. 1932)
100 plates of MSS from archbishops Hildebald (A.D. 785-819) to Hermann (890-923).

1014

Lex Baiwariorum: Lichtdruckwiedergabe der Ingolstädter Handschrift des bayerischen Volksrechts, ed. K. Beyerle (Munich 1926)
Munich, Universitätsbibliothek, MS. 8° 132. A pocket-size volume, written in Caroline at the beginning of the 9th century in Bavaria. Belonged to Ingolstadt University Library and migrated with the university and library to Landshut and thence to Munich. 92 folios. CF, with transcription, translation, and notes.

1015

Das Perikopenbuch Kaiser Heinrichs II. (Munich 1914)
Munich, Bayerische Staatsbibliothek, MS. Clm 4452. Latin lectionary in Uncial, Rustic Capital, and Caroline minuscule commissioned by Henry II (A.D. 1002-24) for Bamberg Cathedral and, according to Dodwell **991**

and Powell **1001**, written and illustrated before 1014 at Trier ('Liuthar group') rather than at Reichenau. 206 folios. PF. 67 plates.

1016
Petzet, E. and O. Glauning. *Deutsche Schrifttafeln des IX. bis XVI. Jahrhunderts aus Handschriften der K. Hof- und Staatsbibliothek in München.* 5 vols. (I-III, Munich 1910-12; IV-V, Leipzig 1924-30 [as *Deutsche Schrifttafeln ... der Bayerischen Staatsbibliothek*]; repr. in 1 vol. 1975). 75 pls.

1017
Strabo: *Hortulus: Walahfrid Strabo,* ed. R. Payne and W. Blunt (Pittsburgh 1966)
Vatican City, BAV, MS. Reg. lat. 469C, fols. 29v-39v. Caroline. St. Gall, second half of the 9th century. CF of Strabo.

Italy

SCRIPTS AND SCRIPTORIA

1018
Carusi, E. 'Cenni storici sull'abbazia di Farfa' in **49**, 3 (1924) 52-9
A brief survey of the abbey from its foundation in A.D. 857, and a list of surviving MSS. See also **1025, 1032**.

1019
Cau, E. 'La scrittura carolina in Pavia, capitale del regno (secoli IX-XII),' *RM* 2 (1967) 105-32. 12 pls.

1020
————. 'Ricerche su scrittura e cultura a Tortona nel IX e X secolo,' *Rivista di storia della chiesa in Italia* 26 (1972) 79-100. 2 pls.

1021
Ferrari, M. 'In Papia conveniant ad Dungalum,' *IMU* 15 (1972) 1-52. 3 pls.
On the influence of the Irish scholar Dungal at Pavia, to which he took in A.D. 825 various texts he had acquired at St. Germain- des- Prés. See also **1038**.

1022
Giuliano, M.L. *Coltura e attività calligrafica nel secolo XII a Verona* (Padua 1933). 17 pls.

1023

Gray, N. 'The Palaeography of Latin Inscriptions in the Eighth, Ninth, and Tenth Centuries in Italy,' *Papers of the British School at Rome* 16 (1948) 38-171. 3 pls., numerous drawings
The only study of its kind to date.

1024

Kajanto, I. *Classical and Christian Studies in the Latin Epitaphs of Medieval and Renaissance Rome* (Helsinki 1980)
Includes 30 plates (A.D. 969-ca. 1500).

1025

Lindsay, W.M. 'The Farfa Type' in **49**, 3 (1924) 49-51. 3 pls.
A plea for the study of a script which, while associated since 1897 with Farfa monastery, some twenty miles NNE of Rome, 'was the script of Rome and all the Roman region.' (Also known as 'Romanesca' – see Supino Martini **1032**).

1026

Mazzoli Casagrande, M.A. 'I codici Warmondiani e la cultura a Ivrea fra IX e XI secolo,' *RM* 6-9 (1971-4) 89-139. 10 pls.
An examination of six liturgical MSS done for Warmond, bishop of Ivrea (ca. A.D. 969-ca. 1100). See also **223**.

1027

Orlandelli, G. *Rinascimento giuridico e scrittura carolina a Bologna nel secolo XII* (Bologna 1965).

1028

Pagnin, B. 'La formazione della scrittura carolina italiana' in *Atti del Congresso internazionale di diritto romano e di storia del diritto,* I (Milan 1951) 245-66.

1029

Palma, M. 'Da Nonantola a Fonte Avellana: A proposito di dodici manoscritti e di un "domnus Damianus",' *SC* 2 (1978) 221-30. 5 pls.
Discusses 12 MSS now in the Vatican Library (MSS. Vat. lat. 202, 213, etc.) written towards the end of the 11th century at Nonantola for the Benedictine hermitage of Fonte Avellana, north of Fabriano, at, seemingly, the request of 'domnus Damianus,' probably a nephew of Peter Damiani (1007-72). See also **1041**.

1030

————. 'L'origine del Codice Vaticano del *Liber diurnus*,' *SC* 4 (1980) 295-310. 12 pls.

Confirms Nonantola as the origin of a copy of the *Liber diurnus* now in Archivio Segreto Vaticano, Misc. Arm. XI, 19. Dates the copy, and the entry of Caroline writing to Nonantola, to ca. A.D. 825-38, when Ansfridus was abbot. See **815** for Nonantola in the 8th century. See also **944**.

1031
Pirri, P. 'La scuola miniaturistica di S. Eutizio in Valcastoriana presso Norcia nei secoli X-XII,' *Scriptorium* 3 (1949) 3-10. 12 pls.

1032
Supino Martini, P. 'Carolina romana e minuscola romanesca,' *SM* 3rd ser. 15/2 (1974) 769-93. 12 pls.
Examines some of the few MSS of indubitable Roman origin from the 9th century (Vatican City, BAV, MS. Vat. lat. 4965 of A.D. 869-70; Tours, Bibl. municipale, MS. 1027, A.D. 873-6), and concludes from comparison with Farfa MSS of a little later (e.g. Rome, Biblioteca Nazionale, MS. Farfense 29) that 'Farfa' Caroline ('Romanesca') is modelled on 9th-century Roman Caroline. See also **1025**.

1033
————. 'Per lo studio delle scritture altomedievale italiane: La collezione canonica chietina (Vat. Reg. lat. 1997),' *SC* 1 (1977) 133-54
Analysis of the colophon shows that the MS was copied at Chieti, possibly in a 'writing-school' attached to the cathedral, in the mid-9th century.

1034
Supino Martini, P. and A. Petrucci. 'Materiali ed ipostesi per una storia della cultura scritta nella Roma del IX secolo,' *SC* 2 (1978) 45-102. 10 pls.
According to Supino Martini (pp. 45-95) evidence is slight from books, inscriptions, frescoes; there is a total loss of private documents, and nothing from the papal curia. Petrucci (95-101) posits that old majuscule Uncial (see **817**) was taught in clerical schools, at least until mid-century.

1035
Tristano, C. 'Scrittura beneventana e scrittura carolina in manoscritti dell'Italia meridionale,' *SC* 3 (1979) 89-150. 4 pls.
Examining some 29 MSS, shows that Caroline had little impact on Beneventan strongholds until the end of the 12th century, when there was an abortive attempt to fuse the two scripts.

1036
Venturini, M. *Ricerche paleografiche intorno all'arcidiacono Pacifico di Verona* (Verona 1929)

Notes that from ca. A.D. 800 some 218 codices were written for the cathedral of Verona at the instigation of Pacificus (A.D. 776-844). See also **224**.

1037

─────. *Vita e attività dello 'scriptorium' veronese nel secolo XI* (Verona 1930). 4 pls.

1038

Vezin, J. 'Observations sur l'origine des manuscrits légués par Dungal à Bobbio' in **66a**, 125-44.

FACSIMILES

For complete or partial facsimiles of MSS from the period see **223** (Ivrea), **224** (Verona), **356** (Bologna), **376** (Gospels of Matilda); for some samples of early Caroline (almost all Verona or area) see CLA V.553, 601; VII.880, 907, 945, 951 (style of Pacificus); VIII.1057, 1058 (Pacificus), 1065 (Pacificus), 1074 (Pacificus), 1076, 1119, 1148; IX.1248, 1281, 1282 (Pacificus), 1359; XI.1603 (Adelhard codex, ca. A.D. 787). In general see Archivio paleografico italiano **161-75**, especial II, IV (MSS from Rome and Rome area, some in 'Farfa' or 'Romanesca' script), VIII (MSS from some writing centres), IX (royal diplomata), XI (notarial documents), XIV (Sicilian diplomata), XV (Beneventan diplomata); see also **829, 830-67, 1202, 1205**.

1039

Petrus de Ebulo. *Liber ad honorem Augusti,* ed. G.B. Siragusa. 2 vols. Fonti per la storia d'Italia 39 (Rome 1905, 1906)

Bern, Bürgerbibliothek, MS. 120. A poem in honour of Emperor Henry VI written by Peter of Eboli (ob. 1220) in 1195-6. Copied here in late but good Caroline and illustrated with pen-and-ink drawings. The poem is edited, with other items, in vol. I (which shows 1 plate of the poem); vol. II is taken up with 53 plates of drawings (with captions in Caroline) 148 folios. PF. See also **1214**.

1040

Pontificum Romanorum diplomata papyracea quae supersunt in tabulariis Hispaniae, Italiae, Germaniae phototypice expressa, ed. E. Carusi, C. Silva-Tarouca, and C. Erdmann (Rome 1929)

43 plates, with transcriptions, of 15 diplomata, A.D. 819 - 1020-22.

1041

Troparium sequentiarium Nonantulanum, ed. G. Vecchi. Monumenta lyrica Italiae medii aevi 1/1 (Modena 1955)

Rome, Biblioteca Casanatense, MS. 1741. Nonantola, 11th century. 192 folios. CF.

1042

Ugolini, F.A. *Atlante paleografico romanzo,* I: *Documenti volgari italiani* (Turin 1942)

Prints 26 plates covering from the end of the 8th to the 12th century.

England (to ca. 1200)

GENERAL

1043

Cross, J.E. 'The Literate Anglo-Saxon: On Sources and Disseminations,' *PBA* 58 (1972) 3-36

Suggestions for identifying sources, and particularly ideas or sequences of ideas, in Anglo-Saxon writings.

1044

Dumville, D. 'English Libraries before 1066: Use and Abuse of the Manuscript Evidence' in *Insular Latin Studies: Papers on Latin Texts and Manuscripts of the British Isles: 550-1066,* ed. M.W. Herren (Toronto 1981) 153-78

The case for the study of 11th-century MS production. See also **697** and **1046**.

1045

Keynes, S. *The Diplomas of King Aethelred 'The Unready' 978-1016: A Study in their Use as Historical Evidence* (Cambridge 1980).

1046

Rella, F.A. 'Continental Manuscripts Acquired for English Centers in the Tenth and Early Eleventh Centuries: A Preliminary Checklist,' *Anglia* 98 (1980) 107-16.

1047

Robinson, F.C. 'Syntactical Glosses in Latin Manuscripts of Anglo-Saxon Provenance,' *Speculum* 48 (1973) 443-75. 2 pls.

An analysis of a system of codes used by Anglo-Saxon teachers for commenting on word order and grammatical relationships in sentences.

Stresses the importance of these for palaeographical and codicological studies.

SCRIPTS AND SCRIPTORIA

1048
Bishop, T.A.M. 'Notes on Cambridge Manuscripts,' *Transactions of the Cambridge Bibliographical Society* 1 (1949-53) 432-40; 2 (1954-8) 185-90, 323-36; 3 (1959-63) 93-5, 312-23; 4 (1964-8) 70-76
Valuable notes, especially on MSS connected with St. Augustine's, Canterbury, in the 10th century.

1049
————. 'An Early Example of the Square Minuscule,' *Transactions of the Cambridge Bibliographical Society* 4 (1964-8) 246-52
Discusses the date and script of Trinity College, Cambridge, MS. 308, and its place in the 10th-century revival in England.

1050
————. 'An Early Example of Insular Caroline,' *Transactions of the Cambridge Bibliographical Society* 4 (1964-8) 396-400
Cambridge, University Library, MS. Ee. ii. 4, written in West or SW England before the middle of the 10th century.

1051
Brownrigg, L.L. 'Manuscripts containing English Decoration 871-1066, Catalogued and Illustrated: A Review,' *ASE* 7 (1978) 239-66
A critical review of E. Temple, *Anglo-Saxon Manuscripts* (**729**) and a general review of recent scholarship.

1052
Clemoes, P. *Liturgical Influence on Punctuation in Late Old English and Early Middle English Manuscripts* (Binghamton, N.Y. 1980)
A corrected reprint of the edition of 1952.

1053
Colgrave, B. and A. Hyde. 'Two Recently Discovered Leaves from Old English MSS,' *Speculum* 37 (1962) 60-78
Notes on two leaves of the 11th century.

1054
Dodwell, C.R. *The Canterbury School of Illumination 1066-1200* (Cambridge 1954). 73 pls.
A list of MSS illuminated at Canterbury, 1050-1200, and analysis of

the illumination and hands.
1055

————. 'L'Originalité iconographique de plusieurs illustrations anglo-saxonnes de l'Ancien Testament,' *Cahiers de civilisation médiévale* 14 (1971) 319-28. 24 pls.
1056

Gasquet, F.A. and E. Bishop. *The Bosworth Psalter* (London 1908). 4 pls.
On London, BL, Add. MS. 37517. Latin, with Old English glosses, written in the late 10th century. See also **1061**.
1057

Homburger, O. *Die Anfänge der Malschule von Winchester im X. Jahrhundert* (Leipzig 1912). 12 pls.
1058

Ker, N.R. 'Hemming's Cartulary: A Description of Two Worcester Cartularies in Cotton Tiberius A. xiii' in *Studies in Medieval History presented to F.M. Powicke,* ed. R.W. Hunt, W.A. Pantin, and R.W. Southern (Oxford 1948) 49-75. 2 pls.
Notes that Cartulary I is of the beginning of the 11th century and is partly in the hand of Hemming, a monk of Worcester; II is in three main hands of the late 11th century. The hands in I illustrate handwriting of the period immediately after the breakdown of Anglo-Insular script about the year 1000; those in II presage the marked roundness of the early 12th century.
1059

————. *English Manuscripts in the Century after the Norman Conquest* (Oxford 1960). 29 pls. without transcriptions
A lucid account of library script in this period, showing, e.g., how the 'set English hand which came into use in the quarter century after 1125 is partly modelled on the set English hand of the eleventh century.'
1060

————. 'The Handwriting of Archbishop Wulfstan' in *England before the Conquest: Studies presented to Dorothy Whitelock,* ed. P. Clemoes and K. Hughes (Cambridge 1971) 315-31. 1 pl.
An analysis of Wulfstan's hand as seen in marginalia or interpolations in ten MSS used by him as bishop of Worcester or archbishop of York at the beginning of the 11th century.

1061

Korhammer, P.M. 'The Origin of the Bosworth Psalter,' *ASE* 2 (1973) 173-87

See **1056**.

1062

McLachlan, E.P. 'The Scriptorium of Bury St. Edmunds in the Third and Fourth Decades of the XIIth Century: Books in Three Related Hands and their Decoration,' *Mediaeval Studies* 40 (1978) 328-48

Has 5 plates illustrating 7 MSS. See also **1325**.

1063

Pächt, O. *The Rise of Pictorial Narrative in Twelfth-Century England* (Oxford 1962). 12 pls.

On the historiated initial in particular.

1064

Pollard, G. 'Some Anglo-Saxon Bookbindings,' *The Book Collector* 24 (1975) 130-59

A description, with diagrams, of 21 bindings. Some books used by Boniface, Dunstan, and Wulfstan still have original boards. Four extant MSS can be shown to have been bound at Canterbury ca. A.D. 1000.

1065

Rigg, A.G. and G.R. Wieland. 'A Canterbury Classbook of the Mid-Eleventh Century (the 'Cambridge Songs' Manuscript),' *ASE* 4 (1975) 113-30

A codicological analysis of Cambridge, University Library, MS. Gg. v. 35: three classbooks in fact, illustrating kinds of texts used and commented on in schools. For PF see **1076**.

1066

Thomson, R.M. 'The Scriptorium of William of Malmesbury' in **46**, 117-42

Discusses William (ca. A.D. 1095 - ca. 1143) as book-collector, scribe, and mentor of scribes. For some of his MSS see **1094**, 27-30 with 4 plates.

1067

Vezin, J. 'Manuscrits des Xe et XIe siècles copiés en Angleterre en minuscule caroline et conservés à la Bibliothèque nationale de Paris' in *Humanisme actif: Mélanges d'art et de littérature offerts à Julien Cain* (Paris 1968) II, 283-96. 4 pls.

1068

Wormald, F. 'The Survival of Anglo-Saxon Illumination after the

Norman Conquest,' *PBA* 30 (1944) 127-46.
1069
————. 'Decorated Initials in English Manuscripts from A.D. 900 to 1100,' *Archaeologia* 91 (1945) 107-35.
1070
————. 'The Insular Script in Late Tenth-Century English Latin Manuscripts' in *Atti del X Congresso internazionale di scienze storiche* (Florence 1957) 160-64.
1071
————. 'An English Eleventh-Century Psalter with Pictures: British Museum, Cotton MS. Tiberius C. VI,' *The Walpole Society* 38 (1960-62) 1-14. 6 pls.
1072
————. 'The "Winchester School" before St. Aethelwold' in *England before the Conquest* (see **1060**) 305-13. 4 pls.
1073
————. *The Winchester Psalter with 134 Illustrations* (London 1973) On London, BL, MS. Cotton Nero C. IV. Written at Winchester in the mid-12th century in late Caroline, probably for Henry of Blois, bishop of Winchester (A.D. 1129-71). 142 folios. PF.

FACSIMILES

For some complete or partial facsimiles of MSS from this period see **215** (Coupar Angus), **365, 373** (Aethelwold), **382, 385** (Guthlac), **386-7, 399** (Aethelgifu), **409** (Dunstan), **415**; and **738-43, 745-8, 751-4** (all EEMF volumes, e.g. **745**: Blickling Homilies, **747**: Nowell Codex, **748**: Aelfric, **754**: Vercelli Book). See also **331** (*Manuscrits datés*).

1074
Bishop, T.A.M. *English Caroline Minuscule* (Oxford 1971)
Prints 24 plates, with introduction and transcriptions, for the period ca. A.D. 950-1100, when, for Latin MSS at least, English scribes resumed the practice of an international script which they had abandoned in the 8th century (when they adopted and adapted Hiberno-Insular minuscule in place of, generally speaking, an Uncial script of an Italian strain).
1075
Bishop, T.A.M. and P. Chaplais. *Facsimiles of English Royal Writs to*

A.D. 1000 presented to V.H. Galbraith (Oxford 1957). 30 pls. with transcriptions.

1076

Breul, K., ed. *The Cambridge Songs: A Goliard's Song Book of the XIth Century* (Cambridge 1915)

A facsimile, with transcription, of Cambridge, University Library, MS. Gg. v. 35, fols. 432-41. Anglo-Caroline, written in Middle or Lower Rhineland. See also **1065.**

1077

Collins, R.L. *Anglo-Saxon Vernacular Manuscripts in America* (New York 1976)

Includes 12 plates illustrating 11 MSS, including the Blickling Homilies (**745**) and the will of Aethelgifu (**399**), with introduction and descriptions.

1078

Forbes-Leith, W., ed. *The Gospel Book of Saint Margaret* (Edinburgh 1896)

Oxford, Bodleian Library, MS. Lat. liturg. f. 5. An illustrated Gospel book, which may have belonged to St. Margaret, queen of Scotland (A.D. 1045-93). Written in England in Anglo-Caroline, in the first half of the 11th century (ca. 1030-50). 38 folios. CF.

1079

Greg, W.W. *Facsimiles of Twelve Early English Manuscripts in the Library of Trinity College, Cambridge* (Oxford 1913)

MSS of the 11th-15th centuries, with transcriptions.

1080

James, M.R., ed. *The Canterbury Psalter* (London 1935)

Cambridge, Trinity College, MS. 987 (R. 17. 1). A decorated codex done in the mid-12th century in a late Caroline hand at Christ Church, Canterbury, by the monk Eadwine ('Scriptor scriptorum princeps,' as he saw himself). 286 folios. CF.

1081

Johnson, C. and H. Jenkinson. *English Court Hand A.D. 1066 to 1500, Illustrated Chiefly from the Public Records.* 2 vols. (Oxford 1915, repr. New York 1967). 44 pls. with transcriptions. See also **1292.**

1082

Kuypers, A.B. *The Prayer Book of Aedeluald the Bishop, commonly called the Book of Cerne* (Cambridge 1902). 2 pls.

Cambridge, University Library, MS. Ll. i. 10. 99 folios. A non-liturgical collection of prayers, generally Celtic in origin, written in a mixed Anglo-Insular script in the 9th century and added to in various hands until the 15th century. It was at Cerne Abbey, Dorset, in the Middle Ages.
1083

Liber vitae ecclesiae Dunelmensis: A Collotype Facsimile of the Original Manuscript, I: *Facsimile and General Introduction,* ed. A.H. T[hompson]. Surtees Society 136 (Durham—London 1923)
Durham, Cathedral Library, MS. s.n. Original part (fols. 1-42r) was written at Lindisfarne in Anglo-Insular minuscule in the 9th century, the remainder (42v-83v) being a continuation from the 11th-16th centuries. The core of the *Liber* is a list of some 3150 names classified according to their bearers' rank. Shows an extraordinary range of hands. 83 folios. CF.
1084

Pächt, O., C.R. Dodwell, and F. Wormald. *The St. Albans Psalter (Albani Psalter)* (London 1960)
Prints 100 plates from the psalter, 72 from cognate matter. Hildesheim, St. Godehard, MS. s.n. Written before A.D. 1123 at St. Albans, Hertfordshire, probably for Christina, anchoress of Markyate. Migrated in the 16th century to the Benedictines of Lamspringe near Hildesheim; at St. Godehard's since 1803. Text is mostly Latin, with some Anglo-Norman. 418 pages. PF. Preface and description of MS are by Wormald; the full-page miniatures are covered by Pächt, and the initials by Dodwell.
1085

Parker Chronicle and Laws (Corpus Christi College, Cambridge, MS. 173): A Facsimile, ed. R. Flower and H. Smith. EETS o.s. 208 (London 1941, repr. 1973)
Fols. 1r-32r contain the Old English chronicle to ca. A.D. 1000, with sporadic additions to ca. 1070; 32r-32v: acts of Lanfranc; 33r-52v: laws; 53r-55v: lists of popes, archbishops, and bishops. Written in Anglo-Insular majuscule and minuscule, probably at Winchester, at the turn of the 11th century. At Christ Church, Canterbury, by A.D. 1070. 56 folios. CF. See **1471**.
1086

Patterson, R.B. *Earldom of Gloucester Charters: The Charters and Scribes of the Earls and Countesses of Gloucester to A.D. 1217* (Oxford 1973)
Prints 32 plates, with transcriptions, from ca. A.D. 1107. Identifies

scribes by hands, pp. 16-21, and notes (see pp. 29-30) that some professional writers made an effort to write a 'business' hand.

1087
Salter, H.E. *Facsimiles of Early Charters in Oxford Muniment Rooms* (Oxford 1929)
Provides 102 plates, with transcriptions, of charters from ca. A.D. 1097-1251.

1088
Skeat, W.W. *Twelve Facsimiles of Old English Manuscripts* (Oxford 1892)
MSS of the 10th-15th centuries, with transcriptions.

1089
Van Langenhove, G. *Aldhelm's De laudibus virginitatis with Latin and Old English Glosses* (Brussels 1941)
Brussels, Bibliothèque royale, MS. 1650, fols. 3r-57v. England, 10th century. Text in Anglo-Insular, glosses in Anglo-Caroline and Anglo-Insular. CF.

1090
Warner, G.F. and H.J. Ellis. *Facsimiles of Royal and Other Charters in the British Museum,* I: *William I – Richard I* (London 1903)
Prints 50 plates, with transcriptions, of 77 charters from ca. A.D. 1070-1198.

Period of Scholastico-Mercantile Culture ('Gothic')

See in general **7**, 150-55; **148**, 220-44; **152**, 205-58; **157**, 163-86.

From A.D. 1150 onwards there are indications that a growing demand for books, a widening readership, and the increasing use of the written document for business transactions, were bringing about a general abandonment of the old, leisurely Caroline hand. The twelfth-century renaissance, a direct result of the quest for original sources and for a scientific methodology begun during the Gregorian reform (ca. 1050-1100), occasioned a multiplication of schools, scholars, and treatises. After the publication of the two most influential syntheses of the twelfth century – the *Decretum* of Gratian for church law about 1140, the *Liber sententiarum* of Peter Lombard for theology some fifteen years later – whole new classes of legal and theological treatises came into being: glosses and commentaries, *quaestiones* and *repetitiones, summae* and *distinctiones,* and the like. In addition, the growing literacy and self-awareness of the lower clergy at large, a process spurred by the educational decrees of the Third Lateran Council (1179), especially that which established chairs of grammar in every cathedral church, caused a demand outside the schools for cheap, portable books of a none too professional nature; possibly it is not without significance for the emergence of Gothic script that the first popular manuals of theology and law began to appear around the year 1200, at much the same time indeed as full-blown Gothic. Given this growing market for writings, whether academic or popular, it was only a matter of time before the generously-spaced and uncluttered pages of a typical Caroline codex gave way to a more economical layout and to more parsimonious methods of writing. Further, the great upsurge of scholastic learning at Bologna, Paris, and, possibly, Oxford, had brought about the eclipse of monastic or clerical scriptoria as the chief centres of book production. Professional non-monastic scribes were now emerging as a class in scholastic centres; and what this new breed of 'scriveners' needed in order to meet the rising demand for the written word was an expeditious and profitable yet legible method of writing as much as possible in the smallest possible space. Such a method, as it happens, lay readily to hand in the small, clear, and highly-abbreviated style of writing that had developed out of Caroline bookhand in various chanceries and business centres in the twelfth century, and in particular after 1150, when notaries begin to be recognized universally as having a *manus publica* and public trust. This neat, cursive hand enabled a writer to cover a lot of ground quickly with a freely-flowing pen, and was ideal for recording or preserving file-copies (rolls, registers) of state and legal affairs, business transactions, or church correspondence. By 1200 this was an established form of writing, and is best to be seen in the earliest extant series of registers of papal correspondence (A.D. 1198-1216: Innocent III), or in groups of English administrative records from the same period (1199-1216: King John). Accordingly, and in imitation of this administrative hand, a new literary script begins to come to the fore about 1200: a compact, highly-abbreviated script to which Humanists later gave the pejorative name *Gothic.* The chief characteristic of this script is the phenomenon, first recorded by Meyer **1103**, of combining, fusing, or 'biting' the opposite curves of letters where these occur back-to-back, thus achieving a considerable economy of space. When, for example, a letter such as *o* was preceded by a letter such as *p,* or was succeeded by some letter such as *c,* the bow or curve of one letter was merged with the opposite bow or curve of the other. By 1220 this was a steady feature of the new book-hand, a bookhand which in fact happens to be the first really international script, and which was written by everyone from merchants to scholastics, and had its most calligraphic form in the *Littera rotunda* or *Bononiensis,* and its most ubiquitous form in the *Littera notularis.*

GENERAL STUDIES

1091
Bischoff, B. 'La Nomenclature des écritures livresques du IXe au XIIIe siècle' in **1701,** 7-14. 12 figs.
Posits a decisive turn from Caroline to 'Gothic' in N. France or in Norman-dy, notably the introduction of curved or snubbed finial strokes in minims, ca. A.D. 1050-1100.

1092
Boussard, J. 'Influences insulaires dans la formation de l'écriture gothique,' *Scriptorium* 5 (1951) 238-64. 3 pls.
Argues that the presence of snubbed instead of the pointed finials of Caroline in 'Gothic' writing is due to the gradual adoption on the continent in the 11th century of the Insular manner of cutting pens obliquely to the left of the nose of the pen.

1093
Boyle, L.E. 'The Emergence of Gothic Handwriting' in *The Year 1200: A Background Survey,* ed. F. Deuchler (New York 1970) II, 175-83; repr. in *The Journal of Typographic Research* 4 (1970) 307-16.

1094
De la Mare, A.C. and B.C. Barker-Benfield, eds. *Manuscripts at Oxford: An Exhibition in Memory of Richard William Hunt (1908-1979), Keeper of Western Manuscripts at the Bodleian Library Oxford, 1945-1975* (Oxford 1980). 109 figs., mostly of MSS
Particularly valuable for MSS of various phases of scholastic learning.

1095
Dobiaš-Roždestvenskaja, O.A. 'Quelques considérations sur les origines de l'écriture dite "gothique" ' in *Mélanges d'histoire du moyen âge offerts à M. Ferdinand Lot* (Paris 1925) 691-721
Argues that the calligraphic quality, based on geometric schemes and on

light and shade of strokes, derives from Beneventan script, and that the emergence of 'Gothic' in NW France and particularly in Normandy may be traced to the known relationship between the monastery of S. Michele at Gargano, where Beneventan was the common script, and that of Mont St. Michel. But see **1107**.

1096

Frenz, T. 'Gotische Gebrauchschriften des 15. Jahrhunderts: Untersuchungen zur Schrift lateinisch-deutscher Glossare am Beispiel des "Vocabularius Ex quo",' *CM* 7 (1981) 14-30. 2 pls.

An examination based on 102 MSS and nine editions of the very popular dictionary *Ex quo,* written ca. 1400. Latin abbreviations are at pp. 24-6.

1097

Gumbert, J.P. 'A Proposal for a Cartesian Nomenclature' in **54**, 45-52. 4 figs., 2 pls. of 32 samples of MSS

Taking for granted the main criteria which underpin Lieftinck's distinction (**1101**) between 'Textualis,' 'Cursiva,' and 'Hybrida' ('Bastarda'), Gumbert suggests how, by assigning a graphical value to each of the three co-ordinates or criteria in question (head of *a* and *g;* feet of *f* and tall *s;* presence or not of loops), it is possible to plot hands on a spatial diagram such as a cube, according to the presence or absence of some or all of these graphical qualities. Much the same ground is covered in his 'Nomenklatur als Gradnetz: Ein Versuch an spätmittelalterlichen Schriftformen,' *CM* 1 (1975) 122-5, with diagrams, etc. See further the note of J.M. Kitzman, 'The Three-Dimensional Graphing of Scripts,' *Viator* 10 (1979) 433-9 with 4 figs.

1098

Heinemeyer, W. 'Studien zur Geschichte der gotischen Urkundenschrift,' *Archiv für Diplomatik* 1 (1955) 330-81; 2 (1956) 250-323; 5-6 (1959-60) 308-429; also publ. separately as *Studien*... (Cologne–Graz 1962) Has 17 plates, mostly of documents from the Middle Rhine area, A.D. 1140-1500.

1099

Kautzsch, R. *Die Entstehung der Frakturschrift* (Mainz 1922). 7 pls.

1100

Kiseleva, L.I. *Gotičeskij kursiv XIII-XV vekov* (Leningrad 1974)

As summarized in French by the author in *Scriptorium* 30 (1976) 182, concludes, among other things, that Gothic cursive derives from Caroline minuscule.

1101

Lieftinck, G.I. 'Pour une nomenclature de l'écriture livresque de la période dite gothique: Essai s'appliquant spécialement aux manuscrits originaires des Pays-Bas médiévaux' in **1701**, 15-34. 22 figs. (nos. 13-34)

Proposes a nomenclature, now largely accepted, to cover different varieties of Gothic: *Textualis formata, Textualis, Textualis currens, Cursiva textualis, Cursiva formata, Cursiva (currens), Bastarda, Cursiva bastarda,* etc. The three main categories are distinguishable (and recognizable) as follows: *Textualis* has full Gothic *a* and *g* (i.e. with two compartments), it makes the letters *f* and *s* rest with slightly snubbed feet on the line of writing, and it does not go in for loops. *Cursiva,* on the other hand, has very plain forms of *a* and *g,* indulges in loops, and provides *f* and *s* with tails. *Bastarda* (later termed *Hybrida*) is *cursiva* without the loops. There are some modifications of nomenclature in Lieftinck's preface to **333**, I, XIII-XVII. It should be noted, however, that Lieftinck's terminology was devised with respect to MSS written in the Low Countries. See also **1097** and **1568**, 199-214.

1102

Mazal, O. *Buchkunst der Gotik* (Graz 1975). 169 pls. of MSS

Has an excellent chapter (pp. 23-45) on Gothic handwriting, with 40 plates illustrating all types of Gothic (Pearl, Parisiensis, Textura, Rotunda, Bastarda, chancery cursive, etc.) from ca. A.D. 1180-1508.

1103

Meyer, W. 'Die Buchstaben-Verbindungen der sogenannten gotischen Schrift' in *Abhandlungen der Kgl. Gesellschaft der Wissenschaften zu Göttingen,* phil.-hist. Klasse, N.F. 1.6 (Berlin 1897) 1-124. 5 pls.

A pioneer study of the phenomenon of overlapping or 'biting' of curved parts of letters which characterizes Gothic as such (as distinct from earlier manifestations known variously as 'primitive Gothic,' 'early Gothic,' 'proto-Gothic,' etc.), and which seems to have been in vogue by A.D. 1200-20 in most areas of Europe. To be supplemented now to some extent by Oeser **1104**.

1104

Oeser, W. 'Das 'a' als Grundlage für Schriftvarianten in der gotischen Buchschrift,' *Scriptorium* 25 (1971) 25-45. 3 pls.

Seven 'variations' on *a* are documented from a wide range of MSS, and may form a basis on which to grade expressions of textual Gothic.

1105

Pirenne, H. 'L'Instruction des marchands au moyen age,' *Annales d'histoire économique et sociale* 1 (1929) 13-28

By the late 11th century, according to Pirenne, some merchants could read and write simple Latin; by the 12th and 13th centuries it was common for merchants to read and write Latin. This mercantile interest in Latin may account for the re-appearance of cursive script towards the end of the 12th century.

1106

Saint Thomas and Saint Bonaventure in the Vatican Library: Exhibit on their Seventh Centenary (1274-1974). Catalogue (Vatican City 1974). 34 pls.

28 of the plates are of MSS of their works. See also **1193**.

1107

Schiaparelli, L. 'Note paleografiche e diplomatiche ... 3. Influenza della scrittura beneventana sulla gotica?' *Archivio storico italiano* 7th ser. 9 (1929) 3-28; repr. in **68**, 437-62

Rejects outright the thesis of Dobiaš-Roždestvenskaja **1095**, arguing that the two scripts are dissimilar graphically.

1108

Wehmer, C. 'Die Namen der "Gotischen" Buchschriften,' *Zentralblatt für Bibliothekswesen* 49 (1932) 11-34, 169-76, 222-34.

FACSIMILES (GENERAL)

See also general collections such as **416, 419, 420-22, 424-5, 427-30, 433-4, 437, 440, 444-5**.

1109

Crous, E. and J. Kirchner. *Die gotischen Schriftarten* (Leipzig 1928). 64 pls. of MSS and printed books, with transcriptions.

1110

Kirchner, J. *Scriptura Gothica libraria a saeculo XII usque ad finem medii aevi* (Munich–Vienna 1966). 87 facs. with transcriptions

With Thomson **1112**, the best visual survey of 'Gothic' hands. For a review, with much adverse comment, see G.I. Lieftinck, *Scriptorium* 22 (1968) 66-71.

1111

Monaci, E. *Facsimili di documenti per la storia delle lingue e della letteratura romanze* (Rome 1910)

Has a portfolio of 65 plates of medieval Italian and French vernacular MSS.

1112

Thomson, S.H. *Latin Bookhands of the Later Middle Ages, 1100-1500* (Cambridge 1969). 132 pls. with partial transcriptions

For a review, with corrections of dating and transcription, see E. Van Balberghe, *Scriptorium* 25 (1971) 304-16.

1113

Viola, C.E. *Exercitationes palaeographiae iuris canonici, 1ª series.* 2 vols. (Rome 1970)

Provides 30 reproductions, with transcriptions, of texts of medieval canon law, 12th-13th centuries. Has excellent sections (I, 27-60, 176-223) on legal abbreviations and formulaic contractions. See also **1762, 1782-91**.

FACSIMILES AND STUDIES (VARIOUS REGIONS)

Austria, Germany, Switzerland

For some facsimiles see, for Austria: **271, 277, 302, 314-19** (*Manuscrits datés*); for Germany: **286, 300, 370, 421**; for Switzerland: **339-40** (*Manuscrits datés*), **411, 875-89** (Bruckner, *Scriptoria*).

1114

Adami Bremensis Gesta Hammaburgensis ecclesiae pontificum: Codex Havniensis, ed. C.A. Christensen (Copenhagen 1948)

Copenhagen, Koneglige Bibliotek, Gl. Kgl. Samml. 2296 4°. Adam (ob. 1081) taught in the cathedral school at Hamburg in 1066-7 under Archbishop Adalbert. Present codex, in very late Caroline verging on Gothic, is from ca. 1200. 75 folios. CF.

1115

Carmina Burana, ed. B. Bischoff (Munich 1967)

Munich, Bayerische Staatsbibliothek, MS. Clm 4660 (and 4660ª). Gothic. Written in Carinthia or Steiermark, mid-13th century. 119 folios. CF.

1116

Eis, G. *Altdeutsche Handschriften* (Munich 1949). 41 pls. with transcriptions.

1117

Fischer, H. *Schrifttafeln zum althochdeutschen Lesebuch* (Tübingen 1966).
24 pls. with transcriptions.

1118

Hildegard of Bingen. *Gebetbuch der Hl. Hildegard von Bingen: Faksimile
Ausgabe* (Wiesbaden 1981)
Munich, Bayerische Staatsbibliothek, Clm 935. Written in late Caroline,
belonged in the second half of the 12th century to Hildegard (1098-1179).
144 folios. CF (including special plates of 72 illustrations in the MS).
A volume of commentary is promised.

1119

Kirchner, J. *Germanistische Handschriftenpraxis: Ein Lehrbuch für die
Studierenden der deutschen Philologie*. 2nd ed. (Munich 1967). 12 pls.
with transcriptions.

1120

Koch, W. *Die Reichskanzlei in den Jahren 1167 bis 1174: Eine diplomatisch-
paläographische Untersuchung* (Vienna 1973). 32 pls.

1121

————. *Die Schrift der Reichskanzlei im 12. Jahrhundert (1125-1190):
Untersuchungen zur Diplomatik der Kaiserkunde* (Vienna 1979). 94 pls.
A minute examination of 'notarial' hands of the period.

1122

Kocher, A. *Mittelalterliche Handschriften aus dem Staatsarchiv Solothurn*
(Solothurn 1974). 75 pls. with transcriptions of documents from the 8th-
15th centuries.

1123

Das Nibelungen Lied, ed. H. Engels and E. Huber (London 1968)
Donaueschingen, Fürstlich Fürstenbergische Hofbibliothek, MS. 3. The
oldest known copy, shortly before A.D. 1220. 120 folios. CF.

1124

Scheurer, R. and M. Bubloz. *Fac-similés et transcriptions de reconnaissances,
de comptes, et de minutes d'actes notariés, XIVe-XVIIe siècle* (Neuchâtel
[1976]). 34 pls. with transcriptions.

1125

Wehmer, C. 'Augsburger Schreiber aus der Frühzeit des Buchdrucks,'
Beiträge zur Inkunabelkunde N.F. 1 (1935) 78-95; 2 (1938) 108-32.

Belgium, Holland

See for some facsimiles **320-23, 332-3** (*Manuscrits datés*), **368**.

1126
Annales Rodenses: Facsimile-uitgave, ed. P.C. Boeren and G.W.A. Pan-
huysen (Assen, Holland 1968)
Maastricht, Rijksarchief van Limburg, MS. s.n. Chronicle of the abbey of
Rode, A.D. 1104-57. 22 folios. CF (with transcription).
1127
Brouwer, H. *Atlas voor nederlandsche palaeographie* (Amsterdam 1945)
With 48 plates, mainly of charters from Dutch archives, A.D. 1290-1670.
1128
Brugmans, H. and O. Oppermann. *Atlas der nederlandsche palaeographie.*
2nd ed. (The Hague 1916). 28 pls.
1129
Cockshaw, P. 'Mentions d'auteurs, de copistes, d'enlumineurs, et de
libraires dans les comptes généraux de l'état Bourguignon (1384-1419),'
Scriptorium 23 (1969) 122-44.
1130
[Delaissé, L.M.J.]. *Le Siècle d'or de la miniature flamande: Le Mécénat de
Philippe le Bon* (Brussels 1959)
With 64 plates illustrating the patronage of Philip III, Count of Flanders
(A.D. 1419-67).
1131
Hulshof, A. *Deutsche und lateinische Schrift in den Niederlanden (1350-
1650).* Tabulae in usum scholarum 9 (Bonn 1918). 50 pls. with transcriptions.
1132
Lieftinck, G.I. *De Librijen en scriptoria der Westvlaamse Cistercienser-
abdijen Ter Duinen en Ter Doest in de 12ᵉ en 13ᵉ eeuw en de betrekkingen
tot het atelier van de kapittelschool van Sint Donatiaan te Brugge.* Mededelingen van de Koninkl.Vlaamse Academie voor wetenschappen, letteren,
en schone kunsten van Belgie 15.2 (Brussels 1953). 24 facs.; resumé in
French
An examination of Bernard's ideal (constitutions of Citeaux, art. 82) of
unostentatiousness in MSS in the light of extant MSS from two Flemish
Cistercian monasteries. Since MSS from Citeaux itself show that illumina-

tion was not at all uncommon there, the author asks what usefulness has Bernard's ideal when one is attempting to identify MSS as Cistercian.
1133
Nélis, H. 'De l'influence de la minuscule romaine sur l'écriture au XIIe et XIIIe siècles en Belgique,' *Bulletin de l'Institut historique belge de Rome* 3 (1924) 5-30
Shows that the origin of diplomatic cursive in use in Belgian areas was the script used in small papal bulls in the second half of the 12th century.
1134
Pirenne, H. *Album belge de diplomatique: Recueil de fac-similés pour servir à l'étude de diplomatique des provinces belges au moyen âge* (Brussels 1908). 32 pls.
1135
Stiennon, J. *L'Ecriture diplomatique dans le diocèse de Liège du XIe au milieu du XIIIe siècle* (Paris 1960). 358 pls. and figs.
Note especially ch. iv: 'De la caroline à la gothique (1145-1200),' pp. 207-293 and pls. 203-82.
1136
Van den Gheyn, J. *Album belge de paléographie: Recueil de spécimens d'écritures d'auteurs et de manuscrits belges (VIIe-XVIe siècles)* (Brussels 1908). 32 pls. with transcriptions.

England, Scotland, Wales

See in general **151, 155,** and for complete or partial facsimiles **331, 352, 363-4, 367, 371, 374-5, 377-81, 383, 388-9, 393, 395-6, 398, 402.**

1137
Anderson, A.O. and M.O. Anderson, eds. *Chronicle of Melrose* (London 1936) London, BL, MS. Cotton Faustina B. IX. Chronicle (A.D. 731-1275) written at the Cistercian Abbey of Melrose, Roxburghshire, Scotland, by various hands, 1236-75. 74 folios. CF.
1138
Anderson, J. *Selectus diplomatum et numismatum Scotiae thesaurus,* ed. T. Ruddimann (Edinburgh 1739). 180 reproductions.
1139
Baxter, J.H., ed. *An Old St. Andrews Music Book (Cod. Helmst. 628)* (London–Paris 1931)

Wolfenbüttel, Herzog August Bibliothek, MS. Helmst. 628. Textual Gothic
of the first half of the 14th century. Belonged to the cathedral church of
St. Andrews, Scotland, in the Middle Ages. 197 folios. CF.
1140
Bevington, D., ed. *The Macro Plays: The Castle of Perseverance. Wisdom.
Mankind* (New York 1972)
CF, with transcription (English and Latin), of Washington, D.C., Folger
Shakespeare Library, MS. V. a. 354, written ca. 1475.
1141
Bishop, T.A.M. *Scriptores regis: Facsimiles to Identify and Illustrate the
Hands of Royal Scribes in Original Charters of Henry I, Stephen, and
Henry II* (Oxford 1961)
Prints 40 plates, without transcriptions, of documents for the period 1100-
1189. Identifies the hands of 48 royal scribes in about 450 royal charters
(out of some 750 which survive for the period).
1142
Brieger, P., ed. *Trinity College Apocalypse.* 2 vols. (London 1967)
Cambridge, Trinity College, MS. 950 (R. 16. 2). Written and illuminated in
England between A.D. 1225 and 1250, perhaps at the Court of Westminster
32 folios. CF.
1143
Chaplais, P. *English Royal Documents, King John – Henry VI, 1199-1461*
(Oxford 1971). 27 pls. with transcriptions.
1144
————. *English Medieval Diplomatic Practice.* 2 vols. (London 1975).
60 pls. (A.D. 1197-1474) with transcriptions.
1145
Delisle, L. *Recueil des actes de Henri II roi d'Angleterre et duc de Norman-
die concernant les provinces françaises et les affaires de France: Atlas*
(Paris 1909)
30 plates, without transcriptions, illustrating 61 acts (A.D. 1154-89).
1146
Egbert, D.D. *The Tickhill Psalter and Related Manuscripts: A School of
Manuscript Illumination in England during the Early Fourteenth Century*
(New York 1940)
New York, Public Library, Spencer Coll., MS. 26. Psalter illustrated at
Worksop, Notts., A.D. 1303-14, by John Tickhill, Augustinian. 154 folios.
PF. 111 plates and 539 figures.

147

rieve, H.E.P. *Examples of English Handwriting 1150-1750, with Tran-ripts and Translations.* 2nd ed. (Chelmsford, Essex 1959)
8 plates of Essex parish and other records.

148

arrison, F. *Treasures of Illumination: English Manuscripts of the Four-enth Century (c. 1250 to 1400)* (London 1937)
4 plates of Trinity Apocalypse, Queen Mary Psalter, Ormesby Psalter, etc. vith a descriptive essay.

149

lassall, W.O., ed. *The Holkham Bible Picture Book* (London 1954)
ondon, BL, Add. MS. 47680. Anglo-Norman text, written and illustrated
a England ca. A.D. 1327. 42 folios. CF.

150

lenderson, G. 'Studies in English Manuscript Illumination,' *Journal of the Varburg and Courtauld Institutes* 30 (1967) 71-137; 31 (1968) 103-47.
9 pls.
)n Matthew Paris, the Dyson Perrins, Douce, and Lambeth Apocalypses,
tc.

151

Ker, N.R., ed. *The Owl and the Nightingale: Reproduced in Facsimile from he Surviving Manuscripts Jesus College Oxford 29 and British Museum Cotton Caligula A. IX.* EETS o.s. 251 (London 1963)
)xford, Jesus College, MS. 29, fols. 156r-168v; London, BL, MS. Cotton Caligula A. IX, fols. 233r-246v. Two MSS of the second half of the 13th entury, here in facsimile on facing pages. An early Middle English poem vritten in the first case (Jesus College) in a plain and simple 'amateur' Gothic hand, in the second case (BL) in heavy, professional Gothic script. CF.

152

————. *Facsimile of British Museum MS. Harley 2253.* EETS o.s. 255 London 1965)
London, BL, MS. Harley 2253, fols. 49r-140v. Prose and verse in French and English, written in one hand in, probably, A.D. 1340-50, and 'at a critical time in the history of the script, when scribes were trying to find a book hand which was not so difficult to write on a small scale as the raditional textura' (p. xviii). PF (fols. 49r-140v).

1153

————. *The Winchester Malory: A Facsimile.* EETS s.s. 4 (London 19⁷.
London, BL, Add. MS. 59678. A paper MS written in English towards the
of the 15th century by two scribes, one of whom (B) writes a plain secret
hand, the other (A) a mixture of Anglicana and secretary. 473 folios. CF.

1154

Millar, E.G. *English Illuminated Manuscripts from the Xth to the XIIIth
Century* (Paris – Brussels 1926). 100 pls.

1155

————. *English Illuminated Manuscripts of the XIVth to the XVth
Century* (Paris – Brussels 1928). 100 pls.

1156

————. *The Luttrell Psalter* (London 1932)
London, BL, Add. MS. 42130. Illustrated Latin psalter, written in East
Anglia ca. A.D. 1340. 309 folios. PF. 190 plates.

1157

Newton, K.C. *Medieval Local Records: A Reading Aid* (London 1971)
12 plates, with transcriptions and translations, showing English records ca
A.D. 1185-1498.

Ordnance Survey Office, London:

1158

[A] *Domesday Book, or the Great Survey of William the Conqueror,*
ed. W.B. Sanders. 2 vols. (Southampton 1861, 1864)
London, Public Record Office, two MS volumes of unequal size.

1159

[B] *Facsimiles of National Manuscripts from William the Conqueror to
Queen Anne,* ed. W.B. Sanders. 4 vols. (Southampton 1865-8). 341 pls

1160

[C] *Facsimiles of National Manuscripts of Scotland,* ed. C. Innes. 3 vol
(Southampton 1867-72). 272 pls.

1161

[D] *Facsimiles of Anglo-Saxon Manuscripts,* ed. W.B. Sanders. 3 vols.
(Southampton 1878-84). 121 pls.

1162

[E] *Facsimiles of National Manuscripts of Ireland:* see **680-85**.

1163

Parkes, M.B. *English Cursive Bookhands 1250-1500* (Oxford 1959, repr.

ondon 1979). 24 pls., chiefly of Anglicana, with transcriptions.

164

earsall, D. and I.C. Cunningham, eds. *The Auckinleck Manuscript* (London
977)
dinburgh, National Library of Scotland, Advocates' MSS, MS. 19. 2. 1.
. facsimile of one of the most important surviving MSS of medieval English
oetry, written ca. A.D. 1330-40 by six scribes. Has a useful codicological
itroduction. 334 folios. CF.

165

ollard, G. 'William de Brailes,' *The Bodleian Library Record* 5 (1955)
02-9. See also **388**.

166

tickert, M. *Painting in Britain: The Middle Ages* (London 1954). 192 pls.

167

tuggiers, P.G., ed. *The Canterbury Tales. Geoffrey Chaucer. A Facsimile
nd Transcription of the Hengwrt Manuscript with Variants from the
'llesmere Manuscript.* Variorum Edition of the Works of Geoffrey Chaucer
(Norman, Okla.–Folkestone 1979)
.berystwyth, National Library of Wales, MS. Peniarth 392 ('Hengwrt'),
robably the earliest surviving copy (ca. 1400) of *Canterbury Tales;* San
1arino, California, Huntington Library, MS. EL 26 C9. With a careful
Palaeographical Introduction' by A.I. Doyle and M.B. Parkes, pp. xix-xlix.
50 folios. CF with facing text.

168

tycraft, A. *English Medieval Handwriting.* 3rd ed. (York 1973)
2 plates, with transcriptions, of Middle English wills, matrimonial cases,
tc., A.D. 1357-1491.

169

iandler, L.F. *The Peterborough Psalter in Brussels and Other Fenland
Manuscripts, with 346 Illustrations* (London 1974)
Treats of the Peterborough Psalter, Ramsey Psalter, Gough Psalter, Canonici
nd Crowland Apocalypses, all early 14th century.

170

iimpson, G.G. *Scottish Handwriting 1150-1650: An Introduction to the
Reading of Documents* (Edinburgh 1973). 30 pls. with transcriptions.

171

Turner, D.H. *Early Gothic Illuminated Manuscripts in England* (London

1965)
British Library booklet, with 20 plates (4 in colour) of illuminated MSS of the period 1250-1300.
1172
Van den Gheyn, J. *Le Psautier de Peterborough* (Haarlem 1909)
Brussels, Bibliothèque royale, MS. 9961-2. Written in Gothic and illuminated at Peterborough Abbey, Northamptonshire, in the 13th century. 141 folios. PF. 33 plates, 62 figures.
1173
Wright, C.E. *English Vernacular Hands from the Twelfth to the Fifteenth Centuries* (Oxford 1960). 24 pls. with transcriptions.

France

See in general **138, 422-3,** and for various complete or partial facsimiles **288, 290, 324-30** (*Manuscrits datés*), **342-3, 369, 372, 392, 397, 403, 40 414.**

1174
Avril, F. *Manuscript Painting at the Court of France: The Fourteenth Century* (New York 1978). 40 pls.
1175
Beer, E.J. 'Das Scriptorium des Johannes Philomena und seine Illumina-toren: Zur Buchmalerei in der Region Arras-Cambrai 1250 bis 1274,' *Scriptorium* 23 (1969) 24-38. 10 pls.
1176
Branner, R. *Manuscript Painting in Paris during the Reign of Saint Louis: A Study of Styles* (Berkeley, Calif. 1977). 412 illustrations
An attempt to identify and study MS paintshops active in Paris in the middle of the 13th century.
1177
Broc, J., J. Fabre, L. Martin, and B. Montagnes. *Testaments provençaux du moyen âge: Documents paléographiques* (Avignon 1979)
11 facsimiles, with transcriptions, of wills from Provence, mostly in Latin A.D. 1354-1516.
1178
Delisle, L. *Fac-simile de livres copiés et enluminés pour le roi Charles V* (Paris 1903). 15 pls. (A.D. 1362-79).

179

Vammeront, J. *Album paléographique du Nord de la France* (Lille 1896)
5 plates of charters and other documents, A.D. 1036-1655, with partial
transcriptions.

180

Valabert, F. and C. Lassalle. *Album de paléographie et de diplomatique:
fac-similés phototypiques de documents relatifs à l'histoire du Midi de la
France et en particulier à la ville de Toulouse.* 4 pts. (Toulouse–Paris
1912-23). 40 pls. with transcriptions.

181

Gasparri, F. 'Etudes sur l'écriture de la Chancellerie royale française de
Louis VI à Philippe Auguste, d'après vingt-cinq actes originaux jusqu'ici
inconnus,' *BEC* 126 (1968) 297-331. 2 pls. of 4 acts.

182

———. *L'Ecriture des actes de Louis VI, Louis VII, et Philippe Auguste*
(Geneva–Paris 1973). 70 pls. of 79 charters
Studies charters from A.D. 1108-1220. Concludes that, until the beginning of the 13th century, monks whose usual scribal occupation was copying MSS were pressed into service by the royal chancery to write charters.
Hence the script of charters is often 'book hand' as such, and there is no
diplomatic 'homogeneity.' Circa 1180 lay scribes began to take over the
writing of charters, and multiplicity gave way to unity, witnessing to new
economic and social stability and to the strength of royal power.

183

———. 'La Chancellerie du roi Louis VII et ses rapports avec le scriptorium de l'abbaye de Saint-Victor de Paris' in **31**, II, 151-8
The period is A.D. 1131-80.

184

Gessler, J. *Une bibliothèque scolaire du XIᵉ siècle d'après le catalogue
provenant de l'abbaye d'Anchin* (Brussels–Paris 1935)
Edits the catalogue of what is presumed to be the students' library (as
distinct from that of monks) from Brussels, Bibliothèque royale, MS.
828-30, a codex from Anchin near Douai, 313 of whose MSS are now at
Douai.

185

Gould, K. *The Psalter and Hours of Yolande of Soissons.* Speculum Anniversary Monographs 4 (Cambridge, Mass. 1978). 68 pls.
A study of New York, Pierpont Morgan Library, MS. M. 729, ca. 1275-85.

1186

Jeanroy, A. *Le Chansonnier d'Arras, reproduction en phototypie* (Paris 1925)

Arras, Bibliothèque municipale, MS. 139, fols. 129r-160v. Gothic, A.D. 1250-1300.

1187

Martin, H. *Le Miniature française du XIIIe au XVe siècle* (Paris 1923). 134 illustrations.

1188

Meiss, M. *French Painting in the Time of Jean de Berry: The Late Four teenth Century and the Patronage of the Duke.* 2 vols. (London 1967), 845 illustrations; (with K. Morand and E.W. Kirsch) *The Boucicaut Master* (London 1968), 497 ill.; (with S.O. Dunlap Smith and E. Home Beatson) *The Limbourgs and their Contemporaries.* 2 vols. (New York 1974), 898 ill.

For the first two vols. see L.M.J. Delaissé, *The Art Bulletin* 52 (1970) 206-12, with valuable notes on book production during the lifetime of Duke Jean de Berry (A.D. 1340-1416).

1189

Morand, K.B. *Jean Pucelle* (Oxford 1962). 33 pls.

Notes that Pucelle was active as an illuminator at Paris and elsewhere ca A.D. 1320-34.

1190

Romanova, V.L. *Rukopisnaja kniga i gotičeskoe pis'mo vo Francii v XI XIV vv.* (Moscow 1975)

On the Gothic script in France, 13th-14th centuries.

1191

Stones, M.A. 'Secular Manuscript Illumination in France' in *Medieval Manuscripts and Textual Criticism,* ed. C. Kleinhenz (Chapel Hill, N.C. 1976) 83-102. 17 pls.

Covers illumination of MSS of secular content (*Roman de la Rose,* etc.) Excellent bibliography.

1192

Thomas, M. *The Golden Age: Manuscript Painting at the Time of Jean, Duc de Berry* (London 1969). 59 illustrations.

1193

La Vie universitaire parisienne au XIIIe siècle (Paris 1974)

A catalogue, with 7 plates of MSS, of the exposition at the Sorbonne in

1974 to commemorate Robert de Sorbon, Bonaventure, Thomas Aquinas, and the Second Council of Lyons (A.D. 1274). See also **1106**.

Italy

See in general **160-75** (Archivio paleografico italiano), **334-5** (*Manuscrits datés*), **436**; and for various complete or partial facsimiles **196** (Petrarch), **203** (Dante), **206** (Villani), **209, 211** (Boccaccio), **216, 221-2** (Padua), **225, 241** (Catullus), **270, 282, 349, 384**.

194
Berg, K. *Studies in Tuscan Twelfth-Century Illumination* (Oslo – Bergen – Tromsö 1968). 509 figs.

195
Buchthal, H. 'A School of Miniature Painting in Norman Sicily' in *Late Classical and Mediaeval Studies in Honor of Albert Mathias Friend, Jr.* Princeton 1955) 312-39. 6 pls.

196
Casula, F.C. *Breve storia della scrittura in Sardegna: La 'documentaria' nell'epoca aragonese* (Cagliari [1978])
?6 plates, with transcriptions, of documents in Gothic, chancery, and other scripts, 13th-17th centuries.

197
Cau, E. 'Codici cisterciensi di Rivalta Scrivia (secoli XIII-XIV),' *RM* 10-12 1975-7) 19-29. 2 pls. of 4 MSS
Makes important observations, in connection with these MSS from Rivalta Scrivia (Alessandria), on the relationship of documentary hands to the emergence of 'Gothic' script.

198
Cencetti, G. 'Note di diplomatica vescovile bolognese dei secoli XI-XIII' in **4**, 159-223. 4 pls.
Deals with documents of A.D. 1189-1290.

199
Daneu-Lattanzi, A. 'Di un manoscritto miniato eseguito a Palermo nel terzo quarto del secolo XII,' *Accademie e biblioteche* 32 (1964) 225-36, 309-20 Interesting on the introduction of Gothic to Sicily.

200
Dante Alighieri. *Il codice Trivulziano 1080 della Divina Commedia*, ed. L.

Rocca (Milan 1921)
Milan, Biblioteca Trivulziana, MS. 1080. Italian Gothic, written at Florence
in A.D. 1337, by Ser Francesco di Ser Nardo de Barberino. 107 folios. CF.

1201
*Diplomi imperiali e reali delle cancellerie d'Italia pubblicati a facsimile dalle
R. Società romana di storia patria* (Rome 1892-)
Seemingly only one fascicule, with 15 plates, was published. The diplomata
run from A.D. 769-1200.

1202
Federici, V. *La scrittura delle cancellerie italiane dal sec. XII al XVII.* 2
vols. (Rome 1934, repr. Turin 1964)
114 plates, with transcriptions, including plates of literary and documentary hands prior to the span specified in the title.

1203
Gallo, A. 'La scrittura curiale napoletana nel medio evo,' *Bullettino dell'
Istituto storico italiano* 45 (1929) 17-112.

1204
Garrison, E.B. *Studies in the History of Medieval Italian Painting.* 4 vols.
(Florence 1953-62)
Each essay is nicely illustrated.

1205
Mazzoleni, J. *Esempi di scritture cancelleresche, curiali, e minuscole*
(Naples [1972])
30 plates, with transcriptions, mostly of South Italian documentary and
literary scripts, A.D. 762-1493.

1206
*La miniatura italiana in età romanica e gotica: Atti del I Congresso di
storia della miniatura italiana* (Florence 1979)
Acts of a congress at Cortona in 1978. See **1215**.

1207
Orlandelli, G. 'Ricerche sulla origine della "Littera Bononiensis": Scritture
documentarie bolognesi del sec. XII,' *BAPI* 2nd ser. 2-3 pt. II (1956-7)
179-214. 6 pls.

1208
————. 'Osservazioni sulla scrittura mercantesca nei secoli XIV e XV' in
Studi in onore di Riccardo Filangieri (Naples 1959) I, 445-60.

1209
Pagnin, B. *Le origini della scrittura gotica padovana* (Padua 1933). 12 pls.

1210

————. 'La "Littera bononiensis": Studio paleografico,' *Atti del R. Istituto veneto di scienze, lettere, ed arti* 93/2 (1933-4) 1593-1665; repr. in *RM* 10-12 (1975-7) 93-168, with 4 new pls. replacing those of 1933-4
Says that Littera bononiensis was in existence by ca. 1180, and is recognized as distinct, together with Littera parisiensis, etc., in a list of books given in 1219 by Cardinal Guala Bichieri to Vercelli (see **1700**). A list of 206 codices in the Littera is in *RM* at pp. 154-68. See also **1207**.

1211

Petrarch. *Francisci Petrarcae Vergilianus codex,* ed. G. Galbiati (Milan 1930)
Milan, Biblioteca Ambrosiana, MS. A 79 inf. Works of Vergil with scholia of Servius, written in Italian Gothic (Rotunda) towards the end of the 13th century. Belonged to and annotated by Petrarch. 269 folios. CF.

1212

Petrarch. *Petrarque: Vie de César,* ed. L. Dorez (Paris 1906)
Paris, BN, MS. lat. 5784. *De gestis Caesaris.* An autograph of Petrarch just before his death in 1374. 49 folios. CF.

1213

Petrucci, A. *Notarii: Documenti per la storia del notariato italiano* (Milan 1958)
85 plates of documents, all described and transcribed, A.D. 726-1802. See also **1264**.

1214

Petrus de Ebulo: Nomina et virtutes balneorum seu De balneis Puteolorum et Baiarum, ed. A. Daneu-Lattanzi. 2 vols. (Rome 1962)
Rome, Biblioteca Angelica, MS. 1474. Written at Naples ca. 1250-75. 23 folios. CF. See also **1039**.

1215

Pettenati, S. 'Alcuni codici bolognesi del XIII secolo della Biblioteca nazionale di Torino' in **1206**, 327-42
13 plates of MSS written at Bologna in the 13th century.

1216

Pratesi, A. 'La scrittura latina nell'Italia meridionale nell'età di Federico II,' *Archivio storico pugliese* 25 (1972) 299-316.

Papal Curia

See also **201** (Innocent III), **208** (Vatican Library), **427-9** (Exempla scripturarum), **801, 824, 1505** (Vatican Archives).

1217
Bock, F. *Einführung in das Registerwesen des avignonesischen Papsttums* (Rome 1941)
Includes an album of 39 plates illustrating the Registra Avenionensia and related registers of papal letters, A.D. 1317-78.
1218
[Denifle, H.-S. and G. Palmieri]. *Specimina palaeographica ex Vaticani tabularii Romanorum pontificum registris selecta ... ab Innocentio III ad Urbanum V* (Rome 1888). 60 pls.
1219
Katterbach, B. *Specimina supplicationum ex registris vaticanis* (Rome 1927)
50 plates, without transcriptions, of samples from papal registers of letters of supplication in the Vatican Archives, A.D. 1345-1823.

Portugal, Spain

See also **7**, 150-55; **140, 142, 145, 784.**

1220
Arribas Arranz, F. *Paleografía documental hispanica.* 2 vols. (Valladolid 1965). 129 pls. (A.D. 812-1641) with transcriptions.
1221
Burnam, J.M. *Palaeographia iberica: Fac-similés de manuscrits espagnols et portugais (IXe-XVe siècles).* 2 vols. (Paris 1912, 1925). 60 pls. with transcriptions.
1222
Mateu Ibars, J. *Paleografía de Andalucia oriental.* 2 vols. (Granada 1973, 1977)
Vol. I is an album of 93 plates of vernacular documents, A.D. 1368-1796; II includes transcriptions (by E. de Lapresa Molina, etc.), a detailed palaeographical and diplomatic introduction, and a list of abbreviations.

1223
Muñoz y Rivero, J. *Manuel de paleografía diplomática española*. 2nd ed.
(Madrid 1917, repr. 1972)
240 reproductions, with transcriptions, of documents of the 12th-17th
centuries.
1224
Nunes, E. *Album de paleografia portuguesa*, I (Lisbon 1969)
60 plates, with some 170 samples, largely of documents, A.D. 999-1712.

Scandinavia

GENERAL

1225
Brøndum-Nielsen, J. and D.A. Seip. *Palaeografi.* 2 vols. (Stockholm –
Oslo – Copenhagen 1943, 1954)
Vol. I, *Palaeografi A. Danmark og Sverige* (1943), by Brøndum-Nielsen,
has 66 figures of Latin and vernacular, all transcribed. II, *Palaeografi B.
Norge og Island* (1954), by Seip, has 55 figures (without transcriptions).

DENMARK

1226
Nielsen, L. *Danmarks middelalderlige Haantskriften* (Copenhagen 1937)
Provides some 1500 samples from Danish medieval MSS.
1226a
Simon, G. *Gotisk Scrift: Laesning af slaegts- og lokalhistoriske kilder*
(Copenhagen 1977)
On Gothic script in medieval Danish MSS and documents.
1227
Corpus codicum Danicorum medii aevi, ed. J. Brøndum-Nielsen (Copen-
hagen 1960-)
To date, 10 volumes have appeared, e.g. I, *Necrologium Lundense*, ed.
E. Kroman (1960): Lund, Universitetsbiblioteket, MS. medeltid. 6,
spanning the years 1223-1316.

FINLAND

1228

CODICES MEDII AEVI FINLANDIAE, ed. Societas Finlandiae historica
(Copenhagen 1950-)
To date, 2 volumes have appeared:
1229
I. *Registrum ecclesiae Aboensis,* ed. J. Jaakkola (1950)
Stockholm, Antikvitets- och Riksarkivet, MS. A. 10. Written at Abo,
ca. A.D. 1468. Parchment. 333 folios. CF.
1230
II. *Codex Särkilahti (Codex Aboensis Skokloster),* ed. J. Jaakkola
(1950)
Stockholm, Antikvitets- och Riksarkivet, MS. Coll. Skokl. in fol. 70.
Completed at Skokloster in A.D. 1486. Parchment. 127 folios. CF.

ICELAND

1231

Benediktsson, H. *Early Icelandic Script as Illustrated in Vernacular
Texts from the Twelfth and Thirteenth Centuries* (Reykjavik 1965).
78 pls. with transcriptions
With introduction on the beginnings of writing in Iceland ca. A.D. 1150
1232
CORPUS CODICUM ISLANDICORUM MEDII AEVI, ed. E. Munksgaard.
20 vols. (Copenhagen 1930-56)
See e.g.:
VII. *Icelandic Illuminated Manuscripts of the Middle Ages,* ed. H.
Hermannsson (1935). 80 pls.;
XVIII. *The Arna-Magnaean Manuscript 677 4ᵗᵒ: Pseudo-Cyprian Frag-
ments, Prosper's Epigrams, Gregory's Homilies and Dialogues,* ed. D.
Arup Seip (1949)
Copenhagen, Universitetsbiblioteket, MS. AM 677 4ᵗᵒ. Written ca. A.D.
1200. 41 folios. CF.
1233
Early Icelandic Manuscripts in Facsimile, ed. J. Helgason (Copenhagen
1958-)
12 volumes were published to 1980.

1234
Helgason, J. *Handritaspjall* (Reykjavik 1958). 25 pls. of vernacular MSS.
1235
Manuscripta Islandica, ed. J. Helgason (Copenhagen 1954-)
7 volumes were published to 1966.
1236
Spehr, H. *Der Ursprung der isländischen Schrift und ihre Weiterbildung bis zur Mitte des XIII. Jahrhunderts* (Halle am Salle 1929).

NORWAY

1237
Corpus codicum Norvegicorum medii aevi, ed. D. Arup Seip. Folio series (Oslo 1950-), Quarto series (1952-)
2 volumes to 1960 in folio series, 5 volumes to 1974 in quarto.

SWEDEN

1238
CODICES MEDII AEVI E BIBLIOTHECA REGIA HOLMENSI SELECTI
(Stockholm 1920-):
I. *Acta et processus canonizationis Sanctae Birgittae,* ed. I. Collijn (1920)
Stockholm, Kungl. Biblioteket, MS. A. 14. Written in Sweden, A.D.
1378-80. Belonged at one time to Vadstena. Cursive Gothic. Paper. 253
folios. CF. See also **336-8** (*Manuscrits datés*).
1239
CORPUS CODICUM SUECICORUM MEDII AEVI, ed. E. Wessén (Copenhagen
1943-)
20 volumes were published to 1967, e.g. (Latin volumes only):
  1240
  II. *Processus seu negocium canonizacionis B. Katherine de Vadstenis,*
  ed. I. Collijn (1943)
  Stockholm, Kungl. Biblioteket, MS. A. 93. Sweden, A.D. 1477. 152
  folios. CF.
  1241
  III. *Vita et miracula S. Erici regis Sueciae,* ed. A. Nelson (1944)
  Vatican City, BAV, MS. Reg. lat. 525. Sweden, 15th century. 38
  folios (Latin and Old Swedish). CF.

1242

VII. *Liber de miraculis beate Brigide de Suecia: Roma 1378,* ed. I.
Collijn (1946)
Rome, Archivio di S. Lorenzo in Panisperna, MS. s.n. Written at
Rome by Nicholas Misner or Vögeler, a cleric from Brandenburg, in
1378. 54 folios. CF.

1243

XI. *Liber privilegiorum Monasterii Vadstenensis,* ed. E. Nygren
(1950)
Stockholm, Antikvitets- och Riksarkivet, MS. A. 19. Written at
Vadstena, ca. 1400. 183 folios. CF.

1244

XIII, XIV. *Revelationes S. Birgittae,* ed. E. Wessén. 2 vols. (1952,
1956)
Lund, Universitetsbiblioteket, MS. 21 fol. Written in Sweden by
Johannes Johannis Kalmarnensis, ca. 1404-7. 360 folios. CF.

1245

XVI. *Diarium Vadstenense ('Vadstena Klosters Minnesbok'),* ed.
E. Nygren (1963)
Uppsala, Universitetsbiblioteket, MS. C 89. A 'diary' in Latin of the
Brigittine abbey of Vadstena beginning in 1344 and continuing until
the 16th century, in a succession of hands writing a remarkably
uniform (at least until ca. 1500) notular hand. 232 folios. CF.

Slavonic Areas, Eastern Europe

1246

Flodr, M. *Skriptorium olomoucké: K počatkům písařské tvorby v českých
zemích* (Prague 1960)
On the beginnings of written culture in Czech regions.

1247

Geitler, L. *Die albanesischen und slavischen Schriften* (Vienna 1883).
25 pls.

1248

Hocij, M. 'Die westlichen Grundlagen des glagolitischen Alphabets,' *Südost-
deutsche Forschungen* 4 (1940) 509-20.

1249

Jakó, S. and R. Manolescu. *Scrierea latina in evul mediu* (Bucharest 1971)

Makes special reference to the evolution of Latin script in Roumania. Has 91 illustrations, often derivative (from Battelli, Steffens, etc.), but with some original material from Roumanian libraries, e.g. the Batthyaneum at Alba Julia. There are resumés in French and German.

1250
Molnár, J. and S. Györgyi. *Magyar nyelvemlékek* (Budapest 1976) Provides 50 plates illustrating Latin and vernacular hands in Hungary, ca. A.D. 1055-1594.

1251
Vaillant, A. 'L'Ecriture cyrillique et son extension' in **456**, 301-12.

1252
Vîrtosu, E. *Paleografia Româno Chirilică* (Bucharest 1968). 61 pls.

Period of Humanist Culture and Beyond

HUMANISTIC SCRIPT

For some complete or partial facsimiles of humanist manuscripts see **240**, **247**, and **279**.

Humanistic script is the name generally given (see **1269**) to the clear, readable script which appears to have been an invention ca. A.D. 1402 of the young humanist Poggio Bracciolini, probably at the instance of Coluccio Salutati (1331-1406), then about to complete some twenty-five years as chancellor of Florence and, at the age of over seventy, faced, as he had been for some time, with failing eyesight (see **1286**, and for Salutati's own hand, **1264**). The script Poggio devised eliminated Uncial *d*, resorted to round *s* only at the end of a line, and avoided as far as possible that biting of curves which is a Gothic characteristic. It was in effect a revival of Caroline writing – not, however, of the classic Caroline of the ninth century but of the Italian Rotunda of the eleventh or twelfth, a variant which Salutati himself seems to have been fond of, calling it on occasion 'littera antiqua' or 'littera italica' (see **1273**, **1283**). The script quickly won adherents, and Poggio, who joined the papal chancery from Florence in 1404 at the age of twenty-four and worked there as a scriptor for nearly fifty years, had a number of personal disciples, notably Giovanni Aurispa and Sozomen of Pistoia in the first twenty years of the existence of the script. Florence, however, where about 1410 Giovanni Aretino was the first recognizable scrivener to be won over, continued to be the chief centre of the script (see **1276, 1280**) until 1440, and particularly in the period 1420-40 when Ambrogio Traversari and Niccolò Niccoli were among its most strenuous proponents. But there was a difference in Niccoli's case. Where the immediate disciples of Poggio copied faithfully Poggio's round, upright Littera formata, Niccoli appears to have advocated a rapid calligraphic hand as an alternative. By 1430 this 'Niccoli' hand was gaining acceptance as a bookhand, possibly because it appealed to the many notaries who doubled as scriveners and therefore were perfectly at home with rapid hands. Niccoli's rapid hand seems to have been influential at Venice and Padua, and possibly it was in the Veneto that it was turned into 'Italic.' The italic version of Niccoli's hand spread rapidly all over Italy; a form of it was adopted by the papal chancery ca. 1440 (see **1280**), and thence it is known as 'cancelleresca,' a script firmly advocated and propagated by the writing manuals of the sixteenth century, notably by the first writing manual of all, that of Ludovico Arrighi (see **1282**). By now, of course, printed books were the order of the day and the copying of manuscripts had become an artificial, luxury occupation on the part of the few remaining scriveners. But the fine hands of Poggio and Niccoli were not without some impact on printing, too: by 1480-90 the script of Poggio had inspired the Roman font, and in 1501 the Aldine press at Venice developed the Italic font from a crossing of the rapid hand of Niccoli with its italic variation.

General

1253
Alexander, J.J.G. *Italian Renaissance Illuminations* (New York 1977)
Prints 40 plates, with introduction and commentary.
1254
Alexander, J.J.G. and A.C. de la Mare. *The Italian Manuscripts in the Library of Major J.R. Abbey* (London 1969). 80 pls.
1255
Howie, D.I. 'Benedictine Monks, Manuscript Copying, and the Renaissance Johannes Trithemius' *De laude scriptorum*,' *RB* 86 (1976) 129-54.
1256
[Hunt, R.W. and A.C. de la Mare]. *Duke Humfrey and English Humanism*

in the Fifteenth Century (Oxford 1970). 24 pls.
The catalogue of an exhibition at the Bodleian Library, Oxford, to commemorate Humfrey, Duke of Gloucester (1390-1447), whose first gift of books to the University was in 1439, and included a significant number of classical and humanistic texts.

1257
Mardersteig, G. 'Leon Battista Alberti e la rinascita del carattere lapidario romano nel Quattrocento,' *IMU* 2 (1959) 285-307. 6 pls.

1258
Marinelli-Marcacci, O. 'Codici e copisti a Perugia nel secolo XV' in *Xenia medii aevi historiam illustrantia oblata Thomae Kaeppeli O.P.,* ed. R. Creytens and P. Künzle. 2 vols. (Rome 1978) II, 547-66.

1259
Meiss, M. *Andrea Mantegna as Illuminator: An Episode in Renaissance Art, Humanism, and Diplomacy* (New York 1957)
Notes that in NE Italy, Padua in particular, from ca. A.D. 1460, forms and proportions of initials began to be based on seriphed square capitals in Roman inscriptions, possibly through Mantegna.

1260
————. 'Toward a more Comprehensive Renaissance Palaeography,' *The Art Bulletin* 42 (1960) 97-112. 36 figs.
Makes much the same point as the previous entry.

1261
Morison, S. 'Early Humanistic Script and the First Roman Type,' *The Library* 4th ser. 24 (1943-4) 1-29. 21 facs.; repr. with additional material in **65**, I, 206-21
Particularly on the script of Niccolò Niccoli. There is a list of 28 dated MSS in Humanistic script, A.D. 1408-65, at pp. 219-21. See also **1271**.

1262
————. *Byzantine Elements in Humanistic Script illustrated from the Aulus Gellius of 1445 in the Newberry Library* (Chicago 1952). 1 pl.
On Chicago, Newberry Library, MS. Wing Add. 90. Written by Milanus Burrus in A.D. 1445, possibly in Milan.

1263
Ouy, G. 'Autographes calligraphiés et scriptoria d'humanistes en France vers 1400,' *Bulletin philologique et historique: Comité des travaux historiques et scientifiques* 10 (1963) 891-8.

1264

Petrucci, A. *Il protocollo notarile di Coluccio Salutati (1372-1373)* (Milan 1963)

Florence, Archivio di Stato, Notarile Antecosimiano C.586. 42 private documents as entered by Coluccio into his notebook. Provides 16 plates illustrating Coluccio's hand. See also **1284**.

1265

————. 'Scrittura, alfabetismo, ed educazione grafica nella Roma del primo Cinquecento: Da un libretto di conti di Maddalena pizzicarola in Trastevere,' *SC* 2 (1978) 163-207. 12 pls.

There are over 100 hands in this account-book, writing variously in forms of 'mercantesca' (Gothic) or 'Italian' (Humanist).

1266

————, ed. *Libri, scrittura, e pubblico nel Rinascimento: Guida storica e critica* (Rome–Bari 1979)

Reprints essays of C. Bühler, P. Goldschmidt, Alfredo Petrucci, Armando Petrucci, J. Ruysschaert.

1267

Ullman, B.L. *The Humanism of Coluccio Salutati* (Padua 1963). 19 pls.

1268

Weiss, R. *Humanism in England during the Fifteenth Century*. 3rd ed. (Oxford 1967).

Handwriting

1269

Battelli, G. 'Nomenclature des écritures humanistiques' in **1701**, 35-44. 10 figs.

1270

Bernardinello, S. *Autografi greci e greco-latini in Occidente* (Padua 1979)

A palaeographical analysis of Greek and Greco-Latin writing in the West, A.D. 1291-1599, with 110 plates.

1271

Butrica, J.L. 'A New Fragment in Niccoli's Formal Hand,' *Scriptorium* 35 (1981) 290-92

Discusses what is possibly Niccolò Niccoli's earliest piece of writing (Florence, Biblioteca nazionale, MS. II IX 125), 'close to 1400,' when his formal hand is still in an experimental stage.

1272
Caroti, S. and S. Zamponi. *Io scrittoio di Bartolomeo Fonzio umanista fiorentino* (Milan 1974). 48 pls.
A study of the productions of a Florentine exponent (A.D. 1445-1513) of the Littera antiqua.

1273
Casamassima, E. 'Lettere antiche: Note per la storia della riforma grafica umanistica,' *Gutenberg Jahrbuch* 39 (1964) 13-26
On the origin and meaning of the term *littera antiqua* or *litterae antiquae*. See also **1283**.

1274
De la Mare, A.C. *The Handwriting of Italian Humanists,* I (Oxford 1973-)
The first fascicule in this series covers Florence and its libraries, and the hands of Petrarch, Boccaccio, Coluccio Salutati, Poggio Bracciolini, Niccolò Niccoli, etc. in MSS there. Prints 25 plates of hands.

1275
Dunston, A.J. 'The Hand of Poggio,' *Scriptorium* 19 (1965) 63-70, with a reply by B.L. Ullman, pp. 71-5
The MSS discussed are Vatican City, BAV, MSS. Vat. lat. 1843, 1849, and 1852 (1st, 3rd, and 4th decades of Livy).

1276
Elder, J.P. 'Clues for Dating Florentine Humanistic Manuscripts,' *Studies in Philology* 44 (1947) 127-39.

1277
Fairbank, A.J. and R.W. Hunt. *Humanistic Script of the Fifteenth and Sixteenth Centuries* (Oxford 1960)
A pamphlet in the Bodleian Picture Book series, with 24 plates.

1278
Fairbank, A.J. and B. Wolpe. *Renaissance Handwriting: An Anthology of Italic Scripts* (London 1960). 96 pls.

1279
Fairbank, A.J. and B. Dickens. *The Italic Hand in Tudor Cambridge* (London 1962). 24 pls.

1280
Frenz, T. 'Das Eindringen humanistischer Schriftformen in die Urkunden und Akten der päpstlichen Kurie im 15. Jahrhundert,' *Archiv für Diplomatik* 19 (1973) 287-418; 20 (1974) 384-506. 18 pls.
On the stages of Humanist script in the papal curia from its first appear-

ance there under Eugene IV at Florence, A.D. 1434-6, to 1500.

1281
Hessel, A. 'Die Entstehung der Renaissanceschriften,' *Archiv für Urkundenforschung* 13 (1935) 1-14. 2 pls.

1282
Ogg, O. *Three Classics of Italian Calligraphy: An Unabridged Reissue of the Writing Books of Arrighi, Tagliente, Palatino* (New York 1953).

1283
Orlandelli, G. *'Littera nova' e 'Littera antiqua' tra glossatori e umanisti* (Bologna 1964)
See also **1273**.

1284
Ross, B. 'Salutati's Defeated Candidate for Humanistic Script,' *SC* 5 (1981) 187-98
A discussion of stages of experimentation immediately before the 'invention' of humanistic script ca. A.D. 1400, chiefly in MSS written by or connected with Coluccio Salutati (1331-1406).

1285
Tannenbaum, S.A. *The Handwriting of the Renaissance* (New York 1930). 14 pls.

1286
Ullman, B.L. *The Origin and Development of Humanistic Script* (Rome 1960). 70 facs.

1287
Vogel, M. and V. Gardthausen. *Die griechischen Schreiber des Mittelalters und der Renaissance*. Zentralblatt für Bibliothekswesen. Beiheft 33 (Leipzig 1909).

1288
Wardrop, J. *The Script of Humanism: Some Aspects of Humanistic Script 1460-1560* (Oxford 1963). 58 facs.

BEYOND

1289
Dawson, G.E. and L. Kennedy-Skipton. *Elizabethan Handwriting 1500-1650* (London–New York 1966). 50 pls. with transcriptions.

1290
Dülfer K. and H.-E. Korn. *Schrifttafeln zur deutschen Paläographie des*

16.-20. Jahrhunderts. 2 vols. 2nd ed. (Marburg 1967). 50 pls. with transcriptions.
1291

Ficker, J. and O. Winckelmann. *Handschriftenproben des 16. Jahrhunderts nach Strassburger Originalen.* 2 vols. (Strasbourg 1902, 1905). 102 pls. with transcriptions.
1292

Jenkinson, H. *The Later Court Hands in England from the 15th to the 17th Century, Illustrated from the Common Paper of the Scriveners' Company of London, the English Writing Masters, and the Public Records.* 2 vols. (Cambridge 1927, repr. New York 1969). 44 pls. with transcriptions.
1293

Judge, C.B. *Specimens of Sixteenth-Century English Handwriting* (Cambridge, Mass. 1935). 24 pls.
1294

Mazzoleni, J. *L'atto notarile napoletano nei secoli XV e XVI* (Naples 1968). 12 pls. with transcriptions.
1295

Mentz, G. *Handschriften der Reformationszeit* (Bonn 1912). 50 pls. with transcriptions
Deals with hands and autographs from Erasmus onwards.
1296

Michaud, H. *La Grande Chancellerie et les écritures royales au XVIe siècle (1515-1589)* (Paris 1969).
1297

Millares Carlo, A. and J.I. Mantecon. *Album de paleografía hispanoamericana de los siglos XVI y XVII* (Mexico City 1955)
Has 93 plates, which in fact run from A.D. 1176 to 1643.
1298

Osley, A.S. *Scribes and Sources: Handbook of the Chancery Hand in the Sixteenth Century. Texts from the Writing-Masters selected, introduced, and translated by A.S. Osley, with an Account of John de Beauchesne by B. Wolpe* (London–Boston 1980). 21 illustrations.
1299

————. *Luminario: An Introduction to the Italian Writing-Books of the Sixteenth and Seventeenth Centuries* (Nieuwkoop 1972). 116 illustrations.
1300

Petti, A.G. *English Literary Hands from Chaucer to Dryden* (London

1977). 67 pls. with transcriptions
The focus of the volume is largely post-medieval. The commentary includes remarks on punctuation, scribal error, and forgery.
1301
Roth, C. and P. Schmidt. *Handschriftenproben zur Basler Geistesgeschichte des 15. und 16. Jahrhunderts* (Basel 1926). 30 pls. with transcriptions.
1302
Rycraft, A. *Sixteenth and Seventeenth Century Handwriting.* Series I and II. 3rd ed. (York 1972)
In each series gives 12 facsimiles, with transcriptions, of documents in English.
1303
————. *Sixteenth and Seventeenth Century Wills, Inventories, and Other Probate Documents* (York 1973)
Again 12 facsimiles, mainly of documents in English, with transcriptions.
1304
Samaran, C. 'Note pour servir au déchiffrement de la cursive gothique de la fin du XVe à la fin du XVIIe siècle,' *Le Moyen Age* 2nd ser. 24 (1922) 95-106. 3 pls.
1305
Whalley, J.I. *English Handwriting 1540-1853: An Illustrated Survey* (London 1969). 90 facs.

The remainder of this bibliography is not concerned, as immediately above, with writing and centres of writing, but rather bears upon those who did the writing and how they addressed their task (Human Setting), the material on which and the instruments with which they wrote (Physical Setting), what they wrote and its quality (Textual Setting), how what they wrote was and is preserved (Institutional Setting), and, last of all, what general helps there are to a better understanding of what they entrusted to writing (Research Setting). Since most research usually begins from some repository or other of old writing such as a library or an archives, the first of these remaining settings *secundum viam inventionis* is the institutional one. Without medieval, renaissance, and modern repositories, there probably would not be very much to find today of writing from the past.

Institutional Setting

GENERAL

1306
Christ, K. 'Bibliotheksgeschichte des Mittelalters: Zur Methode und zur
neuesten Literatur,' *Zentralblatt für Bibliothekswesen* 61 (1947) 38-56,
149-66, 233-52
For some current bibliography see **22**, 2 (1979) nos. 3393-3518; 3 (1980)
3375A-3474.

1307
Humphreys, K.W. 'The Early Medieval Library' in **66a**, 59-70
Concludes that the position of librarian may have been in existence by the
end of the 8th century, and is tempted to see in Alcuin 'the father of
modern librarianship.' See also for this period (A.D. 700-1000) **594**, which
has the widest treatment of the subject to date.

1308
Lehmann, P. 'Quellen zur Feststellung und Geschichte mittelalterlicher
Bibliotheken: Handschriften und Schriftsteller' in **47**, I, 306-58.

1309
Neuhauser, W., ed. *Beiträge zur Handschriftenkunde und mittelalterlichen
Bibliotheksgeschichte: Referate der 7. Tagung österreichischer Hand-
schriftenbearbeiter in Innsbruck/Neustift (Südtirol), Juni 1979* (Innsbruck
1980). 18 pls.
Contributions on MS collections, medieval libraries, and medieval legal
collections in South and North Tirol.

1310
Savage, E. *Old English Libraries: The Making, Collection, and Use of Books during the Middle Ages* (London 1912, repr. Detroit 1968)
Still valuable, with a useful appendix on book prices. See also **1311, 1392.**

1311
Thompson, J.W. *The Medieval Library* (Chicago 1939; repr. with supplement by B.B. Boyer, New York 1957)
A well-tried book, with valuable pages on 'Paper, the Book Trade, and Book Prices' (630-46) and 'The Wanderings of Manuscripts' (647-61). See also **1310, 1392.**

1312
Unterkircher, F. 'Die älteren Bibliotheken Österreichs' in F. Unterkircher, R. Fiedler, and M. Stickler, *Die Bibliotheken Österreichs in Vergangenheit und Gegenwart* (Wiesbaden 1980) 2-25. 1 pl.

1313
Wilson, N. 'The Libraries of the Byzantine World' in *Greek, Roman, and Byzantine Studies* 8 (1967) 53-80; repr. in **1874,** 276-309 with addenda and corrigenda
Includes S. Italy.

1314
Wormald, F. and C.E. Wright, eds. *The English Library before 1700: Studies in its History* (London 1958)
Has 22 plates, nos. 5 and 10 of which are of medieval catalogues.

LIBRARY ECONOMY

1315
Bury, Richard de. *Philobiblon,* ed. and trans. E.C. Thomas. 2nd ed. (Oxford 1960)
One of the first great modern 'bibliophiles.' His *Philobiblon* (ca. A.D. 1340) has remarks on lending, on the care of books, on student behaviour in libraries.

1316
Garrod, H.W. 'The Library Regulations of a Medieval College,' *The Library* 4th ser. 8 (1927) 312-35
On Merton College, Oxford, and regulations for books 'in electione sociorum,' i.e. for the exclusive use of Fellows of the college. See also **1319, 1321.**

1317

Humphreys, K.W. *The Book Provisions of the Mediaeval Friars, 1215-1400* (Amsterdam 1964). See also **1324**.

1318

Hunt, R.W. 'The Library of the Abbey of St. Albans' in **46**, 251-77
Notes on a borrowers' list of A.D. 1420-37.

1319

Ker, N.R. 'The Books of Philosophy Distributed at Merton College in 1372 and 1375' in *Medieval Studies for J. A. W. Bennett aetatis suae LXX*, ed. P.L. Heyworth (Oxford 1981) 374-94. 2 pls.
See also **1316, 1321**.

1320

Lehmann, P. *Die Bibliotheksräume der deutschen Klöster im Mittelalter* (Berlin 1957). 20 pls.

1321

Powicke, F.M. *The Medieval Books of Merton College* (Oxford 1931)
A classic study of an Oxford college library. Among other things, it lists 63 known books at Merton before A.D. 1325, and 140 philosophical books distributed to the Fellows ('in electione sociorum') in 1372. See also **1316** and **1319**.

1322

Schneider, A. 'Skriptorium und Bibliotheken der Cistercienser' in *Die Cistercienser: Geschichte, Geist, Kunst,* ed. A. Schneider et al. (Cologne 1974) 429-508.

1323

Talbot, C.H. 'The Universities and the Mediaeval Library' in **1314**, 66-84
On the impact of the universities on library economy.

1324

Taylor-Vaisey, R. 'Regulations for the Operation of a Medieval Library,' *The Library* 33 (1978) 47-50
A translation, with commentary, of a chapter of the Dominican Master General Humbertus de Romanis in his *Libellus de instructione officialium Ordinis praedicatorum* ca. 1260, ed. J.J. Berthier, *B. Humberti de Romanis Opera de vita regulari,* 2 vols. (Rome 1888-9, repr. Turin 1956) II, 263-6.

1325

Thomson, R.M. 'The Library of Bury St. Edmunds Abbey in the Eleventh and Twelfth Centuries,' *Speculum* 47 (1972) 617-45
See also **1062**.

1326

Vielliard, J. 'Le Registre de prêt de la bibliothèque du Collège de Sorbonne au XVe siècle' in *The Universities* (see **1335**) 276-92

On books borrowed and borrowers ca. 1403-80.

SOME LIBRARIES AND COLLECTIONS

1327

Butzmann, H. *Die Weissenburger Handschriften*. Kataloge der Herzog August Bibliothek Wolfenbüttel. Neue Reihe 10 (Frankfurt am Main 1964)

A survey of the history of the MSS from Wissembourg, with 13 plates of 8th- to 12th-century MSS and of a few later ones.

1328

Búzas, L. *Deutsche Bibliotheksgeschichte des Mittelalters*. Elemente des Buch- und Bibliothekswesens 1 (Wiesbaden 1975). 1 pl.

Deals mainly with religious orders and their libraries. See also **1411, 1459.**

1329

Ehrle, F. *Historiae bibliothecae Romanorum pontificum tum Bonifatianae tum Avenionensis,* I (Rome 1890)

Only one volume published. See further A. Pelzer, *Addenda et emendanda ad Francisci Ehrle Historiae ... Tomum I* (Vatican City 1947). Between them the *Historia* and *Addenda* publish inventories of the library of Boniface VIII (A.D. 1295, 1327, 1339) and of the later papal library at Avignon (1369, 1375). See also **1330, 1374.**

1330

Faucon, M. *La Librairie des papes d'Avignon: Sa formation, sa composition, ses catalogues (1316-1420), d'après les registres de comptes et d'inventaires des archives vaticanes* (Paris 1886-7)

The range of general documentation is greater than that of Ehrle or Pelzer **1329**, but where Faucon and Ehrle-Pelzer overlap, the work of the latter is to be preferred. See also **1374.**

1331

Ferrari, M. 'Per una storia delle biblioteche francescane a Milano nel medioevo e nell'umanesimo,' *Archivum Franciscanum historicum* 72 (1979) 429-64.

1332

Franklin, A. *Les Anciennes Bibliothèques de Paris: Eglises, monastères, collèges, etc.* 3 vols. (Paris 1867-73)

Invaluable, especially for churches and small colleges. Amply documented.

1333

Kaeppeli, T. 'Antiche biblioteche domenicane in Italia,' *Archivum Fratrum praedicatorum* 36 (1966) 5-80

Gives a list of surviving MSS.

1334

Ker, N.R. *Records of All Souls College Library 1437-1600* (Oxford 1971).

1335

————. 'Oxford College Libraries before 1500' in *The Universities in the Late Middle Ages*, ed. J. Ijsewijn and J. Paquet (Louvain 1978) 293-311

An analysis of published and unpublished inventories.

1336

Marks, R.B. *The Medieval Manuscript Library of the Charterhouse of St. Barbara in Cologne.* 2 vols. (Salzburg 1974). 17 pls.

1337

Piper, A.J. 'The Libraries of the Monks of Durham' in **46**, 213-49.

1338

Rouse, R.H. 'Manuscripts Belonging to Richard de Fournival,' *Revue d'histoire des textes* 3 (1973) 253-69. 6 pls.

Includes one plate of Fournival's MSS in the Bibliothèque nationale, Paris, assembled together. Lists 37 known MSS (some commissioned by Richard himself) from the library of the author of the *Biblionomia,* most of which passed to the Sorbonne on his death in 1260.

CATALOGUES

General

1339

Bartoloni, F. 'I cataloghi delle bibliothece medioevali' in *Relazioni* (see **76**) I, 429-34

Review of scholarship and suggestions for future work.

1340

Becker, G. *Catalogi bibliothecarum antiqui:* I, *Catalogi saeculo XIII*

vetustiores; II, *Catalogus catalogorum posterioris aetatis* (Bonn 1885)
Important for texts of many library catalogues before A.D. 1200. In addition to listing 343 catalogues already in print, presents a new edition of 136. See also **1341**.

1341
De Ghellinck, J. 'En marge des catalogues des bibliothèques médiévales' in **41**, V, 331-63
On the value of catalogues of medieval libraries for the intellectual history and literary tastes of the Middle Ages. Discusses Becker **1340** and Gottlieb **1343**, noting supplements to both in issues of the *Zentralblatt für Bibliothekswesen*.

1342
Derolez, A. *Les Catalogues des bibliothèques.* Typologie des sources du moyen âge occidental, Fasc. 31 (Turnhout 1979)
General coverage. Good bibliography, especially for the Low Countries.

1343
Gottlieb, T. *Ueber mittelalterliche Bibliotheken* (Leipzig 1890)
The only survey, country by country, of catalogues of medieval libraries and of notices of books in wills, whether in print or in MS. Lists 756 catalogues. See also **1341**.

1344
Van Balberghe, E. and G. Zelis. 'Un édition scientifique des catalogues médiévaux des bibliothèques belges,' *Scriptorium* 26 (1972) 323-6
A review of Derolez **1347** which also presents some considerations on the editing of medieval catalogues and a general bibliography of editions.

1345
Vernet, A. 'Etudes et travaux sur les bibliothèques médiévales, 1937-1947,' *Revue d'histoire de l'église de France* 34 (1948) 63-94
Bibliographical.

Some Examples

1346
Bateson, M. *Catalogue of the Library of Syon Monastery, Isleworth* (Cambridge 1898)
A model of its kind. The catalogue, from the early 16th century, gives pressmarks and second folios.

1347

Derolez, A. *Corpus catalogorum Belgii: De middeleeuwse bibliotheeks-catalogi der Zuidelijke Nederlanden* (Brussels 1966-), I: *Provincie West-Vlaanderen* (1966).

1348

Dolbeau, F. 'Un nouveau catalogue des manuscrits de Lobbes aux XIe et XIIe siècles,' *Recherches augustiniennes* 13 (1978) 3-36; 14 (1979) 191-248.

1349

Gullotta, G. *Gli antichi cataloghi e i codici della Abbazia di Nonantola* Studi e testi 182 (Vatican City 1955). With a companion volume by J. Ruysschaert, *Les manuscrits de l'abbaye de Nonantola: Table de concordance annotée et index des manuscrits.* Studi e testi 182 bis (1955)
Prints catalogues of A.D. 1002-35, 1166, 1331, etc.

1350

Humphreys, K.W. *The Library of the Carmelites of Florence at the End of the Fourteenth Century* (Amsterdam 1964).

1351

James, M.R. *The Ancient Libraries of Canterbury and Dover* (Cambridge 1903)
Gives catalogues from 1389 (Dover Benedictines) and the 15th century (St. Augustine's, Canterbury), with second folios.

1352

————. 'The Catalogue of the Library of the Augustinian Friars at York' in *Fasciculus Iohanni Willis Clark dicatus* (Cambridge 1909) 2-96
On the catalogue of 1372, giving second folios, from Trinity College, Dublin, MS. 359.

1353

Milde, W. *Der Bibliothekskatalog des Klosters Murbach aus dem IX. Jahrhundert* (Heidelberg 1968). 24 pls.

1354

MITTELALTERLICHE BIBLIOTHEKSKATALOGE DEUTSCHLANDS UND DER SCHWEIZ. 4 vols. in 8 pts. (Munich 1918-79):

    1355

    I. *Die Bistümer Konstanz und Chur,* ed. P. Lehmann (1918, repr. 1969).

    1356

    II. *Bistum Mainz, Erfurt,* ed. P. Lehmann (1928, repr. 1969).

1357
III.1. *Bistum Augsburg*, ed. P. Ruf (1932, repr. 1969).
1358
III.2. *Bistum Eichstätt*, ed. P. Ruf (1933, repr. 1969).
1359
III.3. *Bistum Bamberg*, ed. P. Ruf (1939, repr. 1969).
1360
III.4. *Register* (1962).
1361
IV.1. *Bistümer Passau und Regensburg*, ed. C.E. Ineichen-Eder (1977
1362
IV.2. *Bistum Freising*, ed. G. Glauche; *Bistum Würzburg*, ed. H. Knau
(1979).
1363
MITTELALTERLICHE BIBLIOTHEKSKATALOGE ÖSTERREICHS. 5 vols. in
6 pts. (Vienna 1915-71):
1364
I. *Niederösterreich*, ed. T. Gottlieb (1915).
1365
II. *Niederösterreich. Register zum I. Band*, ed. A. Goldmann (1929).
1366
III. *Steiermark*, ed. G. Möser-Mersky (1961).
1367
IV. *Salzburg*, ed. G. Möser-Mersky and M. Mihaliuk (1966).
1368
(IVa.) *Nachtrag zu Band I.: Niederösterreich. Bücherverzeichnisse in
Korneburger, Tullner, und Wiener Neustädter Testamenten*, ed. P.
Uiblein (1969).
1369
V. *Oberösterreich*, ed. H. Paulhart (1971).
1370
Nortier, G. *Les Bibliothèques médiévales des abbayes bénédictines de
Normandie: Fécamp, Le Bec, Le Mont Saint-Michel, Saint-Evroul, Lyre,
Jumièges, Saint-Wandrille, Saint-Ouen* (Paris 1971). 8 pls.
A reprint, with additions at pp. 235-9, of articles in *Revue Mabillon*
1957-62. Surviving MSS are identified.
1371
Vernet, A. and J.-F. Genest. *La Bibliothèque de l'abbaye de Clairvaux du

XIIe au XVIIIe siècle, I: *Catalogues et répertoires* (Paris 1979). 8 pls.
1372
Winter, U. *Die mittelalterlichen Bibliothekskataloge aus Corbi: Kommentierte Edition und bibliotheks- und wissenschaftsgeschichtliche Untersuchung* (Berlin 1972).

INVENTORIES, BOOK-LISTS

1373
Balbi, G.P. 'Il libro nella società genovese del sec. XIII,' *La bibliofilia* 80 (1978) 1-45
A survey of book notices in notarial records of Genoa.
1374
BIBLIOTHEQUES ECCLESIASTIQUES AU TEMPS DE LA PAPAUTE D'AVIGNON, I:
Williman, D. *I: Inventaires de bibliothèques et mentions de livres dans les Archives du Vatican (1287-1420) – Répertoire; II: Inventaires de prélats et de clercs non français – Edition* (Paris 1980)
The first in a series of volumes projected by the Institut de recherche et d'histoire des textes, Paris, and published by the Centre national de la recherche scientifique (CNRS). Here Williman prints 114 inventories, and adds considerably to the list which Guidi **1379** published in 1948 of inventories of books in various registers in the Vatican Archives.
1375
Boyle, L.E. and R.H. Rouse. 'A Fifteenth-Century List of the Books of Edmund Norton,' *Speculum* 50 (1975) 284-8
A list of 17 books purchased by Norton, who was a Fellow of Balliol College, Oxford, in 1467 (Washington, D.C., Catholic University of America, MS. 114).
1376
Bresc, H. *Livre et société en Sicile, 1299-1499* (Palermo 1971)
Includes the text of 247 inventories of books.
1377
Edmunds, S. 'The Medieval Library of Savoy,' *Scriptorium* 24 (1970) 318-27; 25 (1971) 253-84; 26 (1972) 269-93
Gives inventories of books of the House of Savoy, generally 14th- and 15th-century, and a list of surviving MSS.

1378

Grierson, P. 'Les Livres de l'abbé Seiwold de Bath,' *RB* 52 (1940) 96-116
On the books given to the abbey of St. Vaast, Arras, in the mid-12th
century.

1379

Guidi, P. *Inventari di libri nelle serie dell'Archivio Vaticano (1287-1459)*
(Vatican City 1948)
A list of inventories of books in various registers of the Archives. Now to
be supplemented for the 14th century by Williman **1374**.

1380

Kaeppeli, T. 'La Bibliothèque de Saint-Eustorge à Milan à la fin du XVe
siècle,' *Archivum Fratrum praedicatorum* 25 (1955) 5-74
Prints the inventory of 1494, with 693 items.

1381

————. *Inventari di libri di San Domenico di Perugia (1430-1480)*
(Rome 1962)
On the inventories of 1430, 1446, 1458, 1474-8, 1480.

1382

Ker, N.R. 'Books at St. Paul's Cathedral before 1313' in *Studies in London
History presented to Philip Edmund Jones,* ed. A.E.J. Hollaender and W.
Kellaway (London 1969) 43-72
Chiefly a list of some 123 service and other books in the treasury in 1255
and another of 1295, with additional items. Many names of donors are
recorded.

1383

Laurent, M.-H. 'Guillaume des Rosières et la bibliothèque pontificale à
l'époque de Clément VI' in *Mélanges Auguste Pelzer* (Louvain 1947) 579-
603
Notes that, as papal collector (A.D. 1343-9), Guillaume forwarded 170
MSS by *jus spolii* from Naples to Avignon.

1384

Mather, R. 'The Codicil of Cardinal Comes of Casate and the Libraries of
Thirteenth-Century Cardinals,' *Traditio* 20 (1964) 319-50
On the codicil of 1287. The libraries are mostly legal.

1385

Omont, H. 'Anciens catalogues de bibliothèques anglaises (XIIe-XIVe
siècle),' *Zentralblatt für Bibliothekswesen* 9 (1892) 201-22
Catalogues of Burton-upon-Trent (1175), Flaxley (13th-century), and

Llanthony (14th-century) monasteries.
1386
Ouy, G. 'Simon de Plumetot (1371-1443) et sa bibliothèque' in **62**, II, 353-81. 2 pls.
Identifies some 73 MSS at Paris and elsewhere from the library which Simon, a canon and King's Counsellor, willed to St. Victor, Paris.
1387
Paravicini-Bagliani, A. *I testamenti dei cardinali del Duecento* (Rome 1980)
Prints 45 wills of 30 cardinals of the 13th century, with notes of the provenance of books possessed by various cardinals.
1388
Rouse, R.H. 'Bostonus Buriensis and the Author of the *Catalogus scriptorum ecclesiae*,' *Speculum* 41 (1966) 471-99. 14 facs.
On the 'Union catalogue' compiled ca. 1360-78 by Henry of Kirkestede, a monk of Bury St. Edmunds, Suffolk, with bibliographical notices of authors and a location list of where books of various authors were to be found in monastic or cathedral libraries in England. For a Franciscan 'Union catalogue' (*Registrum Angliae*), begun, probably at Oxford, in the second half of the 13th century, see R.H. and M.A. Rouse in **1094**, 55-6, with one plate of the *Registrum.*

RECONSTRUCTING MEDIEVAL LIBRARIES

1389
Ker, N.R. *Medieval Libraries of Great Britain: A List of Surviving Books* 2nd ed. (London 1964)
A survey (Abbotsbury – York) based on internal evidence of MSS in Great Britain and elsewhere, and on information from medieval catalogues, where they exist. An appendix, pp. 219-24, lists books formerly owned by parish churches and chapels; at pp. 225-325 there is a list (by medieval house, alphabetically) of donors, scribes, and other persons concerned before 1540 with the books recorded in the survey.
1390
Van Balberghe, E. and G. Zelis. 'Introduction au *Medieval Libraries of Belgium*,' *Scriptorium* 26 (1972) 348-57
The model is Ker **1389**.

1391
Van Balberghe, E. and G. Zelis. 'Medieval Libraries of Belgium: A List of the Surviving Manuscripts, I: *Orval*,' *Scriptorium* 27 (1973) 102-6; '..., II *Aulne*,' *ibid.* 28 (1974) 103-9.

BOOK TRADE

1392
Bell, H.E. 'The Price of Books in Medieval England,' *The Library* 4th ser 17 (1936-7) 312-32
Deals mainly with the 14th and 15th centuries. See also **1310-11**.

1393
Delalain, P.A. *Etude sur le libraire parisien du XIIIe au XVe siècle d'après les documents publiés dans le cartulaire de l'Université de Paris* (Paris 1891).

1394
Pollard, G. 'The University and the Book Trade in Mediaeval Oxford' in *Beiträge zum Berufsbewusstsein des mittelalterlichen Menschen,* ed. P. Wilpert and W. Eckert. Miscellanea mediaevalia (1962-) 3 (Berlin 1964) 336-44.

1395
Stelling-Michaud, S. 'Le Transport international des MSS juridiques bolonais entre 1265 et 1320' in *Mélanges d'histoire économique et sociale en hommage au professeur Antony Babel.* 2 vols. (Geneva 1963) I, 95-1.

Renaissance and After

GENERAL

1396
James, M.R. *The Wanderings and Homes of Manuscripts.* Helps for Students of History 17 (London 1919)
This brief volume is still the only broad account of the movement of MS from the Renaissance onwards.

1397
Lehmann, P. 'Konstanz und Basel als Büchermärkte während der grosse

irchenversammlungen' in **47**, I, 253-80.

ELGIUM, FRANCE

398
erolez, A. *The Library of Raphael de Marcatellis, Abbot of St. Baron's,
hent (1437-1508)* (Ghent 1979)
xamination of some 60 *de luxe* MSS, and of Flemish workshops where
aey were produced.
399
oucet, R. *Les Bibliothèques parisiennes au XVIe siècle* (Paris 1956).
400
uy, G. 'Les Bibliothèques' in **42**, 1061-1108
las a crisp section on MS collections in France. There is a bibliography at
p. 1116-19.

NGLAND

401
3ennett, H.S. *English Books and Readers 1475 to 1557*. 2nd ed.
(Cambridge 1970)
A study of the history of the book trade from Caxton to the incorporation
of the Stationers' Company, London, first published in 1952.
402
De Ricci, S. *English Collectors of Books and Manuscripts (1530-1930) and
heir Marks of Ownership* (Oxford 1930; repr. Bloomington, Ind. 1960).
403
Dickens, B. 'The Making of the Parker Library,' *Transactions of the Cambridge Bibliographical Society* 6 (1972-6) 19-34
On Archbishop Parker's contribution (A.D. 1559-75) to the MS collection at
Corpus Christi College, Cambridge. See also **1409, 1471.**
404
Douglas, D.C. *English Scholars 1660-1730*. 2nd ed. (London 1951)
A useful and readable account of bibliophiles and pioneering scholars such
as William Dugdale, George Hickes, Humphrey Wanley, Henry Wharton,
and Thomas Hearne.

1405
Irwin, R. *The English Library: Sources and History* (London [1966])
Has a useful chapter (VIII) on the dispersal, at Reformation, of monastic
and other libraries.
1406
Jayne, S. *Library Catalogues of the English Renaissance* (Berkeley — Los
Angeles 1956)
Deals with catalogues from 1500-1640.
1407
Ker, N.R. 'The Migration of Manuscripts from the English Medieval
Libraries,' *The Library* 4th ser. 23 (1943) 1-11.
1408
————. 'Cardinal Cervini's Manuscripts from the Cambridge Friars' in
Xenia (see **1258**) I, 51-71
An account of some of about 200 MSS which, at the time of the Dissolu-
tion of religious houses in England, were sent overseas from Cambridge,
came into the possession of Cardinal Marcello Cervini (who became Pope
Marcellus II in 1555) before 1545, and are now among the Ottoboniani
codices in the Vatican Library.
1409
Wright, C.E. 'The Dispersal of Monastic Libraries and the Beginnings of
Anglo-Saxon Studies: Matthew Parker and his Circle,' *Transactions of the
Cambridge Bibliographical Society* 1 (1949-53) 208-37
A preliminary study of Archbishop Matthew Parker and his circle. See
also **1403, 1471**.
1410
————. 'The Dispersal of the Libraries in the Sixteenth Century' in
1314, 148-75.

GERMANY, HOLLAND

1411
Búzas, L. *Deutsche Bibliotheksgeschichte der Neuzeit (1500-1800).*
Elemente des Buch- und Bibliothekswesens 2 (Wiesbaden 1976). 1 pl.
See also **1328, 1459**.
1412
De Meyier, K.A. *Codices Vossiani Latini.* 3 vols. (Leiden 1973-7)

catalogue of the Latin MSS collected by Isaac Vossius (1618-89) now in
eiden University Library.

413
artig, O. *Die Gründung der Münchener Hofbibliothek durch Albrecht V.*
nd Johann Jakob Fugger (Munich 1917)
he standard work on the formation and early history of the present
ayerische Staatsbibliothek in the time of Duke Albert V (A.D. 1550-79).

414
ehmann, P. *Franciscus Modius als Handschriftenforscher* (Munich 1908)
n the researches of the Dutch scholar Modius (1556-97) into MSS, some
ow lost, in N. France, the Low Countries, and Germany (Bamberg, Fulda).

415
———. *Iohannes Sichardus und die von ihm benutzten Bibliotheken*
nd Handschriften (Munich 1911)
n books and MSS known to and used by the great editor of patristic
exts (A.D. 1499-1552).

416
———. *Eine Geschichte der alten Fuggerbibliotheken.* 2 vols. (Tübingen
956, 1960)
)n the Augsburg banking family of the 14th-16th centuries.

TALY, VATICAN

417
)e Marinis, T. *La biblioteca napoletana dei re d'Aragona.* 4 vols. (Milan
947-52); and *Supplemento.* 2 vols. (Verona 1969)
A reconstruction from some 479 scattered MSS of the library of Alfonso
V, the Magnanimous (king of Aragón 1416-58, of Sicily 1416-58, of
Naples 1442-58), and his successors.

418
Hobson, A. *Apollo and Pegasus: An Enquiry into the Formation and Dis-*
ersal of a Renaissance Library (Amsterdam 1975)
A reconstruction, through distinctive 'Apollo and Pegasus' bindings, of a
collection of books and MSS bought and bound in Rome, 1545-7, for
G.B. Grimaldi of Genoa.

419
Laurent, M.-H. *Fabio Vigili et les bibliothèques de Bologne au début du*

XVIe siècle, d'après le ms. Barb. lat. 3185 (Vatican City 1943). 2 pls.
1420
Mercati, G. *Note per la storia di alcune biblioteche romane nei secoli XVI*
XIX (Vatican City 1952). 22 pls.
On the Angelica, Sforziana, and other libraries.
1421
Müntz, E. and P. Fabre. *La Bibliothèque du Vatican au XVe siècle d'après*
des documents inédits (Paris 1887)
See also **1329-30, 1504.**
1422
Pellegrin, E. *La Bibliothèque des Visconti et des Sforza, ducs de Milan, au*
XVe siècle (Florence–Paris 1955) with supplementary vol. of 175 pls.
1423
Robathan, D.M. 'Libraries of the Italian Renaissance' in **1311**, 509-93.
1424
Scrittura, biblioteche, e stampa a Roma nel Quattrocento: Aspetti e
problemi. 2 vols. (Vatican City 1980). 33 pls.
The acts of a seminar of 1979.
1425
Ullman, B.L. and P.A. Stadter. *The Public Library of Renaissance*
Florence: Niccolò Niccoli, Cosimo de' Medici, and the Library of San
Marco (Padua 1972). 2 pls.
San Marco is called the 'first public library of modern times.' In 1444 it
received MSS of Niccoli (ob. 1437, aet. 73), some of which were from the
collection of Coluccio Salutati. The catalogue of 1499-1500 is printed at
pp. 125-267. Today the MSS (listed at pp. 359-68) are mostly in the
Biblioteca Laurenziana.

SWEDEN

1426
Callmer, C. *Königin Christina, ihre Bibliothekare und ihre Handschriften:*
Beiträge zur europäischen Bibliotheksgeschichte (Stockholm 1977)
A well-documented account of the library and librarians (e.g. N. Heinsius
I. Vossius) of Christina (1626-89), of her acquisition of MSS, and of the
transfer of the library to Rome (and eventually to the Vatican Library)
after her abdication in 1654. For her MSS (Codices Reginenses) in the

atican Library see **1509**.

Modern

ENERAL

427
autier, R.H. 'Les Archives' in **42**, 1120-66
rovides a good international bibliography.

428
uide international des archives, I (Paris 1934)
o be supplemented by occasional bibliographies in *Archivum* **1438**.

429
aenel, G. *Catalogi librorum manuscriptorum qui in bibliothecis Galliae,
'elvetiae, Belgii, Britanniae M., Hispaniae, Lusitaniae asservantur* (Leipzig
830)
lthough superseded for most of the 1238 collections recorded here, still
aluable for some small collections in some of these countries.

430
risteller, P.O. *Latin Manuscript Books before 1600: A List of the Printed
atalogues and Unpublished Inventories of Extant Collections.* 3rd ed.
New York 1965)
he best coverage of its kind. Section A lists bibliographies, Section B
orks which cover groups of libraries, e.g. **1491**; Section C proceeds city
y city (Aachen – Zwolle), with cross-references to A and B. The present
ibliography therefore limits itself to a few general works, and to selected
atalogues which have appeared since 1965. For additions to Kristeller see,
.g., A. García y García, 'Catálogos de los códices medievales de las biblio-
cas españolas,' *Salmanticensis* 13 (1966) 680-84; G. Dogaer, 'Quelques
dditions au répertoire de Kristeller,' *Scriptorium* 22 (1968) 84-6; C.H.
ohr, 'Further Additions to Kristeller's *Repertorium*,' *Scriptorium* 26
1972) 343-8.

431
ewanski, R.C. *European Library Directory: A Geographical and Biblio-
raphical Guide* (Florence 1968)
Useful for addresses and general information.

1432
Milkau, F. and G. Leyh. *Handbuch der Bibliothekswissenschaft,* III.1:
Geschichte der Bibliotheken. 3rd ed. (Wiesbaden 1961)
Chapters are by various contributors.
1433
Oesterley, H. *Wegweiser durch die Literatur der Urkundensammlungen.*
2 vols. (Berlin 1885-6, repr. Hildesheim–New York 1969)
A still useful survey of diplomatic archives and relevant publications in
Austria, Belgium, Germany, Holland, Switzerland (in vol. I), and other
countries (vol. II).
1434
Richard, M. *Répertoire des bibliothèques et des catalogues de manuscrits*
grecs (Paris 1958); and *Supplément* (1964).
1435
Richardson, E.C. *A Union World Catalog of Manuscript Books,* III: *A*
List of Printed Catalogs of Manuscript Books (New York 1935, repr. 197
Not entirely outmoded by Kristeller **1430**.
1436
Sales Catalogues. Current and past catalogues of leading antiquarian deal
such as Olschki of Florence; Quaritch, Maggs, and Sotheby of London;
Rosenthal of San Francisco; Witten of New Haven; or Kraus of New Yor
(who has acquired the remnants of the Phillipps collection **1474**). A usef
start is provided by the *List of Catalogues of English Book Sales 1679-*
1900 now in the British Museum (London 1915), where there is a chronc
logical list of some 8000 catalogues.

Kristeller **1430** is indispensable, but since many new catalogues or survey
of MSS have appeared since 1965 and continue to appear, his work has te
be supplemented by consulting, e.g., the section 'Sciences auxiliaires' in
the *RHE* **24**, the general bibliographies in *Scriptorium* **26**, or the section
'Cataloghi di manoscritti' in the new *Medioevo latino* **22** (e.g. 2 [1979]
nos. 3304-92; 3 [1980] 3475-666); and by checking local bibliographies
or, notably, surveys of MSS in preparation for critical editions, as in the
following selection (which also takes in archives):
1437
Analecta Bollandiana (Brussels 1882-)
Since 1970 this generally carries survey articles once or twice a year on
'Catalogues récents de manuscrits,' e.g. for Latin MSS 88 (1970) 188-211

89 (1971) 187-202; 90 (1972) 167-89; 91 (1973) 163-201, 419-32; 92 (1974) 173-206, 371-85; 93 (1975) 183-94, 391-404; 94 (1976) 160-82; 98 (1980) 171-210; 99 (1981) 381-94.

1438
Archivum (Paris 1951-)
Since 1952 this carries surveys to supplement the *Guide international* (**1428**), e.g. 'Bibliographie analytique internationale des publications relatives à l'archivistique et aux archives,' *Archivum* 2 (1952) 105-227; 3 (1953) 109-88; 4 (1954) 217-89; 6 (1956) 177-282; etc.

1439
Beccaria, A. *I codici di medicina del periodo presalernitano (secoli IX, X, e XI)* (Rome 1956)
Describes 145 MSS in various libraries. Incipits are at pp. 403-37.

1440
Dondaine, H.-F. and H.-V. Shooner. *Codices manuscripti operum Thomae de Aquino* (Rome 1967-)
To date, two volumes of a promised four have appeared. All libraries are covered, with exhaustive descriptions of contents of each MS.

1441
Oberleitner, M. et al. *Die handschriftliche Überlieferung der Werke des Heiligen Augustinus* (Vienna 1969-)
There are five volumes (in seven parts) to date. Survey is country by country.

SOME LIBRARIES AND ARCHIVES

It is impossible here to give a list of all catalogues of MSS which have appeared since Kristeller **1430**. The present list notes a few at random (generally those providing lists of incipits of MSS — see also **1930-53**), and, further, by way of illustration, lingers for a moment over certain libraries and countries.

Australia

1442
Sinclair, K.V. *Descriptive Catalogue of Medieval and Renaissance Western Manuscripts in Australia* (Sydney 1969). 17 pls.

Austria

1443
Kern, A. *Die Handschriften der Universitätsbibliothek Graz*. 3 vols.
(Vienna 1942-67)
Incipits are listed in III, 141-240.

Belgium

1444
Bibliotheek der Rijksuniversiteit te Gent: Census van de handschriften
(Ghent 1957).
1445
*Cinq années d'acquisitions 1974-1978: Exposition organisée à la Biblio-
thèque royale Albert Ier* (Brussels 1979)
MSS are described at pp. 17-199, with 24 plates.

Czechoslovakia

1446
Sopko, J. *Codices medii aevi, qui in bibliothecis Slovaciae asservantur ac
olim asservabantur*, I: *Codices Latini medii aevi bibliothecarum Slovaciae*
(Matica Slovenská 1981). 24 pls.
The text is in Czech.

France

1447
*Catalogue général des manuscrits des bibliothèques publiques des départe-
ments* ['Quarto Series']. 7 vols. (Paris 1849-85).
1448
*Catalogue général des manuscrits des bibliothèques publiques de France:
Départements* ['Octavo Series'] (Paris 1886-)
57 volumes were published to 1971.
1449
Catalogue général des manuscrits des bibliothèques publiques de France.
2 vols. (Paris 1909, 1914)
Covers various Parisian schools and institutions.

1450

Delisle, L. *Le Cabinet des manuscrits de la Bibliothèque (impériale) nationale: Etude sur la formation de ce dépot comprenant les éléments d'une histoire de la calligraphie, de la miniature, de la reliure, et du commerce des livres à Paris avant l'invention de l'imprimerie.* 4 vols. (Paris 1868-81, repr. Amsterdam 1969)

Vol. IV is a collection of 48 plates to illustrate 'ancient writing.' Here one may note that acquisitions to the Bibliothèque nationale are regularly recorded, sometimes in much detail, in *BEC* (**15**), e.g. 124 (1966) 137-272 and 127 (1969) 87-212 (with a numerical list of all Latin and French additions, 1868-1968). See also [M. Thomas], *Bibliothèque nationale: Enrichissements 1961-1973* (Paris 1974) 79-174 (Département des manuscrits).

1451

Hauréau, B. *Notices et extraits de quelques manuscrits latins de la Bibliothèque nationale.* 6 vols. (Paris 1890-93)

A rich source of information on MSS collections and various MSS at the BN.

1452

Leroquais, V. *Les Sacramentaires et les missels manuscrits des bibliothèques publiques de France.* 4 vols. (Paris 1924)

One volume is of plates. Here, as in all of Leroquais' catalogues of liturgical books, there is a valuable historical introduction.

1453

————. *Les Livres d'heures manuscrits de la Bibliothèque nationale.* 3 vols. (Paris 1927); and *Supplément* (Macon 1943)

One volume is of plates.

1454

————. *Les Bréviaires manuscrits des bibliothèques publiques de France.* 6 vols. (Paris 1934)

One volume is of plates.

1455

————. *Les Pontificaux manuscrits des bibliothèques publiques de France.* 3 vols. (Paris 1937)

With a portfolio of plates.

1456

————. *Les Psautiers manuscrits latins des bibliothèques publiques de France.* 2 vols. (Macon 1940, 1941)

With a portfolio of plates.

1457
Pellegrin, E. *Manuscrits de Pétrarque dans les bibliothèques de France* (Padua 1966). 13 pls.; repr. from *IMU* 4 (1961), 6 (1963), 7 (1964)
Lists incipits of the Latin works of Petrarch at pp. 346-53.
1458
Wickersheimer, E. *Les Manuscrits latins de médecine du haut moyen âge dans les bibliothèques de France* (Paris 1966)
Covers the period up to the end of the 11th century. Incipits are at pp. 201-10.

Germany

1459
Búzas, L. *Deutsche Bibliotheksgeschichte der neuesten Zeit (1800-1945)* (Wiesbaden 1978)
The last of 3 volumes (for 1 and 2 see **1328, 1411**) in the series Elemente des Buch- und Bibliothekswesens, ed. F. Dressler and G. Liebers.
1460
Hofmann, J. and H. Hauke. *Die Handschriften der Stiftsbibliothek und der Stiftskirche zu Aschaffenburg* (Aschaffenburg 1978). 20 pls.
1461
Milde, W. *Mittelalterliche Handschriften der Herzog August Bibliothek* (Frankfurt am Main 1972)
Has 120 plates (mostly of illuminations) of MSS at Wolfenbüttel from ca. A.D. 800-1500.
1462
Spilling, H. *Die Handschriften der Staats- und Stadtbibliothek Augsburg 2° COD 1-100* (Wiesbaden 1978)
Incipits are at pp. 185-98.
1463
Von Euw, A. and J.M. Plotzek. *Die Handschriften der Sammlung Ludwig.* 3 vols. (Cologne 1979-82); ca. 130 pls. in colour and over 1100 figs.
The entire Ludwig collection (Aachen) was purchased (in 1983) by the J. Paul Getty Museum, Malibu, California, where the MSS will retain their Ludwig shelfmarks as in Von Euw and Plotzek.

Great Britain, Ireland

1464
[Bernard, E.] *Catalogi librorum manuscriptorum Angliae et Hiberniae.* 2 vols. (Oxford 1697)
The only general coverage of its kind, now being replaced for England by Ker **1470**. See also **1481**.

1465
Bulletin of the Institute of Historical Research (London 1927-)
Carries notices from time to time of accessions of historical MSS to the BL, London, and of migrations of historical MSS within the British Isles.

1466
De la Mare, A.C. *Catalogue of the Collection of Medieval Manuscripts bequeathed to the Bodleian Library, Oxford by James P.R. Lyell* (Oxford 1971)
Gives useful information on MS description at pp. xxxi-xxxiii.

1467
Hassall, W.O. *The Holkham Library: Illuminations and Illustrations in the Manuscript Library of the Earl of Leicester* (Oxford 1970)
Has 160 plates of some 39 MSS in this library at Wells, Norfolk. There is good treatment of provenance, and a useful list of MSS no longer at Holkham Hall (some are in the Bodleian Library, Oxford: see further W.O. Hassall, 'The Holkham Library' in **1094**).

1468
Historical Manuscripts Commission Reports (London 1870-)
A series of reports, begun in 1870 and still in progress, on the MS collections, whether literary or documentary, of over 400 private owners and of over 200 corporate bodies (e.g. boroughs, cathedrals, counties, parishes, endowed institutions) in Great Britain and Ireland. Some of the *Reports* (e.g. with respect to Cambridge Colleges in the *First Report*) have been superseded by full-scale catalogues (notably for private owners and corporations, etc. by Ker **1470**), but in many cases the series provides the only account in print to date of various libraries. The first fifteen *Reports* (1870-99), from this point of view, are the most valuable. The 23rd (1959), 24th (1962), and 25th (1967) contain important lists of changes of location of MSS.

1469
Ker, N.R. *The Parochial Libraries of the Church of England* (London

1959). 10 pls.
Discusses the fortunes of these libraries from the 15th century onwards. A
list of medieval MSS in present-day parochial libraries is at pp. 108-11.
1470
————. *Medieval Manuscripts in British Libraries* (Oxford 1969-), I:
London (1969); II: *Abbotsford-Keele* (1977).
1471
James, M.R. *A Descriptive Catalogue of the Manuscripts in the Library of
Corpus Christi College, Cambridge.* 2 vols. (Cambridge 1909, 1912)
James published a great series of catalogues of libraries of Cambridge
colleges, but the Corpus catalogue is the only one singled out here because
of the attention James gives there to the large body of important MSS
donated to the college by Archbishop Matthew Parker. See further **1403,
1409,** and R.I. Page and G.H.S. Bushnell, *Matthew Parker's Legacy: Books
and Plate* (Cambridge 1975) with 33 pls. of MSS.
1472
Morgan, P. *Oxford Libraries Outside the Bodleian.* 2nd ed. (Oxford 1981)
An expanded version of a valuable guide of 1972. Covers colleges and
other repositories.
1473
Munby, A.N.L. *Phillipps Studies.* 5 vols. (Cambridge 1951-60)
An absorbing study of the origins and dispersal of the famous collection
of MSS assembled by the antiquary Sir Thomas Phillipps (1792-1872).
1474
————, ed. *The Phillipps Manuscripts: Catalogus librorum manuscriptorum in bibliotheca D. Thomae Phillipps, Bt., impressum typis Medio-
Montanis 1837-1871* (London [1968])
A reprint of Phillipps' own private and unequal catalogue of 25,837 MSS
(not all medieval), which he had printed in instalments at Middle Hill,
Worcestershire, where the library was located until 1862. Munby provides
an introduction. See also **1436.**
1475
————, ed. *Sale Catalogues of Libraries of Eminent Persons* (London
1971-)
To date, 12 volumes of original catalogues from England have appeared.
1476
Mynors, R.A.B. *Catalogue of the Manuscripts of Balliol College, Oxford*
(Oxford 1963)

One of the better modern catalogues. Includes a valuable introduction relative to the history of medieval libraries and books.

1477

Nickson, M.A.E. *The British Library: Guide to the Catalogues and Indexes of the Department of Manuscripts* (London 1978)

Supplements Skeat **1482**. Gives useful information on reference books (incipits, etc.) available in the Students' Room (Manuscript Reading Room).

1478

Oxford, Bodleian Library: *Summary Catalogue of Western Manuscripts in the Bodleian Library at Oxford which have not Hitherto been Catalogued in the Quarto Series*, ed. F. Madan, H.H.E. Craster, et al. 6 vols. and index vol. (Oxford 1895-1953)

Notices of notable accessions occur from time to time in *The Bodleian Library Record* (Oxford 1938-).

1479

Parkes, M.B. *The Medieval Manuscripts of Keble College, Oxford* (London 1979). 192 pls.

Gives extensive descriptions of 87 MSS, mostly liturgical.

1480

Schenkl, H. 'Bibliotheca patrum Latinorum Britannica,' publ. in 13 pts. (including index) in *Sitzungsberichte der phil.-historischen Klasse der Kaiserlichen Akademie der Wissenschaften Wien*, vols. 121-4, 126-7, 131, 136-9, 143, 150 (Vienna 1891-1907)

A survey of patristic, theological, legal, grammatical, and classical writings (4961 entries in all) in British libraries, library by library. Although now superseded for many areas by Ker **1470** and other modern catalogues, it is still valuable for some small, private, or now-dispersed collections.

1481

Singer, D.W. and A. Anderson. *Catalogue of Latin and Vernacular Alchemical Manuscripts in Great Britain and Ireland, Dating from Before the Sixteenth Century*. 3 vols. (Brussels 1928-31)

There is a table of incipits in III, 801-905.

1482

Skeat, T.C. *British Museum: The Catalogues of the Manuscript Collections.* 2nd ed. (London 1962)

A summary listing. See also **1477**.

1483

Watson, R. *Descriptive List of Fragments of Medieval Manuscripts in the*

University of London Library (London 1976). 3 pls.
Supplements Ker I, **1470**. Lists 56 fragments.
1484
Wright, C.E. *Fontes Harleiani: A Study of the Sources of the Harleian Collection of Manuscripts preserved in the Department of Manuscripts in the British Museum* (London 1972)
An exemplary study of a collection of MSS as it was put together. Plates VI-IX illustrate a wide range of English and continental *ex-libris.*

Holland

1485
Boeren, P.C. *Catalogus van de handschriften van het Rijksmuseum Meermanno-Westreenianum* (The Hague 1979).

Italy

1486
Annuario delle biblioteche italiane (Rome 1969-): I. *(A-F)* [= Abano Terme–Fusignano] (1969); II. *(G-M)* [= Gaeta–Mussomeli] (1971); III. *(N-ROL)* [= Napoli–Rolo] (1973); IV. *(ROM-TORA)* [= Roma–Torana] (1976); V. *(TORI-Z)* [= Torino–Zoppola] (1981)
An up-to-date survey, replacing earlier ones of 1949-52, 1956-9, of all libraries, whether public or private, with details of their history, structure, and holdings, and an essential bibliography.
1487
Abate, G. and G. Luisetto. *Codici e manoscritti della Biblioteca Antoniana.* 2 vols. (Padua 1975)
Descriptions of 789 MSS, including many choir books, with 200 illustrations.
1488
Avitabile, L., M.C. Di Franco, V. Jemolo, and A. Petrucci. 'Censimento dei codici dei secoli X-XII,' *SM* 3rd ser. 9/2 (1968) 1115-94; 11/2 (1970) 1013-1133 (with F. De Marco in place of Petrucci)
Valuable notes on holdings of various Roman libraries (e.g. Casanatense, Accademia nazionale dei Lincei, Biblioteca nazionale centrale) and of some outside of Rome, in preparation for a *Censimento* or survey of MSS in libraries for which there is no published catalogue. See also **1641**.

1489

Catalogo di manoscritti filosofici nelle biblioteche italiane (Florence 1980-), I: *Firenze, Pisa, Poppi, Rimini, Trieste,* ed. T. de Robertis et al. (1980); II: *Busto Arsizio, Firenze, Parma, Savignano sul Rubicone, Volterra,* ed. D. Frioli et al. (1981)
A publication of the Unione Accademica Nazionale (Subsidia al 'Corpus philosophorum medii aevi'). The aim is to record any text bearing on the history of thought from the 6th-16th centuries A.D., but the emphasis is on commentaries on Aristotle. Particular attention is given to 'libraries in centres which are not much visited by scholars' (I, p. VIII). Hence valuable details are given of MSS in some libraries that are not well known or are uncatalogued. There is a list of incipits with each volume.

1490

Kristeller, P.O. *Iter Italicum: A Finding List of Uncatalogued or Incompletely Catalogued Humanistic Manuscripts of the Renaissance in Italian and Other Libraries* (London – Leiden 1963-)
Three of a projected five volumes have appeared to date: *Italy, Agrigento to Novara* (1963); *Italy, Orvieto to Volterra. Vatican City* (1967); *Alia itinera: Australia to Germany* (1983).

1491

Mazzatinti, G., A. Sorbelli, et al. *Inventari dei manoscritti delle biblioteche d'Italia* (Turin 1887, Forlì 1890-1911, Florence 1912-)
100 volumes were published to 1981, including an odd fascicule at Turin in 1887 before the series proper began. Has to be supplemented by the occasional *Aggiunte e correzioni agli Inventari dei manoscritti delle biblioteche d'Italia* (1962-) and by Kristeller **1490**, *Annuario* **1486**, and *Catalogo* **1489**.

Portugal, Spain

1492

García y García, A., F.C. Rodriguez, and M.N. Cumplido. *Catálogo de los manuscritos e incunables de la Catedral de Córdoba* (Salamanca 1976)
MSS are listed at pp. 3-330, incipits at 595-615.

1493

Grubbs, H.A. *The Manuscript Book Collections of Spain and Portugal* (New York 1933); and *A Supplement to the Manuscript Book Collections of Spain and Portugal* (1935)
See also **7**, 320-62 and **1430**.

Russia, Eastern Europe

1494
Grimsted, P.K. *Archives and Manuscript Repositories in the USSR: Moscow and Leningrad.* 2 vols. (Princeton 1972, 1976); *Estonia, Latvia, Belorussia* (1979).
1495
Kiseleva, L.I. *Latinskie rukopisi Biblioteki Akademii Nauk SSSR. Opisanie rukopisei latinskogo alfavita X-XV vv* (Leningrad 1978). 36 pls.
See also **896**.

United States, Canada

1496
De Ricci, S. and W.J. Wilson. *Census of Medieval and Renaissance Manuscripts in the United States and Canada.* 3 vols. (New York 1935-40); complemented by C.U. Faye and W.H. Bond, *Supplement to the Census of Medieval and Renaissance Manuscripts in the United States and Canada* (ibid. 1962).
1497
Ermatinger, C. 'A Checklist of the Vatican Manuscript Codices Available for Consultation at the Knights of Columbus Vatican Film Library,' *Manuscripta* 1 (1957) 27-44, 104-16, 159-74; 2 (1958) 41-9, 84-99, 167-81; 3 (1959) 38-46, 89-99
The collection is housed in the Pius XII Memorial Library, St. Louis, Missouri.
1498
Gabriel, A. *The Ambrosiana Collection at the University of Notre Dame: The Frank M. Folson Ambrosiana Microfilm and Photographic Collection* (Notre Dame 1976)
An exhibition relative to the collection of microfilms of MSS from the Ambrosiana Library, Milan, at the University of Notre Dame, South Bend, Indiana.
1499
Gerard, A. 'Liturgical Manuscripts in the United States and Canada,' *Scriptorium* 28 (1974) 92-100
A chronological list of MSS of the 8th-12th centuries.

1500

Hill Monastic Manuscript Library [Collegeville, Minn.] *Descriptive Inventories of Manuscripts Microfilmed for the Hill Monastic Manuscript Library: Austrian Libraries, I (Geras – Schwaz),* ed. D. Yates (Collegeville, Minn. 1981)

The first volume of a projected series whose purpose is to describe hitherto uncatalogued or inadequately catalogued European collections of MSS now on microfilm at Collegeville. The list of incipits at pp. 255-314 covers Latin, Italian, and German MSS. See also **1502**.

1501

Olevnik, P.P. *Selected Medieval and Renaissance Manuscript Collections in Microform.* University of Illinois Graduate School of Library Science, Occasional Papers 133 (Champaign, Ill. 1978)

A useful survey of microfilm holdings in Canada (Pontifical Institute of Mediaeval Studies, Toronto) and the United States (Library of Congress, Washington, D.C.; Collegeville, Minnesota [see **1502**]; Notre Dame, Indiana [**1498**]; St. Louis, Missouri [**1497**]).

1502

Plante, J.G. *Checklist of Manuscripts Microfilmed for the Monastic Manuscript Microfilm Library, Saint John's University, Collegeville, Minnesota* (Collegeville 1967-), e.g. *Checklist of Manuscripts Microfilmed for the Hill Monastic Manuscript Library II, Spain Part 1* (1978).

1503

Sharpe, J.L. 'A Checklist of Collections of Biblical and Related Manuscripts on Microfilm in the United States and Canada,' *Scriptorium* 25 (1971) 97-109.

Vatican City

1504

Bignami Odier, J. *La Bibliothèque Vaticane de Sixte IV à Pie XI: Recherches sur l'histoire des collections de manuscrits avec la collaboration de José Ruysschaert* (Vatican City 1973). 13 pls.

See also **1421**.

1505

Boyle, L.E. *A Survey of the Vatican Archives and of its Medieval Holdings* (Toronto 1972).

1506
Les Manuscrits classiques latins de la Bibliothèque Vaticane, ed. E. Pellegrin,
J. Fohlen, C. Jeudy, Y.-F. Riou, A. Marucchi (Paris 1975-):
I. *Fonds Archivio San Pietro à Ottoboni* (1975). 32 pls.
II.1. *Fonds Patetta et Fonds de la Reine*, ed. E. Pellegrin (1978). 16 pls.
II.2. *Fonds Palatin, Rossi, Ste.-Marie Majeure, et Urbinate*, ed. J. Fohlen,
C. Jeudy, and Y.-F. Riou (1982). 24 pls.

1507
Salmon, P. *Les Manuscrits liturgiques latins de la Bibliothèque Vaticane.*
5 vols. (Vatican City 1968-72)
Proceeds by subject (Psalters, Antiphonaries, Hymnaries, Collectories, etc.).
Gives detailed descriptions of MSS. Incipits are in V, 136-40.

1508
Schuba, L. *Die medizinischen Handschriften der Codices Palatini Latini in
der vatikanischen Bibliothek* (Wiesbaden 1981)
Incipits are at pp. 579-618.

1509
Wilmart, A. *Codices Reginenses Latini.* 2 vols. (Vatican City 1937, 1945)
A model catalogue. Of 2120 MSS in the Reginensis collection, only 1-500
are covered here by Wilmart (1876-1941). The remainder has yet to be
catalogued. See also **1426**.

Yugoslavia

1510
Kaeppeli, T. and H.-V. Shooner. *Les Manuscrits médiévaux de Saint-
Dominique de Dubrovnik: Catalogue sommaire* (Rome 1965)
At pp. 119-29 the authors print five taxation lists, all probably from
Bologna A.D. 1275-1320, of peciae of civil and canon law texts, including:
that already published by Boháček (see **1748**) from Olomouc, Statni Archiv,
MS. C. O. 209; new lists from Autun, Bibliothèque municipale, MS. 81
(S. 101), fol. 1r; Dubrovnik, Dominikanska Biblioteca, MS. 1, fol. 267v;
and Venice, Biblioteca Nazionale Marciana, MS. Lat. IV. 37, fol. 110v.

Physical Setting

The burden of this section is the precise physical setting of a given piece of
writing or text — as distinct, that is, from the writing or text as such, from
the scribes or scriveners who produced the writing, and from the artists who
embellished it or the readers who glossed or annotated it, all of which are
the object of the next or 'Human Setting.' Hence the present section covers,
for example, the material or support (papyrus, parchment, paper, etc.) on
which the writing is transmitted, the format and the make-up (roll, strip,
codex, gathering, booklet, etc.) of the material, the ruling, if any, of the
writing space and of its surrounds, foliation, pagination, binding, rebinding,
signs of origin or provenance, the ink or other medium of writing. As a
term, *physical setting* is designed to be much wider than *codicology*. The
latter, of course, is a useful term when only codices are in question, but
it is much too narrow when one remembers that the codex or book is not
the only possible physical setting of texts, and that palaeography is concerned with handwriting as such and not simply with handwriting as it is
found in codices. *Physical setting* therefore embraces any and every possible setting, from ostraka, masonry, and tablets to papyrus, parchment,
and paper, including the vast body (far larger, in fact, than that of codices)
of single sheets which transmits business, chancery, notarial, judicial, epistolary, or other 'diplomatic' witnesses to the history of handwriting, and
which all too often is abandoned by the wayside in courses of palaeography.
However, since much of conventional palaeography is limited to literary
texts and hence to codices, much of the present section is given over to the
book as one of the main carriers of handwriting.

MATTER

Papyrus, Parchment, Paper, Tablets

PAPYRUS

1511
Bataille, A. 'Papyrologie' in **42**, 498-527.
1512
Pattie, T.S. and E.G. Turner. *The Written Word on Papyrus* (British Library, London 1974)
The catalogue of an exhibition, with 19 plates, map, and select bibliography.
1513
Pliny the Elder (Gaius Plinius Secundus, A.D. 23/24-79), *Naturalis historia* XIII, xxi. 68 - xxvii. 89 (ed. e.g. H. Rackham [London 1945] IV, 139-53)
On the making and kinds of papyrus.
1514
Santifaller, L. *Beiträge zur Geschichte der Beschreibstoffe im Mittelalter, mit besonderer Berücksichtigung der päpstlichen Kanzlei, 1.* Teil: *Untersuchungen* (Graz–Cologne 1953)
On papyrus, parchment, and paper in general. See also M. Wittek, 'Les Matières à écrire au moyen âge: A propos d'un ouvrage de L. Santifaller,' *Scriptorium* 10 (1956) 270-74.
1515
Turner, E.G. *Greek Papyri: An Introduction.* 2nd ed. (Oxford 1980)
First issued in 1968, now reissued with a supplement on recent developments in papyrology.

PARCHMENT

1516
Reed, R. *The Nature and Making of Parchment* (London 1975)
Provides 14 illustrations. Has no notes or bibliography.
1517
Ryder, M.L. 'Parchment: Its History, Manufacture, and Composition,' *Journal of the Society of Archivists* 2 (1964) 391-9.
1518
Sabbe, E. 'Papyrus et parchemin du haut moyen âge' in *Miscellanea histori-*

ca in honorem Leonis van der Essen. 2 vols. (Brussels 1947) I, 95-103.

1519

Thompson, D.V. 'Medieval Parchment Making,' *The Library* 4th ser. 16 (1935) 113-17

Discusses London, BL, MS. Harley 3915 (Germany, 13th century).

PAPER

See also **1646-52.**

1520

Basanoff, A. 'L'Emploi du papier à l'Université de Paris, 1430-1473,' *Bibliothèque d'humanisme et de renaissance* 26 (1964) 305-25.

1521

De la Mare, A.C. 'The Shop of a Florentine "Cartolaio" in 1426' in *Studi offerti a Roberto Ridolfi,* ed. B. Maracchi Biagiarelli and D.E. Rhodes (Florence 1973) 237-48

Especially of interest for 'waste' materials.

1522

Heawood, E. 'Sources of Early English Paper Supply,' *The Library* 4th ser. 10 (1929) 282-307

A survey up to A.D. 1500.

1523

Irigoin, J. 'Les Origines de la fabrication du papier en Italie,' *Papiergeschichte* 13 (1963) 62-7

See also **1652.**

1524

Labarre, E.J. *Dictionary and Encyclopaedia of Paper and Paper Making.* 2nd ed. (Amsterdam–London 1952), with *Supplement* by E.G. Loeber (1967).

1525

Martini, C. *La bottega di un cartolaio fiorentino dalla seconda metà del Quattrocento* (Florence 1956)

On a paper shop of 1476.

1526

Papiergeschichte (Darmstadt 1951-)

A periodical with the occasional bibliography.

TABLETS

1527
Büll, R. and E. Moser. 'Wachs' in Pauly-Wissowa, *Real-Encyclopädie der classischen Altertumswissenschaft* (**2109**), Supplementband XIII (Munich 1973) cols. 1347-1416
See also the journal *Von Wachs* (Frankfurt 1963-) for various articles by Büll and others on wax tablets.
1528
Petrucci, A. *Le tavolette cerate fiorentine di Casa Majorfi* (Rome 1965)
Provides a bibliography on tablets. See also **569, 665**.

Preparation, Tools, Inks

See also **1092** for Insular pens, and **155** for notes on inks, etc.

PREPARATION (GENERAL)

1529
Brown, J. 'The Distribution and Significance of Membrane Prepared in the Insular Manner' in **66**, 127-35
Surveys the influence of Insular codicology on the Continent before, generally, A.D. 800. Notes that Insular membranes were thick, pricked with a knife in both margins, and were ruled after folding.
1530
Vezin, J. 'La Réalisation matérielle des manuscrits latins pendant le haut moyen âge' in **56**, 15-51. 12 pls.
A straightforward account, with diagrams, of the make-up of the medieval codex to ca. A.D. 1100.
1531
Wattenbach, W. *Das Schriftwesen im Mittelalter.* 3rd ed. (Leipzig 1896, repr. Graz 1958)
An enduring survey, with a wealth of sources, of most aspects of MS production in the Middle Ages. For scribes, see further **1744**. There are incipits at pp. 666-70.

TOOLS, FRAMES, RULING

1532
Coveney, D.K. 'The Ruling of the Exeter Book,' *Scriptorium* 12 (1958) 51-5.
1533
Gilissen, L. 'Un elément codicologique trop peu exploité: La réglure,' *Scriptorium* 23 (1969) 150-62.
1534
————. *Prolégomènes à la codicologie* (Ghent 1977). 95 pls., 63 figs.
Investigates the varieties of writing-frames and their mathematical bases.
1535
————. 'Les Réglures des manuscrits: Reflexions sur quelques études récentes,' *SC* 5 (1981) 231-52
Chiefly with respect to Leroy **1540**.
1536
Jones, L.W. 'Where are the Prickings?' *Transactions and Proceedings of the American Philological Association* 75 (1944) 71-86.
1537
————. 'Pricking Manuscripts: The Instruments and their Significance,' *Speculum* 21 (1946) 389-403. 3 pls.
1538
————. 'Pricking Systems in New York Manuscripts' in **63**, VI, 80-92.
1539
————. 'Ancient Prickings in Eighth-Century Manuscripts,' *Scriptorium* 15 (1961) 14-22.
1540
Leroy, J. *Les Types de réglure des manuscrits grecs* (Paris 1976)
See also **1535**.
1541
Miner, D. 'More about Medieval Pouncing' in *Homage to a Bookman: Essays on Manuscripts, Books, and Printing written for Hans P. Kraus on his 60th Birthday,* ed. H. Lehmann-Haupt (Berlin 1967) 87-107. 15 figs.
Notes on the use of pounce (pumice) for smoothing parchment.
1542
Pattie, T.S. 'The Ruling as a Clue to the Make-up of a Medieval Manuscript,' *British Library Journal* 1 (1975) 15-21.

INKS

1543
De Pas, M. 'La Composition des encres noires' in **1665**, 121-32
Discusses black and carbon inks especially.
1544
————. 'Les encres médiévaux' in **497**, 55-60.
1545
Leclercq, H. 'Encre' in *Dictionnaire d'archéologie chrétienne et de liturgie*,
I (Paris 1922) 39-42.

FORM

Roll and Codex

1546
Mallon, J. 'Quel est le plus ancien exemple connu d'un manuscrit latin en
forme de codex?' *Emerita* 17 (1949) 1-8.
1547
McCown, C.C. 'Codex and Roll in the New Testament,' *Harvard
Theological Review* 34 (1941) 219-50.
1548
Roberts, C.H. 'The Codex,' *PBA* 40 (1954) 169-204
An investigation of the 'triumph' of the codex over the roll. See also **1553**.
1549
Rouse, R.H. 'Roll and Codex: The Transmission of the Works of Reinmar
von Zweter' in **66a**, 107-23. 5 pls.
Suggests that songs in Middle High German and other vernaculars initially
circulated on rolls before being placed in codices.
1550
Santifaller, L. 'Über späte Papyrusrollen und frühe Pergamentrollen' in
Speculum historiale: Festschrift J. Spörl (Munich 1965) 117-33.
1551
————. 'Über Papierrollen als Beschreibstoff' in **69**, V, 361-71.
1552
Skeat, T.C. 'Early Christian Book-Production: Papyri and Manuscripts' in
The Cambridge History of the Bible, II: *The West from the Fathers to the
Reformation*, ed. G.W.H. Lampe (Cambridge 1969) 54-79.

1553

Turner, E.G. *The Typology of the Early Codex* (Philadelphia 1977). 9 pls.
While accepting the Christian role advanced by Roberts **1548** and others in
the 'triumph' of the codex over the roll, argues against the supposed prior-
ity of the parchment book over the papyrus book.

1554

Wieacker, F. *Textstufen klassischer Juristen* (Göttingen 1960)
Much on roll and codex, papyrus and parchment.

The Codex

BOOK PRODUCTION

General

1555

Birt, T. *Das antike Buchwesen in seinem Verhältniss zur Literatur* (Berlin
1882, repr. 1959).

1556

Cavallo, G., ed. *Libri, editori, e pubblico nel mondo antico: Guida storica
e critica* (Rome – Bari 1975)
Includes chapters by E.G. Turner, T. Kleberg, and Cavallo.

1557

Glaister, G.A. *Glossary of the Book.* 2nd ed. (Berkeley, Calif. 1979).

1558

Hunger, H. 'Antikes und mittelalterliches Buch- und Schriftwesen' in
*Geschichte der Textüberlieferung der antiken und mittelalterlichen
Literatur,* I (Zürich 1961) 25-147.

1559

Ivy, G.S. 'The Bibliography of the Manuscript Book' in **1314,** 32-65
Among many things has a good note on holster-books.

1560

Kenyon, F.G. *Books and Readers in Ancient Greece and Rome.* 2nd ed.
(Oxford 1951)
A small, readable volume, first published in 1932.

1561

Presser, H. *Das Buch vom Buch* (Bremen 1962)
On all aspects of the book, with a German version of Richard de Bury's

Philobiblon (**1315**) by L. Mackensen, a bibliography (H. Wegener), and a chronological table of writing.
1562
Schubart, W. *Das Buch bei den Griechen und Römern.* 2nd ed. (Heidelberg 1962). 31 pls.

Medieval

See also **1687**.

1563
Bruckner, A. 'Book, the Medieval' in *New Catholic Encyclopedia* (New York 1967) II, 684-9.
1564
Bühler, C.F. *The Fifteenth-Century Book: The Scribes, the Printers, the Decorators* (Philadelphia 1960).
1565
Calot, F., L.-M. Michon, and P. Angoulvent. *L'Art du livre en France des origines à nos jours* (Paris 1931).
1566
Doyle, A.I., E. Rainey, and D.B. Wilson. *Manuscript to Print: Tradition and Innovation in the Renaissance Book.* Durham University Library Guides (Durham 1975)
Provides 35 illustrations, with commentary.
1567
Doyle, A.I. and M.B. Parkes. 'The Production of Copies of the *Canterbury Tales* and the *Confessio amantis* in the Early Fifteenth Century' in **46**, 163-210
Discusses book production outside of universities and religious houses. Various Latin and vernacular texts were often produced on a piecework system by stationers in large towns, the work being farmed out to free-lance scribes, illuminators, and book-binders.
1568
Gumbert, J.P. *Die Utrechter Kartäuser und ihre Bücher im frühen fünfzehnten Jahrhundert* (Leiden 1974). 50 pls. of MSS
On the technical aspects of 50 extant MSS (at Utrecht, Brussels, Wolfenbüttel) from the library of the Carthusian house of Nieuwlicht (1392-1432). Rich treatment is given to codicological and 'archaeolog-

ical' aspects of the MSS, many of which are in Bastarda. See also
Lieftinck **1101**.
1569
Ross, D.J.A. 'Methods of Book Production in a XIVth Century French
Miscellany (London, B. M., MS. Royal 19 D I),' *Scriptorium* 6 (1952)
63-75
Shows, in the light of this MS (probably from the region of Paris) and
related MSS, how the labour of illumination was divided between the
master of the workshop (who drew sketches in the margins), a draughtsman
(who then drew out the sketched miniatures in the space left in the text by
the scribe), and a painter (who, in this case, did his work very sloppily and,
in another case, did the painting after the MS was bound).

CODICOLOGY

Theory

1570
Ahlfeld, R. 'Handschriftenkunde' in *Dahlmann-Waitz, Quellenkunde*
(see **2**) I, sec. 15
A vast bibliography of codicology.
1571
Canart, P. 'Nouvelles recherches et nouveaux instruments de travail dans
le domaine de la codicologie,' *SC* 3 (1979) 267-307
A survey of writings of Gilissen **1534**, Ouy **1581**, and others.
1572
Delaissé, L.M.J. 'Towards a History of the Medieval Book' in **55**, 75-83
A revised version of a contribution of the same title in *Miscellanea André
Combes,* II (Rome 1967) 27-39.
1573
Derolez, A. 'Codicologie ou archéologie du livre? Quelques observations
sur la leçon inaugurale de M. Albert Gruijs à l'Université catholique de
Nimègue,' *Scriptorium* 27 (1973) 47-9.
1574
Gruijs, A. 'Codicology or the Archaeology of the Book? A False Dilemma,'
Quaerendo 2 (1972) 87-108.
1575
————. 'Paléographie, codicologie, et archéologie du livre, questions de

méthodologie et de terminologie' in **66**, 19-25 (including discussion).
1576
Gumbert, J.P. *Schrift, codex, en tekst: Een rondgang door paleografie en codicologie* (Leiden 1974).
1577
————. 'Ebert's Codicology a Hundred and Fifty Years Old,' *Quaerendo* 5 (1975) 336-9
Reflections on F.A. Ebert, *Handschriftenkunde* I (Leipzig 1825).
1578
Leroy, J. 'La Description codicologique des manuscrits grecs de parchemin' in **497**, 27-44.
1579
Mallon, J. 'L'Archéologie des monuments graphiques,' *Revue historique* 460 (1961) 297-312
Makes pointed remarks relative to codicology.
1580
Muzerelle, D. 'Le Vocabulaire codicologique' in **66a**, 39-46.
1581
Ouy, G. 'Histoire "visible" et histoire "cachée" d'un manuscrit,' *Le Moyen Age* 64 (1958) 115-38.
1582
————. 'Pour une archivistique des manuscrits médiévaux,' *Bulletin des bibliothèques de France* 3 (1958) 897-923.
1582a
————. 'Codicologie latine médiévale,' *Annuaire de l'Ecole pratique des hautes études, IVe Section* 104 (1972) 355-64.

Practice

1583
Beit-Arië, M. *Hebrew Codicology* (Paris 1976). 32 pls.
Provides useful parallels.
1584
Bozzolo, C. and E. Ornato. *Pour une histoire du livre manuscrit au moyen âge: Trois essais de codicologie quantitative* (Paris 1980)
On book production in N. France, make-up of quires, dimensions of MSS.
1585
Gilissen, L. 'La Composition des cahiers: Le pliage du parchemin et

l'imposition,' *Scriptorium* 26 (1972) 3-33. 8 pls.
See also **1533-5**.
1586
Lowe, E.A. 'Some Facts about our Oldest Latin Manuscripts,' *Classical Quarterly* 19 (1925) 197-208; repr. in **60**, I, 187-202.
1587
————. 'More Facts about our Oldest Latin Manuscripts,' *Classical Quarterly* 22 (1928) 43-62; repr. in **60**, I, 250-74
Examines, in these two articles, 150 MSS of the 4th-8th centuries A.D. Tabulates certain features, e.g. running titles, quire marks, number of lines, style of colophon, ruling.
1588
Parkes, M.B. 'The Influence of the Concepts of *ordinatio* and *compilatio* on the Development of the Book' in **45**, 115-44. 8 pls. (IX-XVI)
On the possible effect of scholasticism on the layout of the page in the 13th and 14th centuries.
1589
Pollard, G. 'Notes on the Size of the Sheet,' *The Library* 4th ser. 22 (1941-2) 105-37
On the manner of preparing quires. See also **1536-42**.
1590
Preisendanz, K. 'Quaternio' in **2109**, vol. 24 (1963) cols. 838-49.
1591
Samaran, C. 'Manuscrits "imposés" à la manière typographique' in *Mélanges en l'honneur de M. Fr. Martroye* (Paris 1940) 325-36
On the practice, not apparent in MSS as they stand, of writing a number of pages upon an unfolded sheet of parchment which, as happens in printing, was later folded to produce bifolia.
1592
————. 'Contribution à l'histoire du livre manuscrit au moyen âge: Manuscrits "imposés" et manuscrits non "coupés"' in *Atti del X Congresso internazionale di studi storici* (Florence 1957) 151-5.
1593
Vezin, J. 'Observations sur l'emploi des réclames dans les manuscrits latins,' *BEC* 125 (1967) 5-33.
1594
————. 'Codicologie comparée' in **66**, 153-61
Mainly with respect to catchwords once more.

FORMAT

1595
Garand, M.-C. 'Livres de poche médiévaux à Dijon et à Rome,' *Scriptorium* 25 (1971) 18-24. 6 pls.
A Cistercian breviary, A.D. 1498 (Dijon, Bibliothèque publique, MS. 115), and a repertory of jurisprudence, 1283-4 (Vatican City, BAV, MS. Borgiani lat. 355). See also **653**, and for portable vademecum books of Friars in the 13th and 14th centuries, D.L. D'Avray in **1094**, 61-4 with 2 pls. For 'Holster' books see **1559**.

1596
Robinson, P.R. 'The "Booklet": A Self-contained Unit in Composite Manuscripts' in **57**, 46-69. 7 pls.
Lists features which serve to identify a 'booklet.'

BINDING

1597
Baras, E., J. Irigoin, and J. Vezin. *La Reliure médiévale: Trois conférences d'initiation* (Paris 1978)
Useful, especially the essay of J. Vezin, 'La Reliure occidentale au moyen âge.' See also, for dating by binding, **1636**.

1598
Barker, N. 'Quiring and the Binder' in *Studies in the Book Trade in Honour of Graham Pollard* (Oxford 1975) 11-31
Discusses quire-marks made by 15th-century English binders when rebinding MSS.

1599
De Marinis, T. *La legatura artistica in Italia nei secoli XV e XVI.* 3 vols. (Florence 1960-61). 726 pls. See also **1418**.

1600
Diehl, E. *Bookbinding: Its Background and Technique.* 2 vols. (New York –Toronto 1946).

1601
Gibson, S. *Early Oxford Bindings* (Oxford 1903), with many pls.

1602
Helwig, H. *Handbuch der Einbandkunde.* 3 vols. (Hamburg 1953-5)
One of the most comprehensive books on binding.

1603

————. *Einführung in die Einbandkunde* (Stuttgart 1970)
Has a good introduction, especially for terminology.

1604

Kyriss, E. *Verzierte gotische Einbände im alten deutschen Sprachgebiet.*
4 vols. (Stuttgart 1951-8)
Includes 3 volumes of plates.

1605

Mazal, O. 'Medieval Bookbinding' in *The Book through Five Thousand
Years,* ed. H.D.L. Vervliet (London 1972) 314-38
Has an excellent bibliography.

1606

[Miner, D., ed.] *The History of Bookbinding 925-1950 A.D.* (Baltimore
1957)
The catalogue of an exhibition at the Baltimore Museum of Art, Maryland.

1607

Needham, P. *Twelve Centuries of Bookbinding: 400-1600* (New York–
London 1979)
Description, with 100 illustrations, of 100 samples of binding, all from
printed books and MSS in the Pierpont Morgan Library, New York. The
bulk of the bindings illustrated is of printed books, 1460-1600. Latin MSS
are represented by ten examples in colour of 'Treasure bindings,' 800-1250,
and by some six leather bindings, 1190-1460.

1608

Oldham, J.B. *English Blind-Stamped Bindings* (Cambridge 1952).

1609

————. *Blind Panels of English Binders* (Cambridge 1958).

1610

Pollard, G. 'The Construction of English Twelfth-Century Bindings,' *The
Library* 5th ser. 17 (1962) 1-22
See also **1064.**

1611

————. 'Describing Medieval Bookbindings' in **45,** 50-65. 6 figs.

1612

Van Regemorter, B. 'Evolution de la technique de la reliure du VIIIe au
XIIe siècle, principalement d'après les MSS d'Autun, d'Auxerre, et de
Troyes,' *Scriptorium* 2 (1948) 275-85. 4 pls.

1613
————. 'Le Codex relié depuis son origine jusqu'au haut moyen-âge,' *Le Moyen Age* 61 (1955) 1-26.
1614
————. 'La Reliure byzantine,' *Revue belge d'archéologie et d'histoire de l'art* 36 (1967) 99-142. 20 pls., 13 figs.
1615
Vezin, J. 'Les Reliures carolingiennes de cuir à décor estampé de la Bibliothèque nationale de Paris,' *BEC* 128 (1970) 81-113. 4 pls.

CATALOGUING, DATING, LOCALIZING

General Description (Codicography)

See also **1925-9** (Identifying Texts and Fragments). For catalogues which may serve as models see **1466, 1470, 1509.**

1616
[Beaud-Gambier, M.-J. and L. Fossier] *Guide pour l'élaboration d'une notice de manuscrit* (Paris 1977)
A useful 52-page publication (in typescript) of the Institut de recherche et d'histoire des textes (Bibliographies. Colloques. Travaux préparatoires. Série informatique et Documentation textuelle).
1617
Casamassima, E. 'Note sul metodo della descrizione dei codici,' *Rassegna degli archivi di stato* 23 (1963) 181-205.
1618
Colker, M.L. 'The Cataloguing of Mediaeval Manuscripts: A Review Article,' *Mediaevalia et humanistica* new ser. 2 (1971) 165-73.
1619
Coveney, D.K. 'The Cataloguing of Literary Manuscripts,' *Journal of Documentation* 6 (1950) 125-39.
1620
Dufour, J. 'Les Rouleaux des morts' in **57**, 96-102
On how to describe mortuary rolls and their lists of subscriptions. Provides a good bibliography. See also **983.**

1621

Gruijs, A. and P. Holager. 'A Plan for Computer-assisted Codicography of Medieval Manuscripts,' *Quaerendo* 11 (1981) 95-127, with many figs.
The authors take as their basis the compact economical descriptions used by N.R. Ker **698, 1470**. There is a useful bibliography at pp. 118-19, and a vademecum of binding terms at p. 120.

1622

Köttelwesch, C., ed. *Zur Katalogisierung mittelalterlicher und neuerer Handschriften* (Frankfurt 1963)
A special volume (Sonderheft 1) of *Zeitschrift für Bibliothekswesen und Bibliographie.*

1623

Macken, R. 'Bref Vade-mecum pour la description sur place d'un manuscrit médiéval,' *Bulletin de philosophie médiévale* 21 (1979) 86-97
Mainly with respect to MSS of scholastic writings.

1624

Mazal, O., ed. *Handschriftenbeschreibung in Österreich: Referate, Beratungen, und Ergebnisse der Arbeitstagungen in Kremsmünster (1973) und Zwettl (1974)* (Vienna 1975). 8 pls. showing 77 figs.
Deals with MS description at pp. 135-9, nomenclature of scripts at 142-3.

1625

Ouy, G. 'Projet d'un catalogue de manuscrits médiévaux adapté aux exigences de la recherche moderne,' *Bulletin des bibliothèques de France* 6 (1961) 319-35.

1626

Pfaff, R.W. 'M.R. James on the Cataloguing of Manuscripts: A Draft Essay of 1906,' *Scriptorium* 31 (1977) 103-18
Interesting observations, particularly with respect to cataloguing decorated liturgical books, from one of the pioneers of modern cataloguing.

1627

Porcher, J. 'A propos des catalogues de manuscrits,' *Bulletin des bibliothèques de France* 5 (1960) 79-82
Advocates traditional methods, countered subsequently by Ouy **1625**.

1628

Rambaud-Buhot, J. 'Plan et méthode de travail pour la rédaction d'un catalogue des manuscrits du décret de Gratien,' *RHE* 48 (1953) 211-23.

1629

Reingold, N. 'Subject Analysis and Description of Manuscript Collections,'

Isis 53 (1962) 106-12.
1630
Richtlinien Handschriftenkatalogisierung. 2nd ed. (Bonn—Bad Godesberg 1974)
A succinct guide to cataloguing from the Deutsche Forschungsgemein-schaft, for some comments on which see A. Derolez, 'Les Nouvelles Instructions pour le catalogage des manuscrits en République Fédérale allemande,' *Scriptorium* 28 (1974) 299-300.
1631
Thiel, E.J. 'Die liturgischen Bücher des Mittelalters: Ein kleines Lexikon zur Handschriftenkunde,' *Börsenblatt für den deutschen Buchhandel,* Frankfurter Ausgabe 23 (1967) 2379-95
See also **1452-6, 2120.**
1632
Wilson, W.J. 'Manuscript Cataloging,' *Traditio* 12 (1956) 457-555
Based on his experiences while preparing the *Census* **1496.** Thoughtful, with good bibliography, but a little out-dated by recent codicological research.

Dating, Localizing

The importance of *Manuscrits datés* **313-40** and of *Colophons de manu-scrits occidentaux* **1741** will be obvious here. See also **1646-52** (watermarks).

1633
Autenrieth, J. 'Probleme der Lokalisierung und Datierung von spät-karolingischen Schriften (10. und 11. Jahrhundert)' in **58,** 67-74.
1634
Boyle, L.E. 'The Date of the San Sisto Lectionary,' *Archivum Fratrum praedicatorum* 28 (1958) 381-9
On the importance of liturgical evidence.
1635
Destrez, J. and G. Fink-Errera. 'Des manuscrits apparemment datés,' *Scriptorium* 12 (1958) 56-93
On how to distinguish in colophons the date of composition from the date of a copy.

1636

Gibson, S. 'The Localization of Books by their Bindings,' *Transactions of the Bibliographical Society* 1st ser. 8 (1904-6) 25-38
See also **1597-1615**.

1637

Irigoin, J. 'La Datation des papiers italiens des XIIIe et XIVe siècles,' *Papiergeschichte* 18 (1968) 49-52.

1638

Lowe, E.A. 'Assumptions' in **255**, xii-xiv (CLA IV)
A statement of certain 'assumptions' of Lowe with respect to the dating, localization, and origin of MSS, for one or two refinements of which see F. Masai, *Scriptorium* 3 (1949) 136.

1639

Madan, F. 'The Localization of Manuscripts' in *Essays in History presented to Reginald Lane Poole,* ed. H.W.C. Davis (Oxford 1927; repr. Freeport, N.Y. 1967) 5-29.

1640

Patterson, S. 'Comparison of Minor Initial Decoration: A Possible Method of Showing the Place of Origin of Thirteenth-Century Manuscripts,' *The Library* 5th ser. 27 (1972) 23-30; and, more concretely, 'Minor Initial Decoration used to Date the Propertius Fragment (MS. Leiden Voss. lat. O. 38),' *Scriptorium* 28 (1974) 235-47.

1641

Petrucci, A. 'Istruzione per la datazione,' *SM* 3rd ser. 9/2 (1968) 1115-26
Gives guidelines for dating MSS of the 9th-12th centuries. See also **1488**.

1642

Powitz, G. 'Datieren und Lokalisieren nach der Schrift,' *Bibliothek und Wissenschaft* 10 (1976) 124-37.

1643

Trombelli, G.-C. *Arte di conoscere l'età de' codici latini, e italiani* (Bologna 1756, repr. Milan 1971)
Brief, but still useful, with two pull-outs of samples of scripts.

1644

Van Dijk, S.J.P. 'The Lateran Missal,' *Sacris erudiri* 6 (1954) 125-79
Informal but handy directions on dating and localizing liturgical MSS. See also **1634**.

1645

Vezin, J. 'Le Point d'interrogation, un élément de datation et de localisa-

tion des manuscrits: L'exemple de Saint-Denis au IXe siècle,' *Scriptorium*
34 (1980) 181-96
Gives a list of 25 MSS in which the St. Denis style of punctuation has been
detected. See also **1735-40**.

Watermarks

See also **1520-28**.

1646
Briquet, C.M. *Les Filigranes: Dictionnaire historique des marques du papier
dès leur apparition vers 1282 jusqu'en 1600.* 2nd ed. (Paris 1923; repr.
New York 1966 and, with 150 pp. of additional bibliography and matter
by A. Stevenson, Amsterdam 1968)
In all, there are 16,112 facsimiles of watermarks in this standard work,
first published in 1907.

1647
De Bofarull y Sans, F. de A. *Heraldic Watermarks,* trans. A.J. Henschel
(Hilversum 1956)
First published in Spanish, in 1901.

1648
—————. *Animals in Watermarks* (Hilversum 1959)
First published in Spanish, in 1910.

1649
Mošin, V.A. and S.M. Traljič. *Filigranes des XIIIe et XIVe siècles.* 2 vols.
(Zagreb 1957)
Prints 852 plates illustrating 7,271 watermarks of the 13th and 14th cen-
turies not found in **1646.**

1650
Piccard, G. *Die Kronen-Wasserzeichen* (Stuttgart 1961); *Die Ochsenkopf-
Wasserzeichen,* 3 vols. (1966); *Die Turm-Wasserzeichen* (1970).

1651
Stevenson, A. 'Paper as Bibliographical Evidence,' *The Library* 5th ser. 17
(1962) 197-212. 4 pls.

1652
Zonghi, A. *Le marche principali delle carte fabrianesi dal 1293 al 1599*
(Fabriano 1881); repr. as *Zonghi's Watermarks,* ed. A.F. Gasparinetti

(Hilversum 1953)
Invaluable for information about Fabriano (NE of Assisi; province of Ancona) as a paper-making centre from the late 13th century.

Technological Aids

1653
Barrow, W.J. *Manuscripts and Documents: Their Deterioration and Restoration.* 2nd ed. (Charlottesville, Va. 1972)
Has excellent bibliography; and, for this edition (the first was in 1955), a long foreword by F.G. Poole.

1654
Benton, J.F., A.R. Gillespie, and J.M. Soha. 'Digital Image-Processing Applied to the Photography of Manuscripts,' *Scriptorium* 33 (1979) 40-55. 5 pls.
See also **1664**.

1655
Boutaine, J.L., J. Irigoin, and A. Lemonnier. 'La Radiophotographie dans l'étude des manuscrits' in **1665**, 159-76.

1656
Conservation et reproduction des manuscrits et imprimés anciens. Studi e testi 216 (Vatican City 1976)
Papers from an international colloquium at the Vatican Library in 1975.

1657
Fink-Errera, G. 'Contribution de la macrophotographie à la conception d'une paléographie générale,' *Bulletin de philosophie médiévale* 4 (1962) 100-18. 5 pls.
See also **177**.

1658
Garand, M.-C. and F. Etcheverry. 'Analyse d'écritures et macrophotographie: Les manuscrits originaux de Guibert de Nogent,' *CM* 1 (1975) 112-22. 7 pls.

1659
Haselden, R.B. *Scientific Aids for the Study of Manuscripts* (Oxford 1935).

1660
Irigoin, J. 'Quelques méthodes scientifiques applicables à l'étude historique du papier,' *Papiergeschichte* 21 (1971) 4-9.

1661

Ouy, G. 'Qu'attendent l'archéologie du livre et l'histoire intellectuelle et littéraire des techniques de laboratoire?' in **1665**, 77-94.

1662

Pollard, G. 'On the Repair of Medieval Bindings,' *The Paper Conservator* 1 (1976) 35-6

Notes that fewer than 500 of the bindings done in England before A.D. 1225 survive.

1663

Pratesi, A. 'A proposito di tecniche di laboratorio e storia della scrittura,' *SC* 1 (1977) 199-209

A propos *Les Techniques* **1665**, notes that in the long run these techniques are no substitute for palaeographical skill.

1664

Samaran, C. 'Nouvelles perspectives sur la lecture des textes détériorés par grattage, lavage, ou simple usure' in **62**, II, 597-9

Reflections on Benton et al. **1654**.

1665

Les Techniques de laboratoire dans l'étude des manuscrits. Colloques internationaux du Centre national de la recherche scientifique 548 (Paris 1974)

Various papers by Boutaine (see **1655**), de Pas (**1543**), Ouy (**1661**).

Human Setting

It is the human element, writing, that gives life to the physical setting above. In the present section, however, what is in question is not precisely what is written (that is the subject of the section entitled 'Textual Setting') but rather how what is written is present graphically and visually — in other words, the script or scripts, the presence or not of abbreviations, the embellishments. The written text, of course, is subject to all sorts of human vagaries, and, in the long run, it is the quality or intelligibility of the written text that really matters for students of manuscripts or writing of any kind. But one will hardly be in a position securely to judge of that quality or to pronounce on intelligibility unless, for example, one first masters the abbreviations current in the given period, and is thoroughly sensitive to scribal or artistic conceits and conventions. In more senses than one students of palaeography may be said to be at the mercy of scribes and artists: a scribe may be able to call up a battery of contractions and truncations, some commonplace, some arcane; an artist, in turn, may have unsuspected models or modelbooks at his disposal. Above all, it is well to remember that scribes and artists of the twelfth or any other century were not writing or decorating for an audience of the twentieth century. They were writing and decorating for their contemporaries; and they presume a general background — in the Latin language, for example, in the classics and the writings of church fathers, in the scriptures and scriptural typology — that few if any present-day readers may be presumed to possess. As was noted above in the headnote to **1091-1252** ('Gothic'), writing and decoration ceased to be a preserve of clerics and monasteries from about A.D. 1100, when, in particular, professional scribes (here called 'scriveners') began to emerge as a class. In notarial circles, scriveners were regulated in general by the various licensing bodies (communes, etc.). In university circles, particularly in the

thirteenth and fourteenth centuries, the work of scriveners was controlled
to some extent by university statutes. Hence the special section here on
university scriveners and stationers. The heart of the university control of
copying was the pecia-system, by which texts were leased piece-by-piece
by stationers to scriveners who then made copies or *apopeciae* of each in
turn. The place of the pecia-system in the editing of texts is discussed
below (**1977-2078**, especially **2066-73**) under 'Textual Setting.' Perhaps
it is unwise to separate these two treatments of the pecia-system, but in
the present section the system is considered from a scribal point of view,
whereas in the second instance it is seen in relation to the texts that
resulted from the system.

SCRIBAL TRAINING, SCRIBES, SCRIPTORIA

Scribal Training

1666
Bischoff, B. 'Elementarunterricht und Probationes Pennae in der ersten
Hälfte des Mittelalters' in **67**, 9-20; repr. in **32**, I, 74-87
On the process of teaching to read and write.
1667
Casamassima, E. *Trattati di scrittura del cinquecento italiano* (Milan 1966).
89 pls.
See also **1282**.
1668
Gasparri, F. 'Note sur l'enseignement de l'écriture aux XVe-XVIe siècles:
A propos d'un nouveau placard du XVIe siècle découvert à la Bibliothèque
nationale,' *SC* 2 (1978) 245-61.
1669
————. 'L'Enseignement de l'écriture à la fin du moyen âge: A propos
du *Tractatus in omnem modum scribendi*, ms. 76 de l'abbaye de Kremsmünster,' *SC* 3 (1979) 243-65
The text, composed probably at Melk ca. 1420, is edited from this MS at
pp. 252-65. See also **1675**.
1670
Hajnal, I. *L'Enseignement de l'écriture aux universités médiévales*, ed. L.
Mezey. 2nd ed. (Budapest 1959) with album of facsimiles.

1671

————. 'Universities and the Development of Writing in the XIIth-XIIIth Centuries,' *Scriptorium* 6 (1952) 177-95
A summary, in effect, of **1670** above, and of the theory, adumbrated in the first edition (1943), that the teaching of handwriting in universities — a teaching adapted to the practical demands of chanceries — gave rise to an 'international' diplomatic writing. However, as reviewers have pointed out, the problem is that we know next to nothing about the 'teaching of writing' in the universities.

1672

————. 'A propos de l'enseignement de l'écriture dans les universités médiévales,' *Scriptorium* 11 (1957) 3-28
Further points.

1673

Spilling, H. 'Schreibkünste des späten Mittelalters,' *CM* 4 (1978) 97-119
On training of scribes in Germany in the 15th century. Notes remarkable agreement between *modi scribendi* of Melk and Kremsmünster (see **1669**) and sample sheets of writing-masters of the period. See also **1675**.

1674

Steinberg, S.H. 'Medieval Writing-Masters,' *The Library* 4th ser. 22 (1941) 1-24. 6 pls.; 5th ser. 2 (1948) 203.

1675

————. 'Instructions in Writing by Members of the Congregation of Melk,' *Speculum* 16 (1941) 210-15. 1 pl.
See also **1669, 1673**.

1676

————. 'A Hand-List of Specimens of Medieval Writing-Masters,' *The Library* 4th ser. 23 (1942) 191-4.

1677

Van Dijk, S.J.P. 'An Advertisement Sheet of an Early Fourteenth-Century Writing Master at Oxford,' *Scriptorium* 10 (1956) 47-64. 4 pls.

1678

Wehmer, C. 'Die Schreibmeisterblätter des späten Mittelalters' in **63**, VI, 147-61. 2 pls.

Scribes

1679

Amargier, P. 'Les "Scriptores" du XIe siècle à Saint Victor de Marseille,' *Scriptorium* 32 (1978) 213-20

A list of over 70 scribes, both monks and clerks, who subscribed charters at or for St. Victor, A.D. 1001-96.

1680

Bruckner, A. 'Zum Problem der Frauenhandschriften im Mittelalter' in *Aus Mittelalter und Neuzeit: Festschrift zum 70. Geburtstag von Gerhard Kallen* (Berlin 1957) 171-83.

1681

————. 'Weibliche Schreibtätigkeit im schweizerischen Spätmittelalter' in **33**, 441-8

Two articles on women as scribes. See also **910** on the nuns of Chelles.

1682

Couderc, C. 'Instructions données à un copiste du XVe siècle,' *BEC* 55 (1894) 232

On Paris, BN, MS. Nouv. acq. lat. 572.

1683

Gerson, J. *De laude scriptorum,* in his *Oeuvres complètes,* ed. P. Glorieux. IX (Paris 1973) 423-34

There are three types of scribes, according to Gerson in this work of 1423: scribe-authors, scribes who have a fair idea of what they write, and scribes who have none and are 'quasi pictores.' The work is in praise of the middle grade.

1684

Ker, N.R. 'Eton College Ms. 44 and its Exemplar' in **51**, 48-60

Prints 4 plates comparing the two MSS. The Eton MS was made by perhaps 53 amateurs pressed into service at New College, Oxford, in the early 1480s to copy what is now Balliol College MS. 187 (a 13th-century MS of Albert the Great on Luke and Mark).

1685

Lucas, P.J. 'John Capgrave, O.S.A. (1393-1464), Scribe and "Publisher",' *Transactions of the Cambridge Bibliographical Society* 5 (1969-71) 1-35.

1686

Mynors, R.A.B. 'A Fifteenth-Century Scribe: T. Werken,' *Transactions of the Cambridge Bibliographical Society* 1 (1949-53) 97-104. 2 pls.

On the fate of a professional scribe after books began to be printed: the Dutch scribe Werken, and his work for William Gray and others in London.
1687
Orlandelli, G. *Il libro a Bologna dal 1300 al 1330: Documenti, con uno studio su il contratto di scrittura nella dottrina notarile Bolognese* (Bologna 1959)
On writing-contracts and theory at Bologna. Edits 367 contracts between stationers and scribes, and provides an index of books and copyists.
1688
Parkes, M.B. 'A Fifteenth-Century Scribe: Henry Mere,' *Bodleian Library Record* 6 (1957-61) 654-9. 2 pls.
Considers him possibly a foreign scribe in the service of Christ Church, Canterbury, ca. 1450.
1689
Pickford, C.E. 'A Fifteenth-Century Copyist and his Patron' in *Medieval Miscellany presented to Eugène Vinaver,* ed. F. Whitehead (Manchester 1965) 245-62
On the work of Micheau Gonnot in the years 1463-74, when he copied five MSS (all now in libraries in Paris) of vernacular texts for Jacques d'Armagnac, duke of Nemours.
1690
Trithemius, J. *In Praise of Scribes: De laude scriptorum,* ed. K. Arnold, trans. R. Behrendt (Lawrence, Kans. 1974)
The celebrated work of Trithemius (1462-1516), theologian and historian, abbot of Sponheim (1483-1506), then of St. James of Würzburg. Written in 1492 to encourage monk-scribes to perseverance in the age of printing. See further **1255**.

Scriptoria

1691
[Dressler, F., ed.] *Scriptorum opus: Schreiber-Mönche am Werk. Prof. Dr. Otto Meyer zum 65. Geburtstag* (Wiesbaden 1971)
Includes a plate from Bamberg, Staatliche Bibliothek, MS. Patr. 5 (12th century), of scribes at work. There is a commentary by Dressler at pp. 5-14.
1692
Garand, M.-C. 'Manuscrits monastiques et scriptoria aux XIe et XIIe siècles'

in **57**, 9-33. 6 pls.
On the problem of identifying products of various monastic scriptoria.
Includes a bibliography of studies on scriptoria.
1693
Kneepkens, C.H. and H.F. Reijnders, eds. *Magister Siguinus, Ars lectoria:
Un art de lecture à haute voix du onzième siècle* (Leiden 1979)
Although the text edited here (from a writer probably of S or SW France)
is concerned primarily with correct pronunciation and accentuation of
words (of which there are endless lists), the author clearly has scribes in
mind also ('caveat scriptor,' he notes on occasion), and the tract is valuable for an appreciation of the varieties of 'perplexio' that could beset
scribes when listening to dictation or reading out aloud to themselves as
they wrote.
1694
Martin, H. 'Notes sur les écrivains au travail' in *Mélanges offerts à M. Emile
Chatelain* (Paris 1910) 535-44. 1 pl. of 2 figs.
Argues that pictures in MSS of scribes at work are highly stylized and, in
general, do not reveal much about, e.g., the position of the hand or the
way in which the writing instrument was held.
1695
Skeat, T.C. 'The Use of Dictation in Ancient Book Production,' *PBA* 42
(1956) 179-208.
1696
Vezin, J. 'La Répartition du travail dans les "scriptoria" carolingiens,'
Journal des Savants (1973) 212-27. 4 pls.

SCRIPTS, HANDS

Scripts

1697
Bartoloni, F. 'Paleografia e diplomatica, III: La nomenclatura delle scritture documentarie' in *Relazioni* (see **76**) I, 434-43. 10 pls. of samples
On the need for a distinction between canonized and non-canonized
documentary scripts. Presents some guidelines for a nomenclature of the
latter.

1698

Gasparri, F. 'Pour une terminologie des écritures latines: Doctrines et méthodes,' *CM* 2 (1976) 16-25

A review of past and present terminology.

1699

————. 'La terminologie des écritures' in **66a**, 31-7.

1700

Hessel, A. and W. Bulst. 'Kardinal Guala Bichieri und seine Bibliothek,' *Historische Vierteljahrschrift* 27 (1932) 772-94

On the important gift in 1219 to the library of Vercelli Duomo of books of Bichieri variously described as 'littera bononiensis,' 'littera parisiensis,' 'littera anglicana,' 'littera antiqua,' 'littera lombarda,' 'littera aretina.'

1701

Nomenclature des écritures livresques du IXe au XVIe siècle (Paris 1954). 44 figs.

Proceedings of the Premier colloque international de paléographie latine, Paris 1953, containing the papers of Battelli **1269**, Bischoff **1091**, and Lieftinck **1101**. Some reactions to this influential colloquium may be seen in *Scriptorium* 9 (1955) 290-93 (L.M.J. Delaissé); *Revue belge de philologie et d'histoire* 34 (1956) 174-81 (G. Despy); *La bibliofilia* 58 (1956) 44-7 (A. Pratesi); *Eunomia* 1 (1957) 35-40, 95-7 (Spunar **1703**); *BEC* 123 (1965) 558-61 (E. Poulle – in the context of the first volume for Low Countries of *Manuscrits datés* **333**, with Lieftinck's second thoughts on some of his nomenclature). The three papers are united in showing that terminology and classification cannot be arbitrary, but must reflect what happened as writing developed.

1702

Oeser, W. 'Die Brüder des gemeinsamen Lebens in Münster als Bücherschreiber,' *Archiv für Geschichte des Buchwesens* 5 (1962) 197-398. 25 pls.

Active in Holland and NW Germany from the end of the 14th century, the Brothers of the Common Life at Münster generally wrote in Textus and Textus rotundus. Bastarda appears about 1425.

1703

Spunar, P. 'Sur les questions de la terminologie paléographique des écritures livresques du 9e au 16e siècle,' *Eunomia* (Supplement to *Listy filologické*, Prague) 1 (1957) 35-40, 95-7

With respect to *Nomenclature* **1701**, he would include indications of time and place in nomenclature.

1704

Wagner, L. *Proba centum scripturarum: Ein Augsburger Schriftmusterbuch aus dem Beginn des XVI. Jahrhunderts,* ed. C. Wehmer. 2 vols. (Leipzig 1963)

CF of a MS of 53 folios with 100 samples of scripts (some with outlandish names), which Leonhard Wagner (1454-1522), a Benedictine at Augsburg who in his lifetime wrote some 50 MSS, put together at the request of Maximilian I, duke of Bavaria.

Hands, Autographs

1705

Bischoff, B. 'Eine Sammelhandschrift Walahfrid Strabos (Cod. Sangall. 878)' in *Aus der Welt des Buches: Festschrift Georg Leyh* (Leipzig 1950) 30-48. 2 pls. of Walahfrid's hand; repr. in **32**, II, 34-51 and pls. II-III.

1706

Bishop, T.A.M. 'Autographa of John the Scot' in *Jean Scot Erigène et l'histoire de la philosophie.* Colloques internationaux du Centre national de la recherche scientifique 561 (Paris 1977) 89-94. 2 pls.

With respect to MSS. Rheims 875 and Laon 81.

1707

Boyle, L.E. *'E cathena et carcere:* The Imprisonment of Amaury de Montfort, 1276' in **45**, 379-97

Prints one plate of the hand of Amaury from Bodleian Library MS. Auct. D. 4. 13.

1708

Bredero, A.H. 'Un brouillon du XIIe siècle: L'autographe de Geoffroy d'Auxerre,' *Scriptorium* 13 (1959) 27-60. 3 pls.

On the original of his *Vita prima sancti Bernardi Claraevallensis* (Paris, BN, MS. lat. 7561, pp. 65-87), with a host of corrections (A.D. 1153-5) in a variety of scripts which may — or may not — be Geoffroy's.

1709

Brugnoli, G. 'Note sulla minuscola Farfense, 1: La scrittura di Gregorio da Catino,' *Rivista di cultura classica e medioevale* 3 (1961) 332-41

Says that from A.D. 1090-1130, Gregory wrote out four of his own compositions (one at the age of 32, another at 'around 70,' as he informs us) in a calligraphic hand of the 'Farfa type.'

1710

D'Alverny, M.-Th. 'L'Ecriture de Bernard Itier et son évolution,' *Mediaevalia et humanistica* 14 (1962) 47-54. 6 pls.

A cautionary tale. Bernard (1163-1225), when *armarius*, wrote extensively on scraps of parchment or on blank pages and the margins of MSS at St. Martial in Limoges, and although much of his writing belongs to 1200-25, when Gothic had come into its own, his hand on its own shows no sign of it, and in fact suggests a much earlier period.

1711

Dondaine, A. *Secrétaires de Saint Thomas* (Rome 1956)

A companion volume of 40 plates illustrates the hands of some of the secretaries of Aquinas and also those of Aquinas himself and Albert the Great (see **1715, 1719, 1722**).

1712

Garand, M.-C. 'Le Scriptorium de Guibert de Nogent,' *Scriptorium* 31 (1977) 3-29. 3 pls.

Establishes the presence of his hand in three MSS of his works which were written towards the end of his life (ob. 1124) when he was abbot of Nogent-sous-Coucy, and given by him to the abbey.

1713

—————. 'Auteurs latins et autographes des XIe et XIIe siècle,' *SC* 5 (1981) 77-104. 4 pls.

Taking autographs of some non-professional scribes such as Adémar of Chabannes, Bernard Itier, Orderic Vitalis, or William of Malmesbury, Garand attempts to see what they have in common and whether there may be a 'typology' of autographs of this kind. For autographs see also **1922**.

1714

Gilissen, L. *L'Expertise des écritures médiévales: Recherche d'une méthode avec application à un manuscrit du XIe siècle. Le Lectionnaire de Lobbes (Codex Bruxellensis 18018)* (Ghent 1973). 44 pls. of MSS, 132 figs.

In disengaging some twenty hands, demonstrates, with much originality, the value of morphological comparisons: graphic forms, grouping of certain letters, punctuation, styles of abbreviation. There are valuable discussions of the work, in particular with respect to Gilissen's seeming dismissal of *ductus* as a criterion for distinguishing hands, in *Scriptorium* 29 (1975) by A. d'Haenens (pp. 175-98) and E. Ornato (198-234) — with a reply to both by Gilissen (235-44). See also **1721**.

1715

Gils, P.-M. 'Le Ms. Napoli, Biblioteca nazionale I. B. 54, est-il de la main de S. Thomas?' *Revue des sciences philosophiques et théologiques* 49 (1965) 37-59

Has four plates comparing the Naples MS with samples of autographs of Aquinas. See also **1711**.

1716

Ker, N.R. 'William of Malmesbury's Handwriting,' *English Historical Review* 59 (1944) 371-6. 3 pls.

See also **1066, 1713**.

1717

Mabille, M. 'Pierre de Limoges, copiste de manuscrits,' *Scriptorium* 24 (1970) 45-7. 4 pls.

On six MSS at the BN, Paris, identified as being in the hand of this well-known theologian and astronomer (ca. A.D. 1230-1306).

1718

Meyvaert, P. 'The Autographs of Peter the Deacon,' *Bulletin of the John Rylands Library* 38 (1955) 114-38. 4 pls. of 7 MSS.

Argues that the supposed autograph copies of Peter's works in Beneventan script are not his: his normal hand, as may be seen from undoubted autographs at Monte Cassino ca. A.D. 1134-8, was strongly influenced by Caroline minuscule.

1719

Ostlender, H. 'Die Autographe Alberts des Grossen' in *Studia Albertina – Festschrift für Bernhard Geyer* (Münster in Westphalia 1952) 1-21. 4 pls.

See also **1711, 1722**.

1720

Ouy, G. and C.M. Reno. 'Identification des autographes de Christine de Pizan,' *Scriptorium* 34 (1980) 221-38. 2 pls.

Claims that MS. Phillipps 128 (now in private hands in France), containing her *Livre de l'advision*, is in the hand of Christine (ca. 1364 - ca. 1430).

1721

Poulle, E. 'Paléographie et méthodologie: Vers l'analyse scientifique des écritures médiévales,' *BEC* 132 (1974) 101-10

Reviewing Gilissen **1714**, insists, where Gilissen is muted, on the *ductus*, 'the dynamic component of morphology.'

1722

Stegmüller, F. 'Albertus Magnus: Autographum Upsaliense' in his *Analecta*

Upsaliensia theologiam medii aevi illustrantia, I (Uppsala 1953) 147-238
Prints four plates of two unnumbered folios in Uppsala, Universitetsbiblio-
teket, MS. C 232, containing a section of Albert's commentary on II *Sent.*
in a hand which is without doubt that of Albert. Lists autograph MSS of
Albert at pp. 149-50. See also **1711, 1719.**
1723
Vaughan, R. 'The Handwriting of Matthew Paris,' *Transactions of the
Cambridge Bibliographical Society* 1 (1949-53) 376-94
Provides six plates and a list of MSS in or carrying Matthew's hand.

COPYING TECHNIQUES, SCRIBAL WAYS

Techniques, Devices

GENERAL

1724
Boyle, L.E. 'The Nowell Codex and the Poem of *Beowulf,*' in *The Dating
of Beowulf,* ed. C. Chase. Toronto Old English Series 6 (Toronto 1981)
23-32
Discusses the procedures of two Anglo-Saxon scribes of ca. A.D. 1000 when
copying *Beowulf* and other poems into what is now the Nowell codex (see
747), noting in particular the sensitivity of each to harmonious 'openings.'
1725
Destrez, J. 'L'Outillage des copistes du XIIIe e du XIVe siècles' in *Beiträge
zur Geschichte der Philosophie und Theologie des Mittelalters: Texte und
Untersuchungen,* Supplementband III: *Aus der Geisteswelt des Mittelalters.
Studien und Texte Martin Grabmann...gewidmet,* ed. A. Lang et al.
(Münster in Westphalia 1935) I, 19-34
Includes one plate illustrating some parchment and paper reference-aids for
scribes found in various MSS, e.g. to help them to find the order of folios
within a gathering, and the order of gatherings in relation to one another.
1726
Hurm, O. *Schriftform und Schreibwerkzeug: Die Handhabung der Schreib-
werkzeuge und ihr formbildender Einfluss auf die Antiqua bis zum Ein-
setzen der Gotik* (Vienna 1928)
A basic work on how scribes held their pens when writing.

1727
Lehmann, P. 'Blätter, Seiten, Spalten, Zeilen,' *Zentralblatt für Bibliotheks-wesen* 53 (1936) 333-61, 411-42; repr. in **47**, III, 1-59
Notes, e.g., that lines were numbered, at least at Oxford, from the mid-13th century to the beginning of the 14th.

1728
Metzger, B.M. 'When did Scribes Begin to Use Writing Desks?' in his *Historical and Literary Studies* (Leiden 1968) 123-37. 16 pls.
Suggests that this was during the 8th and 9th centuries A.D., but gradually.

1729
Natale, A.R. 'Marginalia: La scrittura della glossa dal V al IX secolo (nota paleografica)' in *Studi in onore di Monsignore Carlo Castiglioni* (Milan 1957) 613-30. 6 pls.

CITATION MARKS

1730
McGurk, P. 'Citation Marks in Early Latin Manuscripts,' *Scriptorium* 15 (1961) 3-13. 4 pls.

INDEXES

1731
Rouse, R.H. 'La Diffusion en occident au XIIIe siècle des outils de travail facilitant l'accès aux textes autoritatifs' in *L'Enseignement en Islam et en Occident au moyen âge.* Islam et Occident au moyen âge 1 (Paris 1978) 113-47
Notes, and advances an explanation for, the emergence in the 13th century of new 'instruments de travail' such as biblical concordances, alphabetical arrangement of material, indexes, and library catalogues, all of which the stationers at Paris and elsewhere helped to popularize. For two plates of indexing symbols, see **1094**, 57-9.

LINE OF WRITING

1732
Ker, N.R. 'From "Above top line" to "Below top line": A Change in Scribal Practice,' *Celtica* 5 (1960) 13-16

OMISSION SIGNS

1733
Lowe, E.A. 'The Oldest Omission Signs in Latin Manuscripts: Their Origin and Significance' in **63**, VI, 36-79. 10 pls.; repr. in **60**, II, 349-80 and pls. 61-70
Discusses especially Visigothic and Insular MSS.

PARAGRAPH SIGNS

1734
Sorbelli, A. 'Dalla scrittura alla stampa: il segno di paragrafo' in **44**, 335-47
Includes two plates illustrating various paragraph signs in MSS and printed books.

PUNCTUATION

1735
Greidanus, J. *Beginselen en ontwikkeling van de interpunctie, in't bijzonder in de Nederlanden* (Utrecht 1926)
Regarded as an important work on punctuation.
1736
Jenkinson, H. 'Notes on the Study of English Punctuation of the Sixteenth Century,' *Review of English Studies* 2 (1926) 152-8.
1737
Hubert, M. 'Corpus stigmatologicum minus,' *Archivum Latinitatis medii aevi* 37 (1969-70) 5-171, with index in 39 (1973-4) 55-84
A survey of references to or treatments of punctuation from Aristotle to Aquinas, mainly in printed sources. Some of the texts retrieved are commented on in **1738**.
1738
————. 'Le Vocabulaire de la "ponctuation" aux temps médiévaux: Un cas d'incertitude lexicale,' *Archivum Latinitatis medii aevi* 38 (1971-2) 57-168
Prints four plates (from the prototype of the Dominican liturgy, ca. 1256, now Rome, Santa Sabina, General Archives of the Dominican Order, MS. XIV L 1). Shows that in literary, liturgical, and other texts there was a

considerable gap between theoreticians and practitioners of punctuation. For the interrogation mark, see Vezin **1645**.

1739
Moreau-Maréchal, J. 'Recherches sur la ponctuation,' *Scriptorium* 22 (1968) 56-66
A survey and some suggestions.

1740
Parkes, M.B. 'Punctuation, or Pause and Effect' in *Medieval Eloquence,* ed. J.J. Murphy (Berkeley, Calif. 1978) 127-42.

Scribal Ways

1741
Colophons de manuscrits occidentaux des origines au XVIe siècle. 6 vols. (Fribourg 1965-82): I. *A-D:* 1-3561 (1965); II. *E-H:* 3562-7391 (1967); III. *I-J:* 7392-12130 (1973); IV. *L-O:* 12131-14888 (1976); V. *P-Z:* 14889-18951 (1979); VI. *Lieux. Anonymes:* 18952-23774 (1982)
An invaluable survey of scribal colophons by the Benedictines of Le Bouveret monastery, Switzerland. See also A. Derolez, 'Observations on the Colophons of Humanistic Scribes in Fifteenth-Century Italy' in **66a**, 249-61.

1742
Jeudy, C. 'Signes de fin de ligne et tradition manuscrite,' *Scriptorium* 27 (1973) 252-62. 2 pls.
Discusses the phenomenon of expunged 'fillers' which begins towards the end of the 13th century, and its value in sorting out a textual tradition.

1743
Ker, N.R. 'Copying an Exemplar: Two Manuscripts of Jerome on Habakkuk' in **62**, I, 203-10. 4 pls.
Comparison of a fragment at Canterbury with Trinity College, Cambridge, MS. 84 (written at Christ Church, Canterbury before 1089) shows that the former is probably a direct copy of the latter and that the scribe was innovative in adopting a different layout to that of his exemplar.

1744
Lindsay, W.M. 'Scribes and their Ways' in **49**, 2 (1923) 20-30; 3 (1924) 63-6

A supplement to the lengthy pages of Wattenbach on scribes in general (**1531**, 416-534).

UNIVERSITY SCRIVENERS AND STATIONERS

See also **2066-73** and the headnote on p. 254 above.

1745
Battelli, G. 'De quodam exemplari Parisino apparatus decretorum,' *Apollinaris* 21 (1948) 135-45; repr. in **30**, 109-21
Discusses Vatican City, BAV, MS. Borghes. 26, and irregular peciae there.
1746
————. 'Ricerche sulla pecia nei codici del "Digestum vetus" ' in *Studi in onore di C. Manaresi* (Milan 1953) 309-30; repr. in **30**, 149-70
Examines various MSS, especially Vatican City, BAV, MS. Vat. lat. 1409.
1747
————. 'Le pecie della glossa ordinaria al Digesto, al Codice, e alle Decretali in un elenco bolognese del Trecento' in *Atti del II Congresso internazionale della Società italiana di storia del diritto* (Florence 1970) 3-22; repr. in **30**, 399-418
A discussion of Vatican City, BAV, MS. Vat. lat. 3980, fols. 2r-7v.
1748
Boháček, M. 'Nuova fonte per la storia degli stazionari bolognesi,' *Studia Gratiana* 9 (1966) 407-40
Edits from Olomouc, Statni Archiv, MS. C. O. 209, a 'Taxatio librorum' from the end of the 13th century (see **1510**) and texts on the office of stationer, the duties of scriveners, and the care of exemplars (or peciae MSS).
1749
Brounts, A. 'Nouvelles précisions sur la "pecia": A propos de l'édition léonine du Commentaire de Thomas d'Aquin sur l'*Ethique* d'Aristote,' *Scriptorium* 24 (1970) 343-59
See also **2071**.
1750
Christ, K. 'Petia, ein Kapitel mittelalterlicher Buchgeschichte,' *Zentralblatt für Bibliothekswesen* 55 (1938) 1-44
With respect to Destrez **1752**.

1751

Destrez, J. 'La "pecia" dans les manuscrits du moyen âge,' *Revue des sciences philosophiques et théologiques* 13 (1924) 182-97.

1752

————. *La Pecia dans les manuscrits universitaires du XIIIe et du XIVe siècle* (Paris 1935). 36 pls.

A fundamental work on the methods employed by the universities of Paris and Bologna to supervise the copying of MSS piece by piece from an approved exemplar deposited at university stationers.[*Note.* Strictly speaking, only university exemplars thus divided into *peciae* for piecemeal copying are *peciae MSS.* Copies made from peciae are, to coin a term, *apopeciae* rather than *peciae.*]

1753

Destrez, J. and M.D. Chenu. '*Exemplaria* universitaires des XIIIe et XIVe siècles,' *Scriptorium* 7 (1953) 68-80

Lists 82 extant university exemplars (peciae MSS), and various medieval notices or legislation relative to university exemplars from A.D. 1215 to ca. 1405.

1754

Fink-Errera, G. 'Jean Destrez et son oeuvre *La "pecia" dans les manuscrits universitaires du XIIIe et du XIVe siècle,*' *Scriptorium* 11 (1957) 264-80

Some inedited papers of Destrez are printed at pp. 265-77, followed by a bibliography.

1755

————. 'Une institution du monde médiéval: La "pecia",' *Revue philosophique de Louvain* 60 (1962) 184-243

Pp. 187-210 and 218-43 also appear in Italian as 'La produzione dei libri di testo nelle università medievali' in **589**, 131-65.

1756

————. 'De l'édition universitaire' in *L'Homme et son destin: Actes du premier Congrès international de philosophie médiévale* (Louvain–Brussels 1958) I, 221-8.

1757

Frati, L. 'Gli stazionari bolognesi nel medio evo,' *Archivio storico italiano* 5th ser. 45 (1910) 380-90

Prints an inventory of exemplars (peciae) in the shop of a Bolognese stationer in 1289.

1758

Gils, P.-M. 'Pour une étude du MS. Pamplona, Catedral 51,' *Scriptorium* 32 (1978) 221-30. 3 pls.

A note on a much-corrected exemplar from Paris of the commentary of Thomas Aquinas on III *Sent.* of Peter Lombard. It is the oldest exemplar extant (ante 1272), and is the source, at various stages of correction, of at least 25 extant copies (apopeciae) of the commentary, written in 1252-6. The Pamplona exemplar and these copies carry many notes (of which 15 examples are shown in the plates) from scriveners as they made mistakes, became irritable, or were interrupted in their work. The notes show, e.g., that a scrivener might be occupied in copying two different works at one and the same time. They provide a window on the university book trade, on the working of the pecia-system, and on the mores of scriveners.

1759

Pollard, G. 'The *Pecia* System in the Medieval Universities' in **46**, 145-61. 3 pls.

Lists criteria for identifying a pecia, i.e. that from which a scribe made his copy. Dates the beginning of the system to Bologna ca. A.D. 1200.

1760

Robson, C.A. 'The Pecia of the Twelfth-Century Paris School,' *Dominican Studies* 2 (1949) 267-79

This is not, strictly speaking, a study of the university pecia-system, but rather advances a theory about the division of certain literary works into peciae of six to eight folios.

1761

Sella, P. 'La "pecia" in alcuni statuti italiani,' *Rivista di storia del diritto italiano* 2 (1929) 541-51

Notes that the term *pecia* has various meanings in university statutes. For the place of peciae and apopeciae MSS in editions of texts, see **2066-73**.

COMPENDIOUS (INCOMPLETE) WRITING

Common Observance

MANUALS

Entries here are in chronological order. For lists of abbreviations of the
'Common observance' in the Middle Ages, see **148**, 100-14; **151**, 64-70;
155, 28-43; **158**, 128-34; **159**, 192-213.

1762
Modus legendi abbreviaturas in utroque iure
A short dictionary for non-jurists ca. 1450, expanding an alphabetical
'Declaratio de breviaturis' which had been attached, ca. 1350, to codices
of the *Summa casuum* ('Pisanella') of Bartholomew of San Concordio (ob.
1347). At least 68 printed editions and expansions appeared between
1476 (Nuremberg) and 1623 (Rome). See further H. Omont, 'Dictionnaire
d'abréviations latines publié à Brescia en 1534,' *BEC* 63 (1902) 5-9, with
8 plates on which is reproduced all of a *Nuova regoletta nella quale troverai
ogni sorta de abbreviatura usuale* (Brescia 1534), carrying a little over 900
sigla (mostly non-legal).
1763
Manutius, A. *De veterum notarum explanatione quae in antiquis monu-
mentis occurrunt* (Venice 1566, repr. Milan 1971).
1764
Baring, D.E. *Clavis diplomatica, tradens specimina veterum scripturarum,
nimirum alphabeta varia, compendia scribendi medii aevi, notariorum
veterum signa nonnulla curiosa, una cum alphabeto instrumenti et abbre-
viaturis, singula tabulis aeneis exhibita.* 2 vols. (Hannover 1737).
1765
Walterus [Walther], J.L. *Lexicon diplomaticum, abbreviationes syllabarum
et vocum in diplomatibus et codicibus a saeculo VIII. ad XVI. usque
occurrentes exponens* (Göttingen 1745-7; 2nd ed. Ulm 1756, repr. New
York 1966)
Two volumes in one, illustrated.
1766
Chassant, A.A. *Dictionnaire des abréviations latines et françaises usitées
dans les inscriptions lapidaires et métalliques, les manuscrits et chartes du*

moyen âge. 5th ed. (Paris 1884, repr. Hildesheim 1965)
Valuable for areas not covered by other dictionaries or lists.
1767
De la Braña, R.A. *Siglas y abreviaturas latinas... y un catálogo de las abreviaturas que se usan en los documentos pontificios* (Léon 1884, repr. Hildesheim—New York 1978).
1768
Volta, Z. *Delle abbreviature nella paleografia latina* (Milan 1892, repr.
1971). 36 pls.
Good on monograms, monuments, dates.
1769
Schiaparelli, L. *Avviamento allo studio delle abbreviature latine nel medioevo* (Florence 1926). 4 pls.
See also **663**.
1770
Martin, C.T. *The Record Interpreter: A Collection of Abbreviations, Latin
Words, and Names used in English Historical Manuscripts and Records.*
2nd ed. (London 1910).
1771
Wright, A. *Court-Hand Restored, or, The Student's Assistant in reading old
Deeds, Charters, Records, etc., neatly engraved on twenty-three copper
plates... with an Appendix containing the Ancient Names of Places in
Great Britain and Ireland.* 10th ed., ed. C.T. Martin (London 1912)
First published in 1773.
1772
Cappelli, A. *Lexicon abbreviaturarum: Dizionario di abbreviature latine ed
italiane usate nelle carte e codici specialmente del medio evo.* 3rd ed.
(Milan 1929, numerous reprints; 2nd German ed. Leipzig 1928)
Has 9 plates, all of documents, with transcriptions, and an excellent introduction on the methods of abbreviation. This, the standard and only comprehensive dictionary of abbreviations, has to be supplemented for philosophical, theological, and general scholastic usage by **1775, 1786-91, 1799**.
1773
Laurent, M.-H. *De abbreviationibus et signis scripturae gothicae* (Rome
1939)
A small, well-argued attempt to establish the logic of the medieval system
of abbreviations.

1774
López de Toro, J. *Abreviaturas hispánicas* (Madrid 1957)
Gives additions to Cappelli **1772** from Spanish sources.
1775
Pelzer, A. *Abréviations latines médiévales: Supplément au Dizionario di abbreviature latine ed italiane de Adriano Cappelli.* 2nd ed. (Louvain– Paris 1966)
Notes philosophical abbreviations in particular. See also **1786-91, 1799.**

STUDIES

General

1776
Bains, D. *A Supplement to Notae Latinae (Abbreviations in Latin MSS. of 850 to 1050 A.D.)* (Cambridge 1936, repr. Hildesheim 1965)
Also carries a list of corrections to Lindsay's *Notae* (**1779**) by the author himself.
1777
Lehmann, P. *Sammlungen und Erörterungen lateinischer Abkürzungen in Altertum und Mittelalter* (Munich 1929)
Prints some lists of sigla from the 14th and 15th centuries at pp. 28-60, including (pp. 33-5) the text of a tract 'Quedam regule de modo titulandi seu apificandi pro novellis scriptoribus copulate' (compilate?), attributed to John Gerson (1363-1429).
1778
Lindsay, W.M. 'The Abbreviation-Symbols of *ergo, igitur,*' *Zentralblatt für Bibliothekswesen* 29 (1912) 56-64
Arguing against Steffens **1784** and his theory that the abbreviation symbols used by scribes of Irish minuscule were fashioned at Bobbio from *notae iuris* and then exported to Ireland, Lindsay notes that Steffens takes *notae iuris* in too wide a sense and that the term should only be used (as Isidore *Etym.* I.23 used it) of abbreviations of technical legal words (e.g. *dolus malus*) and not of abbreviations of common words (e.g. *prae* and *pro*). In the case of the common medieval abbreviations of *ergo* ($\overset{\circ}{g}$) and *igitur* ($\overset{i}{g}$), these forms were developed by Irish scribes in Ireland before A.D. 700, were taken over by Welsh scribes by the 9th century, and had become general in Europe by the close of the 11th century.

1779

————. *Notae Latinae: An Account of Abbreviations in Latin MSS of the Early Minuscule Period (c. 700-850)* (Cambridge 1915, repr. Hildesheim 1965)

See also Bains **1776** for a supplement and corrections.

1780

Rand, E.K. 'On the Symbols of Abbreviations for *-tur*,' *Speculum* 2 (1927) 52-65

Posits that a new siglum (superscript *2*) was introduced for *-tur*, because similar signs for *-tur* and *-tus* were causing confusion; it first appeared ca. A.D. 800 at Tours, and by 820 was common.

1781

Reiche, R. *Ein rheinisches Schulbuch aus dem 11. Jahrhundert* (Munich 1976)

On Bonn, Universitätsbibliothek, MS. S. 218, with some basic sigla at fol. 25b (pl. 3).

1782

Robert, U. 'Note sur l'origine de l'*e* cédillé dans les manuscrits' in *Recueil de travaux d'érudition dediés à la mémoire de Julien Havet (1853-1893)* (Paris 1895) 633-7

Suggests that it originated ca. the 7th century A.D. in a ligature formed by joining *a* and *e*.

1783

Santifaller, L. *Die Abkürzungen in den ältesten Papsturkunden (788-1002)* (Weimar 1939).

1784

Steffens, F. 'Ueber die Abkuerzungsmethoden der Schreibschule von Bobbio' in **36**, 244-54

See Lindsay **1778** and Lowe **255** (CLA IV. xxiii-xxiv) for refutations of the theory of Steffens that Bobbio rather than the British Isles was the cradle of 'Irish' abbreviations. See also **874**.

1785

Traube, L. *Lehre und Geschichte der Abkürzungen* (Leipzig 1899); repr. in **70**, I, 129-56

This is the first proper study of the history of abbreviations, and it inspired the work of Lindsay **1779**, Steffens **1784**, Schiaparelli **1769**, etc. The most complete recent history is that in Cencetti **152**, 353-475.

Law, Logic

1786
Bryson, W.H. *Dictionary of Sigla and Abbreviations to and in Law Books before 1607* (Charlottesville, Va. 1975)
See also **1113**, I, 27-60, and G. Mollat, *Introduction à l'étude du droit canonique et du droit civil* (Paris 1930) pp. 31-71, for useful lists of legal sigla and abbreviations.

1787
Kantorowicz, H. 'Die Allegationen im späteren Mittelalter,' *Archiv für Urkundenforschung* 13 (1935) 15-29
On the sigla of authorities in legal MSS.

1788
Magnin, E. 'Abréviations' in *Dictionnaire de droit canonique*, I (Paris 1935) 106-15
On legal abbreviations (classical, medieval, modern).

1789
Meersseman, G. 'Einige Siglen der mittelalterlichen Logik,' *Freiburger Zeitschrift für Philosophie und Theologie* 2 (1955) 87-9.

1790
Seckel, E. 'Paläographie der juristischen Handschriften des 12. bis 14. und der juristischen Drucke des 15. und 16. Jahrhunderts,' *Zeitschrift der Savigny-Stiftung für Rechtsgeschichte*, Roman. Abt. 45 (1925) 1-16 (also publ. separately, Weimar 1925)
A lexicon of legal abbreviations and of sigla of the names of glossators. Not as comprehensive as it sounds.

1791
Sella, P. *Sigle di giuristi medievali, in ispecie dello Studio Bolognese, tratte dai codici vaticani* (Bologna 1932).

Nomina Sacra

1792
Traube, L. *Nomina sacra: Versuch einer Geschichte der christlichen Kürzung* (Munich 1907)
In this famous monograph Traube sees the origin of the medieval abbreviation-system in the Christian adoption, first in Greek, then in Latin, of the Hebrew conviction that Yahweh was the most personal name of God and

was so sacred that it should not be pronounced or written out in full. Although the theory was generally accepted, it was dealt a serious blow by Schiaparelli **1803**.

1793
Natale, A.R. 'Note paleografiche: *Singula littera:* Le origini sacrali dell' abbreviazioni per sigla,' *Aevum* 24 (1950) 1-9.

1794
Paap, A.H.R.E. *Nomina sacra in the Greek Papyri of the First Five Centuries A.D.: The Sources and some Deductions* (Leiden 1959).

1795
Turner, C.H. 'The Nomina Sacra in Early Latin Christian Manuscripts' in **41**, IV, 62-74
Accepts and restates Traube's position (see **1792**) with respect to the presence of *nomina sacra* in Christian Latin literature.

Numerals

1796
Bischoff, B. 'Die sogennanten "griechischen" und "chaldäischen" Zahlzeichen des abendländischen Mittelalters' in **44**, 327-34; repr. in **32**, I, 67-73.

1797
Hill, G.F. *The Development of Arabic Numerals in Europe exhibited in sixty-four Tables* (Oxford 1915)
In tables I-XVI there is a presentation of the forms Arabic numerals take in MSS from the 10th-16th centuries.

Reportationes

1798
Havette, R. *Les Procédés abréviatifs et sténographiques employés pour recueillir les sermons à l'audition du XIIe au XVIIe siècles* (Paris 1903).

1799
Piltz, A. *Studium Upsalense: Specimens of the Oldest Lecture Notes Taken in the Medieval University of Uppsala* (Uppsala 1977)
An 'Index notarum' (pp. 315-41) carries 444 abbreviations not found in Cappelli **1772**.

Limited Observance

NOTAE IURIS

1800

Bischoff, B. and D. Nörr. *Eine unbekannte Konstitution Kaiser Julians (c. Juliani de postulando)* (Munich 1963). 3 pls.
A copy of the constitution of 17 January 363, containing many ancient *notae,* now in Florence, Biblioteca Laurenziana, MS. Plut. XXXVIII, 24.

1801

Mommsen, T. 'Notarum laterculi' in *Grammatici Latini* by H. Keil, IV (Leipzig 1864, repr. Hildesheim 1961) 265-352
An edition of various *notae iuris* and other compendia, including the earliest known collection of notae, that of Valerius Probus (*Libri iuris notarum* of about A.D. 50, edited at pp. 271-6) and the *Notae litterarum more vetusto* of the Cassinese librarian, Peter the Deacon, from the early 12th century (ed. pp. 331-46).

1802

Rand, E.K. 'A Nest of Ancient *Notae,*' *Speculum* 2 (1927) 160-76
On the notae in Tours, Bibliothèque municipale, MS. 286: Augustine, *De musica.*

1803

Schiaparelli, L. 'Note paleografiche: Segni tachigrafici nelle *Notae iuris,*' *Archivio storico italiano* 72 (1914) 241-75, and 'Le *Notae iuris* e il sistema delle abbreviature medievali,' *ibid.* 275-322; repr. as one continuous article in **68**, 94-186
Notes, among other things, that the principle of contraction, which is the heart of the medieval abbreviation system, is found as early as the 2nd century A.D.

TIRONIAN NOTES

1804

Boge, H. *Griechische Tachygraphie und Tironische Noten: Ein Handbuch der Schnellschrift der Antike und des Mittelalters* (Berlin 1973).

1805

Carpentier, P. *Alphabetum tironianum seu notas Tironis explicandi methodus* (Paris 1747)

This Maurist scholar was the first scholar to engage himself in deciphering Tironian notes.

1806

Chatelain, E. *Introduction à la lecture des notes tironiennes* (Paris 1900, repr. New York [1963]). 18 pls.

1807

Jusselin, M. 'Notes tironiennes dans les diplômes mérovingiens,' *BEC* 68 (1907) 481-508. 2 pls.

1808

Kopp, U.F. *Lexicon Tironianum: Nachdruck aus Kopps 'Palaeographia critica' von 1817 mit Nachwort und einem Alphabetum Tironianum von Bernhard Bischoff* (Osnabrück 1965)
A reprint from vol. II of Kopp's four-volume *Palaeographia critica* (Mannheim 1817-19).

1809

Mentz, A. 'Die Tironischen Noten: Eine Geschichte der römischen Kurzschrift,' *Archiv für Urkundenforschung* 16 (1939) 287-384; 17 (1942) 155-303. 5 pls.
The most complete survey to date, also printed separately as *Geschichte der Kurzschrift* (Wolfenbüttel 1949; 2nd ed. 1974, ed. F. Haeger).

1810

Schmitz, W., ed. *Commentarii notarum tironianarum, cum prolegomenis, adnotationibus criticis et exegeticis notarumque indice alphabetico* (Leipzig 1893)
Provides 132 plates to illustrate the *Commentarii*, a great lexicon of some 13,000 Tironian signs which survives in 17 MSS, the most authoritative of which, probably, is Kassel, Hessische Landesbibliothek, MS. Philol. fol. 2 (see **915** for facsimile edition).

1811

─────. *S. Chroedegangi Metensis episcopi (742-766) Regula canonicorum aus dem Leidener Codex Vossianus Latinus 94 mit Umschrift der Tironischen Noten* (Hannover 1889). 17 pls.
Leiden, BRU, MS. Voss. lat. F. 94, fols. 8v-16v (wanting the beginning). Written by one hand, partly in Caroline, partly in Tironian, in the late 9th century in France, possibly in the area of Tours.

1812

─────. *Miscellanea Tironiana* (Leipzig 1896)
Includes a facsimile of Vatican City, BAV, MS. Reg. lat. 846, fols. 99r-114v.

TACHYGRAPHY

1813
Costamagna, G. *Il sistema tachigrafico sillabico usato dai notai medioevali italiani (sec. VIII-XI): Regole fondamentali* (Genoa 1953).
1814
———. 'La tachigrafia dei papiri latini medioevali italiani,' *BAPI* 2nd ser. 2-3 (1956-7), Pt. I, 213-20. 1 pl.
1815
———. *Tachigrafia notarile e scritture segreti medioevali in Italia.* Fonti e studi del Corpus membranarum italicarum 1 (Rome 1968). 4 pls.

CRYPTOGRAPHY

1816
Bischoff, B 'Übersicht über die nichtdiplomatischen Geheimschriften des Mittelalters,' *Mitteilungen des Instituts für österreichische Geschichtsforschung* 62 (1954) 1-27. 2 pls. of tables; repr. in **32**, III, 120-48
Considers the cryptography of the Middle Ages primitive compared to that of the Renaissance or of today. See also **279**.
1817
Galland, J.S. *An Historical and Analytical Bibliography of the Literature of Cryptology* (Evanston, Ill. 1945).
1818
Havet, J. 'L'Ecriture secrète de Gerbert,' *Académie des inscriptions & belles lettres: Comptes rendus* 4th ser. 15 (1887) 94-112
Posits that Gerbert d'Aurillac, while abbot of Bobbio, might have learned there the old Italian (Pavian) form of tachygraphy to which, as Pope Sylvester II (A.D. 999-1003), he resorted on occasion, as may be seen from notes of his which Havet deciphers in 'La Tachygraphie italienne du Xe siècle,' *ibid.* pp. 351-74. See also **1815**.
1819
Richard, J. 'Cryptographie dans l'antiquité et le haut moyen âge' in **42**, 616-32
For some other forms see R. Derolez, *Runica manuscripta: The English Tradition* (Bruges 1954).

MUSICAL NOTATION

1820
Wagner, P. *Neumenkunde.* 2nd ed. (Leipzig 1912)
See also **2194-2203.**

ORNAMENTATION, PAINTING

Surveys

1821
Bradley, J.W. *A Dictionary of Miniaturists, Illuminators, Calligraphers, and Copyists – From the Establishment of Christianity to the Eighteenth Century.* 3 vols. (London 1887-9, repr. New York 1958).
1822
D'Ancona, P. and E. Aeschlimann. *Dictionnaire des miniaturistes du moyen âge et de la renaissance dans les différentes contrées de l'Europe.* 2nd ed. (Milan 1949, repr. 1969).
1823
Donati, L. *Bibliografia della miniatura.* 2 vols. (Florence 1972)
Very helpful. Current bibliography may be found in *Zeitschrift für Kunstgeschichte: Bibliographischer Teil,* section 'Buchmalerei.'

Studies

GENERAL

1824
Backhouse, J. *The Illuminated Manuscript* (Oxford 1979)
Prints 70 plates, with commentary, of 70 MSS now in the British Library, London.
1825
Diringer, D. *The Illuminated Book, its History and Production.* 2nd ed. (London 1967)
A useful, general book, with 260 illustrations.

1826
Grabar, A. and C. Nordenfalk. *Early Medieval Painting from the Fourth to the Eleventh Century* (New York 1957)
The section on book-illumination is by Nordenfalk.

1827
Guilmain, J. 'Zoomorphic Decoration and the Problem of the Sources of Mozarabic Illumination,' *Speculum* 35 (1960) 17-38. 63 figs.

1828
Harthan, J. *Books of Hours and their Owners* (London 1977)
Describes some 34 Books of Hours owned by members of the houses of Capet, Valois-Orléans-Angoulême, Anjou, Burgundy, Brittany.

1829
Herbert, J.A. *Illuminated Manuscripts* (London 1911; repr. with additional bibliography by J.I. Whalley, Bath 1972). 51 pls. mainly of English MSS.

1830
Klemm, E. *Die romanischen Handschriften der Bayerischen Staatsbibliothek*, I: *Die Bistümer Regensburg, Passau, und Salzburg.* 2 vols. (Wiesbaden 1980). 707 pls.

1831
Koehler, W. *Buchmalerei des frühen Mittelalters: Fragmente und Entwürfe aus dem Nachlass*, ed. E. Kitzinger and F. Mütherich (Munich 1972).

1832
Manuscrits à peintures du XIIIe au XVIe siècle (Paris 1955)
An exhibition catalogue from the Bibliothèque nationale, Paris, with a good introduction.

1833
Pächt, O. and J.J.G. Alexander. *Illuminated Manuscripts in the Bodleian Library.* 3 vols. (Oxford 1966-73), I: *German, Dutch, Flemish, French, and Spanish Schools* (1966); II: *Italian School* (1970); III: *British, Irish, and Icelandic Schools* (1973)
In each volume there is a list of 'Dated or Datable MSS' by country, and an index of artists and scribes. Vol. I lists 906 MSS and provides 66 plates; II, 1053 MSS and 88 plates; III, 1346 MSS and 120 plates, with Addenda to I and II.

1834
Pächt, O. and D. Thoss. *Die illuminierten Handschriften und Inkunabeln der österreichischen Nationalbibliothek*, I: *Französische Schule.* 2 vols. (Vienna 1974). 383 pls.

1835
Pächt, O. and U. Jenni. *Die illuminierten Handschriften und Inkunabeln...*, III: *Holländische Schule* (Vienna 1978). 334 pls.
1836
Robb, D.M. *The Art of the Illuminated Manuscript* (Cranbury, N.J. 1973). 30 pls., 216 figs.
Gives a useful bibliography at pp. 337-45.
1837
Weitzmann, K. *Illustrations in Roll and Codex: A Study of the Origin and Method of Text Illumination* (Princeton 1947). 205 pls.
Note especially the influential pp. 182-92 ('The Relation between Textual Criticism and Picture Criticism'), based on Hort's preface in **1986**, in which Weitzmann advances the idea of an 'iconographic stemma.'
1838
————. *Ancient Book Illumination* (Cambridge, Mass. 1959). 64 pls., 136 figs.
1839
————. *Studies in Classical and Byzantine Manuscript Illumination*, ed. H.L. Kessler (Chicago 1971). 320 figs.
See in particular pp. 96-125 (figs. 69-103), where he argues ('Book Illustration of the Fourth Century: Tradition and Innovation') that the 4th century A.D. was the time when 'almost every conceivable type of full-page miniature came into being,' coinciding (but by chance) with 'the great technical revolution of the parchment codex.'
1840
————. *Late Antique and Early Christian Book Illumination* (New York 1977). 48 pls., 14 figs.
1841
Wormald, F. 'Bible Illustration in Medieval Manuscripts' in *The Cambridge History of the Bible*, II: *The West from the Fathers to the Reformation*, ed. G.W.H. Lampe (Cambridge 1969) 309-37.

ARTISTS AND SCRIBES

1842
Calkins, R.G. 'Distribution of Labor: The Illuminators of the Hours of Catherine of Cleves and their Workshop,' *Transactions of the American Philosophical Society* 69/5 (1979) 1-85. 57 figs.

1843

Masai, F. 'De la condition des enlumineurs et de l'enluminure à l'époque romane,' *BAPI* new ser. 2/3 (1956-7) II, 135-44

Examining Paris and Bamberg sacramentaries (the chief repositories of Liège miniatures of the 11th century), notes how important it is not to confuse the place for which MSS are written with place of origin. In the Romanesque period monks were more Maecenases than artists. Scribes and illuminators could be from distant places and simply hired for a job; more often than not they were laypeople.

1844

Pächt, O. 'Hugo Pictor,' *Bodleian Library Record* 3 (1951) 96-103. 3 pls.

Notes that Oxford, Bodleian Library, MS. Bodley 717 (Jerome on Isaiah), written probably in Normandy in the late 11th century, carries one of the earliest known self-portraits of an artist-scribe.

1845

Randall, L.M.C. *Images in the Margins of Gothic Manuscripts* (Berkeley, Calif. 1966)

158 plates provide 739 illustrations of marginalia (caricatures, doodles, and the like) in MSS of the 13th-15th centuries.

1846

Scott, K. 'A Mid-Fifteenth-Century Illuminating Shop and its Customers,' *Journal of the Warburg and Courtauld Institutes* 31 (1968) 170-96. 5 pls.

Assembles evidence of an English 'shop' from six MSS.

INITIALS

1847

Alexander, J.J.G. 'Scribes as Artists: The Arabesque Initial in Twelfth-Century English Manuscripts' in **46**, 87-116. 12 pls.

Of wider import than England.

1848

————. *The Decorated Letter* (New York 1978). 40 pls.

1849

Gutbrod, J. *Die Initiale in Handschriften des achten bis dreizehnten Jahrhunderts* (Stuttgart 1965). 137 pls.

1850

Nordenfalk, C. *Die spätantiken Zierbuchstaben* (Stockholm 1970)

Argues that the earliest initials, those e.g. in the Vergilius Augusteus (see **200**), seem to have been done by the scribes of the MSS themselves, using ruler and compass.

1851

Porcher, J. 'Aux origines de la lettre ornée médiévale' in **69**, V, 273-6. 4 pls. Illustrates the intermediate stage (Sacramentary of Gellone, etc.) between the 'synthetic' initial of the Merovingians and Insular scribes, and the 'historiated' initial (Sacramentary of Drogo **296**, etc.) of the 9th century, with its straight imitation of models from classical antiquity.

1852

Valentine, L.N. *Ornament in Medieval Manuscripts: A Glossary* (London 1965). many illustrations.

1853

Van Moé, E.-A. *Illuminated Initials in Mediaeval Manuscripts* (London 1950). 80 pls. of initials, etc.

Translated from the French, *La Lettre ornée dans les manuscrits du VIIIe au XIIe siècle* (Paris 1943), by J. Evans, with a foreword by F. Wormald.

MINIATURES

1854

Boeckler, A. *Abendländische Miniaturen bis zum Ausgang der romanischen Zeit.* Tabulae in usum scholarum 10. 2 vols. (Berlin–Leipzig 1930) One volume is text, the other provides 106 plates.

1855

Boutemy, A. and L.M.J. Delaissé. 'L'Histoire de la miniature,' *Scriptorium* 4 (1950) 264-74

A propos Réau **1860**.

1856

Jones, L.W. and C.R. Morey. *The Miniatures of the Manuscripts of Terence prior to the Thirteenth Century.* 2 vols. (Princeton 1930-31) Vol. I has 796 plates, II has 69 and the text. See also **202** for a facsimile of Vatican City, BAV, MS. Vat. lat. 3868 (Corvey Terence).

1857

MacKinney, L. *Medical Illustrations in Medieval Manuscripts* (London 1965). 61 pls., 95 figs. Includes a checklist (compiled with T. Herndon) to A.D. 1550 of medical miniatures in extant MSS.

1858

Melnikas, A. *The Corpus of the Miniatures in the Manuscripts of the Decre-tum.* 3 vols. Studia Gratiana 16-18 (Rome 1975)
These 3 volumes form Tomus I of *Corpus picturarum minutarum quae in codicibus manu scriptis iuris continentur:* I covers all of Pt. One (*Distinctiones*) of the *Decretum,* and a portion of Pt. Two, *Causae* 1-8; II deals with Pt. Two, *Causae* 9-26; III with Pt. Two, *Causae* 27-36, and all of Pt. Three (*De consecratione*). The miniatures for each *distinctio* or *causa,* or for *quaestiones* and chapters within these, are examined following the order of the three parts of the *Decretum.* There are numerous colour plates and black-and-white figures in each case (and with separate numeration). Each set of miniatures is accompanied by an essay on the legal and historical background to the theme of the miniatures in question. But see the critical review of C. Nordenfalk, *Zeitschrift für Kunstgeschichte* 43 (1980) 318-37.

1859

Omont, H. *Miniatures des plus anciens manuscrits grecs de la Bibliothèque nationale du VIe au XIVe siècle.* 2nd ed. (Paris 1929). 138 pls.

1860

Réau, L. *Histoire de la peinture au moyen âge: La Miniature* (Melun 1946). 96 pls.

1861

Smeyers, M. *La Miniature.* Typologie des sources du moyen âge occidental 8 (Turnhout 1974)
A succinct typological and bibliographical survey.

TECHNIQUES

1862

Blanchon-Lasserve, P. *Ecriture et enluminure des manuscrits du IXe au XIIe siècle: Histoire et technique* (Solesmes [1926]). 88 pls.
A good introduction to techniques.

1863

Dodwell, C.R., ed. *Theophilus: The Various Arts* (London—Edinburgh 1961)
Latin text and facing translation (with commentary) of *De diversis artibus,* written, probably, between A.D. 1110 and 1140 in NW Germany. The treatise embraces most of the medieval skills and crafts, e.g. materials for painting on books and walls, for embellishing book-covers, etc.

1864
Gray, N. *Lettering as Drawing* (London–New York 1971). 192 illustrations.
1865
Guerrieri, G. 'Il facsimile del *De arte illuminandi*' in **1206**, 577-617
A facsimile of Naples, Biblioteca nazionale, MS. XII. E. 42 is at pp. 583-600, with an Italian translation at 601-17. The tract was written ca. 1350, the MS is ca. 1400.
1866
Lehmann-Haupt, H. *The Göttingen Model Book: A Facsimile Edition and Translation of a Fifteenth-Century Illuminators' Manual* (Columbia, Mo. 1972)
Göttingen, Niedersächsische Staats- und Universitätsbibliothek, MS. Uffenb. 51. Written at Mainz, ca. 1450, in Rhenish-Franconian dialect. 11 folios. CF (colour).
1867
Roosen-Runge, H. *Farbgebung und Technik frühmittelalterlicher Buchmalerei: Studien zu den Traktaten 'Mappae Clavicula' und 'Heraclius'.* 2 vols. (Munich 1967)
A study of two technological treatises of the late 10th century.
1868
Scheller, R.W. *A Survey of Medieval Modelbooks* (Haarlem 1963).

Textual Setting

The purpose of palaeography is to make a piece of old writing to communicate. This the palaeographer will achieve first and foremost by reading the text in question and finding out what exactly it has to say. But this is not communication to the full. A text does not float in the air. It solidly stands, so to speak, on two supports, one physical, the other textual, each of which must be investigated if the palaeographer is fully to evaluate just what the text is that rests on them. A line of Latin poetry scribbled on a Roman wall or in a medieval miscellany may easily be read at first glance, but until the date of the wall or miscellany (the physical support) has been established, and until (the second support) the corpus of Latin poetical tradition has been sifted, one may not be able to state with certainty to what poet or period the line may pertain, and hence not in any position to make the line communicate to the full. The importance of the physical support of a text needs no stressing: it has been the focus of the three preceding settings, all of which are concerned whether directly (physical and human settings) or indirectly (institutional) with the physical transmission of writing. The importance of the second or textual support is not always given prominence in surveys of palaeography; it belongs, it is sometimes said, to some other discipline such as classical philology or textual criticism. Yet a course in palaeography is as incomplete without a consideration of textual transmission and textual history as it is without an awareness of, shall we say, codicology, or, more generally, of the physical setting of a text. To rule out the transmission, the identification, or the critical evaluation of texts from palaeography is to run the risk of forgetting that the goal of palaeography is to make a text communicate as fully as possible It certainly falls short of an integral approach to palaeography.

The present section is therefore devoted to what I have termed 'Textual

Setting.' Most of the section is perforce given over to the editing of texts. This is for the very good reason that students rarely take a course in palaeography in order simply to be able to read manuscripts. More often than not they hope one day to transcribe and edit unpublished texts, or, perhaps, to re-edit texts which are reputed to have inadequate editions. They should therefore be made aware of the main works on the editing of diplomatic and literary texts, not to speak of (in the case of the latter) the niceties of the Recensionist and Optimist approaches.

TRANSMISSION AND TRADITION

For current bibliography see *L'Année philologique* (**14**), C. Critique des textes; and *Medioevo latino* (**22**), 'Filologia e storia della tradizione': 2 (1979) nos. 3519-39 and 3 (1980) 5206-41.

General

1869
Badel, P.Y. *Introduction à la vie littéraire du moyen âge* (Paris 1969)
Has good pages (224-9) on edition of texts, and bibliography (229-35).
1870
Bolgar, R.R. *The Classical Heritage and its Beneficiaries from the Carolingian Age to the End of the Renaissance* (Cambridge 1954)
A fine survey.
1871
————, ed. *Classical Influences on European Culture A.D. 500-1500* (Cambridge 1971)
Proceedings of an international conference at Cambridge in 1969, with contributions by L. Bieler (**600**), G. Billanovich, B. Bischoff, R.W. Hunt (**1892**), E.J. Kenney, etc.
1872
La cultura antica nell' Occidente latino dal VII all' XI secolo. 2 vols. Settimane di studio 22 (Spoleto 1975)
Long contributions on the transmission of texts in various areas, by G. Billanovich and M. Ferrari (NW Italy), B. Bischoff **1885** (general), T.J. Brown **694** (British Isles), G. Cavallo (Beneventan-Cassinese area), M.C.

Díaz y Díaz (Iberian Peninsula), A. Vernet (France), etc.
1873
Hall, F.W. *A Companion to Classical Texts* (Oxford 1913)
See especially pp. 108-98, 286-357 ('Nomenclature of MSS').
1874
Harlfinger, D., ed. *Griechische Kodikologie und Textüberlieferung* (Darmstadt 1980)
A collection in 656 pages of articles, mainly on textual transmission, reprinted (the editor's own article excepted) from various writings over the years 1905-75 of, e.g., A. Dain, H. Hunger, J. Irigoin, P. Maas, G. Pasquali, M. Richard, R. Sabbadini, N. Wilson. There is an extensive bibliographical supplement by the editor at pp. 657-78.
1875
Hunger, H., ed. *Geschichte der Textüberlieferung der antiken und mittelalterlichen Literatur.* 2 vols. (Zürich 1961, 1964).
1876
Pfeiffer, R. *History of Classical Scholarship from 1300 to 1850* (Oxford 1976)
A companion volume to *History of Classical Scholarship from the Beginnings to the End of the Hellenistic Age* (1968). Apart from a nod to Petrarch, Boccaccio, and Coluccio Salutati, ignores the Middle Ages, and in effect the period is 1500-1850.
1877
Reynolds, L.D. and N.G. Wilson. *Scribes and Scholars: A Guide to the Transmission of Greek and Latin Literature.* 2nd ed. (Oxford 1974)
A revised and enlarged edition of an invaluable volume, first published in 1968, with a particularly lucid chapter (pp. 186-213) on textual criticism. Has 16 plates, with notes thereon.
1878
Sabbadini, R. *Le scoperte dei codici latini e greci nei secoli XIV e XV.*
2 vols. (Florence 1905, 1914; repr. with author's addenda and corrigenda, 1967).
1879
Severyns, A. *Texte et apparat: Histoire critique d'une tradition imprimée* (Brussels 1962)
On the fluctuations of a printed, and therefore supposedly static, text.
1880
Weiss, R. *The Renaissance Discovery of Classical Antiquity* (Oxford 1969).

Classical Texts

1881

Beeson, C.H. 'The Text History of the Corpus Caesarianum,' *Classical Philology* 35 (1940) 113-25.

1882

Billanovich, G. 'Petrarch and the Textual Tradition of Livy,' *Journal of the Warburg and Courtauld Institutes* 14 (1951) 137-208.

1883

————. *I primi umanisti e le tradizioni dei classici latini* (Fribourg 1953).

1884

Bischoff, B. 'Hadoardus and the Manuscripts of Classical Authors from Corbie' in **28**, 39-57; and, in German, in **32**, I, 49-63.

1885

————. 'Paläographie und frühmittelalterliche Klassikerüberlieferung' in **1872**, I, 59-87; repr. in **32**, III, 55-73; republ. in revised version in *Studien und Mitteilungen zur Geschichte des Benediktiner-Ordens* 92 (1981) 165-90

On the work of various scriptoria during the Caroline renewal, e.g. that at Ferrières directed by Lupus.

1886

Brown, V. *The Textual Transmission of Caesar's Civil War* (Leiden 1972).

1887

De Ghellinck, J. 'Les Catalogues des bibliothèques et les classiques' in his *L'Essor de la littérature latine au XIIe siècle*. 2nd ed. (Brussels 1955) 292-312.

1888

Fohlen, J. 'Trois manuscrits parisiens des *Epistulae ad Lucilium* de Sénèque,' *RHT* 1 (1971) 73-92

With respect to Reynolds **1904**.

1889

————. 'Recherches sur le manuscrit palimpseste Vatican, Pal. lat. 24,' *SC* 3 (1979) 195-222

On ten fragments of Seneca, Lucan, Cicero, etc., copied originally in Italy in the 3rd-6th centuries A.D. and palimpsested there in the 6th-8th centuries.

1890

Hedberg, S. *Contamination and Interpolation: A Study of the 15th-Century Columella Manuscripts* (Uppsala 1968).

1891
Housman, A.E., ed. *Marci Manilii Astronomicon,* I (London 1903, repr. Hildesheim 1972) preface
The central parts of this preface, and of prefaces of Housman to other critical editions of classical authors, are now collected together in A.E. Housman, *Selected Prose,* ed. J. Carter (Cambridge 1961).

1892
Hunt, R.W. 'The Deposit of Latin Classics in the Twelfth-Century Renaissance' in **1871**, 51-5.

1893
Hunt, R.W. et al. *The Survival of Ancient Literature* (Oxford 1975)
The catalogue, with 26 plates, of an exhibition in the Bodleian Library of Greek and Latin classical MSS, mainly from Oxford libraries.

1894
Jahn, O. 'Über die Subscriptionen in den Handschriften römischer Classiker' in *Berichte über die Verhandlungen der k. Sächsischen Gesellschaft der Wissenschaften zu Leipzig,* phil.-hist. Klasse 3 (Leipzig 1851) 327-72
A famous paper on a series of signed collations of various classical texts between the end of the 4th and the beginning of the 6th century A.D.

1895
Kenney, E.J. *The Classical Text: Aspects of Editing in the Age of the Printed Book* (Berkeley, Calif. 1974)
Has a good bibliography on the printing of classical texts and on aspects of editing.

1896
————. 'The Manuscript Tradition of Ovid's *Amores, Ars amatoria,* and *Remedium amoris,' Classical Quarterly* n.s. 121 (1962) 1-31
Suggests that the most ancient MSS are derived from an archetype of ca. A.D. 800.

1897
Knowles, M.D. 'The Preservation of the Classics' in **1314**, 136-47.

1898
Lehmann, P. 'The Benedictine Order and the Transmission of the Literature of Ancient Rome in the Middle Ages' in **47**, III, 172-83.

1899
Manitius, M. *Handschriften antiker Autoren in mittelalterlichen Bibliothekskatalogen* (Leipzig 1935, repr. Wiesbaden 1968)
A useful survey of printed catalogues.

1900
Minio-Paluello, L. 'Tradizione testuale latina delle opere di Aristotele nel medio evo' in **1959**, I, 499-528.
1901
Munk Olsen, B. 'Les Classiques latins dans les florilèges médiévaux antérieurs au XIIIe siècle,' *RHT* 9 (1979) 47-121; 10 (1980) 115-64
An examination of the typology of more than 70 *florilegia* of the 9th-12th centuries. Incipits of passages found in the florilegia are at pp. 154-64 of *RHT* 10.
1902
———. *L'Etude des auteurs classiques latins aux XIe et XIIe siècles*, I: *Catalogue des manuscrits classiques latins copiés du XIe au XIIe siècle. Apicius – Juvenal* (Paris 1982)
Extensively annotated.
1903
Paratore, E. 'Il problema degli "Pseudepigrapha" ' in **1959**, II, 619-51
A wide survey of classical literature.
1904
Reynolds, L.D. *The Medieval Tradition of Seneca's Letters* (Oxford 1965).
4 pls.
See further **1888**.
1905
Rouse, R.H. 'The *A* Text of Seneca's Tragedies in the Thirteenth Century,' *RHT* 1 (1971) 93-121. 5 pls.
1906
———. 'Florilegia and Latin Classical Authors in Twelfth- and Thirteenth-Century Orléans,' *Viator* 10 (1979) 131-60.
1907
Rouse, R.H. and M.A. Rouse. 'The *Florilegium Angelicum:* Its Origin, Content, and Influence' in **45**, 66-114
On the transmission of classical and patristic texts through a collection of extracts compiled in France, probably at Orléans, in the latter part of the 12th century.
1908
Rouse, R.H. and M.A. Rouse. 'The Medieval Circulation of Cicero's "Posterior Academics" and the *De finibus bonorum et malorum*' in **46**, 333-67.

1909
Schmidt, P. *Die Überlieferung von Cicero's Schrift 'De legibus' in Mittelalter und Renaissance* (Munich 1974).
1910
Traube, L. 'Die römische Literatur im Mittelalter (Überlieferungsgeschichte)' in **70**, II, 121-37.
1911
Ullman, B.L. 'A List of Classical Manuscripts (in an eighth-century codex) perhaps from Corbie,' *Scriptorium* 8 (1954) 24-37
See now **1884**.

Biblical, Patristic, and Liturgical Texts

1912
Bardy, G. 'Copies et éditions au Ve siècle,' *Revue des sciences religieuses* 23 (1949) 38-52.
1913
Bévenot, M. *The Tradition of Manuscripts: A Study in the Transmission of St. Cyprian's Treatises* (Oxford 1961)
A fine example of how to handle 'contamination.'
1914
Cross, F.L. 'Early Western Liturgical Manuscripts,' *Journal of Theological Studies* new ser. 16 (1965) 61-7
Points out that, unlike literary texts, liturgical texts were written for a practical purpose and were not obliged to be accurate reproductions of existing models.
1915
De Ghellinck, J. 'Diffusion et transmission des écrits patristiques' in his *Patristique et moyen âge: Etudes d'histoire littéraire et doctrinale.* 2 vols. (Brussels 1947) II, 181-377.
1916
Gorman, M. 'The Maurists' Manuscripts of Four Major Works of St. Augustine: With some Remarks on their Editorial Techniques,' *RB* 91 (1981) 238-79
An analysis, the first, it appears, of the principles and practices of the Maurist editors of works of Augustine, especially in the case of the *De Genesi ad litteram* (1689).

1917
Marrou, H.I. 'La Technique de l'édition à l'époque patristique,' *Vigiliae Christianae* 3 (1949) 208-24.
1918
Metzger, B.M. *The Text of the New Testament: Its Transmission, Corruption, and Restoration.* 2nd ed. (Oxford 1968). 16 pls.
Includes a succinct chapter (pp. 156-85) on modern methods of textual criticism.
1919
Wilmart, A. 'La Tradition des grands ouvrages de Saint Augustin' in *Miscellanea Agostiniana.* 2 vols. (Rome 1930, 1931) II, 257-315.

Medieval Texts

1920
Bursill-Hall, G.L. 'Teaching Grammars of the Middle Ages: Notes on the Manuscript Tradition,' *Historiographia linguistica* (Amsterdam) 4 (1977) 1-29
A census of MSS of the most widely-circulating treatises on grammar. See also **1932**.
1921
Goldschmidt, E.P. *Medieval Texts and their First Appearance in Print* (London 1943)
Includes a valuable table of editions before 1550 of writings on mysticism (pp. 122-38).
1922
Lehmann, P. 'Autographe und Originale namhafter lateinischer Schriftsteller des Mittelalters' in **47**, I, 359-81.
1923
Rambaud-Buhot, J. 'La Critique des faux dans l'ancien droit canonique,' *BEC* 126 (1968) 1-62
An interesting study up to the time of Gratian (ca. 1141) of the transmission of, and ecclesiastical attitudes towards, falsified texts of church legislation and documents. Notes that up until the Gregorian reform (ca. 1050-1100) falsifiers had a field day, because no authoritative legislation existed to stop them.

1924
Rouse, M.A. and R.H. Rouse. 'The Texts called *Lumen animae,*'
Archivum Fratrum praedicatorum 41 (1971) 5-113
An exemplary study of the transmission of a 'wild' text relating to pastoral
care in the 14th and 15th centuries.

IDENTIFYING TEXTS AND FRAGMENTS

General

1925
Bischoff, B. and H. Bloch. 'Das Wiener Fragment der *Historiae* des Sallust
(P. Vindob. L 117),' *Wiener Studien* N.F. 13 (1979) 116-29
A good example of how to identify and restore fragments, here a fragment
not later than the 4th century A.D. (see CLA X.1539).
1926
Ker, N.R. *Fragments of Medieval Manuscripts used as Pastedowns in
Oxford Bindings, c. 1515-1620* (Oxford 1954)
A model of what may be achieved with fragments. Shows how law texts in
MS form were handed over for use in binding, A.D. 1490-1540, as college
libraries replaced them with printed editions; so also with liturgical texts
from 1540-50 onwards.
1927
Lehmann, P. 'Mittelalterliche Büchertitel' in **47**, V, 1-93
Fundamental for popular or 'pet' titles of books in inventories and cata-
logues. But see now W. Fitzgerald, '*Ocelli nominum:* Names and Shelf
Marks of Famous/Familiar Manuscripts (I),' *Mediaeval Studies* 45 (1983)
214-97.
1928
Pellegrin, E. 'Fragments et Membra Disiecta' in **57**, 70-95. 4 pls.
A 'Martyrology' of mutilated or fragmentary MSS, with useful pages on
procedures for the identification of fragments. See also her studies of
membra disiecta from Fleury, **963-4.**
1929
Watson, R. 'Medieval Manuscript Fragments,' *Archives* 13 (1977) 61-73
A thoughtful treatment of the problem, with excellent bibliography.

Incipits

For the identification of texts in MSS, and to some extent for that of texts in MSS fragments, collections of incipits or *initia* are of prime importance. A general guide to collections of incipits is A. Pelzer, *Répertoires d'Incipit pour la littérature latine philosophique et théologique du moyen âge.* 2nd ed. (Rome 1951); repr. with additions by J. Ruysschaert in A. Pelzer, *Etudes d'histoire littéraire sur la scholastique médiévale* (Louvain – Paris 1964) 35-69. In addition to the works cited below (many of which are not in Pelzer), lists of incipits are to be found in works noted in other parts of this bibliography, e.g. **1374, 1443, 1458, 1462, 1481, 1489, 1508, 1531, 2119, 2123-4, 2126, 2131, 2137, 2140, 2143.**

1930
Barré, H. *Les Homéliaires carolingiens de l'école d'Auxerre* (Vatican City 1962)
Gives sermon incipits at pp. 147-344.
1931
Bloomfield, M.W., B.-G. Guyot, D.R. Howard, and T.B. Kabealo. *Incipits of Latin Works on the Virtues and Vices, 1100-1500 A.D., including a section of Incipits of Works on the Pater Noster* (Cambridge, Mass. 1979).
1932
Bursill-Hall, G.L. 'A Checklist of Incipits of Medieval Latin Grammatical Treatises: A-G,' *Traditio* 34 (1978) 439-74; now replaced by his *Census of Medieval Latin Grammatical Manuscripts* (Stuttgart – Bad Cannstatt 1981)
The procedure is alphabetical, Aberystwyth – Zwickau, with incipits at pp. 295-359.
1933
Clément, J.M. *Initia patrum Latinorum.* 2 vols. (Turnhout 1971, 1979)
Gives the initia of works published in both the Series Latina and the Continuatio mediaevalis of the Corpus Christianorum.
1934
Hauréau, B. *Initia operum scriptorum Latinorum medii potissimum aevi ex codicibus manuscriptis et libris impressis alphabetice digessit B. Hauréau.* 6 vols. (Turnhout 1974)
An invaluable collection of incipits, drawn mainly from Parisian and Vatican MSS and reproduced here from a handwritten copy ca. 1900. See also **1944** for two volumes of appendices.

1935

Kibre, P. 'Hippocrates Latinus: Repertorium of Hippocratic Writings in the Latin Middle Ages,' *Traditio* 31 (1975) 99-126; 32 (1976) 257-92; 33 (1977) 253-95; 34 (1978) 193-226; 35 (1979) 273-302.

1936

Lindberg, D.C. *A Catalogue of Medieval and Renaissance Optical Manuscripts* (Toronto 1975)

Arranged by author, with a list of incipits at pp. 119-29.

1937

Little, A.G. *Initia operum Latinorum quae saeculis xiii. xiv. xv. attribuuntur secundum ordinem alphabeti disposita* (Manchester 1904, repr. New York 1958).

1938

Lohr, C.H. 'Medieval Latin Aristotle Commentaries,' *Traditio* 23 (1967) 313-413 (A-F); 24 (1968) 149-245 (G-I); 26 (1970) 135-216 (J); 27 (1971) 251-351 (J-M); 28 (1972) 281-396 (N-Ri); 29 (1973) 93-197 (Ro-W); 30 (1974) 119-44 (supplement)

Arranged by author, but without a cumulative list of incipits, publication of which is promised in *Catalogo di manoscritti filosofici* **1489**.

1939

————. 'Renaissance Latin Aristotle Commentaries,' *Studies in the Renaissance* 21 (1974) 228-89 (A-B); *Renaissance Quarterly* 28 (1975) 689-741 (C); 29 (1976) 714-45 (D-F); 30 (1977) 681-741 (G-K); 31 (1978) 532-603 (L-M); 32 (1979) 529-80 (N-Ph); 33 (1980) 623-734 (Pi-Sm).

1940

Mohan, G.E. 'Incipits of Logical Writings of the XIIIth-XVth Centuries,' *Franciscan Studies* new ser. 12 (1952) 349-489.

1941

————. 'Initia operum Franciscalium (XIII-XV s.),' *Franciscan Studies* 35 (1975) 1*-92* (A-C); 36 (1976) 93*-177* (D-H); 37 (1977) 179*-375* (I-Q); 38 (1978) 377*-498* (R-Z).

1942

Schaller, D., E. Könsgen, and J. Tagliabue. *Initia carminum Latinorum saeculo undecimo antiquiorum: Bibliographisches Repertorium für die lateinische Dichtung der Antike und des früheren Mittelalters* (Göttingen 1977)

Lists some 18,000 incipits from the 3rd century B.C. to ca. A.D. 1000.

1943

[Schaller, H.M.] *Inizienverzeichnis zu August Potthast, Regesta Pontificum Romanorum (1198-1304).* Monumenta Germaniae historica. Hilfsmittel 2 (Munich 1978).

1944

Schmeller, A.G. and G. Meyer. *Schedarium initia amplectens praesertim ex codicibus Monacensibus Gottingensibus Bruxellensibus collecta.* 2 vols. (Turnhout 1974)

An appendix to **1934**.

1945

Schneyer, J.-B. *Repertorium der lateinischen Sermones des Mittelalters für die Zeit von 1150 bis 1350.* 9 vols. (Münster in Westphalia 1969-80)

Gives incipits of sermons and sermon-collections.

1946

—————. *Wegweiser zu lateinischen Predigtreihen des Mittelalters* (Munich 1965)

Initia are on pp. 1-546, followed, 546-55, by a list of principal editions of sermons, with initia.

1947

Schumann, O. *Lateinisches Hexameterlexikon: Dichterisches Formelgut von Ennius bis zum Archipoeta* (Munich 1979-)

Useful for verification of random or isolated citations of verse in MSS. Covers from the 3rd century B.C. to ca. A.D. 1160. Two volumes have appeared to date: A-C (1979), D-H (1980).

1948

Spade, P.V. *The Medieval Liar: A Catalogue of the Insolubilia-Literature* (Toronto 1975)

Arranged by author, with a list of incipits at pp. 121-3.

1949

Stegmüller, F. *Repertorium commentariorum in Sententias Petri Lombardi.* 2 vols. (Würzburg 1947)

Arranged alphabetically by author, with an index of incipits. To be supplemented by V. Doucet, 'Commentaires sur les *Sentences:* Supplément au répertoire de M. Frédéric Stegmueller,' *Archivum Franciscanum historicum* 47 (1954) 88-170, 400-27, with incipits at pp. 115-28.

1950

—————. *Repertorium biblicum medii aevi.* 9 vols. (Madrid 1950-80)

An alphabetical list of all commentaries on the Bible, with extant MSS. The

core of the work is vols. I-VII; VIII-IX (1976-7) carry supplementary
material for the authors in the first seven volumes; IX also has addenda
and corrigenda.

1951

Thorndike, L. and P. Kibre. *A Catalogue of Incipits of Mediaeval Scientific
Writings in Latin.* 2nd ed. (Cambridge, Mass. 1963)
For additions and further bibliography see H. Silvestre, 'Les Incipits des
oeuvres scientifiques latines du moyen âge, à propos du nouveau Thorn-
dike-Kibre,' *Scriptorium* 19 (1965) 273-8. See also P. Kibre, 'Further
addenda and corrigenda,' *Speculum* 43 (1968) 78-114.

1952

Vattasso, M. *Initia patrum aliorumque scriptorum ecclesiasticorum Latinorum ex Mignei Patrologia et ex compluribus aliis libris.* 2 vols. (Rome
1906, 1908)
To be taken in conjunction with **1933**.

1953

Walther, H. *Carmina medii aevi posterioris Latina,* I: *Initia carminum ac
versuum medii aevi posterioris Latinorum* (Göttingen 1959); II: *Proverbia
sententiaeque Latinitatis medii aevi,* 6 vols. (ibid. 1963-9)
II includes five volumes of initia and one of indexes; I and II are to be
supplemented in turn by J. Stohlmann, 'Nachträge zu Hans Walther, *Initia
carminum ac versuum medii aevi,*' *Mittellateinisches Jahrbuch* 9 (1973)
320-44 and 12 (1977) 297-315; 'Nachträge zu Hans Walther, *Proverbia...,*'
ibid. 12 (1977) 316-29 and 13 (1978) 315-33.

ASSESSING A TEXTUAL TRADITION

1954

Avalle, D'A.S. *Principî di critica testuale* (Padua 1972).

1955

Bartoloni, F. 'Paleografia e critica testuale' in *Relazioni* (see **76**) I, 423-9.

1956

Bieler, L. *The Grammarian's Craft: An Introduction to Textual Criticism.*
3rd ed. (New York 1965)
A judicious review of the principal approaches to textual criticism which
first appeared in *Folia* (Studies in the Christian Perpetuation of the Classics,
New York) 2 (1947) 94-105 and 3 (1948) 23-32, 47-55; was reprinted in a

revised edition *ibid.* 10/2 (1958) 3-42; and appeared again, as above, in a
3rd edition in 1965 as a special issue of *Folia* (now *Classical Folia*).
1957
Bowers, F. *Bibliography and Textual Criticism* (Oxford 1964).
1958
Brink, C.O. 'Studi classici e critica testuale in Inghilterra,' *Annali della
Scuola normale superiore di Pisa* 8 (1978) 1071-1228
On the predecessors of Bentley **1978.**
1959
La critica del testo. 2 vols. (Florence 1971)
Proceedings, generally with respect to legal texts, of the Secondo Congresso
internazionale della Società italiana di storia del diritto, with contributions
by García y García (see **2063**), Minio-Paluello (**1900**), etc.
1960
Denholm-Young, N. 'Textual Criticism' in *Cassell's Encyclopedia of World
Literature.* 2nd ed. (London 1973) I, 548-53.
1961
Feld, M.D. 'The Early Evolution of the Authoritative Text,' *Harvard
Library Bulletin* 26 (1978) 81-111
On the styles of editorial approach to the Bible and other texts in the cen-
tury or so after the invention of printing.
1962
Fränkel, H. *Testo critico e critica del testo* (Florence 1969)
A translation of *Einleitung zur kritischen Ausgabe der 'Argonautica' des
Apollonios* (Göttingen 1964) pp. 123-54.
1963
Fuhrmann, H. 'Überlegungen eines Editors' in **1965**, 1-34
A well-documented survey of editorial theory and practice in various
medieval fields over the past two centuries.
1964
Gottesman, R. and S. Bennett, eds. *Art and Error: Modern Textual Editing*
(London 1970)
Reprints essays by various writers, notably W.W. Greg (see **2005**) and
A.E. Housman (**2039**).
1965
Hödl, L. and D. Wuttke, eds. *Probleme der Edition mittel- und neulatein-
ischer Texte* (Boppard 1978)
Proceedings of a colloquium of the Deutsche Forschungsgemeinschaft at

Bonn in 1973, with contributions by M.-Th. d'Alverny (see **2061**), P.M.
De Contenson (**2037**), H. Fuhrmann (**1963**), W. Ott (**2030**), etc.
1966
Kenney, E.J. 'Textual Criticism' in *Encyclopedia Britannica, Macropedia*
XVIII (New York 1974-5) 189-95.
1967
Kleinhenz, C., ed. *Medieval Manuscripts and Textual Criticism* (Chapel
Hill, N.C. 1976)
Various essays, e.g. by G. Kane (see **2050**), E. Rossini (**2090**).
1968
Laufer, R. *Introduction à la textologie: Vérification, établissement, édition
des textes* (Paris 1972).
1969
McDonald, A.H. 'Textual Criticism' in *Oxford Classical Dictionary.* 2nd
ed. (Oxford 1970) 1048-50.
1970
Marichal, R. 'La Critique des textes' in **42**, 1247-1366
One of the best surveys, with good bibliography.
1971
Martens, G. and H. Zeller, eds. *Texte und Varianten: Probleme ihrer
Edition und Interpretation* (Munich 1971).
1972
Prete, S. *Observations on the History of Textual Criticism in the Medieval
and Renaissance Periods* (Collegeville, Minn. 1970).
1973
Spongano, R., ed. *Studi e problemi di critica testuale* (Bologna 1961)
Papers from a Bologna conference of 1960.
1974
Thorpe, J. *Principles of Textual Criticism* (San Marino, Calif. 1972)
Six thoughtful essays on modern textual problems.
1975
Van Groningen, B.A. *Traité d'histoire et de critique des textes grecs*
(Amsterdam 1963).
1976
West, M.L. *Textual Criticism and Editorial Technique Applicable to Greek
and Latin Texts* (Stuttgart 1973)
Intended to replace to a great extent both **1992** and **2041**.

ESTABLISHING A TEXTUAL TRADITION

There follows a chronological survey of Recensionist ('Lachmannian') and Optimist ('Bédier') approaches.

1977

Robortello, F. *De arte critica sive ratione corrigendi antiquorum libros disputatio* (Udine 1557)
The first treatise, apparently, on textual criticism.

1978

Bentley, R. *A Dissertation upon the Epistles of Phalaris* (Oxford 1697, enlarged ed. 1699)
An attack on the blind acceptance of MSS occasioned by the edition of the Letters of Phalaris by Hon. Charles Boyle in 1695. Bentley's famous dictum, 'Nobis et ratio et res ipsa centum codicibus potiores sunt,' occurs in his edition of Horace *ad Carmen* iii, 27, 15 (Oxford 1711), but in its full context ('Nobis et ratio et res ipsa ... potiores sunt, praesertim accedente vaticani veteris suffragio') it is less doctrinaire than it seems.

1979

Bengel, J.A. *Apparatus criticus ad Novum Testamentum* (Tübingen 1734, 2nd ed. 1763)
The first scholar to advance the idea of grouping MSS by 'families, nations and tribes,' he provided the spur for Griesbach **1980**.

1980

Griesbach, J.J. *Novum Testamentum.* 2nd ed. (Halle 1796)
Held firmly that no final results can be obtained until one has made a complete classification of all MSS according to 'families,' and laid down 15 rules of textual criticism. The 'genealogical' approach of Bengel and Griesbach was taken a stage further by Zumpt **1981**.

1981

Zumpt, K.G. *Ciceronis Verrinarum libri VII* (Berlin 1831)
The first to use the term *stemma codicum,* and, seemingly, to illustrate it.

1982

Ritschl, F.W. *Thomae magistri sive Theoduli monachi Ecloga vocum Atticarum* (Halle 1832).

1983

Lachmann, K. *Novum Testamentum graece et latine.* 2 vols. (Berlin 1832, 1850)

Insisted (preface to vol. I, pp. i-viii, xliv) on a thorough examination (*recensio*) of all MSS as fundamental to an edition.

1984

Madvig, J.N. *De emendandis Ciceronis orationibus pro P. Sestio et in P. Vatinium* (Copenhagen 1834)

Introduced the term *codex archetypus* to describe the unique source from which all extant MSS ultimately derive.

1985

Ritschl, F.W. *De Dionysii Halic. Antiquitatibus Romanis* (Bresslau 1838)

One of the first, if not the first, to base a genealogical survey or stemma codicum on 'common errors.' About 1910 this method came to be termed the 'Lachmann method.'

1986

Westcott, B.F. and F.J.A. Hort. *The New Testament in Greek* (Cambridge 1882; repr. London 1956, etc.)

The classic preface (by Hort) sets out, for the first time in any language, a complete theory of textual criticism. Shows the clear influence of Griesbach and Lachmann and of the German 'genealogical' tradition of the 1830s. On Westcott and Hort see S. Neill, *The Interpretation of the New Testament 1861-1961* (Oxford 1964) 61-81.

1987

Bédier, J., ed. *'Lai de l'ombre' par Jean Renart* (Paris 1913)

An edition, later repudiated (see **1994**), along Recensionist lines.

1988

Clark, A.C. *The Descent of Manuscripts* (Oxford 1918)

The place of omissions in the Recensionist technique.

1989

Kantorowicz, H. *Einführung in die Textkritik: Systematische Darstellung der textkritischen Grundsätze für Philologen und Juristen* (Leipzig 1921)

Recensionist.

1990

Quentin, H. *Mémoire sur l'établissement du texte de la Vulgate* (Rome – Paris 1922)

Taken with the *Essais* **1991**, a brilliant if, to some scholars, baffling modification of Recensionist techniques: common 'textual variants,' not common 'errors,' are what matter.

1991

————. *Essais de critique textuelle (Ecdotique)* (Paris 1926)

Answers critics such as E.K. Rand in *Harvard Theological Review* 17 (1924) 197-264, restates his position of 1922, and argues that to arrive at a stemma codicum one takes the surviving MSS not as a whole, but in overlapping sets of three, and then the common variants statistically, set by set.

1992

Maas, P. 'Textkritik' in *Einleitung in die Altertumswissenschaft*, I, 3rd ed. ed. A. Gercke and E. Norden (Berlin 1927); issued separately, with additions and a reply to Bédier **1994**, as *Textkritik* (Leipzig 1937, 2nd ed. 1950, 3rd ed. 1957, 4th ed. 1960); whence, from 3rd ed. (1957), *Textual Criticism*, trans. B. Flower (Oxford 1958)

The standard manual of Recensionist technique. Makes no mention of Quentin. See also **1976**.

1993

Greg, W.W. *The Calculus of Variants: An Essay on Textual Criticism* (Oxford 1927)

Like Quentin, advocates classification of MSS by textual comparison of two MSS or more in groups or sets.

1994

Bédier, J. 'La Tradition manuscrite du 'Lai de l'ombre': Réflexions sur l'art d'éditer les anciens textes,' *Romania* 54 (1928) 161-96, 321-56; also publ. separately (Paris 1929, repr. 1970)

A famous attack on Lachmann (= 'Recensionism') as a result of editorial experiences of 1890 and 1913. Opts for a 'best manuscript' theory (= 'Optimism'). See also **1987**.

1995

Shephard, W.P. 'Recent Theories of Textual Criticism,' *Modern Philology* 28 (1930) 129-41

Examines Quentin and Greg closely. For Greg's reply, see *ibid*. pp. 401-4.

1996

Collomp, P. *La Critique des textes* (Paris 1931)

Recensionist. Indebted to Maas, critical of Quentin's 'mechanism.'

1997

Pasquali, G. *Storia della tradizione e critica del testo* (Florence 1934, 2nd ed. 1952)

Recensionist, but critical of Lachmann (to whom, possibly, he attributes too much) and Maas. Quentin is mentioned in passing. Introduces the idea of 'open' and 'closed' recension. To some extent rehabilitates *codices descripti* or MSS usually eliminated because they are direct copies.

1998

Severs, J.B. 'Quentin's Theory of Textual Criticism,' *English Institute Annual 1941* (New York 1942) 65-93

Advances on, and certainly clarifies, Quentin.

1999

Andrieu, J. 'Principes et recherches en critique textuelle,' *Mémorial Marouzeau* (Paris 1943) 458-74

A general statement of Recensionist principles.

2000

————. 'Problèmes d'histoire des textes,' *Revue des études latines* 24 (1946) 271-314.

2001

Fourquet, J. *Le Paradoxe de Bédier* (Paris 1946)

On the problem of *bifides*.

2002

Colwell, E.C. 'Genealogical Method: Its Achievements and its Limitations,' *Journal of Biblical Literature* 66 (1947) 109-33; repr. with corrections in Colwell **2036**, 63-83

An important methodological article.

2003

Fourquet, J. 'Fautes communes ou innovations communes?' *Romania* 70 (1948-9) 85-95

More appreciative of Bédier's position on bifides than in **2001**.

2004

Dain, A. *Les Manuscrits* (Paris 1949, 2nd ed. 1964, 3rd ed. 1975)

Dismisses Bédier, chides Quentin, but allows (in 2nd ed., 1964) that 'properly mathematical methods' may have something to offer. A lucid and influential work.

2005

Greg, W.W. 'The Rationale of Copy-Text,' *Studies in Bibliography* 3 (1950-51) 19-36; repr. in **1964**, 17-33

A salutary essay on the 'tyranny of the copy-text.'

2006

Irigoin, J. 'Stemmas bifides et états de manuscrits,' *Revue de philologie* 3rd ser. 28 (1954) 211-17

A good statement of the problems inherent in the bifides.

2007

Castellani, A. *Bédier avait-il raison? La Méthode de Lachmann dans les*

éditions de texte du moyen âge (Fribourg 1957)
A sturdy defence of 'Lachmannism.'
2008
Harkins, P.W. 'Bisensory Collation of MSS: A Modern Method for Collating MSS,' *Manuscripta* 2 (1958) 162-6
On the possibilities of (first generation) computers.
2009
Dearing, V.A. *A Manual of Textual Analysis* (Berkeley, Calif. 1959)
A variant on Quentin's method, but with Greg's terminology. See J. Froger in *Revue des études latines* 42 (1964) 187-92.
2010
Kane, G., ed. *Piers Plowman: The A Version* (London 1960)
A trenchant rejection (at pp. 53-114) of Recensionism in favour of a refinement of Bédier Optimism: the 'corrected base manuscript.'
2011
Timpanaro, S. *La genesi del metodo del Lachmann* (Florence 1963)
Shows that what passes generally for 'Lachmannism' (= Recensionism) in, e.g., Pasquali **1997** owes more to Zumpt **1981**, Ritschl **1985**, and Madvig **1984** than to Lachmann. Has good pages on Bédier and bifides (112-35). The German translation, *Die Entstehung der Lachmannschen Methode* (Hamburg 1971), carries an extensive bibliography of textual criticism at pp. 153-71. See also P. Ganz, 'Lachmann as an Editor of Middle High German Texts' in **2074**, 12-30.
2012
Froger, J. 'La Collation des manuscrits à la machine électronique,' *BIRHT* 13 (1964-5) 135-71.
2013
Greg, W.W. *Collected Papers,* ed. J.C. Maxwell (Oxford 1966).
2014
Dearing, V.A. 'Some Notes on Genealogical Methods in Textual Criticism,' *Novum Testamentum* 9 (1967) 278-97.
2015
Alberti, G.B. 'Recensione chiusa e recensione aperta,' *Studi italiani de filologia classica* 40 (1968) 44-60
On the importance of understanding just what Pasquali **1997** meant by these terms.
2016
Froger, J. *La Critique des textes et son automatisation* (Paris 1968)

A landmark, at least in European circles. Relies, as did Quentin, on 'common textual variants,' but replaces the famous 'comparison of the MSS in threes' by certain group-comparisons. See the review of V. A. Dearing, *Computers and the Humanities* 4 (1969) 149-54.

2017

Griffith, J.G. 'A Taxonomic Study of the Manuscript Tradition of Juvenal,' *Museum Helveticum* 25 (1968) 101-38

An application to text-classification of the statistical principles used, among other areas, in that of biology. Especially significant for 'contaminated' traditions.

2018

————. 'Numerical Taxonomy and Some Primary Manuscripts of the Gospels,' *Journal of Theological Studies* new ser. 20 (1969) 389-406

A further application of the above.

2019

Fischer, B. 'The Use of Computers in New Testament Studies, with Special Reference to Textual Criticism,' *Journal of Theological Studies* new ser. 21 (1970) 297-308.

2020

Computers and Medieval Data Processing (Montreal 1971-)

A periodical (*CAMDAP*) which includes discussions of computers and editing; notices of projects, seminars, meetings; and current bibliography relative to editing.

2021

Love, H. 'The Computer and Literary Editing: Achievements and Prospects' in *The Computer in Literary and Linguistic Research,* ed. R.A. Wisbey (Cambridge 1971) 47-56.

2022

Brunhölzl, F. 'Zu den sogenannten codices archetypi der römischen Literatur' in **33**, 16-31.

2023

Ott, W. 'Computer Applications in Textual Criticism' in *The Computer in Literary Studies,* ed. A.J. Aitken et al. (Edinburgh 1973) 199-223.

2024

Whitehead, F. and C.E. Pickford. 'The Introduction to the *Lai de l'ombre:* Sixty Years Later,' *Romania* 94 (1973) 145-56; repr. in **1967**, 103-16

See **1987, 1994.**

2025

Dearing, V. A. *Principles and Practice of Textual Analysis* (Berkeley, Calif. 1974)

Shows more awareness of computers than in **2014**.

2026

Duplacy, J. 'Classification des états d'un texte, mathématiques et informatique: Repères historiques et recherches méthodologiques,' *RHT* 5 (1975) 249-309

An informed account, with copious bibliography of advances in Recensionism since Quentin, and of the impact of computer technology on the classification of texts.

2027

Boyle, L. E. 'Optimist and Recensionist: "Common Errors" or "Common Variations"?' in *Latin Script and Letters A.D. 400-900: Festschrift presented to Ludwig Bieler,* ed. J.J. O'Meara and B. Naumann (Leiden 1976) 264-74

An attempt to reconcile the two 'systems.'

2028

Irigoin, J. 'Quelques réflexions sur le concept d'archétype,' *RHT* 7 (1977) 235-46

A review of the history of the term from Cicero onwards.

2029

Bowers, F. 'Greg's "Rationale of Copy-Text" Revisited,' *Studies in Bibliography* 31 (1978) 90-161

A summary of the controversy. See **1993, 1995, 2005.**

2030

Ott, W. 'Bibliographie Computer-Anwendung im Editionswesen' in **1965**, 175-85

Goes as far as 1977.

2031

—————. 'A Text Processing System for the Preparation of Critical Editions,' *Computers and the Humanities* 13 (1979) 29-35

On the methods of the Tübingen 'Software package' known as TU-STEP (Tübingen System of Text-processing Programs): mainly valuable for setting up a critical text, with apparatus, in print.

2032

La Pratique des ordinateurs dans la critique des textes. Colloques interna-

tionaux du Centre national de la recherche scientifique 579 (Paris 1979)
Papers by J. Froger (see **2033**), W. Ott, P. Tombeur, etc.
2033
Froger, J. 'La Méthode de Dom Quentin, la méthode des distances et le
problème de la contamination' in **2032**, 13-22.

ESTABLISHING AND EDITING A TEXT

General

2034
Bieler, L. 'Editing Saint Columbanus: A Reply,' *Classica et mediaevalia* 22
(1961) 139-50
A reply to Mundó **2040** and to M. Esposito, *Classica et mediaevalia* 21
(1960) 184-203.
2035
Clericus [= LeClerc], J. *Ars critica.* 2 vols. (Amsterdam 1697)
The first, it seems, to introduce the principle of *lectio difficilior.*
2036
Colwell, E.C. *Studies in Methodology in Textual Criticism of the New
Testament* (Leiden 1969)
Includes essays from over some thirty years. See also **2002**.
2037
De Contenson, P.M. 'L'Edition critique des oeuvres de S. Thomas d'Aquin:
Principes, méthodes, problèmes, et perspectives' in **1965**, 55-74
A general 'policy statement' by the then director of the 'Editio Leonina'
of the works of Aquinas. See also **2068-72**.
2038
Epp, E.J. 'The Eclectic Method in New Testament Textual Criticism:
Solution or Symptom?' *Harvard Theological Review* 69 (1976) 211-57.
2039
Housman, A.E. 'The Application of Thought to Textual Criticism,'
Proceedings of the Classical Association 18 (1921) 67-84
A celebrated paper which has been reprinted many times, e.g. in *Selected
Prose* (see **1891**) 131-50; in **1964**, 1-16; and in *The Classical Papers of A.
E. Housman,* ed. J. Diggle and F.R.D. Goodyear, 3 vols. (Cambridge 1972)
III, 1058-69.

2040

Mundó, A. 'L'Edition des oeuvres de S. Colomban,' *Scriptorium* 12 (1958) 289-93

See **2034**.

2041

Stählin, O. *Editionstechnik*. 2nd ed. (Leipzig 1914)

See **1976**.

2042

Timpanaro, S. *Il Lapsus Freudiano: Psicanalisi e critica testuale* (Florence 1974); trans. as *The Freudian Slip: Psychoanalysis and Textual Criticism* (London 1976)

An ebullient and learned look at the relevance or non-relevance of Freud's *Psychopathology of Everyday Life* (1904; English trans. 1960) to textual criticism and especially to 'lapses' of the scribal error type.

Copyists, Contamination, Corruption

2043

Andrieu, J. 'Pour l'explication psychologique de fautes de copiste,' *Revue des études latines* 28 (1950) 279-92.

2044

Axelson, B. *Korruptelenkult: Studien zur Textkritik der unechten Seneca-Tragödie Hercules Oetaeus* (Lund 1967).

2045

Bergh, B. *Palaeography and Textual Criticism.* 2 vols. (Lund 1979-80)

A valuable guide to the type of errors caused by a misunderstanding or misinterpretation, on the part of medieval scribes, of certain abbreviations.

2046

Birt, T. *Kritik und Hermeneutik nebst Abriss des antiken Buchwesens* (Munich 1913)

Particularly helpful on techniques of emendation.

2047

Chaytor, H.J. 'The Medieval Reader and Textual Criticism,' *Bulletin of the John Rylands Library* 26 (1941-2) 49-56

Points out that the ancient practice of reading aloud to oneself continued during the Middle Ages and would result in a mainly auditive memory, causing a scribe to write, e.g., *es* for *est*. A summary of this helpful note is in Chaytor, *From Script to Print,* 2nd ed. (Cambridge 1950) 148-52.

2048
Dondaine, A. 'Un cas majeur d'utilisation d'un argument paléographique en critique textuelle (Vat. lat. 781),' *Scriptorium* 21 (1967) 261-76. 4 pls. A survey, with illustrations, of difficult or unlikely words in certain MSS of the *Quaestiones de veritate* of Aquinas which only can be explained if one allows that the archetype of these MSS was MS. Vat. lat. 781, a copy dictated to a secretary who wrote a semi-cursive hand full of graphic 'traps' into which the scribes of the *De veritate* MSS fell all too easily.

2049
Havet, L. *Manuel de critique verbale appliquée aux textes latins* (Paris 1911; repr. Rome 1967)
A classic and exhaustive survey of all the various ways in which texts may be altered in transmission — by copyists, correctors, rubricists, etc.

2050
Kane, G. 'Conjectural Emendation' in *Medieval Literature and Civilization: Studies in Memory of G.N. Garmonsway,* ed. D.A. Pearsall and R.A. Waldron (London 1969) 155-69; repr. in **1967**.

2051
Lindsay, W.M. *An Introduction to Latin Textual Emendation* (London 1896)
On scribal errors, as seen in the MS tradition of Plautus.

2052
Ogilvie, R.M. 'Monastic Corruption,' *Greece and Rome* 2nd ser. 18 (1971) 32-4
A splendid note on the way in which a biblical and liturgical upbringing could influence monastic scribes when copying classical texts.

2053
Peri, V. '<Correctores immo corruptores>: Un saggio di critica testuale nella Roma del XII secolo,' *IMU* 20 (1977) 19-125
Includes an edition at pp. 88-125 of 'Libellus de corruptione et correptione psalmorum et aliarum quarundam scripturarum' of Nicola Maniacutrà, a Cistercian of Tre Fontane, Rome, written ca. A.D. 1140-45. Nicola contributes examples of various scribal errors and some vignettes of Roman scriptoria. Montpellier, Bibliothèque de l'Ecole de médecine, MS. H. 294.

2054
Shipley, F.W. *Certain Sources of Corruption in Latin Manuscripts* (New York 1904)

A study of the types of error which might occur when a Carolingian scribe was faced with an Uncial exemplar (in this case, the third decade of Livy).
2055
Vinaver, E. 'Principles of Textual Emendation' in *Studies in French Language and Literature presented to Professor Mildred K. Pope* (Manchester 1939) 351-69; also in **1967**, 139-66
A sharp rejection of Recensionism. Valuable for plumbing the possibilities of error on the part of scribes. See the review by W.W. Greg, *The Library* 4th ser. 20 (1939-40) 426-9, and the remarks of Bieler **1956**.
2056
Willis, J. *Latin Textual Criticism* (Urbana, Ill. 1972)
Useful on drawing up a stemma, and on conjectural emendation.

Diplomatic Edition

2057
Masai, F. 'Principes et conventions de l'édition diplomatique,' *Scriptorium* 4 (1950) 177-93.
2058
Vanderhoven, H., F. Masai, and P.B. Corbett. *Regula magistri: La Règle du maître. Edition diplomatique des manuscrits latins 12205 et 12634 de Paris* (Brussels 1953). 4 pls.
A celebrated, if not entirely convincing, example of a 'diplomatic' edition. See the review by L. Bieler, *Speculum* 30 (1955) 690-92.

Diplomatic Texts

2059
Falconi, E. *L'edizione diplomatica del documento e del manoscritto* (Parma 1969). 26 pls. with transcriptions.
2060
Petrucci, A. 'L'edizione delle fonti documentarie: Un problema sempre aperto,' *Rivista storica italiana* 75 (1963) 69-80.

Scholastic Texts

GENERAL

2061
D'Alverny, M.-Th. 'Notes et observations au sujet des éditions de textes médiévaux' in **1965**, 41-54
A hard look at the problem of editing medieval texts, especially scholastic texts – e.g. the Latin versions of Arabic philosophical and medical treatises, the scribes of which, professionals for the most part, were less conscientious than were scribes, monks in particular, who copied classical, patristic, or sacred texts.

2062
Díez. G.M. 'Algunas normas criticas para la edición de textos jurídicos,' *Anuario de historia del derecho español* 35 (1965) 527-51
Discusses norms for the edition of the *Collectio canonica Hispana*. See **2063**.

2063
García y García, A. 'Presupuestos para la edición critica de textos jurídicos medievales' in **1959**, I, 257-67.

2064
Petri Lombardi libri IV Sententiarum studio et cura PP. Collegii S. Bonaventurae III editio, pars I: Prolegomena (Quaracchi 1971)
A valuable introduction (by I. Brady) on the edition of a text with a cloud of witnesses.

2065
Thomson, S.H. 'Editing of Medieval Latin Texts in America' in *Progress of Medieval and Renaissance Studies in the United States and Canada: Bulletin* 16 (1941) 37-49
A survey of recent editions; some general principles are enounced.

PECIAE

See also **1745-61** and the headnote on p. 254 above.

2066
Battelli, G. 'La "pecia" e la critica del testo dei manoscritti universitari medievali,' *Archivio storico italiano* 93 (1935) 244-52; repr. in **30**, 1-11
Useful reflections on the work of Destrez **1752**.

2067

Axters, E. 'La Critique textuelle médiévale doit-elle être désormais établie en fonction de la "pecia"? Une réponse à Monsieur l'abbé Destrez,' *Angelicum* 13 (1935) 262-95

See **1752**.

2068

Bataillon, L.J. 'Problèmes posés par l'édition critique des textes latins médiévaux,' *Revue philosophique de Louvain* 75 (1977) 234-49

A general description of the process of editing, with special reference to university exemplars (peciae) and copies thereof.

2069

Dondaine, A. 'L'Edition des oeuvres de Saint Thomas,' *Archiv für Geschichte der Philosophie* 43 (1961) 171-90

Warns that university exemplars have to be taken with great care when one is editing. See also **2070**.

2070

————. 'Exemplars de la *Summa contra gentiles*' in **62**, II, 287-99

An evaluation of three university exemplars against extant parts of the autograph of this work of Aquinas. The result is unflattering to the exemplars.

2071

[Gauthier, R.A., ed.] *Sancti Thomae de Aquino Sententia libri Ethicorum.* 2 vols. Sancti Thomae de Aquino opera omnia 47 (Rome 1969)

At I, 73*-87* is the most complete and documented study of peciae since Destrez **1752**; at 88*-154*, a detailed examination of the Parisian peciae of the *Sententia* as seen in the 31 peciae MSS on which the edition is based; at 179*-190*, a list of the numerous occasions on which the editor has had to resort to conjecture. For a review, see R. Macken, 'Un apport important à l'ecdotique des manuscrits à pièces,' *Scriptorium* 27 (1973) 319-37.

2072

Reilly, J.P. 'A Preliminary Study of a Pecia,' *RHT* 2 (1972) 239-50, with 4 graphs

The text is Aquinas on Aristotle's *Metaphysics*.

2073

Saffrey, H.-D. *S. Thomae de Aquino super librum De causis Expositio* (Fribourg—Louvain 1954) preface

The first recognition (at pp. xl-lxxiii) of the phenomenon of multiple university exemplars.

Vernacular

2074
Ganz, P.F. and W. Schröder, eds. *Probleme mittelalterlicher Überlieferung und Textkritik* (Berlin 1966)
Papers from an international seminar at Oxford in 1966 on problems of editing Middle High German texts. See **2011**.

2075
D'Ardenne, S.R.T.O. 'The Editing of Middle English Texts' in *English Studies Today,* ed. C.L. Wrenn and G. Bullough (Oxford 1951) 74-84.

2076
Donaldson, E.T. *Speaking of Chaucer* (London 1970)
See especially pp. 102-18: 'The Psychology of Editors of Middle English Texts.'

2077
Rigg, A.G., ed. *Editing Medieval Texts: English, French, and Latin Written in England* (New York–London 1977)
A survey of problems, presented at a colloquium in Toronto in 1976, by M. Godden (Old English), A. Hudson (Middle English), I. Lancashire (Medieval Drama), B. Merrilees (Anglo-Norman), and A.G. Rigg (Medieval Latin).

2078
Schoeck, R.J., ed. *Editing Sixteenth-Century Texts* (Toronto 1966)
Proceedings of a colloquium at Toronto in 1965.

PRINTING AN EDITED TEXT

2079
Académie royale de Belgique, Commission royale d'histoire. *Instructions pour la publication de textes historiques* (Brussels 1955).

2080
Balić, C. 'La tecnica delle edizioni critiche' in *Il libro e le biblioteche.* Atti del primo Congresso bibliologico francescano internazionale, 20-27 febbraio 1949. 2 vols. (Rome 1950) I, 189-219
A general survey, with special reference to edition of works of John Duns Scotus.

2081
Bidez, J. and A.B. Drachmann. *Emploi des signes critiques: Dispositions*

de l'apparat dans les éditions savantes de textes grecs et latins, ed. A.
Delatte and A. Severyns (Brussels–Paris 1938)
A guide sponsored by the Union académique internationale.
2082
Brearley, D.G. 'Texts and Studies in Latin Orthography to 1977,' *Classical World* 72 (1979) 385-92
The period covered is 1948-77. A valuable survey of modern editorial attitudes to orthography.
2083
Comité international des sciences historiques: Commission internationale de diplomatique. *Normalisation internationale des méthodes de publication des documents latins du moyen âge* (Paris 1974)
An exhaustive treatment of the scientific publication of original documents.
2084
Dondaine, A. 'Abréviations latines et signes recommandés pour l'apparat critique des éditions de textes médiévaux,' *Bulletin de la Société internationale pour l'étude de la philosophie médiévale* 2 (1960) 142-9.
2085
————. 'Variantes de l'apparat critique dans les éditions de textes latins médiévaux,' *Bulletin de la Société internationale pour l'étude de la philosophie médiévale* 4 (1962) 82-100.
2086
Hunnisett, R.F. *Editing Records for Publication* (London 1977). 2 pls. (transcribed and calendared)
Gives rules for presenting records in print, and principles for resolving the problems of editing records.
2087
Kuttner, S. 'Notes on the Presentation of Text and Apparatus in Editing Works of the Decretists and Decretalists,' *Traditio* 15 (1959) 452-64.
2088
Legge, M.D. 'Anglo-Norman and the Historian,' *History* 26 (1941) 163-75
On rules of transcription for editors of Anglo-Norman texts.
2089
Mohlberg, L.C. *Norme per le pubblicazioni di opere scientifiche* (Rome 1956).
2090
Rossini, E. 'Introduction to the Edition of Medieval Vernacular Documents (XIII and XIV Centuries)' in **1967**, 175-210. 5 pls.

2091

[Association Guillaume Budé] *Règles et recommandations pour les éditions critiques,* [I] *Série grecque,* prepared by J. Irigoin; [II] *Série latine,* by J. André (Paris 1972)
Lists rules for Budé texts.

Research Setting

Palaeography in any form is an exacting discipline. On the one hand it demands a thorough competence in the language of the text or piece of writing under scrutiny, and in the handwriting, scribal practices, and abbreviations of the period. On the other, it requires a vast general knowledge. For diplomatic documents (and often for literary, too) it presumes an acquaintance with chronology, monetary systems, and legal terminology, and with local usages, conventions, and modes of address. For literary texts it is important to have a battery of dictionaries, aids, and manuals at the ready, particularly if one has to essay a complete survey of the institutional, physical, human, and textual settings of a given text, as suggested above. This last section therefore attempts to present some of the dictionaries, aids, and manuals from various disciplines upon which one has to fall back repeatedly when cataloguing rolls, codices, or registers, or when identifying, for example, prayers or proverbs that occur in miscellanies or are scribbled on the dorse of a legal document. The section is manifestly incomplete. It is a pointer to some common tools of research, nothing more. But, as a setting, it is a necessary part of an 'integral' palaeography course.

The promotion of the concept of an integral palaeography has been, indeed, the chief aim of this volume. A secondary aim has been to present the idea of the 'compleat' palaeographer. The latter, it must be admitted, is an almost impossible ideal. The requirements are far too demanding. Palaeographers (and here I am speaking solely of Latin palaeography) who are experts, for example, in classical or pre-Carolingian palaeography are not necessarily at home in the period of Gothic writing. Those whose expertise is literary texts are often baffled by notarial or chancery products. Scholars who may read manuscripts of scholastic philosophy or theology as one would a printed book, may have to throw up their hands in despair when confronted with a legal tract. The 'compleat' palaeographer, in fine, would be one who could move with equal nonchalance through a classical text, a notarial register, a commentary on Roman law, an exposition of scripture, treatises on grammar, mathematics, astronomy, or astrology; court and visitation records, a philosophical quodlibet, or a theological disputation. There is none such, I suspect. Most palaeographers are happy if they are wholly at ease in just one area of palaeography. But being a 'partial' and not a 'compleat' palaeographer does not at all mean that one is thereby tied to a palaeography of the 'piecemeal' kind. Like the present writer, one may be narrowly specialized yet engage wholeheartedly in an integral palaeography. It is the only kind, he is sure, that has any validity.

LATIN LANGUAGE

2092
Allen, W.S. *Vox Latina: A Guide to the Pronunciation of Classical Latin* (Cambridge 1965)
Particularly helpful for a proper understanding of accent (see pp. 64-94), without which there is little hope of enlisting the aid of the *cursus* (see Di Capua **2097**) when editing medieval literary or documentary texts.
2093
Blaise, A. *Dictionnaire latin-français des auteurs chrétiens* (Strasbourg 1954, 4th ed. Turnhout 1975)
Compiled from Christian authors ca. A.D. 200-750.
2094
————. *Dictionnaire latin-français des auteurs du moyen-âge: Lexicon Latinitatis medii aevi praesertim ad res ecclesiasticas investigandas pertinens.* Corpus Christianorum, Continuatio mediaevalis (Turnhout 1975).
2095
Bonioli, M. *La Pronuncia del latino nelle scuole dall'antichità al rinascimento,* I (Turin 1962)
To be taken with **2092**.
2096
Curtius, E.R. *European Literature and the Latin Middle Ages,* trans. W.R. Trask (New York 1953).

2097
Di Capua, F. *Fonti ed esempi per lo studio dello 'stilus curiae romanae' medioevale* (Rome 1941)
Gives sample passages in which to see the *cursus* in play.

2098
Du Cange, C.D. *Glossarium ad scriptores mediae et infimae Latinitatis.* 2 vols. (Paris 1678, etc.)
The standard edition is *Glossarium mediae et infimae Latinitatis,* ed. L. Favre, 10 vols. (Niort 1883-7, repr. Paris 1937-8).

2099
Fisher, J.L. *A Medieval Farming Glossary of Latin and English Words taken mainly from Essex Records* (London 1968).

2100
Gooder, E.A. *Latin for Local History: An Introduction.* 2nd ed. (London 1978).

2101
Lange, W.-D. *Philologische Studien zur Latinität westhispanischer Privaturkunden des 9.-12. Jahrhunderts* (Leiden – Cologne 1966).

2102
Latham, R.E. *Revised Medieval Latin Word-List from British and Irish Sources* (London 1965)
Eventually will be replaced by the *Dictionary of Medieval Latin from British Sources,* ed. R.E. Latham, now in progress in fascicules (London 1975-).

2103
La Lexicographie du latin médiéval et ses rapports avec les recherches actuelles sur la civilisation du moyen-âge. Colloques internationaux du Centre national de la recherche scientifique 589 (Paris 1981)
See, notably, P. Tombeur, 'L'Informatique et le travail lexicographique,' pp. 461-73. See also **2115**.

2104
Manitius, M. *Geschichte der lateinischen Literatur des Mittelalters.* 3 vols. (Munich 1911-31).

2105
McGuire, M.R.P. and H. Dressler. *Introduction to Medieval Latin Studies: A Syllabus and Bibliographical Guide.* 2nd ed. (Washington, D.C. 1977)
This second edition of McGuire's original work in 1964 provides one of the most thorough surveys of medieval Latin in all its manifestations: language,

rhetoric, law, music, palaeography, diplomatics, textual criticism, etc.
2106
Niermeyer, J.F. *Mediae Latinitatis lexicon minus* (Leiden 1976)
A great lexicon in French and English, the first fascicule of which appeared in 1954. A companion volume, *Mediae Latinitatis lexicon minus: Abbreviationes et index fontium,* ed. C. van de Kieft (Leiden 1976), provides a view of Niermeyer's sources and a rich bibliography of Medieval Latin.
2107
Norberg, D. *Manuel pratique de latin médiéval* (Paris 1968).
2108
Palmer, L.R. *The Latin Language* (London 1954)
A readable outline history of the language and its grammar from classical times to the Middle Ages.
2109
Paulys Real-Encyclopädie der classischen Altertumswissenschaft, ed. G. Wissowa, I. Reihe (A-Q), 24 vols. (Stuttgart 1893-1963); II. Reihe (R-Z), 10 vols. (ibid. 1914-72); *Supplementbände* (1903-), 15 vols. to 1978
Cited usually as Pauly-Wissowa, *Real-Encyclopädie.*
2110
Prinz, O. and J. Schneider. *Mittellateinisches Wörterbuch bis zum Ausgehenden 13. Jahrhundert* (Munich 1967-)
An introductory volume, *Abkürzungs- und Quellen Verzeichnisse* (1959), contains a tabular list of authors and editions used for the *Wörterbuch.*
2111
Raby, F.J.E. *A History of Christian-Latin Poetry from the Beginnings to the Close of the Middle Ages.* 2nd ed. (Oxford 1953).
2112
————. *A History of Secular-Latin Poetry in the Middle Ages.* 2nd ed. (Oxford 1957).
2113
Souter, A. *Glossary of Later Latin to 600 A.D.* (Oxford 1949).
2114
Strecker, K. *Introduction to Medieval Latin.* 6th ed. (Dublin – Zürich 1971)
A translation and revision by R.B. Palmer of *Einführung in das Mittellatein,* 3rd ed. (Berlin 1939). The translation appeared originally in 1957 and was reprinted in 1963, with additional bibliography. The above 'edition' of 1971 is a simple reprint of that of 1963.

2115

Tombeur, P. 'Informatique et étude de textes: Pour une meilleure connaissance du vocabulaire médiolatin,' *Archivum Latinitatis medii aevi* 40 (1975-6) 124-38

On the Centre de traitement electronique des documents (CETEDOC) at the Université catholique de Louvain, Louvain-la-Neuve, and its projects with respect to Medieval Latin. Among other things it is publishing in microfiche form the beginnings of a 'Thesaurus patrum Latinorum,' a series of computer concordances to all volumes of the Corpus Christianorum, Series Latina. It is hoped that the result will be a series of concordances that will cover the whole of patristic writing in the CCSL and its Continuatio mediaevalis. See also **2103**.

2116

Wingo, E.O. *Latin Punctuation in the Classical Age* (The Hague 1972).

LITERARY, LITURGICAL, LEGAL, THEOLOGICAL AIDS

2117

Bale, J. *Scriptorum illustrium maioris Brytanniae quam nunc Angliam et Scotiam vocant catalogus.* 2 vols. (Basel 1557-79, repr. Farnborough, Hants. 1971).

2118

——————. *Index Britanniae scriptorum,* ed. R.L. Poole and M. Bateson (Oxford 1902).

2119

Bibliotheca hagiographica Latina antiquae et mediae aetatis. 2 vols. Brussels 1898-1911); and *Supplementum* (1911)

An indispensable bibliography of lives of saints, with MSS, incipits, and printed editions, in the Subsidia hagiographica series of the Bollandists.

2120

Blaise, A. and A. Dumas. *Le Vocabulaire latin des principaux thèmes liturgiques* (Turnhout 1966)

On Latin liturgical vocabulary; includes a dictionary of liturgical themes. For a lexicon of codicology for cataloguing liturgical MSS, see **1631**. For types of liturgical MSS see **1452-6**.

2120a

Bruylants, F. *Les Oraisons du missel romain: Texte et histoire.* 2 vols.

(Louvain 1952)
Vol. II lists 1182 incipits. Valuable for tracking stray prayers in MS miscellanies.

2121
Buchwald, W., A. Hohlweg, and O. Prinz. *Tusculum-Lexikon griechischer und lateinischer Autoren des Altertums und des Mittelalters.* 2nd ed. (Munich 1963)
Crisp notices, with essential bibliography, of classical, patristic, scholastic, and humanist authors.

2122
Catalogus translationum et commentariorum: Mediaeval and Renaissance Latin Translations and Commentaries (Washington, D.C. 1960-)
A project of the Union académique internationale, four volumes of which have appeared to date (1960, 1971, 1976, 1980). Lists and describes the Latin translations of ancient Greek authors and the Latin commentaries on ancient Latin (and Greek) authors (from before A.D. 600) that were composed before 1600.

2123
Chevalier, C.U.J. *Repertorium hymnologicum: Catalogue des chants, hymnes, proses, séquences, tropes en usage dans l'église latine depuis les origines jusqu'à nos jours.* 6 vols. (Louvain 1892-1912, Brussels 1920-21)
An alphabetical list, with 42,060 entries, by incipit. The last two volumes (1920-21) carry addenda, preface, and tables.

2124
Dekkers, E. *Clavis patrum Latinorum a Tertulliano ad Bedam.* 2nd ed. (Steenbrugge 1961)
Essential, with P. Glorieux, *Pour revaloriser Migne* (Lille 1952), as a companion to Migne's Patrologia Latina, where many texts are of dubious or incorrect attribution. Lists initia at pp. 557-84.

2125
De Raze, H., E. de Lachaud, and J.B. Flandrin. *Concordantiarum sacrae scripturae manuale* (Lyons 1851, etc.; repr. Barcelona 1954)
Handy and reliable when identifying scriptural references or echoes, and not outmoded by Fischer **2129**.

2126
Díaz y Díaz, M.C. *Index scriptorum Latinorum medii aevi Hispanorum* (Madrid 1959)
Proceeds by centuries, from the 6th to the 14th. Lists initia at pp. 483-523.

2127

Dictionnaire d'archéologie chrétienne et de liturgie, ed. F. Cabrol and H. Leclercq. 15 vols. (Paris 1907-53).

2128

Dictionnaire de théologie catholique, ed. A. Vacant, E. Mangenot, and E. Amann. 15 vols. (Paris 1903-50).

2129

Fischer, B. *Novae concordantiae bibliorum sacrorum iuxta Vulgatam versionem critice editam.* 5 vols. (Stuttgart–Bad Cannstatt 1977)

A computerized index to the critical edition of the Vulgate (Rome 1926-).

2130

Gamber, K. *Codices liturgici Latini antiquiores.* 2 vols. 2nd ed. (Fribourg 1968)

A survey of sacramentaries and other liturgical books up to ca. A.D. 800.

2131

Glorieux, P. *Répertoire des maîtres en théologie de Paris au XIIIe siècle.* 2 vols. (Paris 1933)

A list of MSS of works of each master. Incipits are given in II, 378-459.

2132

Grässe, J.G.T. *Trésor de livres rares et précieux ou Nouveau dictionnaire bibliographique.* 7 vols. (Dresden 1859-69).

2133

Grant, M. *Greek and Latin Authors: 800 B.C.-1000 A.D.* (London 1979)
A biographical handbook, with useful bibliographies.

2134

Grégoire, R. 'Repertorium liturgicum Italicum,' *SM* 3rd ser. 9 (1968) 465-592; 11 (1970) 537-56; 14 (1973) 1123-32

A list, with some printed extracts, of all liturgical MSS written in Italy, 7th-12th centuries.

2135

Histoire littéraire de la France. 12 vols. [by Benedictines of the Congregation of St. Maur] (Paris 1733-63); vol. XIII- (Paris 1814-), continued by a Commission of the Institut de France

Provides lengthy biographies, often of medieval authors.

2136

Kaeppeli, T. *Scriptores Ordinis praedicatorum medii aevi* (Rome 1970-)
Three volumes to date (but excluding Albert the Great and Thomas Aquinas). The arrangement of authors is alphabetical, and generally all extant

MSS of each work are recorded.

2137

Kuttner, S. *Repertorium der Kanonistik (1140-1234): Prodromus corporis glossarum,* I (Vatican City 1937)

On commentators and commentaries on the *Decretum* of Gratian and the *Quinque compilationes,* with a note of MSS in each case, and a list of incipits.

2138

—————. *Index titulorum decretalium ex collectionibus tam privatis quam publicis conscriptus* (Milan 1977)

Invaluable for tracking down citations, in legal texts of the Middle Ages, of papal legislation as it is found in official or non-official collections of papal legislation in the period 1140-1317.

2139

Lexikon für Theologie und Kirche. 2nd ed., by J. Hofer and K. Rahner. 11 vols. (Freiburg im Breisgau 1957-67)

The most comprehensive of its kind.

2140

Salmon, P. *Analecta liturgica: Extraits des manuscrits liturgiques de la Bibliothèque Vaticane. Contribution à l'histoire de la prière chrétienne* (Vatican City 1974)

Lists incipits at pp. 329-44.

2141

Schulte, J.F. von. *Die Geschichte der Quellen und Literatur des canonischen Rechts von Gratian bis auf die Gegenwart.* 3 vols. (Stuttgart 1875-1880)

The most comprehensive general coverage (vols. I-II) of works of medieval canon law.

2142

Tanner, T. *Bibliotheca Britannico-Hibernica: sive De scriptoribus qui in Anglia, Scotia, et Hibernia ad saeculi XVII initium floruerunt... commentarius* (Oxford 1748; repr. Tucson, Ariz. 1963)

Arranged alphabetically, with incipits of individual works as they occur.

2143

Wilmart, A. *Auteurs spirituels et textes dévots du moyen-âge latin: Etudes d'histoire littéraire* (Paris 1932, repr. 1971)

A formidable collection of articles on textual problems in this literature, with a useful list (pp. 587-91) of incipits of hymns, prayers, and blessings discussed in the work.

HISTORICAL SOURCES AND AIDS

2144

Boyce, G.C. *Literature of Medieval History 1930-1975: A Supplement to Louis J. Paetow's 'A Guide to the Study of Medieval History'*. 5 vols. (New York 1981)
See also **2147**.

2145

Chevalier, C.U.J. *Répertoire des sources historiques du moyen âge: Bio-bibliographie*. 2 vols. (Paris 1905, 1907).

2146

Graves, E.B. *A Bibliography of English History to 1485* (Oxford 1975)
Based on and replacing C. Gross, *The Sources and Literature of English History from the Earliest Times to about 1485* (London 1900, 2nd ed. 1915).

2147

Paetow, L.J. *A Guide to the Study of Medieval History*. 2nd ed. (New York 1931; repr. New York 1980, with revisions and corrections by G.C. Boyce and an addendum by L. Thorndike)
For continuation see **2144**.

2148

Potthast, A. *Bibliotheca historica medii aevi*. 2 vols. 2nd ed. (Berlin 1896)
Now slowly being replaced by **2149**.

2149

Repertorium fontium historiae medii aevi primum ab Augusto Potthast digestum, nunc cura collegii historicorum e pluribus nationibus emendatum et auctum (Rome 1962-), I: *Series collectionum* (1962); II: *Fontes A-B* (1967); III: *Fontes C* (1970); IV: *Fontes D-E-F-Gez* (1976); [V] *Additamenta I: Series collectionum continuata et aucta (1962-1972)* (1977).

2150

Van Caenegem, R.C. and F.L. Ganshof. *Guide to the Sources of Medieval History* (Amsterdam 1978)
Has useful sections on libraries (pp. 131-8), catalogues of modern libraries (138-44) and archives (145-55), diplomatics (330-32), palaeography (333-41).

CHRONOLOGY

2151
L'Art de vérifier les dates des faits historiques, ed. N.V. de St. Allais et al. 44 vols. 4th ed. (Paris 1818-44)
The fourth edition of a work first published in Paris in 1750 'par un religieux de la congrégation de St.-Maur,' which had a second, enlarged edition in 1770, and a third, in three volumes, 1783-7.

2152
Cappelli, A. *Cronologia, cronografia, e calendario perpetuo.* 2nd ed. (Milan 1930)
Invaluable, particularly for German and Italian areas.

2153
Cheney, C.R. *Handbook of Dates for Students of English History* (London 1945, 2nd ed. 1970)
The best of its kind. Valuable for problems of the date of Easter, church festivals, regnal years, medieval reckonings of time.

2154
Eubel, C. *Hierarchia Catholica medii aevi,* I: *Ab anno 1198 usque ad annum 1431 perducta.* 2nd ed. (Münster in Westphalia 1913, repr. Pavia 1960); II: *Ab anno 1431 usque ad annum 1503 perducta.* 2nd ed. (ibid. 1914, repr. Pavia 1960).

2155
Gams, B. *Series episcoporum ecclesiae Catholicae.* 2nd ed. (Leipzig 1885, repr. 1931)
Still the only general survey from the earliest years of the church until modern times, although for the period from 1198 it has been superseded by Eubel **2154.**

2156
Grotefend, H. *Taschenbuch der Zeitrechnung des deutschen Mittelalters und der Neuzeit.* 10th ed., ed. T. Ulrich (Hanover 1960).

2157
Grumel, V. *La Chronologie* (Paris 1958)
Clear and well-presented, but the focus is Byzantine chronology, being vol. I of *Traité d'études byzantines,* ed. P. Lemerle.

2158
Hampson, R.T. *Medii aevi kalendarium, or Dates, Charters, and Customs of the Middle Ages with Kalendars from the Tenth to the Fifteenth Cen-*

tury and an alphabetical digest of obsolete names of days forming a glossary of the dates of the Middle Ages with tables and other aids for ascertaining dates. 2 vols. (London 1841, repr. New York 1978)
Still very useful, particularly for some uncommon information, e.g. on popular customs and superstitions associated with various feasts of the church.
2159
Powicke, F.M. and E.B. Fryde. *Handbook of British Chronology.* 2nd ed. (London 1961)
Includes medieval dioceses and bishops for Irish, Scottish, and Welsh churches.
2160
Ware, R.D. 'Medieval Chronology: Theory and Practice' in *Medieval Studies* (see **120**) 213-37
A good, practical survey.

TOPOGRAPHY

2161
Calmette, J. *Atlas historique,* II: *Le Moyen Age.* 4th ed. (Paris 1959)
Useful, but not as graphic as Engel **2165**.
2162
Chevalier, C.U.J. *Répertoire des sources historiques du moyen âge: Topo-bibliographie.* 2 vols. (Paris 1894, 1903).
2163
Cottineau, L.H. *Répertoire topo-bibliographique des abbayes et prieurés.* 2 vols. (Macon 1939)
Now supplemented by a third volume, ed. G. Poras (Macon 1970), with a bibliography of works used by Cottineau, expansions of his sigla, and (pp. 289-361) a list of the Latin place-names of the monasteries and priories in the volumes.
2164
Grässe, J.G. *Orbis Latinus: oder Verzeichnis der wichtigsten lateinischen Orts- und Ländernamen.* 2nd ed. (Berlin 1909)
Now replaced by H. and S.-C. Plechl, *Orbis Latinus: Lexikon lateinischer geographischer Namen des Mittelalters und der Neuzeit,* 3 vols. (Brunswick 1972), which is also available in summary form: *Orbis Latinus Handausgabe*

(ibid. 1971). The Plechl expansion of Grässe is not as comprehensive as it purports to be, and has to be supplemented by local lists in various countries, where these are available.

2165
Engel, J., ed. *Grosser historischer Weltatlas, Zweiter Teil: Mittelalter.* 2nd ed. (Munich 1979)
Well-designed and in colour. Has good indexes, and useful maps which chart, e.g., medieval mints and the vagaries of Easter reckonings.

DIPLOMATICS, OTHER DISCIPLINES

Diplomatics

2166
Boyle, L.E. 'Diplomatics' in *Medieval Studies* (see **120**) 69-101.
2167
Bresslau, H. *Handbuch der Urkundenlehre für Deutschland und Italien.* 2 vols. 2nd ed. (Leipzig 1912, 1931); repr. as '3rd edition' (Berlin 1958), followed by an *Index,* ed. H. Schulze (Berlin 1960)
The standard general manual for German, Italian, and papal diplomatics.
2168
De Boüard, A. *Manuel de diplomatique française et pontificale.* 2 vols. (Paris 1929, 1948). 2 albums of pls. (1929, 1949-52) with transcriptions
See further **442**.
2169
[Gilson, J.P.] *Legal and Manorial Formularies edited from Originals at the British Museum and the Public Record Office in Memory of Julius Parnell Gilson* (Oxford 1933)
Invaluable for beginners in these areas. Presents the text of two formularies — both rolls — from, probably, a little before A.D. 1300, one a formulary of deeds, the other a *Forma computi* or steward's vademecum. Includes one plate of each.
2170
Giry, A. *Manuel de diplomatique* (Paris 1893, repr. 1925)
A seasoned manual of general diplomatics, with good sections on chronology and currency relative to French areas. No plates.

2171

Hall, H.A. *A Formula Book of English Official Historical Documents*, I: *Diplomatic Documents* (Cambridge 1908); II: *Ministerial and Judicial Records* (ibid. 1909)
Very helpful in the face of MS material of this kind. See also **1157** for English local records, and **1170** for Scottish documents.

2172

Pryor, J.H. *Business Contracts of Medieval Provence: Selected Notulae from the Cartulary of Giraud Amalric of Marseilles 1248* (Toronto 1981). 1 pl. with transcription
An excellent vocabulary of, and notes on, a wide range of contracts, all of which are given in full.

2173

Tessier, G. *La Diplomatique.* Que sais-je? 536. 3rd ed. (Paris 1966)
A concise general introduction.

2174

————. 'Diplomatique' in **42**, 633-76
Includes a select bibliography.

Epigraphy

2175

Bloch, R. *L'Epigraphie latine.* Que sais-je? 534 (Paris 1952)
Does not go beyond the Roman period.

2176

Deschamps, P. 'Etude sur la paléographie des inscriptions lapidaires de la fin de l'époque mérovingienne aux dernières années du XIIe siècle,' *Bulletin monumental* 88 (1929) 5-81. 35 pls.

2177

Diehl, E. *Inscriptiones Latinae Christianae veteres.* Tabulae in usum scholarum 4 (Bonn 1912)
Provides 50 plates, with transcriptions, illustrating some 500 inscriptions of the 1st-15th centuries A.D.

2178

Favreau, R. *Les Inscriptions médiévales.* Typologie des sources du moyen âge occidental 35 (Turnhout 1979)
See especially pp. 49-60 on writing.

2179

Gordon, A.E. and J.S. Gordon. *Contributions to the Palaeography of Latin Inscriptions* (Berkeley, Calif. 1957). 17 pls.

An outgrowth of *Album* (Part One) **2180** on lettering, ductus, tall-I, abbreviations, etc.

2180

—————. *Album of Dated Latin Inscriptions: Rome and the Neighborhood.* 4 vols. (Berkeley – Los Angeles 1958-65)

Three volumes of texts, each with an accompanying album of plates, and a volume of indexes. 176 plates illustrate some 365 inscriptions, ca. 83 B.C. to A.D. 525.

2181

Kloos, R.M. *Einführung in die Epigraphik des Mittelalters und der frühen Neuzeit* (Darmstadt 1980). 8 pls.

2182

Koch, W. 'Zur Technik der Transkription von Inschriften des Mittelalters und der Neuzeit,' *Mitteilungen des Instituts für österreichische Geschichtsforschung* 80 (1972) 390-97.

2183

Lafaurie, J. 'Epigraphie monétaire aux Xe et XIe siècles' in *Congrès international de numismatique, Paris, 6-11 juillet 1953: Rapports,* II (Paris 1957) 545-50.

2184

Pritchard, V. *English Medieval Graffiti* (Cambridge 1967)

A survey, county by county, with 230 figures and some transcriptions.

2185

Silvagni, A. *Monumenta epigraphica Christiana saeculo XIII antiquiora quae in Italiae finibus adhuc exstant.* 4 vols. (Vatican City 1938-44)

Proceeds region by region, with varying numbers of plates.

Heraldry, Numismatics, Sigillography

2186

Bascapè, G.C. 'La sigillografia in Italia: Notizia. Saggio bibliografico,' *Archivi d'Italia* 21 (1954) 191-243.

2187

—————. *Sigillografia: Il sigillo nella diplomatica, nel diritto, nella storia, nell'arte,* I: *Sigillografia generale. I sigilli pubblici e quelli privati* (Milan 1969).

2188

Demay, G. *La Paléographie des sceaux* (Paris 1881)
Fundamental.

2189

Grierson, P. 'Numismatics' in *Medieval Studies* (see **120**) 103-50
Has an excellent bibliography. See also **2183**.

2190

[Jenkinson, H.] *A Guide to Seals in the Public Record Office* (London 1954). 12 pls.
Part I (pp. 1-33) presents a fine introduction to the study of seals, forgery included.

2191

Hector, L.C. *Palaeography and Forgery* (London – York 1959). 4 pls.
A short, informed paper on forgery in general and on that of seals in particular.

2192

Meurgey de Tupigny, J. 'Heraldique' in **42**, 740-67
Includes a handy lexicon of terms. See also **2193**.

2193

Pastoureau, M. 'L'Héraldique au service de la codicologie' in **58**, 75-88.

Musicology

2194

Corbin, S. *Répertoire de manuscrits médiévaux contenant des notations musicales* (Paris 1965-)
The three volumes to date, the last published in 1974, cover Parisian libraries, with many plates. The procedures are generally those adopted for *Manuscrits datés* **313**.

2195

————. *Die Neumen* (Cologne 1977). 41 pls.
The third fascicule of vol. I in *Paläographie der Musik,* ed. L. Shrade; contains a bibliography to 1975.

2196

Escudier, D. 'Les Manuscrits musicaux du moyen âge (du IXe au XIIe

siècles)' in **57**, 34-45
Includes a selective bibliography.
2197
Floros, C. *Universale Neumenkunde.* 3 vols. (Kassel 1970)
Vol. I deals with Byzantine and Slavonic neums; II with Latin neums; III,
which has 127 plates of various liturgies, with Byzantine, Slavonic, and
Gregorian tone-figures and formulae. A summary is in the author's
Einführung in die Neumenkunde (Wilhelmshaven 1980).
2198
Frere, W.H. *Bibliotheca musico-liturgica: A Descriptive Handlist of the
Musical and Latin-Liturgical Manuscripts of the Middle Ages preserved in
the Libraries of Great Britain and Ireland.* 2 vols. (London–Oxford 1894-
1932). 17 pls.
2199
Hughes, A. *Medieval Music.* Toronto Medieval Bibliographies 4. 2nd ed.
(Toronto 1980)
A comprehensive bibliographical guide.
2200
Huglo, M. 'Codicologie et musicologie' in **62**, I, 71-82. 2 pls.
Deals with roll and codex, copyists and *notatores.* Notes the case of
Adémar of Chabannes (ca. A.D. 988-1034), who was both copyist and
notator. Argues that musicology is a step beyond codicology; it looks at
texts and signs of notation: 'L'examen purement paléographique céde le
pas aux analyses philologiques et sémiologiques.'
2201
————. 'Règlement du XIIIe siècle pour la transcription des livres notés'
in *Festschrift Bruno Stäblein zum 70. Geburtstag,* ed. M. Ruhnke (Kassel
1967) 121-33
On Carthusian, Cistercian, Cluniac, Dominican, and Franciscan regulations.
2202
Karp, T. 'Medieval Music in Perspective' in *Medieval Studies* (see **120**)
343-63
Provides a bibliography at pp. 363-72.
2203
Suñol [= Sunyol], G. *Introduction à la paléographie musicale grégorienne*
(Tournai 1935)
A translation of the original Catalan edition (Montserrat 1925).

VARIA

2204

Meyer, O. and R. Klauser. *Clavis mediaevalis: Kleines Wörterbuch der Mittelalterforschung* (Wiesbaden 1962). 8 pls.

A handy and reliable illustrated dictionary of palaeographical, diplomatic, musicological, numismatic, and other terms. Includes a good, basic bibliography.

2205

Mullins, E. L. C. *Texts and Calendars: An Analytical Guide to Serial Publications* (London 1958)

The focus is English and Welsh history. Lists in particular the publications of various antiquarian and other societies (Chatham, William Salt, Surtees, etc.) relative to these areas.

2206

Oxford Dictionary of the Christian Church, ed. F. L. Cross and E. Livingstone. 2nd ed. (Oxford 1974)

Whether in the revised and expanded version of 1974 or the original edition of 1957, this is the best-informed handbook of liturgy, patristics, theology, scholasticism, and general church history.

2207

Rouse, R. H. *A Guide to Serial Bibliographies for Medieval Studies* (Berkeley, Calif. 1969)

Covers some 283 journals in various languages.

Index locorum, nominum, rerum

This index is as comprehensive as possible, and it is followed by an index of manuscripts cited explicitly in the bibliography. References are to entry numbers, not to page numbers. An asterisk before a number (e.g. *516) indicates the preface or headnote that precedes that number. An asterisk before a place-name (e.g. *Bamberg) notes that the place in question is also to be found in the index of manuscripts. A few abbreviations are used: ab.: abbot, abp.: archbishop, bp.: bishop, card.: cardinal, mon.: monastery, nr.: near.

*Aachen 12, 263, 292, 956, 978, 1430; exhibition at 923; Sammlung Ludwig 1463
Aarau, Switzerland 340
Aargau, Switzerland 882
Abano Terme 1486
Abate, Giuseppe 1487
Abbeville 257
Abbey, John R., library of 1254
Abbeys, survey of medieval 2163
Abbotsbury 1389
Abbotsford 1470
Abbreviations, common 1762-99; special 1800-20; at Bobbio 255, 1778, 1784; at Corbie 900; history of 135, 152, 813, 1096, 1222, 1785; in inscriptions 2179; Insular 663, 691, 1776, 1778-9, 1784; legal 1113, 1762, 1786-8, 1790-91; at Lorsch 871; in music 1820, 2194-2203;

Polish 149; at St. Gall 874; scholastic 1775, 1786-91, 1799; and scribal lapses 2043, 2045, 2049; styles of 1714
*Aberystwyth, Wales 1932
Abo, Finland 1229
Académie royale de Belgique 2079
Accentuation of Latin 1693, 2092
Account books 890, 1129, 1265
Ada, Gospels 923; 'Group' 631, 985
Adalbert, abp. Hamburg 1114
Adam of Bremen 1114
Adémar of Chabannes 246, 1713, 2200
Adimarus, Joannes 72
Advertisement sheets of scripts 1668, 1677-8
Aed, ab. Terryglass, Ireland 659
Aedeluald, prayerbook of 1082
Aelfric, ab. Eynsham 748
Aeschlimann, Erhard 1822

in Normandy 945
Anglo-Norman hands 983
Anglo-Saxon charters 182, 700, 703, 707; MSS 693, 698, 700, 703, 707, 710, 729, 945, 1161; studies, beginnings of 1409
Anglo-Saxon England (ASE) 13
Angoulvent, Paul 1565
Angrisani, Maria 792
Anjou, house of 157, 1828
Annales Rodenses 1126
*Ann Arbor, Michigan, papyri at 183 (ChLA), 263 (CLA)
Anne, queen of England 1159
L'Année philologique 14, *1869
Annuario delle biblioteche italiane 1486
Ansfridus, ab. Nonantola 1030
Anthony, St., ab. 392
Antiphonaries 278, 306, 345-52, 358, 364-5, 782, 789-90, 1006, 1507
Antiqua, littera: see Hand
Apices of letters 524
Apicius, proverbial gourmet 1902
Apocalypses 367, 372, 381, 389, 1150, 1169, 1171; Bamberg 1001, 1005; Beatus 783; Trier 295; Trinity 1142, 1148
'Apollo and Pegasus' bindings 1418
Apollonios, *Argonautica* of 1962
'Apopeciae' *1666, 1752, 1758-9
Apparatus criticus 2084-5
Apparatus decretorum 1745
Appenzell, Switzerland 340
Apuleius 230; Apuleius Barbarus 382
Apulia, Beneventan MSS from 853
Aquinas, Thomas, St. 1106, 1193 1440, 1711, 1737, 1749, 1758, 2037, 2048, 2069-73, 2136; hand of 1711, 1715; cf. Leonine commission

Aragón, library of kings of 1417
Archaeology, dictionary of 2127
Archaeology of book 1573-5, 1579; cf. Codicology
Archetype 1896, 1984, 2022, 2028, 2048
Architecture, Insular 610
Archives 24, 1427-8, 1433, 1438, 2150
Archivio paleografico italiano 160-75, *1039, *1194
Archivio Segreto Vaticano: see *Vatican Archives
Archivum 1438
Archpoet 1947
Aretina, littera 1700
Aretino, Giovanni *1253
Arian scholia 177
Aristotle, works of 374, 1489, 1737, 1749, 1900, 1938-9
Armagh, Book of 618, 676, 681
Arn, abp. Salzburg 277
Arndt, Wilhelm F. 416
Arngart, Olof 737
Arnold, Klaus 1690
Arnulf, emperor 972
*Arras 1378; book-production in area of 1175; chansonnier of 1186
Arribas Arranz, Filemón 1220
Arrighi, Ludovico *1253, 1282
L'Art de vérifier les dates 2151
De arte illuminandi 1865
Art forms, Italo-Byzantine 984
Artists, at work 1842; mobility of 1843; cf. Ornamentation
Aschaffenburg, Bavaria 1460
Ashmole, Elias, MSS of: see *Oxford, Bodleian Library
'Assumptions' of E.A. Lowe 255, 1638
Asturia 765
Atkinson, Robert 667

Computers and Medieval Data Processing 2020

Computus 2169

Condatomagos, Auvergne 556

Conjectures, conjectural emendation 2050, 2071

Constance, Switzerland 250, 1355; book-trade at 1397; writing-centres around 877-85

Constantinople 407; scriptorium at 534, 576, 580

'Contamination' of texts 1890, 1913, 2017, 2033

Contraction, principle of 1803; cf. Abbreviations

Contracts, business, samples of 2172

Contreni, John J. 623, 948

*Copenhagen 391, 1114, 1232

Copying devices, techniques 1724-40

Copy-text 2005, 2029

Corbett, Philip B. 2058

Corbie, France 72, 212, 406, 894-903, *912, *916, 937, 941-3, 949, *971, 1372, 1884, 1911; nun scribes at 894

Corbin, Solange 2194-5

Córdoba *760; MSS of cathedral of 1492

Cormery abbey, France 979

Cornelius Nepos, work of 420

Cornwall, and Brittany 691

Corpus, agrimensorum 242; *Christianorum* 1933, 2115; *codicum Danicorum* 1227; *codicum Islandicorum* 1232; *codicum Norvegicorum* 1237; *codicum Suecicorum* 1239-45; *stigmatologicum* 1737

Corruption of texts 1918, 2043; causes of 2047, 2049; cf. Contamination

Cosmographia of Vergil of Salzburg 415

Costamagna, Giorgio 83, 1813-15

Cottineau, Laurent H. 2163

Cotton, Henry, MSS of: see *London, BL

Couderc, Camille 1682

Coulon, Rémi 444

Coupar-Angus, Scotland 215

Court hands, England 1081, 1292

'Court' school, circle, at Aachen 292, 917, 923, 978; at St. Denis, Paris 972; cf. 'Palace' school

Courtois, Christian 527

Coveney, Dorothy K. 1532, 1619

Covers: see Binding

Coxe, Henry O. 367

Craster, Herbert H.E. 1478

Creeds, MSS of 309

Cremona 842

Creytens, Raymond 1258

La critica del testo (colloquium) 1959

Cross, Frank L. 1914, 2206

Cross, James E. 1043

Crous, Ernst 1109

Crowland, Lincolnshire 385; Apocalypse of 1169

Crump, Charles G. 123

Cryptography 279, 1816-19

Cumplido, Manuel N. 1492

Cunningham, Ian C. 1164

Currency, medieval 157, 2170, 2183

Cursive hands 368, 375, 414, *516, 518, 530, 536, 573, *760, 814, 824, 827, 1100-2, 1105, 1133, 1163, 1168, 1170, 1304. For Roman cursive, see Hand, Common.

Cursus, medieval 2092, 2097

Curtius, Ernst R. 2096

Customs, popular 2158

Cuthbert, St. 400

Cyprian of Carthage, St., writings of 263, 1913

1058, 1094, 1256, 1277, 1318,
1871, 1892-3
Hurm, Otto 1726
Hybrida (Bastarda) 333, 1097, 1101,
1568, 1702
Hyde, Ann 1053
Hymnaries 1507
Hymnology, guide to 2123
Hymns, Book of, Irish 616, 685

Iberian peninsula, circulation of MSS
in 762; cf. Portugal, Spain
Iceland 1231-6
Iconography 562, 725, 1055; in
Anglo-Saxon England 1063;
cf. Typology
Igitur, abbreviation for 1778
Ihm, Maximilian 433
Ijsewijn, Jozef 1335
Illumination 13, 957, 1461, 1824-46,
1853, 1862; Cistercian 1132;
English 1142, 1146, 1148-50,
1154-6, 1165-6, 1169, 1171-2:
Anglo-Saxon 701, 1055, 1068;
Flemish 1398; French 1174-6,
1178, 1185, 1187-9, 1191;
Icelandic 1232; Insular 310, 378,
637-8, 645, 651, 654, 657-8, 671,
705, 723-4; Italian 1194-5, 1199,
1204, 1206; at Lorsch 991;
Mozarabic and Spanish 763-4;
at Reichenau 991; renaissance
1253; Roman 1839-40;
romanesque 1830; at St. Gall
999; techniques of 1569;
Visigothic 724, 763-4, 781;
workshops 1146, 1175-6, 1188,
1567, 1569, 1842, 1846; cf.
Miniatures, Ornamentation
Illuminators, manuals for 1866;
professional 1842-3
Illustration, medical 1857

Imperial chancery: see Diplomatics
Incipits, general 1374, 1443, 1458,
1462, 1481, 1489, 1492, 1500,
1507-8, 1531, *1930, 1930-53,
2119, 2123-4, 2126, 2131, 2137,
2140, 2143; alchemical 1481;
Aristotle, commentaries on
1938-9; Bible commentaries
1950; florilegia 1901; Franciscan
works 1941; Gospel books 596;
grammatical texts 1932; hymns
2123; insolubilia 1948; Latin
verse 1942, 1947, 1953; liturgical
texts 1507; logical works 1940;
Lombard (*Sentenciae*) commentaries 1949; medical texts 1439,
1458, 1508, 1935; optical texts
1936; patristic writings 1933,
1952; Petrarch, Latin works of
1457; philosophical texts 1489;
prayers 2120a, 2143; proverbs,
Latin 1953; sermons 1930,
1945-6; virtues and vices,
treatises of 1931
Index titulorum decretalium 2138
Indexes in MSS 1731
Indexing symbols 1731
Ineichen-Eder, C.E.: see Eder,
Christine E.
'in electione sociorum,' books
1316, 1319, 1321
Ingolstadt university 1014
Ingreus, scribe of Corbie *916
Inguanez, Maurus 852, 866
Inisfallen, Annals of 666
Initia: see Incipits
Initials 288, 376, 657, 1259, 1847-
1853; arabesque 1847; Beneven-
tan 857; in English MSS 1063,
1069; historiated 1851; minor,
decoration of 1640; 'synthetic'
1851; techniques of drawing 1850

Inks, 1543-5

Innes, Cosimo 1160

Innocent III, pope 201, *1091, 1218

Innsbruck, book inventories from 1309

Inscriptions 2175-85; abbreviations in 1766; dated 2180; Greek 491; Latin 165, 539-40, 1023-4; renaissance, in relation to Roman 1257, 1259

Insolubilia, incipits of 1948

Instrumenta, legal: see Diplomatics (and diplomata)

Insular, Caroline 1050, 1074; hands, writing, studies of 600-759, cf. Anglo-Insular, Hiberno-Insular, Wallico-Insular; palaeography, concept and state of 253 (CLA), *600, 613, 617, 652; presence in continental centres 606, 613, 694, *727, 806, 868, 870-71, 945, 948, 969, 988, 993, 1021; 'symptoms' 694, 901

Interlace decoration in Insular MSS 635

International Medieval Bibliography 20

Interpolation 1890

Interrogation, point of, and dating of MSS 1645

Inventari dei manoscritti delle biblioteche d'Italia 1491

Inventories of books 1373-88

Iona, Scotland *600, 651, 671

Irblich, Eva 12, 971

Ireland 253 (CLA), 258, 308, 412, 600-85, 1464, 1481; book-satchels in 664; and continental Europe 603, 606, 613; illumi-nated MSS from, in Bodleian Library 1833; literature of 604, 605; MSS illuminated in 728; MSS surviving in Irish language 612, 666-70; and Northumbria 602, 651, 672; and origin of medieval abbreviation system 874, 1778, 1784; and Visigothic Spain 609, 724-5

Irigoin, Jean 1523, 1597, 1637, 1655, 1660, 1874, 2006, 2028, 2091

Irish Manuscripts Commission 673-9

Irwin, Raymond 1405

Isidore, of Padua 221; of Seville 234, 775

Isleworth, Middlesex 1346

Italy 160-75, 254-5 (CLA), 334-5, 787, 2134; book production in 832, 834, 994, 1253; Caroline period in 1018-42; Christian inscriptions in 2185; Gothic period in 1194-1219, cf. Gothic script; humanism in 1253-5, 1257-62, 1264-7; humanist script in *1253, 1269-88; libraries in: *medieval* 1331, 1333, 1349-50, 1380, *modern* 1486-91; pre-Caroline scripts in: *North* 792-829, *South* 830-67; Uncial in 578-9, 817, 828, 1034; writing masters in 1282, 1299

Ithael, Welsh scribe 310

*Ivrea, Italy 223, 1026

Ivy, G.S. 1559

Jaakkola, Jalmari 1229-30

Jackson, Donald 466

Jacob, Ernest F. 123

Jahn, Otto 1894

Jakó, Sigismund 1249

James, Montague R. 372, 374-5, 377, 379-81, 383-4, 386-7, 389, 391, 1080, 1351-2, 1396, 1471, 1626

McLachlan, Elizabeth P. 1062
MacNeill, Eóin 633, 666
MacNiocaill, Gearóid 650
MacRegol (Rushworth) Gospels 681
Macrobius, Ambrosius Theodosius
    692
Macrophotography 177, 1654,
    1657-8
Macro Plays 1140
Madalberta, nun-scribe of Meaux
    946
Madan, Falconer 1478, 1639
Maddalena of Trastevere, account
    book of 1265
*Madresfield Hours 402
*Madrid 234
Madvig, J. Nicolai 1984
Maffei, Scipione 73-4, 88
Magnani, Luigi 206, 223
Magnin, E. 1788
Mai, Angelo 111
Mainz 280, 287, 645, 872, 1356
Maiolus (Maieul), ab. Cluny 954
Mairold, Maria 319
Majuscule, Greek 481
Malibu, California, J. Paul Getty
    Museum 1463
Mallon, Jean 81, 521, 535-42, 549,
    559, 565, 568, 581, 1546, 1579
Malmédy nr. Liège 967
Malmesbury, Wiltshire, scriptorium
    at 1066; cf. William of
Malone, Kemp 747
Malory, Thomas 1153
Mammacini, Romolo 208
Manaresi, Cesare 548
Mangenot, Eugène 2128
Manheim, Ralph 450
Maniacutrà, Nicola 2053
Manilius, Marcus, works of 1891
Manitius, Max 1899, 2104
Manolescu, Radu 1249

Manorial formularies 2169
Mantecon, José I. 1297
Mantegna, Andrea 1259
Mantua 376
Manuscripta 21
Manuscripts, description of 1466,
    1479, 1509; destruction, disper-
    sal of 1405, 1408-10, 1926;
    'families' of 1979-80; migration
    of 1311, 1407; cf. in general
    Codices, Libraries
Manuscrits à peintures 1832
Manuscrits datés 82, 87, 313-40,
    2194
Manutius, Aldo, the Elder 1763
Mappae Clavicula 1867
Maracchi Biagiarelli, B. 1521
Marazuela, T.A. 770
Marcellarii, John 392
Marcellus II, pope 1408
Marche region, Italy 846-7
Mardersteig, Gustav 1257
Margaret, St., queen of Scotland,
    Gospel book of 1078
Marginalia 660, 1845
Maria-Laach nr. Koblenz 260
Marianus Scotus 645
Marichal, Robert 81, 98-9, 124-5,
    178, 181-90, 324, 408, 521,
    543-50, 581, 1970
Marinelli-Marcacci, Olga 1258
Marks, Richard B. 1336
Markyate nr. Luton, Hertfordshire
    1084
Marouzeau, Jules 1999
Marrou, Henri I. 1917
Marseilles 1679, 2172
Marsh-Micheli, G.I.: see Micheli
Martens, Günter 1971
Martial (Marcus Valerius Martialis)
    420
Martin of Ireland, at Laon 948

Index codicum

References are to entry numbers, not to page numbers.

Bern
- Bürgerbibliothek, 120: 1039; 318: 982
- Stadt- und Universitätsbibliothek, 363: 227
Bonn
- Universitätsbibliothek, S. 218: 1781
Bremen
- Universitätsbibliothek, b. 21: 1010
Brogyntyn, Oswestry, Shropshire, s.n.: 395
Brussels
- Bibliothèque royale, 1650: 1089; 1828-30: 1184; 9961-2: 1169, 1172; 14650-59: 413; 18018: 1714
Cambrai
- Bibliothèque municipale, 940: 414
Cambridge
- Corpus Christi College, 53: 380; 173: 1085; 286: 825; 415: 980
- Fitzwilliam Museum, BL 1: 404; 38-1950: 391; 192: 397; 298: 370; 330: 388; 368: 397
- St. John's College, 59: 640
- Trinity College, 84: 1743; 308: 1049; 881: 375; 950: 372, 1142, 1148; 987: 1080
- University Library, Ee. ii. 4: 1050; Ee. iii. 59: 377; Gg. v. 35: 1065, 1076; Ii. iv. 26: 386; Kk. v. 16: 744; Ll. i. 10: 1082; Mm. ii. 9: 364; Nn. ii. 41: 577
Canosa di Puglia
- Tesoro della Cattedrale, s.n.: 838
Chartres
- Bibliothèque municipale 47: 351
Chatsworth House, Derbyshire, s.n.: 678
Chicago, Illinois
- Newberry Library, Wing 7: 401; Wing Add. 90: 1262
Cologne
- Dombibliothek, 63, 65, 67: 910
Copenhagen
- Koneglige Bibliotek, Gl. Kgl. Samml. 2296 4°: 1114; Thott 547 4°: 391
- Universitetsbiblioteket, AM 677 4to: 1232
Darmstadt
- Hessische Landes- und Hochschulbibliothek 4262: 722
Dijon
- Bibliothèque publique, 115: 1595
Donaueschingen
- Fürstlich Fürstenbergische Hofbibliothek, 3: 1123

Heidelberg
— Universitätsbibliothek, lat. 1613: 228
Hildesheim
— St. Godehard, s.n.: 1084
Holkham Hall, Wells, Norfolk, 458: 374
Ivrea
— Biblioteca capitolare, 86: 223
Karlsruhe
— Badische Landesbibliothek, Frag. Augiense 20: 650
Kassel
— Hessische Landesbibliothek, Anhang 19: 741; Philol. fol. 2: 915, 1810
Killiney, Co. Dublin
— Dun Mhuire Franciscan Library, A. 2: 616, 685
Klagenfurt
— Landesarchiv für Kärnten, Sammelhs. 6/19: 271
Kremsmünster
— Stiftsbibliothek, Cim. 1: 293; 76: 1669; 243: 286
Laon
— Bibliothèque municipale, 81: 1706; 239: 350
Lausanne
— Bibliothèque cantonale et universitaire, 5011: 411
Leeuwarden
— Provinciale Bibliotheek van Friesland, 55: 998
Leiden
— Bibliotheek der Rijksuniversiteit (BRU), B.P.L. 16B: 240; B.P.L. 52:
  406; B.P.L. 76A: 245; B.P.L. 118: 237; B.P.L. 2391a: 626; Periz.
  Q. 21: 247; Scalig. 69: 415; Voss. lat. F. 30: 233; Voss. lat. F. 84: 239;
  Voss. lat. F. 94: 1811; Voss. lat. O. 15: 246; Voss. lat. O. 38: 1640;
  Voss. lat. Q. 94: 238; Voss. lat. Q. 110: 244
Leningrad
— Publichnaja Biblioteka, Lat. Q. V. I. 3: 528; Lat. Q. V. I. 18: 737
León
— Archivo Catedral, 8: 782
London
— British Library (BL), Add. MSS — 10546: 971; 12194: 363; 30337: 865;
  34209: 347; 37517: 1056, 1061; 40618: 639; 42130: 1156; 47680:
  374, 1149; 47967: 738; 49598: 373; 49999: 388; 54000: 396; 54180:
  397; 59678: 1153. Cotton MSS — Augustus II. 18: 709; Caligula A. IX:
  1151; Claudius B. IV: 753; Faustina B. IX: 1137; Faustina C. I: 692;
  Julius E. IV: 371; Nero A. I: 752; Nero C. IV: 1073; Nero D. IV: 756,
  758; Tiberius A. III: 307; Tiberius A. XIII: 1058; Tiberius B. V: 387;

Ottob. lat. 501: 195. Pal. lat. MSS – 24: 1889; 50: 978; 65: 215; 143: 216; 493: 714; 830: 645; 1071: 209; 1631: 199; 1729: 203. Reg. lat. MSS – 316: 212; 317: 265; 469C: 1017; 525: 1241; 689A: 414; 694: 215; 703A: 981; 703B: 981; 846: 1812; 1653: 414; 1709: 244; 1997: 1033. Vat. lat. MSS – 202: 1029; 213: 1029; 781: 2048; 1409: 1746; 1843: 1275; 1849: 1275; 1852: 1275; 3195: 196; 3196: 207; 3225: 193, 213; 3226: 560, 583; 3256: 200, 299; 3867: 194, 562; 3868: 202, 1856; 3964: 208; 3966: 208; 3980: 1747; 4965: 1032; 5750: 197; 5757: 205; 9820: 210; 10673: 354; 10696: 571; 12910: 620
Venice
– Biblioteca Nazionale Marciana, Lat. IV. 37: 1510; Giustiniani Recanati s.n.: 553
Vercelli
– Biblioteca capitolare, 117: 218, 754
Verona
– Biblioteca capitolare, XV (13): 576; XXXVII (35): 220, 224; XXXVIII (36): 220, 224; LXXXV (80): 268
Vienna
– Österreichische Nationalbibliothek (ONB), lat. MSS – 15: 232, 573; 16: 418; 93: 282; 162: 407; 338: 300; 370: 272; 411: 291; 449: 269; 507: 302; 515: 274; 652: 287; 751: 280; 795: 277; 958: 281, 418; 1826*: 391; 1857: 273; 1861: 303; 1907: 289; 2160*: 418; 2398: 279; 2554: 290; 2687: 284. Papyrussammlung L 117: 1925. Series nova MSS – 2644: 270; 2700: 278
Washington, D.C.
– Catholic University of America, 114: 1375
– Folger Shakespeare Library, V. a. 354: 1140
Windsor Castle, Berkshire, s.n.: 403
Wolfenbüttel
– Herzog August Bibliothek, Aug. 2° 36. 23: 242; Aug. 2° 82. 6: 235; Gud. 224: 236; Helmst. 254: 1004; Helmst. 628: 1139
Worcester
– Cathedral Library, F. 160: 352
Würzburg
– Universitätsbibliothek, M. p. th. f. 12: 670; M. p. th. f. 62: 276; M. p. th. qu. 22: 993
Yale: see New Haven
Zadar, Yugoslavia
– Convent of St. Mary, s.n.: 861

Explicit liber domni Leonardi Boyle ordinis praedicatorum non absque alacri studio tribus saeculis post impressum *De re diplomatica* venerabilis domni Johannis Mabillon ordinis Sancti Benedicti, anno incarnationis Domini Nostri millesimo nongentesimo octogesimo primo compilatus. Impressus apud Toronto impensis virorum honestorum Pope Sociorumque civium eiusdem, Johanne Paulo Secundo pontifice maximo illustrissimo suaviter sedente, Elizabetha Secunda regina gloriosissima feliciter regnante, anno incarnationis Domini Nostri M°DCCCC°LXXX°IV°.
Finit feliciter. Deo gratias.
Amen.